Study Guide

Biological Psychology

Ninth Edition

Elaine M. Hull
State University of New York at Buffalo

THOMSON

WADSWORTH

Australia • Brazil • Canada • Mexico • Singapore • Spain • United Kingdom • United States

Thomson Higher Education
10 Davis Drive
Belmont, CA 94002-3098
USA

For more information about our products, contact us at:
Thomson Learning Academic Resource Center
1-800-423-0563

For permission to use material from this text or product, submit a request online at
http://www.thomsonrights.com.
Any additional questions about permissions can be submitted by email to **thomsonrights@thomson.com.**

TABLE OF CONTENTS

THE MAJOR ISSUES

Introduction

Biological psychology is the study of the physiological, ontogenetic (developmental), evolutionary, and functional explanations of behavior. Bird song provides an example of the four types of explanation. Increased testosterone levels during mating season cause a brain area that is important for singing to increase in size, providing a physiological mechanism for singing. Ontogenetic explanations focus both on the genes that prepare for a behavior and on experience during a sensitive period, when a bird must hear the appropriate song. Evolutionary explanations discuss the selection of traits in terms of their adaptive value to the organism. Similar behavior patterns in two different species suggests that those species evolved from a common ancestor. Functional explanations describe the advantages conferred by each trait. For example, a male bird's song attracts a female and deters competition from other males.

Human behavior is also subject to biological explanation. There are a number of theories about the relationship of the mind to the brain. According to the dualist position, the mind and the brain exist independently, but somehow interact. However, that "somehow" causes a problem. Monism holds that there is only one kind of substance, though various theorists differ as to whether that substance is mental, physical, or some combination of the two. The materialist position (a form of monism) holds that everything that exists is material (physical). Mentalism suggests that only the mind really exists. The identity position (another form of monism) proposes that mental processes are the same thing as brain activity but are described in different terms.

David Chalmers proposed that there are "easy problems" concerning the specific application of the term consciousness to wakefulness vs. sleep, or to the focusing of attention, for example. However, the "hard problem" is how *any* kind of brain activity is associated with consciousness. One approach is to determine what brain activity is necessary and sufficient for consciousness. A major difficulty in studying consciousness is that it is not directly observable. This has led some to a solipsist position: I alone am conscious. However, while few people doubt that other people are conscious, they do question whether other animals, plants, or inanimate objects, including robots, are conscious. Neuroscience cannot resolve the issues of the essence and functional significance of the mind or of its relationship to the brain, but it can contribute relevant data.

Genes are the units of heredity; they maintain their structural identity from one generation to another. DNA (deoxyribonucleic acid, the substance of genes) serves as a template for the synthesis of messenger RNA (ribonucleic acid), which in turn provides a template for the production of structural proteins and enzymes. Chromosomes and the genes they contain come in pairs, one from each parent. An individual with identical genes of a given pair is said to be homozygous for that gene; an individual with an unmatched pair of genes is heterozygous for that gene. Genes may be dominant or recessive; dominant genes have strong effects in either homozygous or heterozygous individuals, whereas recessive genes have effects only in the homozygous condition. When chromosomes pair up during reproduction, they sometimes break apart and one part attaches to the other chromosome; this is called "crossing over." If two genes are close together on a chromosome, they are less likely to be separated by crossing over than if they are far apart. Sex-linked genes are usually found on the X chromosome; any characteristic produced by a recessive X-linked gene will be observed primarily in males, who do not have a second X chromosome to overrule the recessive gene. Sex-limited genes are found on autosomal chromosomes, and are therefore equally present in both sexes; however, their expression is activated by sex hormones that are more abundant in one sex than the other. Genetic variation is produced by recombination of genes during sexual reproduction and by random mutations. Mutations resulting in an altered protein are almost always maladaptive. Mutations that alter the amount or timing of protein production are often neutral or occasionally advantageous.

Heritability describes the extent to which variations in a characteristic are due to genetic, as opposed to environmental, variations. It is determined either by comparing the resemblance between monozygotic (identical) twins with that between dizygotic (fraternal) twins or by comparing the resemblance of adopted children to their adoptive vs. biological parents. Genetic influences on behavior may be either relatively direct, via control of brain chemicals, or indirect, by affecting height, attractiveness, or physical activity, for example. Furthermore, certain environmental conditions, such as malnutrition or severe stress, early in development can attach a methyl group to a gene and inactivate it. Heritability may be overestimated if members of a population live in similar environments, if genetic and prenatal influences are confounded, and if the effects of a trait are magnified by their influence on the social environment. Even traits with high heritability in "standard" conditions may be influenced by environmental interventions. For example, phenylketonuria (PKU) results from a recessive gene that prevents metabolism of the amino acid phenylalanine. The resulting high levels of phenylalanine lead to brain malformations and mental retardation. However, a diet low in phenylalanine can greatly reduce the abnormalities.

Evolution is a change over generations in the frequencies of various genes in a population. Genes that confer a reproductive advantage will become more prevalent in later generations. Neither use nor disuse of a given structure or behavior can cause an evolutionary increase or decrease in that feature, contrary to the theory of Lamarckian evolution. Furthermore, humans have not stopped evolving; medical treatments and welfare programs may increase survival, but may not enhance an individual's reproductive success. Evolution does not necessarily imply improvement, since previous success does not guarantee future success in a changing world. Evolution is based on the benefit for genes, not for individuals or species. Genes for altruistic behavior, for example, may be favored by reciprocal altruism or by kin selection. Evolutionary psychology seeks functional explanations for the evolution of social behaviors. However, these explanations are often speculative. Furthermore, even if genes do predispose us towards certain behavior patterns, we still have flexibility in acting on those predispositions.

The issue of animal experimentation has become controversial. The usefulness of animal research rests both on the similarity across species of many biological functions and on the difficulty or impossibility of conducting such research on humans. In addition, we are interested in animals, both for their own sake and for the light they can shed on human evolution. Some animal rights activists, the "abolitionists", believe that all animals have the same rights as humans and should never be used by humans for any purpose. "Minimalists" believe that some animal research is necessary, but that it should be minimized. Valuable clinical treatments of human disorders have been gleaned from animal experiments. However, even though experimenters attempt to minimize pain, and even though animal care committees (which include veterinarians and community members as well as scientists) oversee the research, a certain amount of distress accompanies much animal experimentation. In this case, as in many other ethical issues, it is difficult to resolve the competing values.

Learning Objectives

Module 1.1 The Mind-Brain Relationship

1. Be able to describe four kinds of biological explanations of behavior and give an example of each.

2. Understand the two major positions concerning the relationship between the brain and conscious experience.

3. Know which kinds of problems are thought to be "hard" or "easy."

4. Be able to describe the professionals who conduct neuroscience research and who provide clinical treatment for psychological, neurological, and psychiatric disorders.

Module 1.2 The Genetics of Behavior

1. Understand the concept of Mendelian genetics.

2. Be able to describe the relationship between DNA, RNA, and proteins.

3. Understand the concepts of dominant and recessive genes, sex-linked and sex-limited genes, and sources of variation in the course of evolution.

4. Understand the concept of heritability and reasons why it can be overestimated.

5. Be able to discuss natural selection and the goals and criticisms of evolutionary psychology.

Module 1.3 The Use of Animals in Research

1. Understand the reasons for animal research.

2. Be able to discuss the ethical debate concerning the use of animals in research.

3. Be able to describe the regulatory committees that oversee animal research.

Key Terms and Concepts

Module 1.1 The Mind-Brain Relationship

1. Biological explanations of behavior

   No need for organism to understand function of behavior

   Physiological explanation

   Reduces a behavior to activity of the brain and other organs
   Testosterone and bird song: increase in size of a brain area

   Ontogenetic explanation

   Describes the development of a structure or behavior
   Song development: requires both genes and hearing song during early sensitive period

   Evolutionary explanation

   Examines a structure or behavior in terms of evolutionary history
   Common ancestor

   Functional explanation

   Describes why a structure or behavior evolved as it did

   Genetic drift within isolated community
   Male sings to attract mate and defend territory

2. The brain and conscious experience: mind-body or mind-brain problem

   Dualism: mind and body—different kinds of substance; exist independently but interact

   Rene Descartes

   Pineal gland

   Conflict: law of conservation of matter and energy

   Monism: only one kind of existence

   Materialism
   Mentalism
   Identity

   Mental and brain processes described in different terms
   Mind is brain activity

   Function of consciousness?

   Solipsism: I alone exist.

   David Chalmers

   Easy problems: difference between wakefulness and sleep; mechanisms that focus attention
   Hard problem: how any brain activity is associated with consciousness

Problem of other minds

    Other mammals? Insects? Rocks?

    Just-fertilized egg?

    Computers? robots?

Research approaches

    Visual stimulus for 29 ms: Conscious stimulus → same brain areas, but stronger activation

Try it yourself

    Binocular rivalry: brain activity matches aspects of the stimulus

Career opportunities

    Research fields

        Neuroscientist

        Behavioral neuroscientist

        Cognitive neuroscientist

        Neuropsychologist

        Psychophysiologist

        Neurochemist

        Comparative psychologist

        Evolutionary psychologist

    Practitioner fields

        Clinical psychologist

        Counseling psychologist

        School psychologist

    Medical fields

        Neurologist

        Neurosurgeon

        Psychiatrist

    Allied medical fields

        Physical therapist

        Occupational therapist

        Social worker

3. In closing: The biology of experience

Module 1.2 The Genetics of Behavior

1. Mendelian genetics

    Genes: units of heredity that maintain structural identity from one generation to another

        Chromosomes

Deoxyribonucleic acid (DNA)

Template for ribonucleic acid (RNA)
Translation of mRNA

Structural proteins or enzymes
Homozygous vs. heterozygous
Dominant vs. recessive
Recessive gene: effects only in homozygous condition
Blue eyes
Inability to taste phenylthiocarbamide (PTC)

Chromosomes and crossing over

General independence of inheritance of genes on different chromosomes
Some dependence if genes are on same chromosome
Crossing over: attachment of part of one chromosome on another

Sex-linked and sex-limited genes

Sex-linked: genes on sex chromosomes
Autosomal genes
X and Y chromosomes
Y chromosome: genes for only 27 proteins
X chromosome: genes for ~1500 proteins
Most sex-linked genes on X chromosome
Sex-limited genes: genes activated by sex hormones

Sources of variation

Recombination
Mutation
Altered protein: almost always disadvantageous
Altered amount or timing of protein production: May be neutral or advantageous

2. Heritability and environment

Ways of measuring human heritability

Monozygotic (identical) twins
Dizygotic (fraternal) twins

Overestimating heritability

Similar environments
Monozygotic (identical) twins
Dizygotic (fraternal) twins
Adopted children: resemblance to biological parents → hereditary influence

Possible complications

Overestimating heritability

        Biological mother also provides prenatal environment
        Multiplier effect: environment magnifies early tendencies

    Environmental modification

        Elevated plus maze
        Phenylketonuria (PKU)

           Inability to metabolize phenylalanine
           Brain malformations, mental retardation, irritablity
           Modified by low phenylalanine diet

    How genes affect behavior

        Increasing production of a protein
        Indirect effects
        Change in one behavior due to change in another behavior

3. The evolution of behavior

    Natural selection

        Evolutionary tree
        Genes associated with reproductive success
        Artificial selection

    Common misunderstandings about evolution

        Does use or disuse cause evolutionary change in that feature?

           Lamarckian evolution
        Have humans stopped evolving?
        Does evolution mean improvement?
        Does evolution benefit individual or species?

    Evolutionary psychology (sociobiology)

        Functional explanations

           Altruistic behavior
           Group selection
           Reciprocal altruism
           Kin selection
        Criticism

           Assumption that every behavior must be adaptive

    In closing: Genes and behavior

        Flexibility in acting on predispositions

Module 1.3 The Use of Animals in Research

1. Reasons for animal research

Similar mechanisms of behavior and ease of studying animals

Curiosity about animals

Clues to human evolution

Can't experiment on humans

2. The ethical debate

Animal research → useful discoveries

Minimalists vs. abolitionists

Opposition to environmental protection groups

European Science Foundation proposals

Lab animals: both instrumental and intrinsic value
Reduction, replacement, and refinement
Research to improve animal welfare
Evaluation by others
Assumption: procedure painful to humans is painful to animals
Training of investigators in animal care
Publication policy on ethical treatment of animals

Institutional Animal Care and Use Committees

National laws and professional organization guidelines

In closing: Humans and animals

Difficulty of resolving moral issues

Short-Answer Questions

Module 1.1 The Mind-Brain Relationship

1. *Biological explanations of behavior*

   a. What should we infer about an animal's or human's understanding of his or her behavior?

   b. What are the four major types of explanation of behavior sought by biological psychologists?

   c. What is the effect of testosterone on the brain of male songbirds?

   d. What is an ontogenetic explanation?

   e. What is an evolutionary explanation?

   f. What are the two functions of the male bird's song?

g. What is genetic drift, and under what circumstances does it occur?

2. *The brain and conscious experience*

a. What are the two major positions regarding the mind-brain relationship? List the main variants of these major positions. Give a strength and a weakness of each of these positions.

b. According to David Chalmers, what kinds of issues do "easy problems" deal with?

c. What is the main "hard problem"?

d. What is the problem of other minds? How does solipsism deal with that problem?

e. How do non-solipsists deal with the problem of other minds in humans? In animals, rocks, or computers?

f. Describe an experiment that showed a difference in brain activity when a given stimulus was consciously perceived and when it was not perceived.

g. Describe the main issues studied by neuroscientists, and specifically, behavioral neuroscientists.

h. What is a neuropsychologist? Where do they usually work?

i. What does a psychophysiologist study?

j. What issues do neurochemists investigate?

k. Compare the main issues studied by comparative psychologists with those studied by evolutionary psychologists.

l. Distinguish among neurologists, neurosurgeons, and psychiatrists.

Module 1.2 Nature and Nurture

1. *The genetics of behavior*

a. Briefly, what is a gene?

b. What is the relationship between DNA and RNA? Between one type of RNA and protein molecules?

c. What are two major functions of protein molecules?

d. What does it mean for an individual to be homozygous for a particular gene? Heterozygous?

e. What is a dominant gene? When can the effects of a recessive gene be seen?

f. What is "crossing over"?

g. On which chromosome are almost all sex-linked genes?

h. What is a sex-limited gene? On which chromosomes may it occur? Why are its effects usually limited to one sex?

i. What are two sources of genetic variation?

j. How is heritability of a trait determined?

k. What three factors may lead to overestimation of heritability?

    l.   What is phenylketonuria (PKU)? How can its effects be modified?

    m. What are some of the ways in which genes may influence behavior?

2. *The evolution of behavior*

    a.   What is evolution?

    b.   What is artificial selection?

    c.   Does the use or disuse of a structure or behavior cause an evolutionary increase or decrease in that feature? What is Lamarckian evolution?

    d.   Have humans stopped evolving?

    e.   Does evolution always imply improvement? Why or why not?

    f.   How can a gene that promotes altruistic behavior be maintained in evolution, if it places its possessor in danger?

    g.   What kinds of issues do evolutionary psychologists seek to explain? What is a criticism of this approach?

Module 1.3 The Use of Animals in Research

1. *Reasons for animal research*

    a.   What are four reasons biological psychologists study nonhuman animals?

2. *The ethical debate*

    a.   Compare the positions of the "minimalists" and the "abolitionists" with regard to the conduct of animal research.

    b.   What principles regarding animal research did the European Science Foundation propose?

    c.   What is the role of Laboratory Animal Care Committees? What groups are represented in their membership?

True/False Questions

1. Physiological explanations describe the development of a structure or behavior.

    TRUE or FALSE

2. The observation that a male bird sings to attract a mate and defend his territory is a functional explanation.

    TRUE or FALSE

3. Rene Descartes believed that the pineal gland was the site at which mind and brain interact.

    TRUE or FALSE

4. According to David Chalmers, the hard problem is to discern the mechanisms that focus attention.

   TRUE or FALSE

5. DNA is the template for RNA.

   TRUE or FALSE

6. A sex-limited gene is one whose expression depends on the presence of sex hormones, which are more abundant in one sex or the other.

   TRUE or FALSE

7. An autosomal gene is one located on the X or Y chromosome.

   TRUE or FALSE

8. Heritability may be overestimated in studies of biological children of low-IQ, criminal, or mentally ill parents, even if they were adopted at an early age, because the parents provided not only their genes but also their prenatal environment.

   TRUE or FALSE

9. The mental retardation caused by PKU can be completely ameliorated by providing a low-phenylalanine diet for the first 10-12 years of life.

   TRUE or FALSE

10. A gene can affect behavior directly by increasing or decreasing the production of a structural protein or an enzyme or indirectly by influencing height, weight, or activity level.

    TRUE or FALSE

11. Humans have stopped evolving, thanks to our fabulous medical system and social support network.

    TRUE or FALSE

12. The ethical treatment of animals depends solely on the good will and morals of individual researchers.

    TRUE or FALSE

Fill In The Blanks

1. The observation that testosterone increases the size of a brain area that controls singing is a(n) _____ explanation.

2. The observation that bird song requires both genes and hearing song during the early sensitive period is a(n) _____ explanation.

3. The observation that the tendency of humans to have "goose bumps" in frightening situations is related to the erection of hairs in our hairier ancestors, which made them look larger, is a(n) _____ explanation.

4. The spread of a gene within a small isolated community is called _____ .

5. Rene Descartes was a _____ , who believed that mind and body interact at the _____ .

6. Three types of monism are _____ , _____ , and _____ .

7. The search for neural mechanisms that distinguish waking and sleep is a pursuit of a(n) _____ problem.

8. The belief that "I alone exist" is referred to as _____ .

9. The units of heredity that maintain structural identity from one generation to another are _____ .

10. The function of _____ is to serve as a template for one type of RNA, which in turn is translated into _____ or _____ .

11. An individual who has an identical pair of genes on the two matched chromosomes is said to be _____ for that gene.

12. Two sources of genetic variation are _____ and _____ .

13. The inability to metabolize phenylalanine is called _____ .

14. The proposal that use or disuse can cause evolutionary change in a feature is called _____ .

15. The field of study that seeks functional explanations for how behavior evolved is called _____ .

16. People who believe that no animal should ever be used by humans for any purpose are called _____ .

17. People who believe that animal research is useful, but that it should be closely regulated, are called _____ .

18. Institutional Animal Care and Use Committees that oversee the use of animals in research include _____ , _____ , and _____ as members.

Matching Items

1. _____ Dualist
2. _____ Type of monism
3. _____ Easy problem
4. _____ Hard problem
5. _____ Template for protein synthesis
6. _____ Dizogotic twin
7. _____ Monozygotic twin
8. _____ Sex-limited gene
9. _____ Sex-linked gene
10. _____ PKU
11. _____ Lamarckian evolution

a. Fraternal twin
b. Gene on X chromosome that is expressed mostly in males
c. Inability to metabolize phenylalanine
d. Autosomal gene that depends on sex hormone for expression
e. Belief in evolutionary change caused by use or disuse
f. Identical twin
g. Difference between waking and sleeping
h. Rene Descartes
i. How any brain activity is associated with consciousness
j. Materialism
k. RNA

Multiple-Choice Questions

1. Which of the following is not a major category of biological explanation?
   a. physiological explanations
   b. ontogenetic explanations
   c. evolutionary explanations
   d. mental explanations

2. Most adult male songbirds
   a. sing throughout the year and throughout wide territories.
   b. sing when testosterone levels are high enough to increase the size and activity of a brain area that is critical for singing.
   c. sing because they are consciously aware that their songs will attract females and deter male competitors.
   d. sing the correct song, even if they have never heard the song.

3. The dualist position
   a. is problematic because it does not fit with our commonsense notion of the mind.
   b. proposes that the mind is the same thing as brain activity.
   c. cannot explain how, if the mind is not a type of matter or energy, it could possibly alter the electrical and chemical activities of the brain.
   d. proposes that mind is just an illusion.

4. The view that everything that exists is physical, and that mental events either don't exist or can be explained in purely physical terms, is characteristic of which position?
   a. materialism
   b. dualism
   c. mentalism
   d. functionalism

5. David Chalmers proposed that the "hard problem" concerning consciousness
   a. is how neural mechanisms differentiate between wakefulness and sleep and allow us to focus our attention.
   b. is why and how *any* kind of brain activity is associated with consciousness.
   c. really consists of an enormous number of easy problems.
   d. is impossible to answer, under any circumstances.

6. A solipsist
   a. assumes that other people, animals, and computers are conscious because they look and/or act much like I do.
   b. assumes that other people are conscious, but animals and computers are not.
   c. assumes that I alone exist, or I alone am conscious.
   d. is frequently a member of an organization called Solipsists United.

7. The order of bases on DNA
   a. determines the order of bases on RNA, which in turn determines the order of amino acids in proteins.
   b. directly determines the order of amino acids in proteins, which in turn determines the order of bases in RNA.
   c. is less important for genetic function than is the total number of particular bases.
   d. is more important for determining the shapes of carbohydrates and fats than of proteins.

8. An individual with a pair of identical genes at a given site on a pair of chromosomes
   a. is homozygous for that gene.
   b. is heterozygous for that gene.
   c. must have crossing over at that gene.
   d. must not have the ability to taste phenylthiocarbamide.

9. Crossing over refers to
   a. chickens getting to the other side of the road.
   b. heterozygous genes now becoming homozygous.
   c. homozygous genes now becoming heterozygous.
   d. the breaking of paired chromosomes during reproduction, with a part of one chromosome now attaching to the paired chromosome.

10. Sex-linked genes are usually genes
    a. on autosomal chromosomes that are expressed only under hormonal conditions that are usually found only in one sex.
    b. on autosomal chromosomes that are expressed in both sexes.
    c. on the X chromosome, which cannot be overridden by a second X chromosome in males.
    d. that most frequently engage in crossing over.

11. Mutations
    a. result from the recombination of genes from the two parents.
    b. are random genetic changes that are almost always maladaptive if they lead to an altered protein.
    c. are so extremely rare that they almost never affect inheritance.
    d. are random genetic changes that are always maladaptive if they affect the amount or timing of protein production.

12. Heritability can be overestimated
    a. if populations are studied in extremely varied environmental conditions.
    b. because a democratic society treats all individuals similarly.
    c. because parents provide their offspring both genes and prenatal environment.
    d. all of the above.

13. Phenylketonuria (PKU)
    a. is a heritable condition.
    b. results from inability to metabolize phenylalanine, which results in high levels of that amino acid, which in turn results in brain damage and mental retardation.
    c. effects can be minimized by a low phenylalanine diet throughout the affected individual's life.
    d. all of the above.

14. The survival of genes for altruistic behavior
    a. can be explained by either reciprocal altruism or kin selection.
    b. can be explained by the fact that altruism to strangers is not in fact harmful to the individual.
    c. can be explained by both a and b.
    d. cannot be explained at all and is likely to die out in later generations.

15. Animal research
    a. yields no useful discoveries.
    b. is regulated by Institutional Animal Care and Use Committees, which are composed of veterinarians, community representatives, and scientists.
    c. depends entirely on the wisdom and good intentions of individual researchers for maintaining good care of the animals.
    d. all of the above.

16. "Abolitionist" animal advocates
    a. agree that some animal research is acceptable if an important goal can be achieved with minimal suffering.
    b. maintain that use of primates in experimentation should be abolished, but that "lower" animals may be used.
    c. maintain that all animal experimentation, as well as any other use of animals, should be totally eliminated.
    d. can not be explained at all and is likely to die out are also called "minimalists".

Solutions

True/False Questions

1.	F	5.	T	9.	F
2.	T	6.	T	10.	T
3.	T	7.	F	11.	F
4.	F	8.	T	12.	F

Fill In The Blanks

1. physiological
2. ontogenetic
3. evolutionary
4. genetic drift
5. dualist; pineal gland
6. materialism; mentalism; identity
7. easy
8. solipsism
9. genes
10. DNA; structural proteins; enzymes
11. homozygous
12. recombination; mutation
13. phenylketonuria (PKU)
14. Lamarckian evolution
15. evolutionary psychology
16. abolitionists
17. minimalists
18. veterinarians; community members; scientists

Matching Items

1.	H	5.	K	9.	B
2.	J	6.	A	10.	C
3.	G	7.	F	11.	E
4.	I	8.	D		

Multiple-Choice Questions

1.	D	4.	A	7.	A
2.	B	5.	B	8.	A
3.	C	6.	C	9.	D

10. C   13. D   16. C
11. B   14. A
12. C   15. B

NERVE CELLS AND NERVE IMPULSES

Introduction

Neurons, like all animal cells, are bounded by a fatty membrane, which restricts the flow of chemicals into and out of the cell. Animal cells also contain structures, such as a nucleus, ribosomes, mitochondria, and an endoplasmic reticulum, that are important for various genetic, synthetic, and metabolic functions. A neuron is composed of (1) dendrites, which receive stimulation from other cells; (2) the soma or cell body, which contains the genetic and metabolic machinery and also conducts stimulation to the axon; and (3) the axon, which carries the nerve impulse to other neurons, frequently across long distances. Sensory neurons are highly sensitive to specific external stimuli; motor neurons stimulate muscles and glands; and local neurons have either no axon or a very short one and can convey information only to adjacent neurons. One can infer a great deal about a neuron's function from its shape. For example, a neuron that integrates input from many sources has many branching dendrites. The nervous system also contains many support cells called glia, which help synchronize the activity of axons, remove waste, build myelin sheaths, and guide neurons during development and during regeneration of peripheral axons.

A blood-brain barrier prevents many substances, including most viruses and bacteria and most forms of nutrition, from entering the brain. In most parts of the brain, glucose is the only nutrient that can cross the barrier in significant amounts. Therefore, the brain is highly dependent on glucose and on thiamine (vitamin B_1), which is needed to metabolize glucose. Fat soluble molecules and small uncharged molecules can cross the barrier freely. The barrier depends on tight junctions between endothelial cells lining the capillaries.

The ability of a neuron to respond quickly to stimulation depends on the resting potential. A metabolically active sodium-potassium pump establishes concentration gradients by transporting sodium (Na^+) ions out of the cell and potassium (K^+) ions into the cell. There is a resultant negative charge inside the cell, because three sodium ions are pumped out for every two potassium ions pumped in. Selective permeability of the membrane increases this potential by allowing potassium ions to flow out, down their concentration gradient; the loss of the positive potassium ions leaves the inside of the neuron even more negative. The relative impermeability of sodium results in minimal inflow of positive ions to offset the potassium outflow. The concentration and electrical gradients exert opposing influences on potassium. The electrical gradient (the negative charge inside the cell) attracts more potassium inside the cell than would be there if the concentration gradient were the only influence. Sodium ions, however, are attracted to the inside by both the electrical and concentration gradients. Therefore, when the sodium channels are opened, there is considerable impetus for sodium to flow into the cell.

A neuron may receive input that either hyperpolarizes it (makes the inside more negative) or depolarizes it (makes the inside less negative). If the membrane is depolarized to a threshold level, it briefly loses its ability to exclude sodium ions, and these ions rush in through voltage-activated sodium channels. They cause the inside of the neuron to become positive, at which point the membrane quickly becomes impermeable to sodium again. However, as the neuron becomes more depolarized, voltage-activated potassium channels open, resulting in even greater permeability than usual to potassium, which is repelled out of the neuron by both the positive electrical gradient and its own concentration gradient. The exit of the positively charged potassium ions returns the neuron approximately to its previous resting potential. This rapid exchange of ions is called the action potential. All action potentials of a given axon are approximately equal in size, shape, and velocity, regardless of the size of the depolarization that gave rise to them. This principle is called the all-or-none law. Immediately after an action potential, a neuron is resistant to re-excitation, because sodium channels are closing and are resistant to reopening. During the 1 millisecond absolute refractory period, no stimulus can initiate a new impulse; during the subsequent relative refractory period of about 2-4 milliseconds, slight hyperpolarization resulting from potassium outflow makes it difficult, but possible, to produce an action potential.

Once an action potential occurs, entering sodium ions spread to adjacent portions of membrane, thereby depolarizing these areas to their threshold and allowing sodium to rush in there. Thus the action potential is regenerated at each succeeding area of the axon until it reaches the end. The regenerative flow of ions across the membrane is slower than electrical conduction within the axon. In some axons, 1-mm-long segments of myelin (a fatty insulating substance) are wrapped around the axon, with short uncovered segments (nodes of Ranvier) in between. The action potential is conducted passively with some decrement under the myelin sheath. There is still sufficient potential to depolarize the next node of Ranvier to its threshold, and the action potential is regenerated at full strength at each node. The impulse appears to "jump" from node to node. This mode of transmission is called saltatory conduction and is much faster than transmission without myelin. It forces the action potential to use the faster electrical conduction within the axon for a longer distance before engaging in the slower regenerative flow across the membrane. Very small local neurons use only graded potentials, not action potentials, because they transmit information over very short distances.

Learning Objectives

Module 2.1 The Cells of the Nervous System

1. Know the main structures of neurons and the structural differences among neurons.

2. Know the main types of glia and their functions.

3. Be able to describe the advantages and disadvantages of the blood-brain barrier.

Module 2.2 The Nerve Impulse

1. Understand why the neuron uses considerable energy to produce a resting potential.

2. Understand the competing forces of the electrical and concentration gradients on potassium ions and how this competition produces the resting potential.

3. Be able to describe the function and the molecular basis of the action potential.

4. Understand how an action potential is conducted down an axon and how myelin sheaths contribute to this process.

5. Know how local interneurons transmit information without benefit of action potentials.

Key Terms and Concepts

Module 2.1 The Cells of the Nervous System

1. Anatomy of neurons and glia

   Santiago Ramon y Cajal, a pioneer of neuroscience

   The structures of an animal cell

      Membrane

         Two layers of fat molecules
         Protein channels
      Nucleus
      Mitochondrion
      Ribosomes
      Endoplasmic reticulum

   The structure of a neuron

      Motor neuron
      Sensory neuron
      Dendrites

         Synaptic receptors
         Dendritic spines
      Cell body or soma

         Nucleus, ribosomes, mitochondria
      Axon

         Myelin sheath, node of Ranvier
         Presynaptic terminal, end bulb, or bouton
         Afferent axon
         Efferent axon

Interneuron, intrinsic neuron

Variations among neurons

Purkinje cell of cerebellum

Cells in retina

Glia (neuroglia)

Astrocytes

Encircle several presynaptic terminals

Take up, store, and transfer chemicals

Remove waste

Help control blood flow

Microglia

Remove waste, viruses, fungi

Oligodendrocytes (brain and spinal cord) and Schwann cells (periphery)

Form myelin sheaths

Radial glia (type of astrocyte): guide migrating neurons, growing axons and dendrites during development

Schwann cells: guide peripheral axons during regeneration

2. The blood-brain barrier

Why we need a blood-brain barrier

Virus-infected non-neural cells: targeted for destruction

Virus-infected cells in nervous system: virus particles remain

Area postrema: monitors blood chemicals that cannot enter other brain areas

How the blood-brain barrier works

Endothelial cells of capillaries

Small uncharged molecules

Fat-soluble molecules

Active transport system

Glucose

Amino acids

Certain vitamins and hormones

Moves some chemicals from brain to blood

3. The nourishment of vertebrate neurons

Dependence on glucose and oxygen

Due to blood-brain barrier

Ketones

Liver: converts carbohydrates, amino acids, and glycerol into glucose

Requirement for thiamine (vitamin B_1)

Deficiency leads to Korsakoff's syndrome

4. In closing: Neurons

Importance of communication among neurons

Module 2.2 The Nerve Impulse

1. The resting potential of the neuron

Electrical gradient: difference in electrical charge between inside and outside of cell

Phospholipid membrane with embedded proteins

Polarization

Resting potential

Negatively charged proteins inside
Microelectrode

Forces acting on sodium and potassium ions

Selective permeability
Ion channels
Concentration gradient

More sodium outside
More potassium inside
Sodium-potassium pump

Moves three sodium ions out for every two potassium ions in
Active transport
Sodium stays out; some potassium leaks out
Electrical gradient vs. concentration gradient

Both attract sodium in
Electrical gradient: attracts potassium in
Concentration gradient: repels potassium

Why a resting potential? Strong, fast response

2. The action potential

Hyperpolarization, depolarization

Threshold of excitation

The molecular basis of the action potential

Voltage-activated channels
Sodium inflow: depolarization
Potassium outflow: temporary hyperpolarization
Drug effects

Scorpion venom: opens sodium channels and closes potassium channels
Local anesthetic: blocks sodium channels

The all-or-none law

The refractory period

Absolute refractory period
Relative refractory period

3. Propagation of the action potential

Axon hillock

Successive depolarization of adjacent areas

Regenerative ion flow slower than current spread in axon

4. The myelin sheath and saltatory conduction

Myelinated axons

Nodes of Ranvier

Saltatory conduction

Increases speed by increasing distance current spreads within axon
Conserves energy by decreasing sites of sodium inflow

Multiple sclerosis

5. Local neurons

Graded potentials

Depolarization
Hyperpolarization
Horizontal cell in retina
Astrocytes: exchange chemicals with neighboring neurons

Small neurons and big misconceptions

Large neurons easier to study
Small cells functionally important

6. In closing: Neural messages

Communication based on multiple on/off messages

Short-Answer Questions

Module 2.1 The Cells of the Nervous System

1. *Neurons and glia*

   a. What did Ramon y Cajal demonstrate?

   b. List the major structures of animal cells and give the main function of each.

   c. What are the main subdivisions of the neuron and the function of each?

   d. List several anatomical distinctions between dendrites and axons.

   e. What is the myelin sheath?

   f. What is the function of the presynaptic terminal or end bulb?

   g. Describe the structural and functional differences among sensory, motor, and local neurons.

   h. What do the terms afferent and efferent mean? Can an axon be both afferent and efferent? Explain.

   i. What is an intrinsic neuron?

   j. How do glia cells differ from neurons?

   k. What are four functions of glia?

   l. What are two functions of astrocytes?

   m. What two kinds of glia form myelin sheaths?

   n. What is the function of radial glia? What related function do Schwann cells perform?

2. *The blood-brain barrier*

   a. Why do we need a blood-brain barrier? Why don't we have a similar barrier around other body organs?

   b. What happens if a virus does enter the nervous system?

   c. Describe the arrangement of the endothelial cells that form the blood-brain barrier.

   d. What types of chemicals can cross the blood-brain barrier freely?

   e. How does the area postrema differ from most other brain areas? What is its major function.

   f. What is the role of the active transport system? What four types of chemicals are transported in this way?

3. *The nourishment of vertebrate neurons*

   a. What is the major fuel of neurons?

b. Why can't most parts of the adult brain use fuels other than glucose?

c. Why is a shortage of glucose usually not a problem?

d. Why is a diet low in thiamine a problem? What is Korsakoff's syndrome?

Module 2.2 The Nerve Impulse

1. *The resting potential*

    a. What is the composition of the membrane covering the neuron? Describe its structure.

    b. How is the electrical potential across the membrane measured?

    c. What is meant by selective permeability of the membrane? Which chemicals can cross the membrane and which ones cannot? How do a few biologically important ions cross?

    d. What is the sodium-potassium pump? How does its exchange of sodium and potassium ions lead directly to an electrical potential across the membrane?

    e. How does the selective permeability of the membrane increase the electrical potential?

    f. Describe the competing forces acting on potassium ions. Why don't all the potassium ions surrounding a neuron migrate inside the cell to cancel the negative charge there?

    g. What is the advantage of expending energy during the "resting" state to establish concentration gradients for sodium and potassium?

2. *The action potential*

    a. What happens to the electrical potential of a cell if a negative charge is applied? What is this change called?

    b. What happens to the potential if a brief, small positive current is applied? What is this change called?

    c. What happens to the potential if a threshold depolarization is applied?

    d. What does the term "voltage-activated sodium channels" mean?

    e. What causes the initial rapid increase in positivity of the action potential?

    f. What accounts for the ensuing repolarization? Why does the neuron hyperpolarize slightly, rather than stopping at the previous resting potential?

    g. What effect does scorpion venom have on the membrane?

    h. What is the effect of local anesthetic drugs like Novocain and Xylocaine?

    i. What is the all-or-none law? How may a neuron signal "greater than"?

    j. What is the absolute refractory period? What causes it?

    k. What is the relative refractory period? What causes it?

3. *Propagation of the action potential*

    a. How does an action potential propagate down an axon?

4. *The myelin sheath and saltatory conduction*

   a. What is the major advantage of the myelin sheath, and how is this advantage conferred?

   b. What is a node of Ranvier? What would happen if the axon were wrapped with one long expanse of myelin, without any nodes of Ranvier?

   c. What is meant by saltatory conduction?

5. *Signaling without action potentials*

   a. In what ways is transmission by local neurons different from the usual conduction by axons? Why is this local transmission restricted to very short distances?

True/False Questions

1. Ramon y Cajal demonstrated that neurons are continuous with one another, providing a basis for our sense of unified beings.

   TRUE or FALSE

2. The membrane of a cell consists of a bilayer of protein molecules, through which only electrically charged ions and molecules can pass.

   TRUE or FALSE

3. Neurons that are afferent to one structure can also be efferent from another structure.

   TRUE or FALSE

4. Dendrites carry information from one neuron to another, releasing neurotransmitters from their end bulbs (boutons).

   TRUE or FALSE

5. Dendritic spines increase the surface area available for synapses.

   TRUE or FALSE

6. Intrinsic neurons typically have long axons that convey action potentials from one brain area to another.

   TRUE or FALSE

7. Astrocytes are glia that wrap around the terminals of several axons and, by taking up and then releasing chemicals released by axons, may help to synchronize the activity of those axons.

   TRUE or FALSE

8. The major function of the blood-brain barrier is to keep the blood from spilling into the brain.

   TRUE or FALSE

9. The brain depends heavily on glucose, because the blood-brain barrier keeps out most other nutrients.

   TRUE or FALSE

10. The neuron expends considerable energy to produce a resting potential, based on unequal distributions of ions across the membrane, so that a small stimulus that opens ion channels can produce a large, rapid flow of ions.

    TRUE or FALSE

11. The sodium-potassium pump extrudes 3 sodium ions for every 2 potassium ions that it brings in.

    TRUE or FALSE

12. Hyperpolarization decreases the charge across the membrane.

    TRUE or FALSE

13. The absolute refractory period ensures that an action potential is conducted in both directions from a given site on the axon.

    TRUE or FALSE

14. Saltatory conduction increases the speed of conduction of an action potential down an axon.

    TRUE or FALSE

15. A node of Ranvier is the site of release of neurotransmitter from an axon terminal.

    TRUE or FALSE

Fill In The Blanks

1. Some structures common to all cells are the _____ , _____ , _____ , and the _____ .

2. _____ carry information from other neurons toward the soma.

3. _____ _____ are fatty coverings that force the action potential to use faster electrical conduction within an axon for a longer distance before engaging in slower regenerative flow of ions across the membrane.

4. An _____ axon carries information toward a structure.

5. _____ and _____ form myelin sheaths.

6. _____ absorb, store, and release chemicals released from axons.

7. _____ guide neuron migration during early development.

8. The _____ _____ prevents most viruses, bacteria, harmful chemicals, and many nutrients from gaining access to the brain.

9. The cell membrane is composed of a double layer of _____ , with embedded proteins.

10. There is an excess of sodium ions _____ the neuron, and an excess of potassium ions _____ the neuron.

11. The neuron expends energy to produce a resting potential in order to ensure a _____ and _____ response to a stimulus.

12. A _____ is an increase in the voltage across the membrane; it _____ the likelihood of an action potential.

13. In many neurons an action potential begins at the _____ .

14. A _____ of _____ is a break between myelin sheaths.

15. _____ conduction refers to the jumping of the action potential from node to node.

16. Local neurons are able to signal to adjacent neurons without the aid of _____ .

Matching Items

1. _____ Dendrite
2. _____ Soma
3. _____ Axon
4. _____ Efferent axon
5. _____ Afferent axon
6. _____ Myelin sheath
7. _____ Astrocytes
8. _____ Oligodendrocytes
9. _____ Radial glia
10. _____ Sodium
11. _____ Potassium
12. _____ Action potential
13. _____ Resting potential
14. _____ Regenerative ion flow

a. Carries action potentials away from soma
b. Fatty covering on an axon
c. Glia that produce myelin sheaths
d. Receiver of neural input to a neuron
e. Carries information toward a neural structure
f. Location of nucleus, ribosomes, endoplasmic reticulum
g. Ion actively transported out of the cell
h. Carries information away from a neural structure
i. Generated by sodium/potassium pump
j. Glia that absorb, store, and release chemicals
k. Slower than electrical conduction within axon
l. Rapid inflow of sodium and slower outflow of potassium
m. Glia that guide neural migration during development
n. Ion actively transported into the cell

Multiple-Choice Questions

1. The membrane of a cell consists primarily of
    a. two layers of protein molecules.
    b. two layers of fat molecules.
    c. two layers of carbohydrate molecules.
    d. one layer of fat molecules adjacent to a layer of protein molecules.

2. Which of the following is the site of protein synthesis in cells?
    a. ribosomes
    b. endoplasmic reticulum
    c. nucleus
    d. mitochondria

3. Which of the following is the site of chemical reactions that produce energy for the cell?
    a. ribosomes
    b. endoplasmic reticulum
    c. nucleus
    d. mitochondria

4. Which part of the cell consists of a network of thin tubes that transport newly synthesized proteins to other locations?
    a. ribosomes
    b. endoplasmic reticulum
    c. nucleus
    d. mitochondria

5. Which part of the cell contains the chromosomes?
    a. ribosomes
    b. endoplasmic reticulum
    c. nucleus
    d. mitochondria

6. Which part of the neuron is specialized to receive information from other neurons?
    a. dendrites
    b. soma
    c. axon
    d. end bulbs

7. Dendritic spines
    a. are structures inside the dendrite that give it rigidity.
    b. are the sites of all synapses on a neuron.
    c. increase the surface area available for synapses.
    d. are long outgrowths that stretch for several millimeters.

8. Sensory neurons
   a. are afferent to the rest of the nervous system.
   b. are highly sensitive to specific types of stimulation.
   c. sometimes have dendrites that merge directly into the axon, with the soma located on a stalk off the main trunk.
   d. all of the above.

9. Intrinsic neurons
   a. have multiple axons extending to numerous structures.
   b. have dendrites and axons confined within a structure.
   c. are afferent to a given structure.
   d. are efferent to a given structure.

10. Glia
   a. are larger as well as more numerous than neurons.
   b. are found in only a few areas of the brain.
   c. got their name because early investigators thought they glued neurons together.
   d. form synaptic connections with neurons and other glia.

11. Which of the following is not a function of glia?
   a. guiding the migration of neurons and the regeneration of peripheral axons
   b. exchanging chemicals with adjacent neurons
   c. forming myelin sheaths
   d. transmitting information over long distances to other cells

12. The blood-brain barrier
   a. allows some substances to pass freely, while others pass poorly or not at all.
   b. is formed by Schwann cells.
   c. is completely impermeable to all substances.
   d. keeps the blood from washing away neurons.

13. Which of the following is true of the blood-brain barrier?
   a. Electrically charged molecules are the only molecules that can cross.
   b. It results from tight junctions between endothelial cells.
   c. Fat soluble molecules cannot cross at all.
   d. An active transport system pumps blood across the barrier.

14. If a virus enters the brain,
   a. it survives in the infected neuron.
   b. a particle of it is exposed through the neuron's membrane so the infected cell can be killed.
   c. it is immediately removed by glia before it can enter a neuron.
   d. it is impossible for any virus ever to enter the brain.

15. Adult neurons
    a. are like all other cells of the body in depending heavily on glucose.
    b. depend heavily on glucose because they do not have enzymes to metabolize other nutrients.
    c. depend heavily on glucose because other nutrients cannot cross the blood-brain barrier in significant amounts.
    d. cannot use glucose because they do not receive enough oxygen or thiamine through the blood-brain barrier to metabolize it.

16. Potassium
    a. is found mostly outside the neuron.
    b. is pumped into the resting neuron by the sodium-potassium pump, but some flows out as a result of the concentration gradient.
    c. is actively pumped outside the neuron during the action potential.
    d. more than one of the above.

17. The sodium-potassium pump
    a. creates a negative potential inside the neuron by removing 3 sodium ions for every 2 potassium ions that it brings in.
    b. creates a negative potential inside the neuron by removing 2 sodium ions for every 3 potassium ions that it brings in.
    c. creates a positive potential inside the neuron by removing 3 sodium ions for every 2 potassium ions that it brings in.
    d. is basically a passive mechanism that requires no metabolic energy.

18. The resting potential
    a. prepares the neuron to respond rapidly to a stimulus.
    b. is negative inside the neuron relative to the outside.
    c. can be measured as the voltage difference between a microelectrode inside the neuron and a reference electrode outside the neuron.
    d. all of the above.

19. Sodium ions
    a. are found largely inside the neuron during the resting state because they are attracted in by the negative charge there.
    b. are found largely inside the neuron during the resting state because they are actively pumped in.
    c. are found largely outside the neuron during the resting state because they are actively pumped out, and the membrane is largely impermeable to their reentry.
    d. are actively repelled by the electrical charge of the neuron's resting potential.

20. Hyperpolarization
    a. refers to a shift in the cell's potential in a more negative direction.
    b. refers to a shift in the cell's potential in a positive direction.
    c. can trigger an action potential if it is large enough.
    d. occurs in an all-or-none fashion.

21. Depolarization of a neuron can be accomplished by having
    a. a negative ion, such as chloride (Cl-), flow into the cell.
    b. potassium (K+) ions flow out of the cell.
    c. sodium (Na+) ions flow into the cell.
    d. sodium ions flow out of the cell.

22. The all-or-none law
    a. applies only to potentials in dendrites.
    b. states that the amplitude and velocity of the action potential are independent of the intensity of the stimulus that initiated it.
    c. makes it impossible for the nervous system to signal intensity of a stimulus.
    d. all of the above.

23. When a neuron receives a threshold depolarization
    a. an action potential occurs, the size of which reflects the size of the stimulus that gave rise to it.
    b. so much sodium comes in that it almost completely depletes the extracellular fluid of sodium.
    c. sodium flows in only until the potential across the membrane is zero.
    d. the membrane becomes highly permeable to sodium ions for a brief time.

24. The down slope of the action potential graph
    a. is largely a result of sodium ions being pumped back out again.
    b. is the result of potassium ions flowing in briefly.
    c. is the result of sodium ions flowing in briefly.
    d. usually passes the level of the resting potential, resulting in a brief hyperpolarization, due to potassium freely leaving the cell.

25. Which of the following is true?
    a. Local anesthetics block nerve transmission by blocking sodium channels.
    b. Scorpion venom also blocks sodium channels.
    c. Local anesthetics keep sodium channels open and close potassium channels.
    d. None of the above is true.

26. The absolute refractory period is the time during which
    a. a stimulus must exceed the usual threshold in order to produce an action potential.
    b. a neuron is more excitable than usual.
    c. the sodium gates are firmly closed and no new action potentials can be generated.
    d. sodium and potassium ions are rapidly flowing.

27. Propagation of an action potential
    a. is analogous to the flow of electrons down a wire.
    b. is almost instantaneous.
    c. is inherently unidirectional because positive charges can flow only in one direction.
    d. depends on passive diffusion of sodium ions inside the axon, which depolarize the neighboring areas to their threshold.

28. Myelin sheaths
    a. would be much more efficient if they were not interrupted with a lot of leaky nodes.
    b. are interrupted about every 1 mm by a short unmyelinated segment.
    c. are much less effective in speeding transmission than a simple increase in axon size.
    d. are composed primarily of protein.

29. Saltatory conduction refers to
    a. the salt ions used in the action potential.
    b. sodium ions jumping into the neuron, once the sodium channels are opened.
    c. the impulse jumping from one node of Ranvier to the next.
    d. the impulse jumping from one myelin sheath to the next.

30. Myelin sheaths
    a. slow conduction of the impulse by blocking sodium's entry to the cell; their advantage lies in making the impulse all-or-none.
    b. are destroyed in multiple sclerosis.
    c. are found on dendrites.
    d. are found on cell bodies.

31. Nodes of Ranvier
    a. are interruptions of the myelin sheath at about 1 mm intervals.
    b. are sites of abundant sodium channels.
    c. are sites where an action potential is regenerated.
    d. all of the above.

32. Local neurons utilize
    a. graded potentials to convey information over short distances.
    b. graded potentials to convey information over long distances.
    c. action potentials to transmit information over long distances.
    d. action potentials to transmit information over short distances.

Helpful Hints

1. To remember the relative locations of sodium and potassium ions during the resting potential, remember that sodium (Na+) is "Not allowed" inside the neuron and potassium (K+) is labeled "Keep".

2. To appreciate the difference between fast electrical conduction inside the membrane and slow regenerative potentials across the membrane, think of ions simply elbowing their like-charged neighbors a short distance away inside the membrane, while sodium and potassium ions have to swim their equivalent of the length of a pool to cross the membrane.

Crossword Puzzle

Genes, Neurons, and Behavior

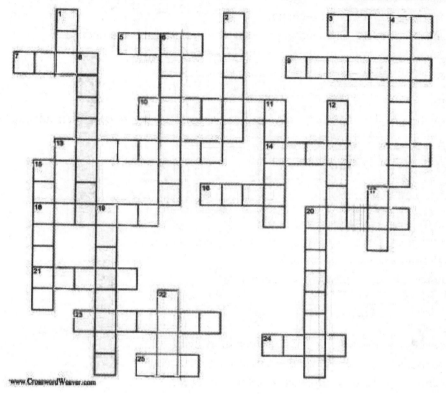

www.CrosswordWeaver.com

ACROSS

3 Small neuron using only graded potentials
5 Problem of how any kind of brain activity is associated with consciousness
7 Unit of heredity
9 Major nutrient for the brain
10 Node of _____: segment of axon not covered by myelin
13 _____ over: attachment of part of one chromosome onto another
14 Part of neuron that receives input
16 Support cells
18 _____ potential: rapid, "all-or-none" exchange of ions
20 Type of acid that makes up proteins
21 Part of dendrite that increases area for synapses
23 Part of axon where action potentials start
24 Template for protein synthesis (abbr.)
25 Major component of membranes

DOWN

1 ____ selection: explanation for altruistic behavior
2 Fatty sheaths covering some axons
4 Refractory period when no new action potential can be started
6 Refractory period when it is more difficult, but possible, to start an action potential
8 Direction away from a structure
11 Type of glia that guide neurons in development
12 Major ion producing EPSPs
15 Theory that mind and body are different kinds of substance that exist independently but interact
17 Substance of genes (abbr.)
19 Theory that mental processes are the same as brain activity
20 Direction toward a structure
22 Cell body

Crossword Puzzle Solution

Genes, Neurons, and Behavior

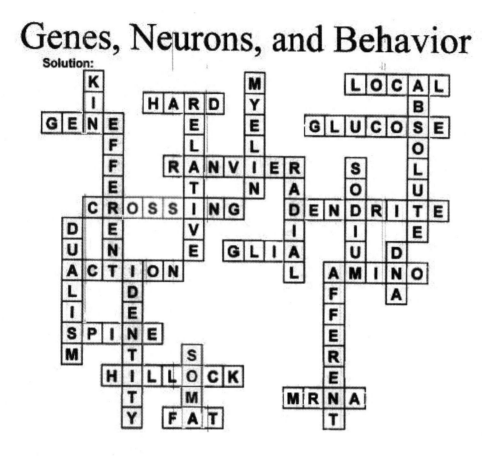

Solutions

True/False Questions

1.	F	6. F	11. T
2.	F	7. T	12. F
3.	T	8. F	13. F
4.	F	9. T	14. T
5.	T	10. T	15. F

Fill In The Blanks

1. nucleus; mitochondria; ribosomes; endoplasmic reticulum
2. Dendrites
3. Myelin; sheaths
4. afferent
5. Oligodendrocytes; Schwann cells
6. Astrocytes
7. Radial glia
8. blood-brain; barrier
9. phospholipids
10. outside; inside
11. strong; fast
12. hyperpolarization; decreases
13. axon hillock
14. node; Ranvier
15. Saltatory
16. action potentials

Matching Items

1.	D	7. J	13. I
2.	F	8. C	14. L
3.	A	9. M	
4.	H	10. G	
5.	E	11. N	
6.	B	12. K	

Multiple-Choice Questions

1.	B	3. D	5. C
2.	A	4. B	6. A

7. C	16. B	25. A
8. D	17. A	26. C
9. B	18. D	27. D
10. C	19. C	28. B
11. D	20. A	29. C
12. A	21. C	30. B
13. B	22. B	31. D
14. A	23. D	32. A
15. C	24. D	

SYNAPSES

Introduction

C. S. Sherrington inferred from careful behavioral observations that neurons do not merge with each other but communicate across tiny gaps called synapses. Reflex arcs that have one or more synapses are slower than simple transmission along the same distance of unbroken axon. Sherrington also inferred that complex integration of stimuli, including spatial and temporal summation of both excitation and inhibition, occurs at synapses. Most of his inferences were later confirmed by electrophysiological recordings using microelectrodes inserted inside neurons. Inhibitory postsynaptic potentials (IPSPs) hyperpolarize the postsynaptic cell, making it more difficult to produce an action potential. Excitatory postsynaptic potentials (EPSPs) depolarize the postsynaptic neuron and may summate spatially and temporally with other EPSPs to reach triggering threshold for an action potential. Most neurons fire action potentials at a spontaneous rate, even without synaptic input. EPSPs increase firing above that rate, whereas IPSPs decrease the firing rate.

EPSPs and IPSPs result from the release of neurotransmitters from presynaptic terminals. The neurotransmitter diffuses to and combines with receptor sites on the postsynaptic neuron, giving rise to either ionotropic or metabotropic changes that produce the postsynaptic potentials. The neurotransmitter then detaches from its receptor and is either transported back into the presynaptic terminal and reused or broken by enzymes into inactive components. Different neurotransmitters have different modes of inactivation, but some form of inactivation is critical to prevent the neurotransmitter from having a prolonged effect on the postsynaptic neuron, which would make it incapable of responding to new stimuli. The effect on the postsynaptic cell depends on the type and amount of neurotransmitter, the nature and number of receptors, the amount of deactivating enzyme present at the synapse, the rate of reuptake, and probably other factors. A number of peptide neurotransmitters are referred to as neuromodulators. They act at metabotropic receptors and modulate the effects of other neurotransmitters, sometimes without direct effects of their own. Hormones are different from neurotransmitters in that they are released from various organs into the blood, which carries them throughout the body. However, some hormones act like metabotropic neurotransmitters, binding to receptors on the cell membrane and activating an enzyme. Most neurons are thought to release the same neurotransmitter or combination of neurotransmitters at all of their terminals, although spinal cord motor neurons appear to be an exception. Although each particular synapse is always excitatory or always inhibitory, each neuron receives many synapses, some of which are excitatory and some of which are inhibitory. Some synaptic mechanisms involve a brief flow of ions; others affect metabolic processes and are of slower onset and longer duration. However, all neurotransmitters must be inactivated, either by reuptake into presynaptic terminals or by enzymes. Neurons can be prevented from releasing excessive amounts of neurotransmitters, either by using autoreceptors that detect the released transmitter or by having the postsynaptic cell release a chemical that diffuses back to the presynaptic cell. The most widely studied neurotransmitter systems are those of the amino acids glutamate, glycine, and gamma-aminobutyric acid (GABA); the monoamines dopamine, norepinephrine, epinephrine, and serotonin; peptides, including endorphins, substance P, and neuropeptide Y; acetylcholine (a modified amino acid); purines, including adenosine and ATP; and gases, such as nitric oxide. Levels of some neurotransmitters can be affected by diet. Genetic differences in the forms of receptor subtypes may contribute to certain personality characteristics, such as a tendency toward risky behaviors, novelty seeking, and even schizophrenia. However, the statistical associations between the alternative receptors and the behavioral tendencies are weak.

Drugs typically either impede or facilitate chemical transmission at a given type of synapse. It may seem surprising that many drugs are derived from plants. Plants may use these chemicals to communicate from one part of the plant to another, or they may have evolved them to entice or repel insects or other animals. Indeed, many of the same chemicals are used for communication throughout both the plant and animal kingdoms. Drugs may either block or activate a certain type of receptor, or they may affect release, reuptake, or enzyme inactivation of the neurotransmitter. Since different neurotransmitters have different behavioral and physiological effects, we can frequently predict the effect of a drug on behavior or physiology if we know its synaptic effect. However, there are individual differences in the effectiveness and side effects of drugs, due in part to differences in the numbers and distributions of the subtypes of receptors affected by the drug. Almost all abused drugs increase dopamine release in the nucleus accumbens either directly or indirectly. Amphetamine increases release of dopamine from the presynaptic terminal, while cocaine blocks the reuptake of dopamine, norepinephrine, and serotonin, thereby prolonging their effects. Methylphenidate (Ritalin) also blocks dopamine reuptake; however, at the low doses prescribed for attention deficit disorder (ADD), orally administered methylphenidate does not produce a rush of excitement or addiction. Methylphenidate used for ADD may even decrease later drug use. Methylenedioxymethamphetamine (MDMA, or "ecstasy") increases release of dopamine and, at high doses, of serotonin, thereby producing hallucinogenic effects. It may also destroy serotonin neurons and thus lead to sleep problems, anxiety, depression, memory deficits, and other disorders. Nicotine stimulates nicotinic acetylcholine receptors, which increase dopamine release in the nucleus accumbens. Opiate drugs stimulate the same receptors as do endorphins (*endo*genous m*orphin*es); they contribute directly to reinforcement and also increase (disinhibit) dopamine and norepinephrine release. Marijuana leaves contain Δ^9-tetrahydrocannabinol (Δ^9-THC) and other cannabinoids, which intensify sensory experience, cause memory and cognitive impairments, and cause time perception to be slowed. Cannabinoid receptors are also stimulated by endogenous chemicals, such as anandamide and sn-2-arachidonylglycerol (2-AG), which are released from the postsynaptic cell to the presynaptic cell to decrease neurotransmitter release. Hallucinogenic drugs, such as lysergic acid diethylamide (LSD) stimulate serotonin type 2A (5-HT$_{2A}$) receptors. Chronic use of all abused drugs results in decreased responsiveness of nucleus accumbens cells that mediate reinforcement. However, we do not understand *why* dopamine in the nucleus accumbens is reinforcing.

Learning Objectives

Module 3.1 The Concept of the Synapse

1. Be able to describe Sherrington's inferences concerning the speed of a reflex and temporal and spatial summation.

2. Understand the mechanisms underlying the excitatory and inhibitory postsynaptic potentials.

3. Understand how synaptic potentials contribute to the firing rates of neurons and the integration of information.

Module 3.2 Chemical Events at the Synapse

1. Be able to describe the contributions of T.R. Elliott and O. Loewi to the question of whether most synaptic transmission is electrically or chemically mediated.

2. Be able to list the six major types of neurotransmitters.

3. Understand the role of diet in the synthesis of neurotransmitters.

4. Understand the processes of transport, release, and diffusion of neurotransmitters.

5. Understand the differences between ionotropic and metabotropic effects of neurotransmitters.

6. Be able to describe the similarities and differences between neurotransmitters and hormones.

7. Understand the difference in control mechanisms of the anterior and posterior pituitary and be able to list some of the hormones released from each.

8. Understand why inactivation of neurotransmitters is important and the two major ways in which this is achieved.

9. Be able to explain how genes controlling receptor subtypes could influence personality.

Module 3.3 Drugs and Synapses

1. Understand why our brains have receptors for plant chemicals.

2. Understand the difference between agonists, antagonists, and mixed agonist-antagonists.

3. Be able to explain the common mechanism of action of nearly all abused drugs.

4. Be able to explain the differences between the effects of amphetamine, cocaine, and methylphenidate.

5. Understand the different ways of increasing dopamine release in the nucleus accumbens used by nicotine, opiates, and marijuana.

6. Understand how drugs affect synaptic activity and behavior.

7. Understand how drugs affect synaptic activity and behavior.

8. Understand how drugs affect synaptic activity and behavior.

9. Be able to list the six major types of neurotransmitters.

Key Terms and Concepts

Module 3.1 The Concept of the Synapse

1. The properties of synapses

   Charles Sherrington's inferences
   Reflex arc
   Coordinated flexing and extending
   Speed of a reflex and delayed transmission at the synapse
   Temporal summation

   John Eccles
   Microelectrode
   Excitatory postsynaptic potential (EPSP)

   Open gates for sodium (Na^+) to enter
   Spatial summation

   Larger EPSPs at more distant synapses
   Inhibitory synapses

   Role of interneurons
   Inhibitory postsynaptic potential (IPSP)

   Open gates for potassium (K^+) to leave or for chloride (Cl^-) to enter

2. Relationship among EPSP, IPSP, and action potential

   Combination of temporal and spatial summation
   Spontaneous firing rate

3. In closing: The neuron as decision maker

   Integration of information

Module 3.2 Chemical Events at the Synapse

1. The discovery that most synaptic transmission is chemical

   T. R. Elliott

   Adrenalin
   Sympathetic nervous system

   O. Loewi

   Vagus nerve
   Accelerator nerve

2. The sequence of chemical events at a synapse

    Types of neurotransmitters

        Amino acids

            Glutamate, GABA, glycine, aspartate, maybe others
        Peptides

            Endorphins, substance P, neuropeptide Y, many others
        Acetylcholine

            A modified amino acid
        Monoamines

            Indoleamine: serotonin
            Catecholamines: dopamine, norepinephrine, epinephrine
        Purines

            Adenosine, ATP, maybe others
        Gases

            Nitric oxide (NO), maybe others
            Control of blood flow

    Synthesis of transmitters

        Role of diet

            Acetylcholine

                Choline
            Catecholamines

                Dopamine, norepinephrine, epinephrine
                Precursors: phenylalanine, tyrosine
            Serotonin

                Tryptophan
                Role of insulin

    Transport of transmitters

        Peptides

            Hours or days to transport to axon terminal
        Small neurotransmitters

            Synthesized in terminals, no problem with transport

    Release and diffusion of transmitters

        Vesicles

            Exception: nitric oxide released as soon as formed
            Some transmitter outside of vesicles
        Voltage-dependent calcium gates

Exocytosis

Combination of transmitters

Motor neurons: different transmitters from different branches

Ability to respond to numerous neurotransmitters, though it releases only a few

Activation of receptors of the postsynaptic cell

Multiple receptor subtypes

Ionotropic effects (rapid, short-lived)

Acetylcholine (nicotinic)

Glutamate

GABA

Glycine

Metabotropic effects and second messenger systems (slow, long-lasting)

G-protein (coupled to guanosine triphosphate, GTP)

Second messenger

Cyclic AMP

Neuromodulators, mainly peptides

Hormones

Released from endocrine glands, travel via blood

Protein hormones, peptide hormones

Some chemicals: both hormone and neurotransmitter

Anterior pituitary (glandular tissue)

Releasing hormones from hypothalamus

Adrenocorticotropic hormone (ACTH)

Thyroid stimulating hormone

Prolactin

Somatotropin (growth hormone, GH)

Gonadotropins: follicle stimulating hormone (FSH), luteinizing hormone (LH)

Posterior pituitary (neural tissue, extension of hypothalamus)

Oxytocin

Vasopressin (antidiuretic hormone)

Inactivation and reuptake of neurotransmitters

Acetylcholinesterase: acetylcholine → acetate + choline

Reuptake

Transporters

Conversion to inactive chemicals

COMT (catechol-o-methyltransferase)

MAO (monoamine oxidase)

Peptide neurotransmitters or neuromodulators: diffuse away

Negative feedback from the postsynaptic cell

> Presynaptic autoreceptors: negative feedback
> Chemical from postsynaptic cell: travels back to presynaptic cell

>> Nitric oxide, anandamide, 2-AG

3. Synapses and drug effects

> One form of dopamine D_2 receptor: predisposition to pleasure-seeking behaviors

>> One form of dopamine D_4 receptor: predisposition to novelty-seeking behaviors
>> Other receptor variants: links to anxiety, neurotic personality

>>> Small, unreliable effects

4. In closing: Neurotransmitters and behavior

> Similarities across species

Module 3.3 Drugs and Synapses

1. Drug mechanisms

> Why are our brains sensitive to plant chemicals?

>> Plants evolved chemicals to affect animals' behavior
>> Plants use the same "neurotransmitters"

> Antagonist

> Agonist

> Mixed agonist-antagonist

> Ways to influence synaptic activity

>> Increase or decrease synthesis of neurotransmitter
>> Cause neurotransmitter to leak from vesicles
>> Increase neurotransmitter release
>> Decrease neurotransmitter reuptake
>> Block neurotransmitter breakdown
>> Directly stimulate or block receptors

> Affinity: ability to bind to a receptor

> Efficacy: tendency to activate a receptor

> Variability of responses to drugs

>> Differences in abundance of receptor subtypes

2. Common drugs and their synaptic effects

Abused drugs → dopamine release in nucleus accumbens

Inhibition of cells that release GABA → disinhibition

Stimulant drugs

Increase dopamine activity directly
Increase signal-to-noise ratio
Amphetamine

Reversal of dopamine transporter
Blockade of receptors that inhibit dopamine release
Also → release of serotonin, norepinephrine, etc.
Cocaine

Blockade of reuptake of dopamine, serotonin, norepinephrine
"Crash" after amphetamine or cocaine: depletion of dopamine
Long-term problems: repeated high doses→ stroke, epilepsy, memory impairment
Methylphenidate (Ritalin)

Blockade of dopamine reuptake
Treatment for attention-deficit disorder (ADD)
Low dose oral pills → slower increase in dopamine than cocaine, not addictive
Prolonged use in childhood → less likely to abuse drugs in adolescence
May lead to increased fear response and depression
Methylenedioxymethamphetamine (MDMA, "ecstasy")

Low doses → dopamine release
High doses → also serotonin release and destruction of serotonin axons
Increase anxiety, depression, sleep and memory problems, attention deficits, impulsiveness
Thinner layers in some brain areas
Nicotine → stimulation of nicotinic acetylcholine receptors → dopamine release in nucleus accumbens

Repeated exposure → cells that produce reinforcement are less responsive
Opiates (morphine, heroin, methadone) → relaxation, less sensitivity to pain and problems

Taken for pain relief under medical supervision: rarely abused
Candace Pert and Solomon Snyder: brain peptides: endorphins
Inhibit ventral tegmental neurons that release GABA → disinhibition of dopamine neurons
Inhibit locus coeruleus → decrease norepinephrine release → decrease memory, stress response
Marijuana (Δ^9-tetrahydrocannabinol, Δ^9-THC)

Decreases pain, nausea, glaucoma, increases appetite
Intensifies sensation, illusion of time passing slowly
Impairs memory, cognition
Slow removal from body → fewer withdrawal symptoms
Cannabinoid receptors: abundant except in brain stem: little effect on breathing, heartbeat
Endogenous cannabinoids: anandamide, sn-2 arachidonylglycerol (2-AG)

Presynaptic receptors → decrease both glutamate and GABA release

Disinhibit dopamine neurons in ventral tegmental area

Relieve nausea: inhibition of serotonin type 3 receptors (5-HT$_3$)

Hallucinogenic drugs → stimulation of serotonin 5-HT$_{2A}$ receptors

3. In closing: Neurotransmitters and behavior

Importance of reuptake transporters, retrograde signalling

Why is dopamine reinforcing?

Why does stimulation of serotonin 5-HT$_{2A}$ receptors → hallucinations?

Short-Answer Questions

Module 3.1 The Concept of the Synapse

1. *The properties of synapses*

   a. What is a reflex?

   b. What experimental evidence did Sherrington have for synaptic delay? For temporal summation?

   c. What evidence did he have for spatial summation? For coordinated excitation and inhibition?

   d. Describe John Eccles's experimental support for Sherrington's inferences.

   e. What is an EPSP, and what ionic flow is largely responsible for it?

   f. What is an IPSP, and what ionic flows can produce it?

2. *The relationship among EPSP, IPSP, and action potential*

   a. What influence do EPSPs and IPSPs have on neurons with a spontaneous rate of firing?

3. *In closing: The neuron as decision maker*

   a. What factors influence a cell's "decision" whether or not to produce an action potential?

Module 3.2 Chemical Events at the Synapse

1. *The discovery that most synaptic transmission is chemical*

   a. What did T. R. Elliott propose?

   b. Describe Loewi's experiment with the two frogs' hearts.

2. *The sequence of chemical events at a synapse*

   a. What are the major events, in sequence, at a synapse?

b. List the major neurotransmitters.

c. How is nitric oxide unlike most other neurotransmitters?

d. How is the synthesis of peptide neurotransmitters different from that of most other neurotransmitters?

e. List the three catecholamines in the order of their synthesis. What is their amino acid precursor?

f. How might one increase the amount of acetylcholine in the brain? Serotonin?

g. How quickly can peptide neurotransmitters be transported to the terminal? Why is this not a problem for smaller neurotransmitters?

h. Describe the process of exocytosis.

i. What generalization can be drawn regarding the release of neurotransmitter(s) at the terminals of a given neuron? What type of neurons provides an exception to this generalization?

j. Contrast ionotropic and metabotropic synaptic mechanisms. List three ionotropic neurotransmitter receptors.

k. Discuss the role of second messengers in producing the metabotropic effects of neurotransmitters. What kinds of changes can they exert?

l. What is a G-protein? What is the "first messenger"? What is one common second messenger?

m. What is a neuromodulator? Through what type of receptor (ionotropic or metabotropic) are neuromodulator's effects produced?

n. What is a major difference between the function of neurotransmitters and hormones? Through what kind of receptor (ionotropic or metabotropic) do many hormones act?

o. Contrast the control of the anterior pituitary and posterior pituitary. What are some hormones released from each?

p. How are acetylcholine, serotonin, and the catecholamines inactivated? Why is inactivation important? Are peptide neurotransmitters inactivated after they are released?

q. What are autoreceptors? What is their presumed function?

r. What is the function of chemicals released by the postsynaptic cell that travels back to the presynaptic terminal? Name two such chemicals.

s. Why should there be multiple receptor types for each neurotransmitter?

t. What sorts of behaviors have been linked to alternative forms of genes for the D2 and D4 dopamine receptors? How strong is the association?

3. *Drugs and synapses*

a. What are two possible explanations for why our brains are sensitive to plant chemicals? How common are neurotransmitter molecules throughout the animal kingdom?

b. List six ways in which drugs may affect synaptic function.

c. What is an agonist? An antagonist?

d. How can one drug be an agonist at a given receptor, while another drug, with similar affinity for that receptor, is an antagonist?

e. What may explain individual differences in responsiveness to drugs?

f. What is the common neural mechanism of nearly all drugs of abuse?

g. Describe a way in which inhibitory effects on neurons could result in excitation of a behavior.

h. Contrast the actions of amphetamine and cocaine. What accounts for the "crash" that occurs after taking amphetamine or cocaine?

i. Why is methylphenidate (Ritalin), taken orally as prescribed, less addictive than cocaine? Is there evidence that taking it for attention-deficit disorder in childhood promotes drug addiction in adolescence?

j. What are the neuronal effects of low and high doses of MDMA ("ecstasy")? What psychological effects are observed after MDMA use in humans?

k. How does nicotine affect dopamine release? How are nucleus accumbens cells altered after repeated exposure to nicotine?

l. What are the psychological effects of opiate drugs? What are endorphins? Who discovered them?

m. How do opiates affect cells in the ventral tegmental area that release GABA? What is the resultant effect on dopamine neurons?

n. What are the effects of opiates on norepinephrine-containing cells in the locus coeruleus? What is the effect of opiates on memory and responsiveness to stress?

o. What is the major chemical in the marijuana plant that produces psychological changes? Name some of the medical and psychological changes produced by marijuana.

p. Why does quitting marijuana not produce sudden withdrawal symptoms?

q. What receptors mediate marijuana's effects? Why does marijuana have little effect on breathing and heartbeat?

r. Name two endogenous chemicals that bind to cannabinoid receptors. Where are cannabinoid receptors located (pre- or postsynaptic)?

s. How does stimulation of cannabinoid receptors result in an increase in dopamine release in the nucleus accumbens?

t. How does marijuana affect appetite?

u. What type of receptor is activated by hallucinogenic drugs?

True/False Questions

1. Reflex arcs always consist of activation of motor neurons by sensory neurons within a single segment of the spinal cord.

    TRUE or FALSE

2. C. S. Sherrington discovered the concepts of spatial and temporal summation in simple experiments involving pinching a dog's foot.

   TRUE or FALSE

3. EPSPs and action potentials are similar in that both result from the influx of sodium ions.

   TRUE or FALSE

4. IPSPs and EPSPs are also similar in that both result from the influx of sodium ions.

   TRUE or FALSE

5. Otto Loewi discovered that synaptic conduction is almost always electrical in nature.

   TRUE or FALSE

6. The three catecholamine neurotransmitters are dopamine, epinephrine, and serotonin.

   TRUE or FALSE

7. Brain levels of acetylcholine may be increased by eating a lot of milk, eggs, and peanuts.

   TRUE or FALSE

8. Nitric oxide is a gaseous transmitter that is synthesized at the time it is needed, rather than being stored in vesicles; it is different from "laughing gas."

   TRUE or FALSE

9. Potassium, flowing in through voltage-dependent potassium channels in axon terminals, directly stimulates the release of vesicles containing neurotransmitters.

   TRUE or FALSE

10. Each neuron is responsive to many neurotransmitters, although it releases only one or a few neurotransmitters.

    TRUE or FALSE

11. Ionotropic effects result from ions crossing the membrane through cylindrical channels; these effects are faster, but more short-lived, than metabotropic effects.

    TRUE or FALSE

12. A second messenger is one that is sent out if the first messenger has no effect.

    TRUE or FALSE

13. Neuromodulators are peptide neurotransmitters that do not directly excite or inhibit a postsynaptic cell, but alter the release of other neurotransmitters or the response of the postsynaptic cell.

    TRUE or FALSE

14. Neuromodulators usually activate ionotropic receptors.

    TRUE or FALSE

15. Receptors for protein and peptide hormones are in the cell membrane and activate second messenger systems similar to those of metabotropic neurotransmitters.

TRUE or FALSE

16. The anterior pituitary is composed of neural tissue; neurons in the hypothalamus send axons into the anterior pituitary, from which hormones are released into the general blood circulation.

TRUE or FALSE

17. Hormones released from the anterior pituitary include adrenocorticotropic hormone (ACTH), thyroid-stimulating hormone (TSH), prolactin, somatotropin (growth hormone, GH), and gonadotropins (follicle-stimulating hormone, FSH; luteinizing hormone, LH).

TRUE or FALSE

18. Inactivation of neurotransmitters is accomplished almost exclusively by enzymes that convert them into inactive chemicals.

TRUE or FALSE

19. Levels of some hormones and neurotransmitters are regulated by negative feedback systems.

TRUE or FALSE

20. Species differences in neurotransmitters and receptors are so large that it is impossible to make useful generalizations about them across species.

TRUE or FALSE

21. Affinity and efficacy are really just two different words for the same factor—the ability of a drug to bind to a receptor.

TRUE or FALSE

22. Nearly all drugs of abuse either directly or indirectly increase the extracellular levels of dopamine in the nucleus accumbens.

TRUE or FALSE

23. Both methylphenidate (Ritalin) and cocaine block reuptake of dopamine; however, methylphenidate, taken orally in low doses, produces a more gradual and smaller increase in dopamine levels and is therefore not usually addictive.

TRUE or FALSE

24. The drug methylenedioxymethamphetamine (MDMA, or "ecstasy") acts via nicotinic receptors and is relatively harmless.

TRUE or FALSE

25. Cannabinoid receptors are a type of opioid receptor.

TRUE or FALSE

26. Endorphins increase dopamine release by inhibiting inhibitory neurons in the ventral tegmental area that contain GABA.

    TRUE or FALSE

27. Anandamide is an endogenous chemical that activates cannabinoid receptors and can thereby inhibit the release of both glutamate and GABA.

    TRUE or FALSE

28. Hallucinogenic drugs exert their effects primarily by increasing dopamine release in the nucleus accumbens.

    TRUE or FALSE

Fill In The Blanks

1. _____ , in the late 1800s, showed that neurons do not physically merge with one another.

2. _____ discovered the properties of spatial and temporal summation using behavioral experiments on dogs' reflexes.

3. Temporal summation in single cells was demonstrated by _____ , using microelectrodes inserted into neurons.

4. EPSPs and action potentials are similar in that they both result from an inflow of _____ ions.

5. EPSPs and IPSPs are similar in that they are both _____ .

6. IPSPs result from the outflow of _____ ions and/or the inflow of _____ __ ions.

7. The periodic production of action potentials without synaptic input is referred to as a _____ .

8. Otto Loewi found that when he stimulated the vagus nerve of one frog and then placed fluid collected from around that heart onto a second frog's heart, the second heart _____ .

9. Amino acid neurotransmitters include _____ , _____ , _____ , and

   _____ .

10. Monoamine neurotransmitters include _____ , _____ , _____ , and

    _____ .

11. Some peptide neurotransmitters are _____ , _____ , and _____ .

12. Insulin release, as a result of eating carbohydrates, can increase the production of _____ in the brain.

13. Enzyme-mediated effects that emerge about 30 ms or more after the release of a neurotransmitter are referred to as _____ effects.

14. _____ and _____ hormones activate metabotropic receptors that activate second messenger systems in a cell.

15. Two hormones released from the posterior pituitary are _____ and _____ .

16. Six hormones released from the anterior pituitary are _____ and _____ .

17. The enzyme that inactivates acetylcholine is _____ .

18. Symptoms of _____ can be alleviated by drugs that block acetylcholinesterase.

19. Serotonin and the catecholamines are inactivated primarily by _____ , which occurs through membrane proteins called _____ .

20. _____ are receptors on presynaptic terminals that are sensitive to the same transmitter they release.

21. Alternative forms of the _____ receptor may be associated with alcoholism and other risky behaviors; alternative forms of the _____ receptor may be associated with a novelty-seeking tendency or schizophrenia. However, the statistical correlations for both associations are weak.

22. An _____ is a drug that mimics or increases the effects of a neurotransmitter; an _____ is a drug that blocks the effects of a neurotransmitter.

23. The degree to which a drug binds to a receptor is called its _____ ; the degree to which the drug is able to activate the receptor is called its _____ .

24. Almost all drugs of abuse increase extracellular levels of _____ in the _____ .

25. _____ reverses the dopamine transporter and blocks receptors that inhibit dopamine release; it also increases release of norepinephrine and serotonin.

26. _____ blocks the reuptake of dopamine, serotonin, and norepinephrine.

27. _____ is used to treat attention-deficit disorder; its effects are similar to those of cocaine, but have a slower onset and offset and therefore less potential for addiction.

28. Long-term use of methylenediioxymethamphetamine (_____ or " _____ ") destroys _____ neurons, increases anxiety, depression, sleep problems, memory deficits, attention problems, and impulsiveness.

29. Nicotine stimulates nicotinic receptors, which are a type of _____ receptor and are found on neurons that release _____ in the nucleus accumbens.

30. Peptides known as _____ are the brain's endogenous morphines. They inhibit ventral tegmental neurons that release _____ , and thereby inhibit an inhibitor of dopamine neurons.

31. Marijuana stimulates _____ receptors, which are also stimulated by endogenous peptides such as _____ and sn-2 arachidonylglycerol (_____).

32. Hallucinogenic drugs stimulate _____ receptors.

Matching Items

1. _____ Sherrington
2. _____ Eccles
3. _____ Loewi
4. _____ EPSP
5. _____ IPSP
6. _____ amino acid
7. _____ indoleamine
8. _____ catecholamine
9. _____ peptide
10. _____ gaseous transmitter
11. _____ modified amino acid
12. _____ ionotropic effect
13. _____ metabotropic effect
14. _____ treatment for myasthenia gravis
15. _____ affinity
16. _____ efficacy
17. _____ agonist
18. _____ antagonist
19. _____ inhibited by cocaine

a. nitric oxide
b. acetylcholinesterase inhibitor
c. mimics or increases effects of transmitter
d. dopamine
e. ability to bind to a receptor
f. transmitter activation of G protein, enzyme
g. blocks effects of transmitter
h. inferred major properties of synapses
i. serotonin
j. showed temporal summation in single neurons
k. graded potential due to potassium out or chloride in
l. ability to activate a receptor
m. endorphin
n. glutamate
o. graded potential due to sodium influx
p. opening of ion channel by transmitter
q. showed synaptic conduction is chemical
r. acetylcholine
s. dopamine transporter

Multiple-Choice Questions

1. C. S. Sherrington
    a. did extensive electrophysiological recording of synaptic events.
    b. inferred the existence and properties of synapses from behavioral experiments on reflexes in dogs.
    c. was a student of John Eccles.
    d. found that conduction along a single axon is slower than through a reflex arc.

2. Which of the following was not one of Sherrington's findings?
    a. The speed of conduction through a reflex arc was significantly slower than the known speed of conduction along an axon.
    b. Repeating a subthreshold pinch several times in rapid succession elicited leg flexion.
    c. Simultaneous subthreshold pinches in different parts of the foot elicited flexion.
    d. Reflex arcs are limited to one limb and are always excitatory.

3. Electrophysiological recording from a single neuron
    a. utilizes a microelectrode inserted into the neuron.
    b. supported Sherrington's inferences.
    c. is a field pioneered by John Eccles.
    d. all of the above.

4. IPSPs
    a. may summate to generate an action potential.
    b. are always hyperpolarizing under natural conditions.
    c. are characterized mainly by a large influx of potassium ions.
    d. are characterized mainly by a large influx of sodium ions.

5. Which of the following is true?
    a. The size of EPSPs is the same at all excitatory synapses.
    b. The primary means of inactivation for all neurotransmitters is degradation by an enzyme.
    c. The size, duration, and direction (hyperpolarizing or depolarizing) of a postsynaptic potential are functions of the type and amount of transmitter released, the type and number of receptor sites present, and perhaps other factors.
    d. A given neuron may release either an excitatory or an inhibitory transmitter (at different times), depending on whether it was excited or inhibited by a previous neuron.

6. EPSPs and action potentials are similar in that
    a. sodium is the major ion producing a depolarization in both.
    b. sodium is the major ion producing a hyperpolarization in both.
    c. potassium is the major ion producing a depolarization in both.
    d. both decay as a function of time and space, decreasing in magnitude as they travel along the membrane.

7. EPSPs
   a. result from a flow of potassium (K+) and chloride (Cl-) ions.
   b. are always depolarizing in natural conditions.
   c. are always large enough to cause the postsynaptic cell to reach triggering threshold for an action potential; otherwise there would be too much uncertainty in the nervous system.
   d. are the same as action potentials.

8. EPSPs and IPSPs
   a. may alter a neuron's spontaneous firing rate.
   b. are always the same size.
   c. usually occur one at a time, so that the neuron does not get confused.
   d. all of the above.

9. T. R. Elliott discovered that
   a. adrenalin slowed a frog's heart.
   b. synaptic transmission is electrical rather than chemical.
   c. adrenalin could mimic the effects of the sympathetic nervous system.
   d. all of the above.

10. Otto Loewi discovered that a substance collected from the vagus nerve innervating one frog's heart and transferred to a second frog's heart
   a. slowed the second frog's heart.
   b. speeded the second frog's heart.
   c. either speeded or slowed the second frog's heart, depending on the quantity applied.
   d. had no effect, thereby showing that synaptic transmission is not chemically mediated.

11. The level of acetylcholine in the brain can be increased by increasing dietary intake of
   a. acetylcholine.
   b. tyrosine.
   c. choline.
   d. tryptophan.

12. Serotonin levels in the brain can be increased by eating a meal that has protein and is high in
   a. choline.
   b. tyrosine.
   c. fat.
   d. carbohydrates.

13. The speed of transport of substances down an axon
   a. is fast enough that even the longest axons require only a few minutes for substances synthesized in the nucleus to reach the terminal.
   b. limits the availability of small neurotransmitters more than that of peptides.
   c. limits the availability of peptides more than that of small neurotransmitters.
   d. is a severe limitation on the availability of all neurotransmitters.

14. Calcium
    a. is responsible for exocytosis of neurotransmitters.
    b. enters the terminal when an action potential opens voltage-dependent calcium gates.
    c. causes the release of neurotransmitters.
    d. all of the above.

15. Vesicles
    a. are tiny nearly-spherical packets filled with neurotransmitters.
    b. are especially important for storing nitric oxide.
    c. are the only places where transmitters are found in axon terminals.
    d. store only excitatory neurotransmitters; inhibitory neurotransmitters are never stored in vesicles.

16. Each terminal of a given axon
    a. releases a different neurotransmitter, thus providing a rich repertoire of effects.
    b. usually releases the same neurotransmitter or combination of neurotransmitters at every terminal of that axon, although one exception to that rule is the motor neurons of the spinal cord.
    c. releases only one neurotransmitter, so as not to "confuse" the postsynaptic cell.
    d. releases all of the neurotransmitters known to exist in the brain.

17. Ionotropic synaptic mechanisms
    a. have slow-onset, long-lasting effects.
    b. use a cyclic AMP second messenger response.
    c. are exemplified by glutamate, GABA, and acetylcholine receptors.
    d. frequently use hormones as transmitters.

18. Metabotropic synapses
    a. may have effects that significantly outlast the release of the transmitter.
    b. are activated when a neurotransmitter binds to its receptor site and thereby induces a change in an intracellular part of the receptor that is coupled to a G-protein.
    c. are characterized by initiation of changes in proteins by cyclic AMP, which in turn open or close ion gates or alter the structure or metabolism of the cell.
    d. all of the above.

19. Neuromodulators
    a. are usually peptides that diffuse widely enough to affect several cells.
    b. are carried in the blood throughout the entire body.
    c. are usually monoamine neurotransmitters.
    d. usually have ionotropic effects.

20. Hormones
    a. are released in small quantities close to the target cells.
    b. may exert their effects through metabotropic receptors on the surface of cells.
    c. usually exert their effects through ionotropic receptors on the surface of cells.
    d. none of the above.

21. The posterior pituitary
    a. is composed of glandular tissue.
    b. releases ACTH, TSH, prolactin, somatotropin, FSH, and LH into the blood stream.
    c. releases oxytocin and vasopressin into the blood stream.
    d. all of the above.

22. Acetylcholinesterase
    a. promotes reuptake of ACh into cholinergic terminals, thereby inactivating it.
    b. is the enzyme that produces ACh.
    c. is the enzyme that cleaves ACh into two inactive parts.
    d. blocks reuptake of choline into cholinergic terminals.

23. Reuptake of neurotransmitters
    a. is the major method of inactivation of ACh.
    b. is the major method of inactivation of serotonin and the catecholamines.
    c. is speeded up by COMT.
    d. is completely blocked by MAO.

24. An antagonist is a drug that
    a. has no affinity for a receptor.
    b. changes EPSPs into IPSPs.
    c. mimics or strengthens the effects of a neurotransmitter.
    d. blocks the effects of a neurotransmitter.

25. Which of the following is true?
    a. Some plant-derived drugs are chemicals that are used by the plants to communicate from one part of the plant to another.
    b. There is a great deal of specificity in neurotransmitters across species; most transmitters used in humans have no counterpart in other species.
    c. A drug with high affinity for a given receptor will always elicit a response from that receptor.
    d. The presence of alternative forms of certain dopamine receptors can explain most cases of alcoholism, novelty-seeking, and schizophrenia.

26. Almost all drugs of abuse
    a. activate serotonin 2A receptors.
    b. activate cannabinoid receptors.
    c. activate opioid receptors.
    d. increase dopamine release in the nucleus accumbens.

27. Methylphenidate (Ritalin)
    a. blocks the reuptake of dopamine.
    b. is used to treat attention-deficit disorder (ADD).
    c. may decrease adolescent drug addiction after treatment of childhood ADD.
    d. all of the above.

28. Anandamide
    a. is an opioid peptide.
    b. is sometimes known as "ecstasy."
    c. is an endogenous chemical that activates cannabinoid receptors.
    d. stimulates serotonin 2A receptors and thereby induces hallucinations.

Crossword Puzzle

Synaptic Symphony

www.CrosswordWeaver.com

ACROSS

1 Temporary hyperpolarization (abbr.)
5 Monoamine transmitter made from tryptophan
10 A peptide neurotransmitter
12 Temporary depolarization (abbr.)
13 Type of summation in which rapidly repeated stimuli have a cumulative effect
15 Cyclic ___: a common second messenger
16 Kind of animal whose reflexes were studied by Sherrington
21 A protein that synthesizes or metabolizes transmitters (and other chemicals)
24 Type of summation in which inputs from nearby locations exert a cumulative effect
26 Negative ion that enters through GABA receptors
27 He stimulated a frog's vagus nerve, showed synaptic transmission is chemical
28 A chain of amino acids
30 Ability to bind to a receptor
31 Inhibitory amino acid (abbr.)
32 Part of pituitary that consists of glandular tissue

DOWN

2 Extracellular space between axon terminal and dendrite
3 Type of receptor that opens ion channels
4 Type of acid used as transmitter or as building blocks of peptides and proteins
6 Nitric _____: a gaseous transmitter
7 Drug that increases activity at a given type of synapse
8 Receptor activated by acetylcholine
9 Monoamine transmitter activated by stimulant drug
11 An automatic muscular response to a stimulus
14 Major means of inactivating released transmitters
17 Excitatory amino acid transmitter
18 Precursor of acetylcholine
19 Storage packet for neurotransmitters
20 Part of pituitary that consists of neural tissue, extension of hypothalamus
22 He used microelectrodes to study electrical potentials
23 Tendency to activate a receptor
25 Positive ion that produces EPSP
29 Enzyme that metabolizes monoamines (abbr.)

Crossword Puzzle Solution

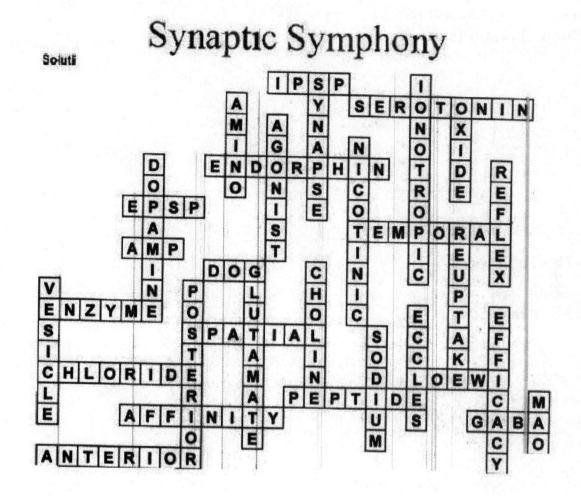

Synaptic Symphony

Soluti

Solutions

True/False Questions

1. F	11. T	20. F
2. T	12. F	21. F
3. T	13. T	22. T
4. F	14. F	23. T
5. F	15. T	24. F
6. F	16. F	25. F
7. T	17. T	26. T
8. T	18. F	27. T
9. F	19. T	28. F
10. T		

Fill In The Blanks

1. Ramon y Cajal
2. Charles Sherrington
3. John Eccles
4. Na+ (sodium)
5. graded potentials
6. K+ (potassium); Cl- (chloride)
7. spontaneous firing rate
8. slowed
9. glutamate; GABA; glycine; aspartate
10. dopamine; norepinephrine; epinephrine; serotonin
11. endorphins; substance P; neuropeptide Y
12. serotonin
13. metabotropic
14. Protein ; peptide
15. oxytocin; vasopressin
16. adrenocorticotropin, thyroid-stimulating hormone, prolactin, growth hormone, follicle-stimulating hormone,; luteinizing hormone
17. acetylcholinesterase
18. myasthenia gravis
19. reuptake; transporters
20. Autoreceptors
21. D2; D4
22. agonist; antagonist

23. affinity; efficacy
24. dopamine; nucleus accembens
25. Amphetamine
26. Cocaine
27. Methylphenidate
28. MDMA; ecstasy; serotonin
29. acetylcholine; dopamine
30. endorphins; GABA
31. cannabinoid; anandamide; 2-AG
32. serotonin 2A

Matching Items

1. H	8. D	15. E
2. J	9. M	16. L
3. Q	10. A	17. C
4. O	11. R	18. G
5. K	12. P	19. S
6. N	13. F	
7. I	14. B	

Multiple-Choice Questions

1. B	11. C	21. C
2. D	12. D	22. B
3. D	13. C	23. B
4. B	14. D	24. D
5. C	15. A	25. A
6. A	16. B	26. D
7. B	17. C	27. D
8. A	18. D	28. C
9. C	19. A	
10. A	20. B	

CHAPTER 4

ANATOMY OF THE NERVOUS SYSTEM

Introduction

The vertebrate nervous system consists of two major divisions, the central (CNS) and the peripheral (PNS) nervous systems. The CNS is composed of the brain and the spinal cord. The PNS is divided into the somatic and the autonomic nervous systems. The somatic system consists of sensory nerves that convey information from sense organs to the spinal cord, and motor nerves carrying messages from the spinal cord to muscles and glands. A pair of sensory nerves enters (one from each side) and a pair of motor nerves exits from the spinal cord through each pair of openings in the vertebral canal. The sensory nerves enter the spinal cord from the dorsal direction, and the motor axons leave from the ventral aspect. Cell bodies of sensory neurons lie in the dorsal root ganglia; those of the motor neurons are in the spinal cord. The autonomic nervous system also sends neurons through the vertebral openings; they synapse in ganglia outside the spinal cord. Ganglia of the sympathetic division of the autonomic nervous system are arranged in an interconnected chain along the thoracic and lumbar sections of the spinal cord. Ganglia of the parasympathetic division of the autonomic nervous system receive input from the cranial nerves and the sacral section of the cord and are located near the organs they innervate. The interconnections of the sympathetic system promote unified action by the body in a fight-or-flight situation, whereas the relative independence of the parasympathetic innervations allows for more discrete energy-saving responses. Most of the final synapses of the sympathetic nervous system use the neurotransmitter norepinephrine, while the final parasympathetic synapses use acetylcholine.

The brain is divided into the hindbrain, the midbrain, and the forebrain. The hindbrain is composed of the medulla, the pons, and the cerebellum. The medulla contains numerous nuclei that control life-preserving reflexes. The pons has many fibers that cross from one side to the other, going to the cerebellum, which is directly behind the pons. The cerebellum helps control movement and is important for shifting attention and for timing. The reticular formation and the raphe system, which modify the brain's readiness to respond to stimuli, have diffusely branching neurons throughout the medulla, pons, and midbrain and send diffusely branching axons throughout the brain. The midbrain is composed of the tectum (or roof), on which are the two superior colliculi and the two inferior colliculi, involved in sensory processing; and the tegmentum, containing cranial nerve nuclei, parts of the reticular formation, extensions of neural systems of the hindbrain, and the substantia nigra, degeneration of which causes Parkinson's disease. The forebrain includes the limbic system, a number of interlinked structures important for motivational and emotional behaviors; the thalamus, which is the main source of sensory input to the cerebral cortex; the hypothalamus, important for motivational and hormonal regulation; the pituitary or "master gland"; the basal ganglia, which influence motor movements, emotional expression, memory, and reasoning; the hippocampus, important in memory functions; and the cerebral cortex, which surrounds the rest of the brain and is responsible for complex sensory analysis and integration, language processing, motor control, and social awareness. The ventricles are fluid-filled cavities within the brain.

The cerebral cortex consists of up to six laminae, or layers, of cell bodies parallel to the surface of the brain. The cells are organized into columns, perpendicular to the laminae; each column contains cells with similar response properties. The occipital lobe of the cerebral cortex is the site of primary visual processing. The parietal lobe processes somatosensory and numerical information and contributes to our spatial sense. The temporal lobe processes auditory information and is important for perception of complex visual patterns, comprehension of language, and emotional and motivated behaviors. The frontal lobe contains the motor cortex, which controls fine movements, and prefrontal cortex, which contributes to social awareness, the expression of emotion, memory for recent details (working memory), and calculation of actions and their outcomes.

Each part of the brain accomplishes a set of more or less specific functions; yet, a sense of unified experience emerges from these separate operations. The question of how the brain integrates various kinds of sensory information into the perception of a unified object is known as the binding problem. How are the various aspects bound together? One possibility is that binding depends on precisely simultaneous activity (gamma waves) in the different brain areas. However, we still do not understand how synchronized gamma waves bind the different aspects into a unified perception. The inferior temporal cortex may contribute to binding by assigning aspects of a perception to a common location in space.

Describing the structure of the brain can be tedious, but understanding the functions of the various structures is daunting. Images of the whole brain can be obtained by computerized axial tomography (CAT or CT scans) or magnetic resonance imaging (MRI). Localized brain activity can be recorded with an electroencephalograph (EEG), which records either spontaneous activity or evoked potentials. Activity can also be recorded by a magnetoencephallograph (MEG), which measures faint magnetic fields. In addition brain activity can be recorded during a task, using electrodes or positron emission tomography (PET), which detects radioactivity from labeled chemicals taken up by the most active brain areas. A less expensive and less dangerous method is functional magnetic resonance imaging (fMRI), which detects changes in hemoglobin molecules as they release oxygen to the most active brain areas. The functions of brain areas can also be inferred from accidental (in humans) or deliberate (in animals) damage or temporary inactivation. Such inferences can be compared with those from electrical or magnetic stimulation of those areas in an intact brain. One problem with inferences about the function of a brain area from correlations between its size or activity and behavior is that correlation does not imply causation. Also, previous experience with a task may alter the brain's activity during a task.

Learning Objectives

Module 4.1 Structure of the Vertebrate Nervous System

1. Be able to identify the directional terms for anatomical structures.

2. Be able to describe the structure of the spinal cord and the locations of its sensory inputs and motor outputs.

3. Know the functions, locations, and organization of the two main branches of the autonomic nervous system.

4. Know the three main divisions of the hindbrain and both their unique and their shared functions.

5. Know the two divisions of the midbrain and the major structures in each.

6. Be able to identify the main structures and functions of the diencephalon, the limbic system, the basal ganglia, and the basal forebrain.

Module 4.2 The Cerebral Cortex

1. Know the locations and functions of the four lobes of the cerebral cortex.

2. Understand the "binding problem" and a possible means of coordinating neural activity throughout a large portion of the brain to form a unified perception.

Module 4.3 Research Methods

1. Understand the uses of and principles underlying the techniques of computerized axial tomography (CAT), magnetic resonance imagine (MRI), electroencephalography (EEG), magnetoencephalography (MEG), positron emission tomography (PET), and functional magnetic resonance imaging (fMRI).

2. Be able to identify the major ways of inactivating parts of the brain, temporarily or permanently, and of stimulating parts of the brain.

3. Understand the problems of interpretation of the effects of lesions.

Key Terms and Concepts

Module 4.1 Structure of the Vertebrate Nervous System

1. Terminology that describes the nervous system

   Central nervous system (CNS): Brain and spinal cord

   Peripheral nervous system (PNS): Somatic and autonomic nervous systems

   Dorsal (toward the back)

   Ventral (toward the stomach)

   Dorsal-ventral axis of human brain at right angles to dorsal-ventral axis of spinal cord

2. The spinal cord

   Bell-Magendie Law

   > Sensory nerves: Enter dorsally
   > Motor nerves: Exit ventrally

   Dorsal root ganglia: Clusters of cell bodies of sensory neurons

   Gray matter: Cell bodies and dendrites

   White matter: Myelinated axons

3. The autonomic nervous system

   Sympathetic nervous system ("fight or flight")

   > Sympathetic chains of ganglia
   > Thoracic and lumbar regions of spinal cord
   > Norepinephrine

   Parasympathetic nervous system (energy conserving)

   > Cranial and sacral regions (craniosacral system)
   > Ganglia near organs
   > Acetylcholine

4. The hindbrain (rhombencephalon): Medulla, pons, cerebellum

   Brain stem (medulla, pons, midbrain, some forebrain structures)

   Medulla

   > Vital reflexes
   > Cranial nerves
   > Reticular formation
   > Raphe system

   Pons ("bridge")

   > Fibers crossing
   > Cranial nerves
   > Reticular formation
   > Raphe system

   Cerebellum

   > Control of movement
   > Balance and coordination
   > Shifting attention
   > Timing

5. The midbrain (mesencephalon)

    Tectum

        Superior and inferior colliculi

    Tegmentum

        Cranial nerves
        Reticular formation
        Substantia nigra

6. The forebrain (prosencephalon)

    Cerebral hemispheres

    Cerebral cortex

    Limbic system: Border around brain stem

        Olfactory bulb
        Hypothalamus
        Hippocampus
        Amygdala
        Cingulate gyrus of cerebral cortex

    Thalamus (part of diencephalon)

        Transmits sensory information (except olfaction) to cortex

    Hypothalamus (part of diencephalon, ventral to thalamus)

        Motivated behaviors
        Control of pituitary gland

    Pituitary gland

        Controls other glands

    Basal ganglia

        Caudate nucleus
        Putamen
        Globus pallidus
        Connections with frontal cortex
        Control of movement
        Aspects of memory and emotional expression
        Parkinson's disease
        Huntington's disease

    Basal forebrain

        Nucleus basalis: acetylcholine to cortex

      Arousal, wakefulness, attention

      Parkinson's disease

      Alzheimer's disease

   Hippocampus

      Storing new memories

7. The ventricles

   Central canal of spinal cord

   Two lateral ventricles, third and fourth ventricles

   Cerebrospinal fluid (CSF)

      Cushion, buoyancy, reservoir of hormones and nutrition

   Choroid plexus: Forms CSF

   Meninges

   Subarachnoid space: Reabsorption of CSF into blood vessels

   Hydrocephalus

8. In closing: Learning neuroanatomy

Module 4.2 The Cerebral Cortex

1. Organization of the cerebral cortex

   Connections between hemispheres

      Corpus callosum

      Anterior commissure

   Cortex: Higher percentage of brain in primates

   Laminae: Layers parallel to surface

   Columns: Perpendicular to laminae

2. The occipital lobe (posterior, or caudal, end of cortex)

   Primary visual cortex

   Striate cortex

   Cortical blindness

3. The parietal lobe (between occipital lobe and central sulcus)

Central sulcus

Postcentral gyrus: Primary somatosensory cortex

    Four bands parallel to central sulcus

        Two light-touch bands
        One deep-pressure band
        One light-touch and deep-pressure band

Interpretation of visual and auditory input, numerical information

4. The temporal lobe (lateral, near temples)

    Primary auditory cortex

    Language comprehension

    Complex visual patterns

    Klüver-Bucy syndrome

5. The frontal lobe (from central sulcus to anterior end of brain)

    Precentral gyrus: Primary motor cortex

    Prefrontal cortex

        Prefrontal lobotomies

            Lack of initiative
            Failure to inhibit unacceptable impulses

    Modern view of functions of the prefrontal cortex

        Working memory: Memory for recent events
        Delayed-response task

    Follow two or more rules at same time

    Modify behavior according to context

6. How do the parts work together?

    Operation as a whole vs. collection of parts

    The binding problem

        How brain areas influence one another to produce perception of single object
        "Association area"

            Advanced processing on a particular sensory system, not combining 2 systems
        Synchronized gamma waves (30-80 action potentials/second)
        Parietal cortex: Location of object in space

7. In closing: Functions of the cerebral cortex

Elaborating sensory material

Module 4.3 Research Methods

1. Correlating brain anatomy with behavior

Phrenology

Computerized axial tomography (CAT or CT scan)

Pass x-rays through the head

Magnetic resonance imaging (MRI)

Atoms with odd-numbered atomic weights: inherent rotation
Magnetic field aligns rotation of atoms
Brief radio frequency field → tilt axes
Field turned off → atoms relax, give off electromagnetic energy
Advantage: good spatial resolution without radioactivity
Disadvantage: lie motionless in confining, noisy apparatus

Problem: Correlation does not mean causation

2. Recording brain activity

Electroencephalograph (EEG)

Spontaneous brain activity
Evoked potentials (evoked responses)

Magnetoencephalograph (MEG)

Minute magnetic fields generated by brain activity
Good temporal resolution, but poor spatial resolution

Positron emission tomography (PET)

Radioactive chemical absorbed by most active neurons
Radioactive decay → positron collides with electron → two gamma rays
Gamma ray detectors
High spatial resolution
Dangerous because of radioactivity

Functional magnetic resonance imaging (fMRI)

Changes in hemoglobin molecules as they release oxygen in active areas
Less dangerous and less expensive than PET
Problem with interpretation of results

What is comparison task?

Experience alters results

3. Effects of brain damage

Paul Broca

Part of left frontal lobe: Broca's area → ability to speak

Lesion: Damage to an area

Ablation: Removal of an area
Chemical inactivation or electrode-induced lesion in animals
Stereotaxic instrument, atlas
Sham lesion

Gene-knockout approach: directed mutation of a gene

Transcranial magnetic stimulation: Disruption of local activity by intense magnetic field

Difficulty of determining exact function

4. Effects of brain stimulation

Electrical stimulation in animals

Brief, moderate intensity magnetic fields in humans

Injection of chemical that stimulates one kind of receptor

5. Brain and intelligence

Comparisons across species

Brain-to-body ratio

Comparisons across humans

Moderate positive correlation between brain size and IQ
Significant correlation between IQ and specific brain areas
Men: Larger brains than women, but equal IQs
Women: more and deeper gyri → more surface area
Men and women: equal gray matter; men: more white matter

No practical applications

6. In closing: Methods and their limits

Short-Answer Questions

Module 4.1 Structure of the Vertebrate Nervous System

1. *The spinal cord*

   a. Draw a cross section of the spinal cord, including sensory and motor nerves, dorsal root ganglia, and dorsal and ventral directions.

   b. What is the Bell-Magendie Law?

   c. What makes up gray matter? White matter?

   d. The autonomic nervous system

   e. Of what two parts does the autonomic nervous system consist? Give the location and basic function of each.

   f. Which transmitter is used by the postganglionic parasympathetic nerves? Which is used by most sympathetic postganglionic nerves?

2. *The hindbrain*

   a. What are the three components of the hindbrain? Give one "specialty" of each.

   b. What are cranial nerves? Where are their nuclei?

   c. What are the anatomical locations and functions of the reticular formation and the raphe system?

3. *The midbrain*

   a. What are the two major divisions of the midbrain? Name two structures in each division.

4. *The forebrain*

   a. What are the major structures comprising the limbic system? What are the general functions of this interconnected system?

   b. Describe the relationship of the thalamus to the cerebral cortex.

   c. Where is the hypothalamus, and what kinds of behavior does it help regulate?

   d. Where is the pituitary? What is its function? What structure largely controls it?

   e. Where are the basal ganglia? Which structures make up the basal ganglia? Briefly describe their function.

   f. Where is the hippocampus? To what psychological process has it been linked?

   g. The ventricles

   h. What are the ventricles? Where is cerebrospinal fluid (CSF) formed? In which direction does it flow? Where is it reabsorbed into blood vessels?

   i. What are the functions of CSF?

Module 4.2 The Cerebral Cortex

1. *Organization of cerebral cortex*

    a. What is the relationship of gray matter to white in the cortex? Compare this relationship to that in the spinal cord.

    b. How many layers (laminae) does human neocortex have? Describe the input to lamina IV and the output from lamina V.

    c. What is the relationship of columns to laminae? What can be said about all the cells within one column?

2. *The occipital lobe*

    a. What are the location and functions of the occipital lobe?

3. *The parietal lobe*

    a. What are the location and functions of the parietal lobe?

4. *The temporal lobe*

    a. Where is the temporal lobe? What are some temporal lobe functions?

5. *The frontal lobe*

    a. What are the location and functions of the frontal lobe? Distinguish between the precentral gyrus and the prefrontal cortex.

    b. What were the results of prefrontal lobotomies?

    c. What is working memory? What is one task that shows impairment after prefrontal lesions?

6. *How do the parts work together?*

    a. What is the binding problem?

    b. What are gamma waves? What may be the role of the inferior temporal cortex in binding the different aspects of sensory objects?

Module 4.3 Research Methods

1. *Correlating brain activity with behavior*

    a. What was phrenology?

    b. Describe computerized axial tomography (CAT).

    c. What is the basis for magnetic resonance imaging? What is one drawback of this method?

    d. What is a limitation of inferences of function from correlations with measurable features of the brain?

2. *Recording brain activity*

    a. Describe the process of electroencephalography (EEG). What two types of activity can it measure?

b. How does magnetoencephalography (MEG) differ from electroencephalography? Does it have better spatial or temporal resolution than EEG?

c. What is the principle on which positron emission tomography (PET) is based?

d. What are two advantages of functional magnetic resonance imaging (fMRI) over PET? What is the physical basis for fMRI?

e. What is a problem with inferring function from records of brain activity?

3. *Effects of brain damage*

a. What did Paul Broca discover?

b. What is a stereotaxic instrument used for?

c. What are four methods of deliberately inactivating some type or location of brain activity?

d. What is the main problem with inferences about function based on these approaches?

e. Effects of brain stimulation

f. Compare the magnetic stimulation used to stimulate certain brain areas with that used to inactivate brain areas.

g. What is a problem with inferences about the functions of brain areas based on localized stimulation?

True/False Questions

1. Sensory nerves enter the spinal cord from the dorsal side, and motor nerves exit from the ventral side.
TRUE or FALSE

2. Ganglia of the sympathetic nervous system lie along the cervical and sacral parts of the spinal cord.
TRUE or FALSE

3. The postganglionic transmitter of the parasympathetic nervous system is norepinephrine.
TRUE or FALSE

4. The reticular formation and raphe system are found in the pons and medulla; they regulate arousal and the readiness to respond, respectively.
TRUE or FALSE

5. The substantia nigra is found in the tectum of the midbrain and controls vital reflexes.
TRUE or FALSE

6. The limbic system comprises the olfactory bulb, the hypothalamus, the hippocampus, the amygdala, and the cingulate gyrus of the cerebral cortex.
TRUE or FALSE

7. The main function of the hypothalamus is to transmit information to the cortex.
TRUE or FALSE

8. The basal ganglia are concerned with the control of movement and also some aspects of memory, reasoning, and emotional expression.

    TRUE or FALSE

9. A major function of the hippocampus is control of the pituitary gland.

    TRUE or FALSE

10. The ventricles contain cerebrospinal fluid (CSF) that is produced by the choroid plexus and provides cushioning and buoyancy to the brain.

    TRUE or FALSE

11. Laminae of the cerebral cortex are the same thing as columns.

    TRUE or FALSE

12. The occipital lobe is the site of primary auditory cortex.

    TRUE or FALSE

13. The temporal lobe is essential for the understanding of spoken language and also contributes to complex visual perceptions.

    TRUE or FALSE

14. The prefrontal cortex is the primary motor cortex.

    TRUE or FALSE

15. Magnetoencephalography is a technique that detects the electromagnetic energy given off after atoms with odd numbers of electrons relax after a strong radiofrequency field is turned off.

    TRUE or FALSE

16. PET scans are safer and less expensive than fMRI scans.

    TRUE or FALSE

17. Paul Broca discovered that people who had lost their ability to speak usually had damage to a part of the left frontal lobe.

    TRUE or FALSE

18. A stereotaxic instrument is used to direct electrodes to a precise area of the brain.

    TRUE or FALSE

Fill In The Blanks

1. The Bell-Magendie Law states that sensory neurons enter the spinal cord from the _____ direction, and motor neurons exit the spinal cord from the _____ direction.

2. The autonomic nervous system consists of the _____ nervous system, with ganglia located _____ , and the _____ nervous system, with ganglia located _____ .

3. The hind brain consists of the _____ , the _____ , and the _____ .

4. In addition to containing the reticular formation and the raphe system, the medulla contains cranial nerve nuclei that control _____ .

5. The pons gets its name (Latin for "bridge") from _____ .

6. The cerebellum was originally thought to be important only for controlling _____ ; however, we now know that it also contributes to _____ and _____ .

7. The _____ of the midbrain contains the superior and inferior colliculi; the _____ of the midbrain contains nuclei of cranial nerves, part of the reticular formation, and the substantia nigra.

8. The main structures that comprise the limbic system are the _____ , the _____ , the _____ , the _____ , and the _____ of the cerebral cortex.

9. The main function of the _____ is to transmit sensory information (except olfaction) to the cerebral cortex.

10. The hypothalamus sends hypothalamic hormones to the _____ gland, and also helps to regulate various _____ behaviors.

11. The basal ganglia comprise the _____ , the _____ , and the _____ .

12. The basal ganglia have important connections with the _____ and are important for the control of _____ and aspects of _____ and _____ .

13. The _____ in the basal forebrain sends acetylcholine to the cortex and promotes arousal, wakefulness, and attention.

14. The main function of the _____ is storing new memories.

15. The _____ forms cerebrospinal fluid.

16. The _____ of the cerebral cortex are layers of cell bodies that lie parallel to the surface of the cortex; the _____ of the cortex are perpendicular to the laminae and contain neurons that have similar properties.

17. Primary visual cortex is located in the _____ lobe.

18. The parietal lobe contains the postcentral gyrus, which is the primary _____ cortex.

19. A tumor in the temporal lobe may give rise to _____ or _____ hallucinations.

20. The main divisions of the frontal lobe are the _____ , which serves as the primary motor cortex, and the _____ , which contributes to working memory and modifies behavior according to the context.

21. The question of how the various areas of the brain work together to form a unitary perception is known as the _____ . This function may be mediated by _____ waves of neural firing throughout much of the cortex.

22. The technique of _____ records magnetic fields generated by brain activity. It has good _____ resolution, but poor _____ resolution.

23. The technique of _____ (_____) uses the inherent rotation of atoms with odd-numbered atomic weights. A powerful magnetic field aligns the axes of rotation, which are tilted by a radiofrequency field. When the radiofrequency field is turned off, the atoms release electromagnetic energy as they relax. This technique has good _____ resolution.

24. The method of recording brain activity that measures changes in hemoglobin molecules as they release oxygen in active brain areas is _____ .

25. Paul Broca discovered that loss of speech was frequently correlated with brain damage in the _____ .

26. Different intensities and durations of magnetic fields can be used either to _____ or to _____ localized brain areas.

Matching Items

1. _____ CAT scans
2. _____ Intense, prolonged magnetic fields
3. _____ Brief, moderate intensity magnetic fields
4. _____ PET scans
5. _____ fMRI
6. _____ Dorsal root ganglia
7. _____ Motor axons
8. _____ Sympathetic nervous system
9. _____ Medulla
10. _____ Pons
11. _____ Midbrain
12. _____ Thalamus
13. _____ Hypothalamus
14. _____ Basal ganglia
15. _____ Occipital lobe
16. _____ Temporal lobe
17. _____ Parietal lobe
18. _____ Frontal lobe

a. Contains "vital nuclei"
b. Site of axons crossing to other side
c. Contains primary motor cortex
d. X-rays used to show brain structure
e. Exit through the ventral side of the spinal cord
f. Hemoglobin molecules releasing oxygen
g. Relays information to cerebral cortex
h. Method of temporarily inactivating an area
i. Movement, memory, emotional expression
j. Primary visual cortex
k. "Fight or flight" system
l. Cell bodies of sensory neurons
m. Primary somatosensory cortex
n. Site of tectum and tegmentum
o. Primary auditory cortex
p. Method of stimulating a brain area
q. Motivated behaviors, controls pituitary
r. Radioactive chemicals in most-active areas

Multiple-Choice Questions

1. Which is true concerning the spinal cord?
   a. Sensory neurons enter on the ventral side; motor neurons exit on the dorsal side.
   b. Cell bodies of sensory neurons lie outside the CNS in the dorsal root ganglia.
   c. Cell bodies of motor neurons lie outside the CNS in the ventral root ganglia.
   d. All of the above are true.

2. The parasympathetic nervous system
   a. is sometimes called the "fight or flight" system.
   b. has a chain of interconnected ganglia along the thoracic and lumbar parts of the spinal cord.
   c. uses norepinephrine as its transmitter to end organs, whereas the sympathetic system uses acetylcholine.
   d. is an energy-conserving system.

3. Concerning the cranial nerves,
    a. nuclei for the first four enter the forebrain and midbrain; nuclei for the rest are in the medulla and pons.
    b. nuclei for all twelve are in the medulla and pons.
    c. all have both sensory and motor components.
    d. all have only sensory or only motor components.

4. The hindbrain
    a. consists of four parts: the superior and inferior colliculi, the tectum, and the tegmentum.
    b. contains the reticular formation and raphe system.
    c. controls the pituitary gland.
    d. consists of the pons, which is adjacent to the spinal cord; the medulla, which is rostral to the pons; and the cerebellum, which is anterior to the pons.

5. The medulla
    a. contains prominent axons crossing from one side of the brain to the other.
    b. is part of the limbic system.
    c. contains nuclei that control vital functions.
    d. is especially important for working memory.

6. The cerebellum
    a. contributes to the control of movement, shifting of attention, and timing.
    b. is concerned mostly with visual location in space.
    c. is located immediately ventral to the pons.
    d. all of the above.

7. The components of the midbrain include
    a. the superior and inferior colliculi in the tectum, involved in sensory processing.
    b. the tegmentum, containing nuclei of the third and fourth cranial nerves, part of the reticular formation, and pathways connecting higher and lower structures.
    c. the substantia nigra, origin of a dopamine-containing pathway that deteriorates in Parkinson's disease.
    d. all of the above.

8. The limbic system
    a. is a set of isolated areas that are important for different aspects of memory.
    b. is a set of interlinked structures that are important for motivated and emotional behaviors.
    c. is another term for the basal ganglia.
    d. gets its name from the Latin word for bridge.

9. The hypothalamus
    a. contains parts of the reticular formation and raphe system.
    b. is part of the basal ganglia.
    c. is important for motivated behaviors and hormonal control.
    d. is connected only with the brain stem.

10. The basal ganglia
    a. are composed primarily of the caudate nucleus, putamen, and globus pallidus.
    b. control movement directly via axons to the spinal cord.
    c. are primarily concerned with sensory processing.
    d. all of the above.

11. The hippocampus
    a. controls breathing, heart rate, and other vital reflexes.
    b. provides the major control for the pituitary gland.
    c. is part of the basal ganglia.
    d. none of the above.

12. The thalamus contains
    a. the superior and inferior colliculi.
    b. nuclei that project to particular areas of cerebral cortex.
    c. nuclei that regulate the pituitary.
    d. nuclei having to do with motivated behaviors, such as eating, drinking, sex, fighting, arousal level, and temperature regulation.

13. Cerebrospinal fluid
    a. is formed by cells lining the four ventricles.
    b. flows from the lateral ventricles to the third and fourth ventricles, and from there either to the central canal of the spinal cord or to the space between the brain and the meninges, where it is reabsorbed into the blood vessels.
    c. cushions the brain and provides buoyancy.
    d. all of the above.

14. The laminae of the cortex
    a. usually consist of only two layers, one of axons and one of cell bodies.
    b. are the same thickness throughout the brain of a given species, but differ across species.
    c. consist of up to six layers, which vary in thickness across the various brain areas.
    d. are present only in humans; other mammals have cortical cells and axons mixed together.

15. Which of the following is true of cortical columns?
    a. Columns run parallel to the laminae, across the surface of the cortex.
    b. There are six columns in the human brain, and only one or two in other mammals.
    c. Cells within a column have similar response properties.
    d. The properties of cells within a column change systematically from top to bottom; cells at the top may respond to one stimulus, while those at the bottom respond to a different one.

16. Which is true of the occipital lobe?
    a. It is located at the posterior end of the cortex and contains the primary visual cortex.
    b. It is located at the sides of the brain and is concerned mostly with perception of complex visual patterns.
    c. It is located immediately behind the central sulcus and contains the postcentral gyrus.
    d. It is located at the top of the brain and contributes to somatosensory processing.

17. Which is true of the parietal lobe?
    a. It contains the primary receiving area for axons carrying touch sensations and other skin and muscle information.
    b. It has 4 bands on the postcentral gyrus that receive light-touch, deep-pressure, or both.
    c. It contributes to our sense of our body in space, relative to visual and auditory stimuli.
    d. All of the above are true.

18. The temporal lobe
    a. is located immediately in front of the central sulcus.
    b. is involved in some complex aspects of visual processing as well as auditory processing.
    c. has as its only function the processing of simple auditory information.
    d. none of the above.

19. Damage to the frontal lobe
    a. may cause losses of initiative and of social inhibitions and produce difficulties with delayed response tasks.
    b. is still a widely used surgical technique for mental patients because of its remarkable calming and normalizing tendencies without noticeable side effects.
    c. produces drastic impairments in intelligence.
    d. all of the above.

20. Gamma waves
    a. are synchronized waves of activity (30 to 80 per second) in various brain areas, which may reflect binding of sensory aspects into a unified perception.
    b. are synchronized by the prefrontal cortex, indicating that prefrontal cortex is the site of unified experience.
    c. are especially important for our numerical sense.
    d. are synchronized waves of activity localized within a specific brain area, and are important for shifting attention to the sensory aspect that is processed by that area.

21. CAT scans
    a. use intense magnetic fields to inactivate brain areas temporarily.
    b. use x-rays to describe brain structure.
    c. use changes in hemoglobin as it releases oxygen to areas with high metabolic activity.
    d. use brief, moderate magnetic fields to stimulate brain areas.

22. A problem in trying to infer behavioral function from measures of brain structure or activity is:
    a. Correlation does not imply causation.
    b. Cases of brain damage often are not specifically localized to one area.
    c. It is difficult to determine which aspect of a complex task is controlled by the brain area that was inactivated.
    d. All of the above are true.

Helpful Hints

1. To remember the 12 cranial nerves, use this mnemonic device:

    a. On (Olfactory)

    b. Old (Optic)

    c. Olympia's (Oculomotor)

    d. Towering (Trochlear)

    e. Tops, (Trigeminal)

    f. A (Abducens)

    g. Firm, (Facial)

    h. Staid (Statoacoustic)

    i. German (Glossopharyngial)

    j. Viewed (Vagus)

    k. A lot of (Accessory)

    l. Hops (Hypoglossal)

2. To remember the functions of the hypothalamus, think of the "4 Fs": Fighting, Fleeing, Feeding, and Reproductive Behavior.

Solutions

True/False Questions

1. T	7. F	13. T
2. F	8. T	14. F
3. F	9. F	15. F
4. T	10. T	16. F
5. F	11. F	17. T
6. T	12. F	18. T

Fill In The Blanks

1. dorsal; ventral
2. sympathetic; along the spinal cord; parasympathetic; near the organs they innervate
3. medulla; pons; cerebellum
4. vital reflexes
5. axons crossing from one side to the other
6. movement; timing; shifting attention
7. tectum; tegmentum
8. olfactory bulb; hypothalamus; hippocampus; amygdala; cingulate gyrus
9. thalamus
10. pituitary; motivated
11. caudate nucleus; putamen; globus pallidus
12. frontal lobe; movement; memory, reasoning,; emotional expression
13. nucleus basalis
14. hippocampus
15. choroid plexus
16. laminae; columns
17. occipital
18. somatosensory
19. auditory; visual
20. precentral gyrus; prefrontal cortex
21. binding problem; gamma
22. magnetoencephalography; temporal; spatial
23. magnetic resonance imaging; MRI; spatial
24. functional magnetic resonance imaging (fMRI)
25. left frontal lobe
26. inactivate; stimulate

Matching Items

1. D	7. E	13. Q
2. H	8. K	14. I
3. P	9. A	15. J
4. R	10. B	16. O
5. F	11. N	17. M
6. L	12. G	18. C

Multiple-Choice Questions

Matching Items

1. B	10. A	19. A
2. D	11. D	20. A
3. A	12. B	21. B
4. B	13. D	22. D
5. C	14. C	
6. A	15. C	
7. D	16. A	
8. B	17. D	
9. C	18. B	

DEVELOPMENT AND PLASTICITY OF THE BRAIN

Introduction

The central nervous system develops from two long thin lips on the surface of the embryo that merge to form a fluid-filled tube. The forward end of the tube enlarges to become the forebrain, midbrain, and hindbrain; the rest becomes the spinal cord. Cerebrospinal fluid continues to fill the central canal of the spinal cord and four hollow ventricles of the brain.

There are five major stages in the development of neurons: proliferation, migration, differentiation, myelination, and synaptogenesis. During proliferation, cells lining the ventricles divide. Some of the new cells remain in place as stem cells and continue dividing, whereas others, destined to become neurons and glia, migrate to their new destinations. Differentiation includes formation of the axon and dendrites and determination of shape and chemical components. Myelination is the formation, by glial cells, of insulating sheaths around axons, which increase the speed of transmission. Synaptogenesis, the formation of functional synapses, continues throughout life. The traditional view that vertebrates do not generate any new neurons in adulthood has been shown to be inaccurate in at least some cases. Undifferentiated stem cells in the interior of the brain continue to divide and some migrate to the olfactory bulb and become glia or neurons. New neurons also have also been found in the song control areas of songbirds and in the hippocampus of birds and mammals.

As the brain grows, axons must travel long distances to reach their appropriate targets. They are guided by concentration gradients of chemicals, such as the protein TOP_{DV}, which guides retinal axons to the appropriate part of the tectum. Axons are attracted by some chemicals and repelled by others. After axons reach the general area of their target, they begin to form synapses with postsynaptic cells. These target cells receive an overabundance of synapses; they gradually strengthen some synapses and reject others. Initially, there are many tentative connections between axons and target cells; later, fewer but stronger attachments develop. The overproduction of neurons and subsequent pruning of unsuccessful connections provide a process of selection of the fittest or most informative connections.

There is an initial overproduction of neurons; those that fail to form synapses with appropriate target cells die. The process of programmed cell death, or apoptosis, can be prevented if the neuron receives a neurotrophin from the target cell. Rita Levi-Montalcini discovered the first neurotrophin, nerve growth factor (NGF), which promotes survival of neurons of the sympathetic nervous system. Several additional neurotrophins have been discovered, including brain-derived neurotrophic factor (BDNF). In addition to preventing apoptosis, neurotrophins also enhance branching of axons and dendrites in adulthood. During maturation of the prefrontal cortex in adolescence, the number of neurons decreases while neuronal activity actually increases. Thus, more successful neurons and connections survive at the expense of less successful ones.

Developing brains are not only more responsive to environmental stimuli, they are also more vulnerable to malnutrition, toxic chemicals, and disease. For example, fetal alcohol syndrome is characterized by hyperactivity, attention deficits, impulsiveness, mental retardation and other physical and mental abnormalities. Children with fetal alcohol syndrome have neurons with smaller, less branching dendrites. Alcohol decreases the release of glutamate and neurotrophins and increases activity at inhibitory GABA synapses; as a result more neurons undergo apoptosis. Prenatal exposure to cocaine and to the effects of cigarette smoking also result in physical and intellectual deficits. Even maternal stress can change the mother's behavior in a way that results in emotional and behavioral problems in the offspring.

Environmental enrichment results in a thicker cortex, more dendritic branching, and enhanced performance on learning tasks. Effects of enrichment, or of sensory deprivation, have been observed in several species, including fish, rats, and humans, although it is sometimes difficult to determine cause and effect relationships. At least some of the effects of enrichment may be due to increased physical activity; exercise enhances growth of axons and dendrites and lessens the thinning of the neocortex in old age. People who have been blind since infancy have increased activity in their occipital cortex while performing either a touch discrimination task or a verbal task, and this activity helps them to outperform sighted people in those tasks. Thus, a brain area normally devoted to visual processing becomes reorganized to analyze tactile and auditory information. Extensive training may increase the amount of cortical area devoted to a skill. In professional musicians one area in the right temporal lobe was larger than in nonmusicians. However, cause and effect relationships are not clear. There was also a larger representation of the fingers of left hand in the right postcentral gyrus of people who play stringed instruments, and another study showed thicker gray matter in areas related to hand control and vision in musicians. While such an increase in cortical representation is usually beneficial, it can produce problems if the representations of two fingers overlap.

Brain damage can be caused by a variety of factors, including closed head injury and stroke. Stroke can result either from ischemia due to a blood clot that obstructs an artery, or from hemorrhage, caused by rupture of an artery. Strokes kill neurons either by depriving them of oxygen and glucose or by overexcitation, which allows excess sodium and other positive ions to enter the neuron, blocking metabolism in mitochondria and killing the neurons. Cell death can be minimized by the use of drugs that break up clots and perhaps those that block glutamate receptors, if given early after the stroke. Preventing positive ions from entering neurons or opening potassium channels may also help. However, after the immediate injury, drugs that reduce excitation may result in neural death from understimulation. Potential new treatments include cooling the brain and the administration of neurotrophins or cannabinoids.

Recovery from brain damage depends on a number of physiological mechanisms. Diaschisis, or decreased activity of neurons after loss of input, contributes to impairment following brain damage. It can be reduced by administration of stimulant drugs during the recovery phase. Regrowth of axons can be guided by myelin sheaths in the periphery. However, axons in the central nervous system do not regenerate, in part because of the mechanical barrier of scar tissue and in part because of growth-inhibiting chemicals from the scar tissue or from myelin. Sprouting of axons occurs in response to normal cell death, as well as after brain damage; axons from undamaged neurons develop new terminals that occupy the vacant synapses. Gangliosides may increase sprouting or aid recognition of one neuron by another. Progesterone in women also promotes release of BDNF, which promotes axon sprouting and formation of new synapses. Denervation supersensitivity refers to the increased sensitivity to a neurotransmitter by a postsynaptic cell that is deprived of synaptic input. It can promote recovery, but can also result in prolonged pain. Reorganization of sensory representations can occur by collateral sprouting, sometimes over surprisingly long distances. However, these reorganizations may not be beneficial, as in the case of phantom-limb sensations. Therapies for brain damage include behavioral interventions that help people to reaccess memories or skills or to make better use of their unimpaired abilities. Learned adjustments in behavior allow an individual to make better use of abilities unaffected by the damage and to improve abilities that were impaired by the damage, but not lost.

Learning Objectives

Module 5.1 Development of the Brain

1. Understand the processes of growth and differentiation of the brain.

2. Understand why there is initial overproduction of neurons and how axons follow chemical paths to their destinations and make functional connections, thereby allowing them to survive.

3. Understand the reasons why the developing brain is vulnerable to chemical insults.

4. Be able to describe the effects of experience on the brain.

Module 5.2 Plasticity after Brain Damage

1. Be able to describe the processes by which strokes damage the brain and the means of lessening the damage.

2. Understand the mechanisms of recovery after brain damage and how various therapies promote recovery.

Key Terms and Concepts

Module 5.1 Development of the Brain

1. Growth and differentiation of the vertebrate brain

   Early development of the nervous system

Neural tube → spinal cord, hindbrain, midbrain, forebrain
Cavity of neural tube → central canal of spinal cord, ventricles of brain

Cerebrospinal fluid (CSF)

Growth and development of neurons

Proliferation of new cells

Cells lining ventricles divide

Some → primitive neurons and glia
Others → stem cells that remain in place
Number of days of neuron proliferation: Longer in humans than in chimpanzee

Small genetic change → large difference in outcome
Migration toward eventual destinations

Guides: Immunoglobulins, chemokines
Differentiation, forming axon first and then dendrites

Ferrets: optic nerves to auditory thalamus → vision
Myelination of some axons, continuing for years
Synaptogenesis, continuing throughout life

New neurons later in life

Olfactory receptors
Stem cells
Hippocampal cells in songbirds and mammals

2. Pathfinding by axons

Chemical pathfinding by axons

Specificity of axon connections

Axons to extra leg of salamander
Optic tract axons to tectum of newts

Chemical gradients

TOP_{DV}

Competition among axons as a general principle

Neural Darwinism

3. Determinants of neuron survival

Nerve growth factor (NGF)

Sympathetic nervous system

Rita Levi-Montalcini

Promotes survival and growth, not neuronal birth

Apoptosis vs. necrosis

Other neurotrophins

Brain-derived neurotrophic factor (BDNF) and others

Overproduction of neurons and massive cell death

Release of neurotransmitter plus neurotrophin

Neurotrophins needed from both incoming axons and target cells

Error correction

Match incoming axons to number of recipient cells

Functions of neurotrophins

Prevent apoptosis

Increase branching of both axons and dendrites

4. The vulnerable developing brain

Greater vulnerabililty to malnutrition, toxic chemicals, infections

Impaired thyroid function in infancy: Permanent mental retardation and slow body growth

Fever, low blood glucose → impair neuron proliferation

Fetal alcohol syndrome

Short, less branched dendrites

Alcohol: Inhibits glutamate & neurotrophin release; increases GABA activity

Maternal cocaine or cigarette smoking → multiple deficits

Maternal stress → less care of offspring → emotional, social problems in offspring

5. Fine-tuning by experience

Experience and dendritic branching

Enriched environment

Thicker cortex

More dendritic branches

Improved learning

Effect of exercise

Extensive education in humans

Effects of special experiences

Brain adaptations in people blind since infancy

Occipital cortex: increased responsiveness to touch, sound, verbal stimuli

Effects of prolonged practice

Magnetoencephalography (MEG): Professional musicians stronger response of auditory cortex

Magnetic resonance imaging (MRI): Right temporal cortex of musicians larger

MRI: Increased thickness of gray matter in areas for hand control and vision in musicians
Playing stringed instruments (fingering with left hand): Larger area in right postcentral gyrus
When brain reorganization goes too far

Difficulty distinguishing one finger from another
Focal hand dystonia ("musician's cramp"): due to overlap of cortical representation of two fingers
"Writer's cramp" due to similar problem

6. In closing: Brain Development

Many ways to disrupt development; wonder that it ever works normally

Module 5.2 Plasticity after Brain Damage

1. Brain damage and short-term injury

Tumors, infections, radiation, toxic substances, degenerative conditions

Closed head injury

Rotational force
Blood clots

Reducing the harm from a stroke (cerebrovascular accident)

Ischemia (blood clot closes artery)

Loss of oxygen and glucose
Hemorrhage (rupture of artery)

Excess oxygen, calcium, blood products
Both ischemia and hemorrhage

Edema → increased pressure → possible additional strokes
Impaired sodium-potassium pump →

Increased extracellular potassium, intracellular sodium →
Glutamate release →
Overstimulation →
Accumulation of sodium, other ions →
Block metabolism in mitochondria →
Neurons die, glia proliferate
Means of lessening damage

Tissue plasminogen activator (tPA): Breaks up blood clots
Penumbra (area surrounding immediate damage): Decrease stimulation

Open potassium channels
Glutamate antagonists and positive ion channel blockers: mixed results
Problem: Understimulation

Neurotropins, drugs that block apoptosis: Must be injected into brain
Cooling brain—most effective
Animal studies: Cannabinoids → reduced glutamate release

2. Later mechanisms of recovery

Diaschisis

Amphetamine (releases dopamine and norepinephrine) → enhanced recovery
Blocking dopamine receptors → impaired recovery
Tranquilizers (decrease dopamine and norepinephrine release) → impaired recovery

The regrowth of axons

Myelin sheaths as guides
Scar tissue

Mechanical barrier
Growth-inhibiting chemicals
Myelin: Inhibits axon regrowth in CNS

Sprouting

Neurotrophins → collateral sprouts
Normal condition, not just response to damage
Hippocampus: Input from entorhinal cortex

Cut axons from one entorhinal cortex → other hemisphere sprouts → recovery
Cut axons from both sides → sprouting from unrelated areas → helpful, harmful, or neutral effects
Gangliosides (glycolipids) → may increase sprouting → restoration

Recognition of one neuron by another
Females: progesterone → BDNF → sprouting and new synapses

Denervation supersensitivity

Disuse supersensitivity
Increased receptors or efficacy of receptors
Can induce prolonged pain

Reorganized sensory representations and the phantom limb

Deafferented arm → "arm" area of cortex responds to stimuli from face

Stimuli perceived as from arm
Sexual activity → feel phantom foot
Artificial or transplanted arm or hand → phantom sensations subside
Connections plastic throughout life

Learned adjustments in behavior

Deafferented limbs

One deafferented limb: Lack of spontaneous use

Two deafferented limbs: Monkey learns to use both

Cortical damage → difficulty finding memory trace

Early practice or therapy most helpful after damage

Methods 5.1: Histochemistry

Horseradish peroxidase: Transported from axon terminal to cell body

3. In closing: Brain damage and recovery

Numerous experimental treatments, none fully effective now

Short-Answer Questions

Module 5.1 Development of the Brain

1. *Growth and differentiation of the vertebrate brain*

   a. Describe the formation of the central nervous system in the embryo. What happens to the fluid-filled cavity?

   b. What are the three main divisions of the brain?

   c. What are the five stages in the development of neurons? Describe the processes in each.

   d. Where in the brain are new neurons found in adulthood in birds? In mammals? What are stem cells?

2. *Pathfinding by axons*

   a. What did Weiss observe in his experiments on salamanders' extra limbs? What principle did he conclude directed the innervation of the extra limb? Is this principle still thought to be correct?

   b. What did Sperry observe when he damaged the optic nerve of newts? What happened when he rotated the eye by 180 degrees? How did the newt with the rotated eye see the world?

   c. What conclusion did these results suggest?

   d. What is TOPDV? What is its role in directing retinal axons to the tectum?

   e. What happens to axons that form active synapses? What happens to axons that do not form active synapses?

   f. Describe the principle of neural Darwinism. How does this relate to the initial overproduction and subsequent death of large numbers of neurons?

3. *Determinants of neuronal survival*

   a. Who discovered nerve growth factor? What happens if a neuron in the sympathetic nervous system does not receive enough nerve growth factor?

b. What is apoptosis? What type of chemical can prevent apoptosis?

c. What is another neurotrophin besides nerve growth factor? What functions do neurotrophins serve in adulthood?

d. The vulnerable developing brain

e. What are the effects of thyroid deficiency in adulthood? Compare these with the effects of thyroid deficiency in infancy.

f. Describe fetal alcohol syndrome. How are dendrites affected? What effects of alcohol on synaptic activity may explain the neural deficits.

g. What are the effects of prenatal cocaine exposure? Cigarette smoking during pregnancy?

h. How does stress affect the mother, and how does her behavior influence her offspring?

4. *Fine-tuning by experience*

a. Describe the effects of environmental "enrichment".

b. How may exercise contribute to the effects of enrichment?

c. Describe the changes that occur in the occipital cortex in people who have been blind since infancy. Are these changes helpful?

d. What brain area is larger in professional musicians? What can we conclude about cause and effect in the relationship of brain size, musical ability, and experience?

e. What area is larger in people who had extensive experience playing stringed instruments? What is focal hand dystonia, and what is its physiological basis?

Module 5.2 Plasticity after Brain Damage

1. *Causes of brain damage*

a. What is the most common cause of brain damage in young people? What actually produces the brain damage in these cases?

b. What are the two types of stroke and the cause of each? How does each kill neurons?

c. Describe the sequence of destructive processes in the penumbra.

d. What are six treatments that may minimize damage from stroke?

2. *Mechanisms of recovery after brain damage*

a. List six potential mechanisms for recovery from brain damage.

b. How may learned adjustments in behavior be promoted?

c. What is diaschisis? How is recovery from diaschisis affected by amphetamine or a dopamine antagonist?

d. How may crushed, but not cut, axons in the peripheral nervous system form appropriate connections when they regenerate? Why don't axons in the central nervous system regenerate?

e. Under what conditions is sprouting most likely to be useful? Does sprouting produce beneficial results? What kind of chemical promotes restoration after injury? What hormone in women promotes recovery?

f. What is denervation supersensitivity? What are two mechanisms of supersensitivity?

g. What evidence is there that sensory representations may be reorganized during recovery? What surprised investigators about the brain of a monkey whose limb had been deafferented 12 years earlier?

h. What are some sources of sensory input that can give rise to phantom limbs? What is the relationship between reorganization of somatosensory cortex and the likelihood of phantom sensations?

i. How may behavioral interventions facilitate recovery from brain damage?

3. *Methods box*

a. What is histochemistry? How is horseradish peroxidase used? How was it used to determine the source of inputs to the cerebral cortices of monkeys that had had a forelimb deafferented 12 years earlier?

True/False Questions

1. The cavity of the neural tube fills in with neural tissue as the brain develops.

   TRUE or FALSE

2. The five stages of neural development are proliferation, migration, differentiation, myelination, and synaptogenesis.

   TRUE or FALSE

3. Nerve growth factor (NGF) primarily promotes neuronal birth.

   TRUE or FALSE

4. Apoptosis is the process of increasing the branching of dendrites.

   TRUE or FALSE

5. In addition to preventing programmed cell death, neurotrophins increase the branching of axons and dendrites in adulthood.

   TRUE or FALSE

6. Massive cell death early in development is a sign of a profound disorder.

   TRUE or FALSE

7. Axons follow chemical gradients to get to the area where they can make functional synaptic connections.

   TRUE or FALSE

8. Rats that were reared in an enriched environment had thicker cortex, more dendritic branching, and improved learning.

   TRUE or FALSE

9. Mammals are born with all the neurons they will ever have.

   TRUE or FALSE

10. Professional musicians have a larger area in the right temporal lobe than do non-musicians.

    TRUE or FALSE

11. Fetuses are generally more affected by malnutrition, toxic chemicals, and infections than are adults.

    TRUE or FALSE

12. The two kinds of stroke are ischemic and hemorrhagic.

    TRUE or FALSE

13. The penumbra is the area of most direct damage from a stroke; neurons in the penumbra are killed almost immediately.

    TRUE or FALSE

14. One way to decrease damage immediately after a stroke is to administer a glutamate antagonist; however, this may be harmful if administered later, during recovery.

    TRUE or FALSE

15. Tissue plasminogen activator (tPA) should be administered after a hemorrhagic stroke, but not after an ischemic stroke.

    TRUE or FALSE

16. Heating the brain, mimicking a fever, is the most effective treatment for a stroke.

    TRUE or FALSE

17. A dopamine antagonist is an effective treatment for diaschisis.

    TRUE or FALSE

18. Scar tissue inhibits the growth of axons both by providing a physical barrier and by releasing growth-inhibiting chemicals.

    TRUE or FALSE

19. In studies of laboratory animals males typically recover from brain damage better than females, because the higher levels of progesterone in females impede recovery.

    TRUE or FALSE

20. After one limb was deafferented, the monkey stopped using it; if both arms were deafferented, the monkey learned how to use both arms.

    TRUE or FALSE

Fill In The Blanks

1. Early in development the _____ differentiates into the hindbrain, the midbrain, the forebrain, and the spinal cord.

2. The five stages of neural development are _____ , _____ , _____ , _____ , and _____ .

3. The principle of competition among axons is referred to as _____ .

4. _____ discovered the first neurotrophin, _____ .

5. Programmed cell death, also called _____ , occurs if neurons do not receive sufficient neurotrophins.

6. The cells that give rise to new neurons in the adult brain are called _____ .

7. The developing brain is more vulnerable than is the adult brain to _____ , _____ , and _____ .

8. An area in the _____ lobe of the _____ hemisphere was larger in professional musicians. An area of the _____ gyrus of the _____ hemisphere was larger in people who play stringed instruments.

9. The two types of stroke are _____ and _____ .

10. The area surrounding the direct damage from a stroke is called the _____ .

11. Some potential means of lessening the damage, if applied immediately after a stroke are _____ antagonists and drugs that open _____ channels; however, these may be harmful if applied during recovery.

12. _____ refers to the decreased activity of surviving neurons after other neurons are damaged. A treatment for this condition may be administration of _____ during recovery.

13. Myelin sheaths in the _____ nervous system inhibit axon growth; myelin sheaths in the _____ nervous system serve as guides for regrowth.

14. Two chemicals that may stimulate sprouting after brain damage are _____ , and _____ .

15. Denervation _____ depends on increased receptors or efficacy of receptors.

16. Phantom limb sensations arise primarily because of collateral _____ of axons.

Matching Items

1. _____ Cavity of neural tube
2. _____ Rita Levi-Montalcini
3. _____ Apoptosis
4. _____ Necrosis
5. _____ Neural Darwinism
6. _____ Stem cells
7. _____ Ischemic
8. _____ Hemorrhagic
9. _____ Overexcitation
10. _____ Underexcitation

a. Cell death due to injury or toxic chemical
b. A cause of damage several days after a stroke
c. Stroke caused by ruptured blood vessel
d. A cause of damage immediately after a stroke
e. Programmed cell death
f. Stroke caused by blood clot
g. Cerebral ventricles and spinal central canal
h. Discovered nerve growth factor
i. Undifferentiated cells that can become neurons
j. Axons competing for synapses and survival

Multiple-Choice Questions

1. The neural tube
   a. arises from a pair of long thin lips that merge around a fluid-filled cavity.
   b. develops into the spinal cord; the brain arises from a separate structure.
   c. eventually merges to form a solid structure, squeezing out the primitive cerebrospinal fluid.
   d. none of the above.

2. The five major stages in the development of neurons, in order, are
   a. proliferation, differentiation, migration, myelination, synaptogenesis.
   b. proliferation, growth, synaptogenesis, myelination, migration.
   c. proliferation, migration, myelination, synaptogenesis, growth.
   d. proliferation, migration, differentiation, myelination, synaptogenesis.

3. Which of the following is true?
   a. Myelination is complete by the end of the first year in humans.
   b. Neurons experimentally transplanted from one site to another at an intermediate stage of development may keep some properties of cells in the old location and develop some that are characteristic of their new location.
   c. Dendrites usually form before axons, and are usually fully formed before migration begins.
   d. Neurons are incapable of conducting action potentials until they are fully myelinated.

4. Stem cells
   a. are hippocampal neurons that are especially resistant to damage.
   b. are undifferentiated cells in the interior of the brain that generate daughter cells that migrate to the olfactory bulb or hippocampus and become glial cells or neurons.
   c. are glial cells that guide neurons during migration.
   d. are neurons that develop especially long axons that resemble the stems of plants.

5. When Paul Weiss grafted an extra leg onto a salamander
   a. the extra leg received no neurons and therefore could not move.
   b. the extra leg moved in the opposite direction from the normal adjacent leg.
   c. the extra leg moved in synchrony with the normal adjacent leg.
   d. the leg degenerated because the immune system rejected it.

6. Sperry's work with the eyes of newts led him to conclude that
   a. neurons attach to postsynaptic cells randomly, and the postsynaptic cell confers specificity.
   b. axons follow a chemical trail that places them in the general vicinity of their target.
   c. innervation in the sensory system is guided by specific genetic information, whereas that in the motor system is random.
   d. neurons follow specific genetic information that directs each of them to precisely the right postsynaptic cell.

7. TOP_{DV}
   a. is a trophic factor necessary for the survival of neurons of the sympathetic nervous system.
   b. is a protein that guides axons to the developing legs of newts.
   c. is a protein that causes a group of neurons that possess it to fire together, thereby increasing their chance of survival.
   d. is a protein that is more concentrated in neurons of the dorsal retina and the ventral tectum than in the ventral retina and dorsal tectum.

8. Neural Darwinism
   a. was formulated by Roger Sperry.
   b. has recently been shown to be false.
   c. proposes that synapses form somewhat randomly at first; those that work best are kept, while the others degenerate.
   d. all of the above.

9. Nerve growth factor
   a. was discovered by Roger Sperry.
   b. is important for the survival and growth of sympathetic neurons.
   c. determines the number of neurons that will be formed.
   d. all of the above.

10. Apoptosis
    a. is caused by an excess of neurotrophin.
    b. occurs in only a few areas of the brain.
    c. is the "suicide program" of the cell.
    d. was the first neurotrophin to be discovered.

11. Massive cell death early in development
    a. would be so maladaptive that it hardly ever occurs.
    b. occurs only with sensory deprivation or when the fetus has been exposed to toxins.
    c. occurs as a result of genetic mistakes, which fail to direct the cells to their genetically programmed target. As a result the neurons wander aimlessly until they die.
    d. is a normal result of unsuccessful competition for synapses and growth factors.

12. Mental retardation
    a. can be caused by thyroid deficiency during adulthood.
    b. can be caused by thyroid deficiency in infancy.
    c. is not due to lack or excess of chemicals during development, because the young brain is very plastic and can repair itself easily.
    d. all of the above.

13. Fetal alcohol syndrome
    a. results in hyperactivity, impusliveness, difficulty maintaining attention, varying degrees of mental retardation, motor problems, heart defects, and facial abnormalities.
    b. occurs because alcohol increases glutamate release and decreases GABA release.
    c. results from excessively long, heavily branched dendrites.
    d. all of the above.

14. Children of mothers who smoked during pregnancy have greater risk for
    a. low birth weight and many illnesses early in life.
    b. Sudden Infant Death Syndrome.
    c. intellectual deficits, ADHD, and impairments of the immune system.
    d. all of the above.

15. Environmental enrichment
    a. produces greater dendritic branching and a thicker cortex.
    b. produces changes in the structure of neurons, but no changes in neural function.
    c. produces changes in the function of neurons, but no changes in neural structure.
    d. has beneficial effects only in primates.

16. Which of the following is true?
    a. Professional musicians have a larger area in the right temporal lobe than do nonmusicians.
    b. Exercise generates waste products that are harmful to neural survival.
    c. The occipital cortex in people who have been blind since infancy continues to be selective only to visual stimuli.
    d. All of the above are true.

17. Which of the following is true?
    a. The increase in representation of the left hand in the right postcentral gyrus of stringed instrument players is always beneficial.
    b. There was decreased thickness of gray matter in brain areas for hand control and vision in musicians, because those areas became totally devoted to auditory function.
    c. Stressing a mother rat changes her behavior in ways that increase fearfulness in her offspring.
    d. None of the above

18. The most common cause of brain damage in young adults is
    a. stroke.
    b. disease.
    c. a sharp blow to the head.
    d. a brain tumor.

19. Which of the following occurs in the penumbra around the area of direct damage from stroke?
    a. Edema increases pressure on the brain and increases the probability of additional strokes.
    b. The combination of edema and impairment of the sodium-potassium pump results in glutamate release.
    c. Positive ions accumulate inside neurons, block metabolism in mitochondria and kill neurons.
    d. All of the above are true.

20. Damage from strokes may be minimized by
    a. activating glutamate synapses immediately after the stroke.
    b. giving tissue plasminogen activator, if the stroke is due to ischemia.
    c. creating a fever, which will increase the temperature of the brain and enhance repair processes.
    d. all of the above.

21. Amphetamine administered during practice improves recovery by
    a. producing denervation supersensitivity.
    b. reducing diaschisis.
    c. relieving stress.
    d. stimulating regrowth of axons.

22. Adequate regrowth of an axon does not occur if
    a. the damaged axon is in the spinal cord of fish.
    b. an axon in the peripheral nervous system of mammals is crushed.
    c. the damaged axon is in the central nervous system of mammals.
    d. all of the above.

23. Research on regrowth of axons in mammals has shown that
    a. breaking up scar tissue has been shown to be an effective means of promoting axon regrowth.
    b. myelin in the peripheral, but not central, nervous system helps axons regenerate.
    c. the mammalian central nervous system has evolved advanced chemical stimuli to promote better axon regrowth than that seen in fish.
    d. the reason that neurons in the central nervous system fail to regenerate is that there are no myelin sheaths there.

24. Sprouting
    a. occurs only in response to traumatic brain damage.
    b. is always maladaptive, since the wrong axons make connections.
    c. may be adaptive if sprouts come from closely related axons.
    d. is enhanced by dopamine antagonists.

25. Which of the following is true?
    a. Gangliosides may increase sprouting and promote recognition of one neuron by another.
    b. Progesterone in females may increase BDNF and thereby promote sprouting and new synapses.
    c. Denervation supersensitivity can result in prolonged pain.
    d. All of the above are true.

26. Denervation supersensitivity is the result of
    a. increased output from other presynaptic cells adjacent to the one that has been damaged.
    b. postsynaptic neurons producing receptors for a different transmitter.
    c. changes in the chemical composition of the transmitter, making it more potent.
    d. an increased number of receptors on the postsynaptic cell and increased effectiveness of the receptors.

27. After denervation of a monkey's arm 12 years earlier
    a. neurons that had previously responded to it died because of lack of input.
    b. neurons that had previously responded to it became responsive to stimuli in the face.
    c. no reorganization could occur because all connections are determined only genetically.
    d. no reorganization could occur because connections become permanently fixed during the early critical period.

28. Research on recovery from brain damage has shown that
    a. recovery can occur when an individual is forced to make full use of remaining capabilities.
    b. phantom limbs result from irritation in the remaining stump of the limb.
    c. monkeys with only one arm denervated showed better recovery in the use of that arm than when both arms were denervated..
    d. it is better to wait several weeks after a brain injury before beginning therapy.

Crossword Puzzle

Brain Parts and Development

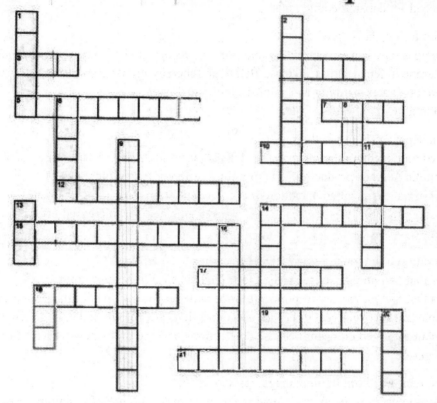

ACROSS

3 Imaging system that detects radioactive chemicals absorbed by the most active neurons (abbr.)
4 Part of forebrain important for memory functions
5 "Hole in the brain" filled with cerebrospinal fluid
7 _____ cell: type of cell that lines the ventricles and produces new neurons and glia
10 Nucleus that is part of basal ganglia
12 Neural "suicide program"
14 Lobe that processes somatosensory information
15 "Fight or flight" system
17 Units of cortex perpendicular to laminae
18 Portion of brainstem that controls vital reflexes
19 _____ problem: How we construct a single object out of many aspects
21 Stage of development when neurons move to their final destinations

DOWN

1 Chemical gradient that guides retinal axons to proper area of tectum (abbr.)
2 Lobe containing primary auditory cortex and important for language comprehension and complex visual patterns
6 Substantia _____: midbrain structure, degeneration of which causes Parkinson's disease
8 Drug used after a stroke to break up blood clots (abbr.)
9 Forebrain structure imortant for motivated behaviors and hormone control
11 Roof of midbrain
13 Fluid that fills the ventricles and cushions the brain (abbr.)
14 Area surrounding site of direct stroke damage
16 Treatment to brain to minimize stroke damage
18 Imaging system that uses a magnetic field to tilt rotation axes of atoms with odd-numbered atomic weights (abbr.)
20 Type of matter composed mostly of cel bodies and dendrites

Crossword Puzzle Solution

Brain Parts and Development

Solution:

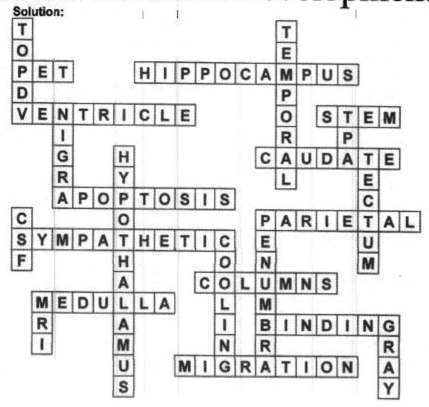

Solutions

True/False Questions

1.	F	9.	F	17.	F
2.	T	10.	T	18.	T
3.	F	11.	T	19.	F
4.	F	12.	T	20.	T
5.	T	13.	F		
6.	F	14.	T		
7.	T	15.	F		
8.	T	16.	F		

Fill In The Blanks

1. neural tube
2. proliferation; migration; differentiation; myelination; synoptogenesis
3. neural Darwinism
4. Rita Levi-Montalcini; nerve growth factor
5. apoptosis
6. stem cells
7. malnutrition; toxic chemicals; infections
8. temporal; right; postcentral; right
9. ischemic; hemorrhagic
10. penumbra
11. glutamate; potassium
12. Diaschisis; amphetamine
13. central; peripheral
14. gangliosides; progesterone
15. supersensitivity
16. sprouting

Matching Items

1.	G	5.	J	9.	D
2.	H	6.	I	10.	B
3.	E	7.	F		
4.	A	8.	C		

Multiple-Choice Questions

1.	A	2.	D	3.	B

4. B	14. D	24. C
5. C	15. A	25. D
6. B	16. A	26. D
7. D	17. C	27. B
8. C	18. C	28. A
9. B	19. D	
10. C	20. B	
11. D	21. B	
12. B	22. C	
13. A	23. B	

VISION

Introduction

Sensory systems, including vision, are concerned with reception (absorption) of physical energy and transduction of that energy into neural activity that encodes some aspect of the stimulus. The structure of each kind of sensory receptor allows it to be stimulated maximally by one kind of energy, and little or not at all by other forms of energy. The brain interprets any information sent by nerves that synapse with those receptors as being about that form of energy. This principle was described by Müller as the law of specific nerve energies.

The retina contains two kinds of receptors. Cones are most densely packed in the fovea, an area in the center of the retina with the most acute (detailed) vision. This acuity is largely the result of the small number of cones that synapse with each bipolar cell. Rods are located more peripherally in the retina than are cones and are more sensitive to low levels of light. Furthermore, each bipolar cell receives input from a large number of rods. This improves sensitivity to dim light but sacrifices acuity.

All mammalian photopigments contain 11-cis-retinal bound to one of several opsins. Light converts 11-cis-retinal to all-trans-retinal, which in turn activates second-messenger molecules. The trichromatic theory states that cones mediate color vision because three different photopigments are found in three types of cones. Each photopigment is maximally sensitive to one wavelength of light but responds less readily to other wavelengths. Thus, each wavelength produces a certain ratio of responses from the three receptor types; the ratio remains essentially constant regardless of brightness. Rods, in contrast to cones, contain only one photopigment and therefore do not contribute directly to our perception of colors. Processing of color vision beyond the receptor level depends on an opponent-process mechanism, in which a given cell responds to one color with increased firing and to another color with a decrease below its spontaneous rate of firing. In addition, color constancy, the ability to recognize the color of an object despite changes in lighting, depends on an area of the cortex that compares colors across all the objects in the visual field. Color vision deficiency occurs when an individual lacks, or has low numbers of, long-, medium-, and/or short-wavelength cones.

Visual input is processed neurally in order to provide an organized, useful representation of the environment. To understand the more complex processing later in the system, we begin with the retina. The direct route of information is from receptor to bipolar to ganglion cell; ganglion cell axons exit through the blind spot of the retina and project primarily to the lateral geniculate nucleus of the thalamus. However, a visual receptor is able not only to stimulate its own bipolar(s) but also to inhibit activity in neighboring bipolars. It accomplishes this feat through the cooperation of horizontal cells, which receive input from a number of receptors and synapse with a number of bipolars. Electrical activity can flow in all directions in horizontal cells. The advantage of this arrangement is that borders are enhanced at the expense of redundant input. The process is called lateral inhibition.

A receptive field of a neuron in the visual system is that area of the visual field in which the presence or absence of light affects that neuron's activity. A receptive field beyond the receptor level represents a composite of the receptive fields of neurons that provide its input. Many contain both excitatory and inhibitory regions. The receptive fields of bipolar, ganglion, and geniculate cells are concentric circles. For some cells light in the center is excitatory, and for other cells it is inhibitory; light in the surround has the opposite effect. Cells in the visual cortex (occipital lobe) have bar shaped receptive fields as a result of summing the receptive fields of their lateral geniculate cell inputs.

Ganglion cells have been divided into three types. Parvocellular neurons are relatively small cells, located in or near the fovea, that respond differentially to colors. Because they have small receptive fields, they are highly sensitive to details. Magnocellular neurons are larger, are spread evenly across the retina, and respond best to moving stimuli and overall patterns. Because their receptive fields are large, they are not sensitive to small details; they also do not respond differentially to colors. A smaller group of cells, koniocellular neurons, respond weakly to light and are poorly understood. At the lateral geniculate nucleus of the thalamus, most parvocellular ganglion cell axons synapse with parvocellular geniculate neurons, and most magnocellular ganglion cell axons synapse with magnocellular geniculate neurons, although a few have connections with other visual areas of the thalamus. Koniocellular neurons send axons to the lateral geniculate nucleus, other parts of the thalamus, and the superior colliculus.

Most of the input from the lateral geniculate goes to the primary visual cortex (area V1), which in turn projects to secondary visual cortex (area V2). From area V2, information branches out to numerous additional areas. At the cortex, the parvocellular and magnocellular systems split into three pathways. A ventral pathway in the temporal lobe processes shape information primarily from the parvocellular system. A primarily magnocellular pathway also projects to the temporal lobe and processes movement information. A second branch of the magnocellular system projects dorsally to the parietal cortex and integrates vision with action. The third pathway processes brightness input from the magnocellular system and color information from the parvocellular system. The shape, movement, and color/brightness pathways remain separate in the temporal cortex and are collectively referred to as the ventral stream, or the "what" pathway. Cells in this area are specialized to recognize objects. The pathway in the parietal cortex is the dorsal stream, or the "where" or "how" pathway. It primarily helps the motor system to find objects and manipulate them.

David Hubel and Torsten Wiesel received the Nobel Prize for their pioneering work on feature detectors in the visual cortex. They distinguished three categories of neurons: simple, complex, and end-stopped, or hypercomplex. Simple cells respond maximally to a bar oriented in a particular direction and in a particular location on the retina. Their receptive fields can be mapped into fixed excitatory and inhibitory areas. Complex cells, on the other hand, have larger receptive fields, respond to correctly oriented bars located anywhere within the field (i.e., they do not have fixed excitatory and inhibitory areas), and respond best to stimuli moving perpendicular to the receptive field axis. End-stopped, or hypercomplex, cells are like complex cells, except for an area of strong inhibition at one end of the field. Cortical cells with similar properties are grouped in columns perpendicular to the surface.

It has been suggested that neurons in area V1 are feature detectors. However, although each neuron has a preferred stimulus, it will respond to other similar stimuli. Therefore, the response of any cell must be compared with responses of many other cells. Furthermore, many cells in V1 respond best to sine wave gratings; however, it is obvious that we do not perceive the world as an assembly of sine waves. Therefore, the role of V1 in visual perception is probably to provide preliminary analyses for other areas that actually identify objects.

After V1, receptive fields become even larger and more specialized. Some cells in V2 respond best to lines, edges, and sine wave gratings; however, others prefer circles, right angles, or other complex patterns. In V4 some cells respond best to a slanted line in a three-dimensional space. Additional processing of shape information is accomplished by the inferior temporal cortex (in the ventral stream, or "what" pathway), which responds preferentially to highly complex shapes. Cells in this area ignore changes in location, size, and perspective; they may contribute to our capacity for shape constancy. Damage to the pattern pathway results in visual agnosia, the inability to recognize visual objects. Some people have difficulty identifying almost all objects; others experience agnosia for only one or a few classes of stimuli. An area in the inferior temporal lobe (the fusiform gyrus) and part of the prefrontal cortex are activated during recognition of faces and, to a lesser degree, other complex figures.

Area V4, or a nearby area, is especially important for color constancy. Animals with damage to this area retain some color vision, but lose the ability to recognize the color of an object across lighting conditions. Area V4 also contributes to visual attention. Some cells in the magnocellular system are specialized for stereoscopic depth perception. They are sensitive to the amount of discrepancy between the images from the two eyes. Another branch of the magnocellular system detects motion. It projects to middle temporal cortex, or MT (area V5), and an adjacent area (medial superior temporal cortex, MST). These areas also receive some information from the parvocellular system about disparity between views of the two eyes. Neurons in these areas respond preferentially to different directions of movement, without analyzing the object that is moving. Many cells in MT respond best to moving borders of single objects, while cells in the dorsal part of MST prefer expanding, contracting, or rotating large scenes. These two types of cells send their output to the ventral part of MST, which allows us to perceive the motion of an object against a stationary field. Damage to MT can result in motion blindness. Nearby temporal lobe areas detect ogical motion, such as swinging of arms and legs, or distinguish between moving objects and visual changes due to head or eye movements (saccades).

The shifting of visual attention from one object to another is correlated with increased activity in parts of the frontal and parietal lobes. As a result, neural activity in visual cortex is altered in a "top-down" process, so that areas most relevant to the focused stimulus show increased activity. Furthermore, although a single neuron may not consistently detect a given stimulus, it contributes to the analysis by a population of neurons. Simultaneous activity in many brain areas gives rise to visual perception.

Human infants are predisposed to pay more attention to faces than to other stimuli. Although cells in the mammalian visual cortex are endowed at the individual's birth with certain adultlike characteristics, normal sensory experience is necessary to develop these characteristics fully and to prevent them from degenerating. If only one eye is deprived of vision during an early sensitive period, the brain becomes unresponsive to that eye. Input from the active eye displaces the early connections made by the inactive eye. If both eyes are kept shut, however, cortical cells remain at least somewhat responsive to both eyes, though their responses are sluggish. Apparently, the changes that occur during the sensitive, or critical, period require GABA, the main inhibitory transmitter. Therefore, both excitatory and inhibitory influences are required to sculpt the neural mechanisms of vision. Visual experience can restore responsiveness to a previously inactive eye, especially if the previously active eye is covered. Other aspects of vision that require early experience for proper development are stereoscopic depth perception, ability to see lines of a given direction, and motion perception. A cataract on the left eye during the early sensitive period can impair recognition of faces, because the left eye projects primarily to the right side of the brain during early development, and the right fusiform cortex is specialized for facial recognition. Furthermore, a lack of detailed vision for many years, due to cataracts or damaged corneas, can result in impaired ability to see details after surgical correction. We are born with pre-wired connections for visual processing; however, we need experience to maintain and develop visual perception.

Learning Objectives

Module 6.1 Visual Coding and the Retinal Receptors

1. Be able to describe the parts of the eye and its connections to the brain.

2. Understand the process by which three types of cones, and the neurons they connect with, can produce a rich spectrum of perceived color.

3. Understand the trade-off between acuity for detail and sensitivity to dim light.

Module 6.2 The Neural Basis of Visual Perception

1. Understand the concept of receptive fields and how they change from the retina to the various areas of the visual cortex.

2. Understand how the parvocellular and magnocellular pathways branch into three pathways in the cerebral cortex and what each of those pathways analyzes.

3. Know the contributions of areas V1, V2, V4, and inferior temporal cortex to shape perception.

4. Be able to describe the brain areas that process color and motion.

Module 6.3 Development of the Visual System

1. Be able to describe the effects of early experiences and of visual deprivation on the development of the visual system.

Key Terms and Concepts

Module 6.1 Visual Coding and the Retinal Receptors

1. General principles of perception

    From neuronal activity to perception

        Receptor potential: A local depolarization or hyperpolarization of a receptor membrane
        Coding does not duplicate shape of object in brain

    Law of specific nerve energies: Activity by a given nerve always sends same kind of information to brain

        Mechanical pressure on eye → perception of light

2. The eye and its connections to the brain

    The route within the retina

        Cornea → pupil → lens → retina
        Image inverted and reversed
        Receptors → bipolar cells → ganglion cells
        Amacrine cells
        Optic nerve
        Blind spot

    Fovea and periphery of the retina

        Macula
        Fovea (pit): Center of macula

            Blood vessels and ganglion cell axons nearly absent
            Midget ganglion cells: Input from single cone
            Good acuity: Sensitivity to detail
            Poor sensitivity to dim light
        Periphery

More receptors converge on bipolar and ganglion cells

>> Better sensitivity to dim light
>> Poorer acuity

> Birds: Two foveas per eye

>> Predatory birds: Greater receptor density on top half of retina (looking down)
>> Prey animals: Greater receptor density on bottom half of retina

3. Visual receptors: Rods and cones

> Rods

>> Most abundant in periphery
>> Responsive to faint light, bleached out by bright light

> Cones

>> Most abundant in and around fovea
>> Essential for color vision, less active in dim light

> Ratio of rods to cones: 20 to 1 in humans; 15,000 to 1 in South American oilbirds

> Photopigments

>> 11-cis-retinal
>> Opsins
>> Conversion of 11-cis-retinal to all-trans-retinal releases energy

4. Color vision

> No single neuron can encode both brightness and color

> Dependent on patterns of responses by different neurons

> The trichromatic theory (Young-Helmholtz)

>> Three types of cone, each maximally sensitive to a different set of wavelengths
>> Psychophysical color matching
>> More long- and medium-wavelength than short-wavelength cones
>> Random distribution of cone types

> The opponent-process theory (Hering)

>> Negative color afterimage
>> Red vs. green, yellow vs. blue, white vs. black

> The retinex theory

>> Color constancy
>> Edwin Land
>> Dale Purves: Perception requires inference

> Color vision deficiency

Most common form: Difficulty distinguishing red from green

Red and green cones make same photopigment
Sex linked (gene on X chromosome)
People with four cone types

5. In closing: Visual receptors

Module 6.2 The Neural Basis of Visual Perception

1. An overview of the mammalian visual system

Retina

Receptors (rods and cones)
Horizontal cells
Bipolar cells
Amacrine cells
Ganglion cells

Axons form optic nerve
Optic chiasm

Lateral geniculate nucleus of the thalamus

Superior colliculus

Hypothalamus

Cerebral cortex: Many visual areas with distinct functions

Axons from cortex back to thalamus

2. Processing in the retina

Lateral inhibition

Horizontal cells (local cells)
Bipolar cells

3. Pathways to the lateral geniculate and beyond

Receptive fields

That part of visual field to which a given neuron responds
Receptive field of ganglion cell: Composite of receptive fields of its inputs

In the retina and lateral geniculate

Parvocellular

Small cell bodies

Small receptive fields
Located in or near fovea
Good acuity and color discrimination
Connect only to lateral geniculate

Magnocellular

Larger cell bodies
Larger receptive fields
Even distribution
Best response to moving stimuli
No color discrimination
Most → lateral geniculate, a few → other visual areas of thalamus

Koniocellular: least responsive, least understood

Project to lateral geniculate, other areas of thalamus, and superior colliculus

Ganglion cell axons: Optic nerve → optic chiasm (half cross there in humans)

Lateral geniculate

Parvocellular geniculate cells: Input from parvocellular ganglion cells
Magnocellular geniculate cells: Input from magnocellular ganglion cells
Some input from koniocellular cells

4. Pattern recognition in the cerebral cortex

Primary visual cortex, striate cortex (V1)

Necessary for conscious vision, visual imagination, visual dreams
Blindsight: After V1 damage, people respond to light they report not seeing

Due to undamaged islands of V1?
Due to input to other brain areas, such as superior colliculus?

Secondary visual cortex (V2)

Reciprocal connections
30-40 visual brain areas in monkeys

Pathways in the visual cortex

Ventral, mostly parvocellular: "What" pathway

Temporal cortex → details of shape

Dorsal, mostly magnocellular: "Where" or "how" pathway

Parietal cortex → aids motor system

Mixed parvocellular and magnocellular: Brightness and color

Some sensitivity to shape
Contributes to ''what" pathway in temporal lobe

The shape pathway

Hubel and Wiesel's cell types in the primary visual cortex

Bar- or edge-shaped receptive fields
Simple cells (V1)

Fixed excitatory and inhibitory zones in receptive fields
Complex cells (V1 and V2)

Larger receptive fields
Cannot be mapped into excitatory and inhibitory zones
Response to moving bar of light
Input from simple cells
End-stopped or hypercomplex cells

Strong inhibitory area at one end of bar-shaped receptive field
Largest receptive field
The columnar organization of the visual cortex

Columns perpendicular to surface
Similar response properties within a column
Are visual cortex cells feature detectors?

Prolonged exposure: Decreased sensitivity to feature
Ambiguity of response of a single cell
Spatial frequencies, sine-wave gratings
Shape analysis beyond area V1

Area V2

Lines, bars, sine wave gratings
Circles, right angles, other complex patterns
Area V4

Slant of line in three-dimensional space
Inferior temporal cortex

Huge receptive fields, always include fovea
Shape constancy
Respond to reversal of contrast or mirror image
Do not respond to figure-ground reversal

5. Disorders of object recognition

Visual agnosia

Prosopagnosia

Fusiform gyrus in inferior temporal cortex (especially right side)
Part of frontal lobe
Some specialization for faces and some general expertise

6. The color, motion, and depth pathways

   Structures important for color perception

   Clusters of neurons in V1 and V2 → V4 → posterior inferior temporal cortex

   Input from parvocellular (color) and koniocellular pathways
   Area V4

   Color constancy
   Visual attention
   Stereoscopic depth perception

   Magnocellular pathway

   Structures important for motion perception

   Area V5 (middle temporal cortex, MT)

   Cells respond best to moving borders
   Medial superior temporal cortex (MST)

   Cells in dorsal MST: Best response to expansion, contraction, or rotation of large scene
   Cells in ventral MST: Best response to movement of object relative to background
   Input to both MT and MST

   Mostly magnocellular (overall patterns)
   Some parvocelular (disparity between left and right eyes)
   Area near MT: Biological motion

   Suppressed vision during eye movements

   Suppression of visual cortex activity during saccades

   Motion blindness

   Also opposite: Movement detection without seeing object

7. Visual attention

   Feedback from other areas to enhance responsiveness of V1 to specific stimulus

   "Top down"
   Similar facilitation of response to specific color or motion

8. In closing: From single cells to vision

   Redundancy: Simultaneous processing of different aspects by different brain areas

Module 6.3 Development of the Visual System

1. Infant vision

Attention to faces and face recognition

    More time looking at faces

        Improved recognition with practice, especially at 6 − 9 months of age

Visual attention and motor control

    Difficulty shifting attention before 6 months of age
    Ability matures until 18 years of age

2. Early experience and visual development

Early lack of stimulation of one eye

    Binocular input to cortex, normally
    Blindness in deprived eye

Early lack of stimulation of both eyes

    Cortical cells

        Sluggish response to both eyes
        No sharp receptive fields
    Sensitive, or critical, period

        Depends on availability of GABA
        Need for excitation of some synapses and inhibition of others
        Duration of sensitive period different for different functions

            Local rearrangements vs. growth over longer distances

Uncorrelated stimulation in both eyes

    Stereoscopic depth perception
    Retinal disparity
    Strabismus
    Synchronous messages

Restoration of response after early deprivation of vision

    Lazy eye, or amblyopia

Early exposure to a limited array of patterns

    Astigmatism

        Force child to use weak eye
    Training in adulthood → increased responsiveness to particular stimuli

        Less effective than earlier training
    Lack of seeing objects in motion

        Stroboscopic illumination
        Motion blindness

117

People with vision restored after early deprivation

    Cataracts removed at 2 − 6 months → subtle problems

    Cataract on left eye of infants → worse problem than on right eye

        Right fusiform gyrus

        Crossed pathway develops faster

    Cataract removal in adulthood → limited improvement

    Infant plasticity greater than in adulthood

3. In closing: The nature and nurture of vision

Some visual abilities at birth

Require experience to maintain and refine them

Short-Answer Questions

Module 6.1 Visual Coding and the Retinal Receptors

1. *General principles of perception*

    a. What is a receptor potential?

    b. Is it necessary for the representation of an image in the brain to resemble the stimulus itself?

    c. State the law of specific nerve energies. Who formulated it?

2. *The eye and its connections to the brain*

    a. What is the fovea? How did it get its name?

    b. How have many bird species solved the problem of getting detailed information from two different directions?

    c. Trace the path of visual information from a receptor to the optic nerve. What is the blind spot?

3. *Visual receptors: Rods and cones*

    a. Compare foveal and peripheral vision with regard to acuity, sensitivity to dim light, and color vision.

    b. What is the specific role of light in the initiation of a response in a receptor? What is a photopigment?

    c. What is the relationship of 11-cis-retinal to all-trans-retinal? What is an opsin?

    d. What kind of electrical response is produced in the receptor, and how does this affect the bipolars with which it synapses?

4. *Color vision*

a. Why does color vision necessarily depend on the pattern of responses of a number of different neurons?

b. How did Young and Helmholtz propose to account for color vision? On what kind of data was their theory based?

c. What kind of theory did Hering propose? What observations supported his theory?

d. What is the current relationship between the three-receptor and the opponent-process theories?

e. What visual ability does the retinex theory explain?

f. What is the genetic basis for the most common form of color vision deficiency? Why do more males than females have this form of color deficiency?

Module 6.2 The Neural Basis of Visual Perception

1. *An overview of the mammalian visual system*

   a. Draw a diagram showing the relationships among the rods and cones, the bipolar and horizontal cells, and the ganglion and amacrine cells.

   b. Axons of which kind of cell form the optic nerve? What is the name of the site where the right and left optic nerves meet? What percentage of axons cross to the opposite side of the brain in humans? What percentage of axons cross to the opposite side of the brain in species with eyes far to the sides of their heads?

   c. Where do most axons in the optic nerve synapse? Where do some other optic nerve axons synapse?

   d. What is the destination of axons from the lateral geniculate nucleus?

2. *Processing in the visual system*

   a. What is lateral inhibition? How does it enhance contrast?

   b. How is lateral inhibition accomplished in the retina?

   c. What is the definition of the receptive field of a neuron in the visual system?

   d. If several bipolar cells provide input to a certain ganglion cell, what can be said about the location of their receptive fields relative to that of the ganglion cell?

3. *Pathways to the lateral geniculate and beyond*

   a. Describe the characteristics of parvocellular ganglion cells.

   b. How do they differ from magnocellular ganglion cells? What are koniocellular ganglion cells?

   c. What happens to the parvocellular and magnocellular pathways in the cortex? What type of information does each of the three main visual pathways process?

   d. In what cortical areas does the ventral stream of visual input end? What aspects of vision are analyzed there?

   e. In what cortical area does the dorsal stream of visual input end? To what process does it contribute?

4. *Pattern recognition in the cerebral cortex*

   a. Describe the evidence that Area V1 is necessary for conscious vision.

   b. What is blindsight? What may explain it?

   c. Describe the three types of information that are analyzed by the "what" pathway? What area of cortex analyzes this information?

   d. What is the functional contribution of the dorsal stream? What cortical area analyzes this information?

   e. For what accomplishment did David Hubel and Torsten Wiesel share the Nobel Prize?

   f. Describe the receptive fields of simple cells.

   g. What is the major difference between responses of simple and complex visual cortical cells?

   h. Describe the receptive field of an end-stopped, or hypercomplex, cell?

   i. What can be said about the receptive fields of neurons in a column in the visual cortex?

   j. What is a feature detector?

   k. What evidence suggests that neurons in area V1 are feature detectors?

   l. What are the problems with that interpretation?

   m. What is the evidence for spatial frequency detectors? What is the problem with the view that neurons in V1 are primarily spatial frequency detectors?

   n. Which areas, beyond V1, are important for shape analysis? What are their major contributions?

5. *Disorders of object recognition*

   a. Describe the symptoms of visual agnosia. What is prosopagnosia?

   b. Which area in the inferior temporal lobe increases its activity when people with intact brains recognize faces?

6. *The color, motion, and depth pathways*

   a. What appears to be the special function of area V4? To what other function does area V4 contribute?

   b. Cells of which pathway are specialized for stereoscopic depth perception? To what aspect of the visual stimulus are they highly sensitive?

   c. Which two areas of the cortex are specialized for motion perception? How "picky" are cells in these areas to the specific characteristics of the stimulus that is moving?

   d. Describe the response characteristics of some cells in area MT.

   e. Describe the preferred stimuli for many cells in the dorsal part of area MST.

   f. What is the role of cells in the ventral part of MST?

   g. Why don't we see a blur when we move our eyes?

   h. Describe the symptoms of motion blindness. Damage to what area might cause motion blindness?

7. *Visual attention*

a. What cortical areas may be important for shifting visual attention? How does activity in the visual cortex change when attention is shifted?

b. Describe the "top-down" process of altering cortical activity when attention shifts.

c. Why is it not a problem if a single cell does not consistently detect a particular aspect of a visual stimulus?

Module 6.3 Development of the Visual System

1. *Infant vision*

   a. To what type of stimuli do infants pay most attention? What aspect of such a stimulus is important for this preference?

   b. How easy is it for infants to shift their attention to other visual stimuli? What brain area controls the ability to shift attention.

2. *Early experience and visual development*

   a. What is the effect of depriving only one eye of pattern vision during the critical period?

   b. What happens if both eyes are kept shut early in life?

   c. What is a sensitive or critical period? What neurotransmitter is important for establishing organization during the critical period?

   d. Define retinal disparity. How does the brain use this information to produce stereoscopic depth perception?

   e. What is strabismus? What ability do people with strabismus lack?

   f. For what human condition does deprivation of visual experience in one eye have relevance? What is the usual treatment for this condition? Why is it important to begin treatment as early as possible?

   g. What happens to the response characteristics of visual cortical cells in a kitten exposed to only horizontal lines early in life?

   h. What is astigmatism? What happens if a child has severe, uncorrected astigmatism during the first few years of life?

   i. What was the effect of rearing kittens in an environment illuminated only by a strobe light?

   j. What visual deficit was observed after cataracts were removed at ages 2 – 6 months? Why does a cataract on the left eye result in greater deficits in face perception than a cataract on the right eye?

True/False Questions

1. In order to perceive the shape of an object, the pattern of activity in the cortex must duplicate that shape in the brain.

    TRUE or FALSE

2. The law of specific nerve energies states that the activity of a given nerve always sends the same kind of information to the brain.

    TRUE or FALSE

3. The order of information transmission in the retina is receptor → ganglion cell →bipolar cell → amacrine cell.

    TRUE or FALSE

4. The fovea is the site at which ganglion cell axons exit the retina.

    TRUE or FALSE

5. The reason that peripheral vision has relatively low acuity, but good sensitivity to dim light, is that many receptors send input to each bipolar, and many bipolars synapse with each ganglion cell.

    TRUE or FALSE

6. Conversion of all-trans-retinal to 11-cis-retinal releases energy that controls the receptor's activity.

    TRUE or FALSE

7. The trichromatic theory was proposed by Young and Helmholst on the basis of psychophysical color matching experiments.

    TRUE or FALSE

8. A likely physiological basis for the opponent-process theory is the depolarization of bipolar cells by some wavelengths and their hyperpolarization by other wavelengths.

    TRUE or FALSE

9. The retinex theory was proposed by Hering to explain negative color afterimages.

    TRUE or FALSE

10. People who have four types of cones are almost always men; they have much better color discrimination than others.

    TRUE or FALSE

11. The receptive field of a ganglion cell is composed of the receptive fields of the cells that send input to it.

    TRUE or FALSE

12. Lateral inhibition is produced by horizontal cells, which inhibit nearby bipolar cells.

    TRUE or FALSE

13. Parvocellular neurons are large cells that are especially important for motion detection.

    TRUE or FALSE

14. The parvocellular and magnocellular pathways remain completely separate throughout the visual cortex.

    TRUE or FALSE

15. The ventral stream ("what") pathway terminates in the temporal cortex.

    TRUE or FALSE

16. The dorsal stream ("where" or "how") pathway also terminates in the temporal lobe.

    TRUE or FALSE

17. Hubel and Wiesel received the Nobel Prize for discovering that cells in the primary visual cortex respond preferentially to bars or edges, rather than spots of light.

    TRUE or FALSE

18. Complex cells have receptive fields that can be mapped into excitatory and inhibitory areas, and those areas recognize complex shapes, such as triangles, squares, or faces.

    TRUE or FALSE

19. Columns in the visual cortex are spread across the surface of the cortex and have response characteristics that vary systematically across the column.

    TRUE or FALSE

20. Sine wave gratings of specific spatial frequencies elicit even greater responses from cells in primary visual cortex than do bars and edges; however, we don't perceive the world as a series of gratings, suggesting that these neurons provide an early stage of analysis.

    TRUE or FALSE

21. Prosopagnosia is a degenerative condition leading to total blindness.

    TRUE or FALSE

22. Cells in the inferior temporal cortex contribute to our capacity for shape constancy.

    TRUE or FALSE

23. Area V4 is especially important for color constancy and visual attention.

    TRUE or FALSE

24. Cells in the MT and MST respond primarily to faces.

    TRUE or FALSE

25. A cataract on the left eye during early development can lead to problems with face recognition, even after the cataract is removed, because the right fusiform gyrus does not get proper stimulation during the early sensitive period.

    TRUE or FALSE

Fill In The Blanks

1. The _____ is a local depolarization or hyperpolarization of a receptor membrane.

2. The _____ cells receive input from the retinal receptors and provide input to the _____ cells.

3. The _____ is an area in the center of the macula that provides the most acute vision, as a result of tight packing of receptors and near absence of _____ and _____ in front of it.

4. Compared to the fovea, the periphery has _____ sensitivity to dim light, both because rods are _____ sensitive than cones and because ganglion cells there have _____ receptive fields than in the fovea.

5. _____ -retinal is converted to _____ -retinal by light; this releases energy that leads to a receptor potential.

6. Helmholtz proposed the _____ theory, based on psychophysical experiments.

7. Hering proposed the _____ theory, based on negative color afterimages.

8. Land proposed the _____ theory to account for color constancy.

9. Axons of _____ cells form the optic nerve, which exits the retina at the _____ .

10. The _____ receives input from ganglion cell axons and sends its output to the primary visual cortex.

11. Lateral inhibition is produced by _____ cells; it is useful for _____ contrast.

12. _____ ganglion cells in the retina have small cell bodies and small receptive fields and are located in or near the fovea.

13. _____ ganglion cells have larger cell bodies and larger receptive fields and are located more evenly across the retina.

14. In the cortex the parvocellular and magnocellular pathways split into three pathways: a mostly parvocellular pathway provides _____ information, a mostly magnocellular pathway that has a ventral branch that is sensitive to _____ and a dorsal branch that integrates vision with _____ , and a mixed parvocellular and magnocellular pathway that is specialized for _____ and _____ .

15. The brain area that confers shape constancy is the _____ cortex.

16. The brain area that confers color constancy is area _____ .

17. The area of the cortex that responds best to moving borders and may record the movement of single objects is the _____ cortex (_____) _____ .

18. The cortical area that responds best to expansion, contraction, or rotation of large scenes is the _____ cortex (_____).

19. Blindsight may be mediated by the _____ or by islands of healthy tissue in otherwise damaged cortex.

20. The neurotransmitter that is important for establishing neural connections during the early critical period is _____ .

21. A human condition similar to that of animals that were deprived of vision in one eye for several days is _____ .

22. Animals raised with uncorrelated stimulation of the two eyes lacked _____ perception.

23. Animals that were raised with only stroboscopic lighting had _____ blindness.

24. People with a cataract on the left eye early in life had problems with _____ even after the cataract was removed.

Matching Items

1. _____ Horizontal cells
2. _____ Blind spot
3. _____ Ganglion cells
4. _____ Fovea
5. _____ Rods
6. _____ Cones
7. _____ Parvocellular neurons
8. _____ Magnocellular neurons
9. _____ Columns of cortex
10. _____ Simple cells
11. _____ Hypercomplex cells
12. _____ Area MST
13. _____ Area MT
14. _____ Area V4
15. _____ Inferior temporal lobe
16. _____ Superior colliculus

a. Small cells, small receptive fields → detailed vision
b. Detects movement of simple objects
c. Detects expansion, contraction, or rotation of field
d. Possible mediator of blindsight
e. Color constancy
f. Cells with similar responses, perpendicular to surface
g. Site where ganglion cells exit the retina
h. Cells in V1 with fixed excitatory & inhibitory areas
i. Lateral inhibition
j. Large receptive field w/ inhibitory area at 1 end
k. Receptors more sensitive to dim light
l. Shape constancy
m. Cells that send axons to lateral geniculate nucleus
n. Receptors with 3 different pigments → color vision
o. "pit" in retina, all cones, most acute vision
p. Large cells, large receptive fields, detect movement

Multiple-Choice Questions

1. The law of specific nerve energies
   a. was proposed by Hering.
   b. states that any activity of a given nerve always conveys the same kind of information to the brain.
   c. states that the information carried by a given nerve changes, depending on the kind of stimulus that gave rise to the nerve's activity.
   d. is no longer thought to be true, and is now only of historical interest.

2. The fovea
   a. is completely blind because axons from ganglion cells exit from the retina there.
   b. covers approximately half the retina.
   c. contains no rods and is bypassed by most blood vessels and axons of distant ganglion cells.
   d. is color blind because it contains no cones but has good sensitivity to dim light.

3. Which of the following is true?
   a. The fovea is more sensitive to dim light than is the periphery.
   b. The fovea has more detailed vision because few receptors synapse with each bipolar.
   c. Cones mediate more detailed vision because of their shape.
   d. Cones are situated peripherally in the retina, rods more centrally, though there is overlap.

4. A photopigment molecule absorbs a photon of light whose energy converts
   a. all-trans-retinal to 11-cis-retinal.
   b. opsin to all-trans-retinal.
   c. 11-cis-retinal to all-trans-retinal.
   d. 11-cis-retinal to opsin.

5. The opponent-process theory
   a. is now thought to describe color processing by neurons after the receptor level, whereas the trichromatic theory describes responses of three kinds of cones.
   b. is now thought to describe color processing at the receptor level, whereas the trichromatic theory describes processing at higher levels.
   c. states that each receptor is sensitive only to a narrow band of wavelengths of light and that wavelength bands of different receptor groups do not overlap.
   d. is true only for rods, not cones.

6. The most common form of color vision deficiency
   a. is more common in women than in men.
   b. has been well known since the earliest civilizations.
   c. is characterized by difficulty distinguishing blue from yellow.
   d. is characterized by difficulty distinguishing red from green.

7. Which of the following best describes the main route of visual information in the retina?
   a. receptor→ganglion cell→bipolar cell
   b. receptor→bipolar cell→ganglion cell
   c. receptor→ganglion cell→amacrine cell
   d. receptor→horizontal cell→amacrine cell

8. Which of the following is true concerning receptive fields?
   a. They are always defined as an area surrounding "their" neuron; the receptive field for a simple cortical cell is itself in the cortex.
   b. The presence of both excitatory and inhibitory areas in the same receptive field is maladaptive and is a holdover from an earlier, inefficient way of processing information.
   c. Receptive fields of simple cortical cells are circular.
   d. For mammalian ganglion cells, they are generally doughnut-shaped, with the center being either excitatory or inhibitory and the surround being the opposite.

9. Lateral inhibition
    a. increases sensitivity to dim light.
    b. ordinarily decreases contrast at borders.
    c. ordinarily heightens contrast at borders.
    d. interferes with processing of color information.

10. Horizontal cells
    a. send axons out of the retina through the blind spot.
    b. send graded inhibitory responses to neighboring bipolar cells.
    c. are located behind the receptors so that they are out of the way of incoming light.
    d. all of the above.

11. Parvocellular ganglion cells
    a. are highly sensitive to both detail and color.
    b. are located primarily in the periphery of the retina.
    c. are among the largest ganglion cells in the retina.
    d. respond only weakly to visual stimuli.

12. Koniocellular ganglion cells
    a. send axons only to the superior colliculus.
    b. connect to the lateral geniculate nucleus, other parts of the thalamus, and the superior colliculus.
    c. are the most important ganglion cells for shape perception.
    d. are located only in the fovea.

13. The parvocellular and magnocellular systems
    a. merge in area V1 and remain one system for subsequent analysis.
    b. remain as two systems throughout visual processing.
    c. divide into three systems, with much of the parvocellular system continuing to analyze details of shape, most of the magnocellular system analyzing movement, and the third system containing parvocellular cells that analyze color and magnocellular cells that analyze brightness.
    d. divide into many concurrent pathways, each analyzing a different color, direction of movement, or shape, but then converge in one master area, where all of these aspects are put together into a unified perception.

14. Simple cells in the visual cortex
    a. respond maximally to bars of light oriented in one direction but not to bars of light oriented in another direction.
    b. respond to "correctly" oriented bars of light only when the bars are in the "correct" part of the retina.
    c. were first described by Hubel and Wiesel.
    d. all of the above.

15. Simple and complex cells differ in that
    a. the receptive field of a simple cell is larger than that of a complex cell.
    b. the receptive field of a complex cell cannot be mapped into fixed excitatory and inhibitory zones, but that of a simple cell can.
    c. simple cells respond only to bars of light, whereas complex cells respond best to small spots of light.
    d. all of the above.

16. Simple and complex cells are similar in that
    a. most of them receive at least some input from both eyes.
    b. most respond maximally to bars of light oriented in a particular direction.
    c. both may be found in the striate cortex.
    d. all of the above.

17. End-stopped, or hypercomplex, cells
    a. have extremely small receptive fields.
    b. are similar to complex cells, except for an inhibitory area at one end of the receptive field.
    c. respond only to very complex stimuli, such as faces.
    d. respond best to small spots of light.

18. Neurons along the track of an electrode inserted perpendicular to the surface of visual cortex
    a. have response characteristics that vary widely, but systematically, from the top to the bottom.
    b. have a random distribution of response characteristics.
    c. have certain response characteristics in common.
    d. cannot have their responses recorded, since the electrode damages them severely.

19. The hypothesis that neurons in the visual cortex are feature detectors
    a. is supported by the observation that prolonged exposure to a given feature seems to fatigue the relevant detectors.
    b. is supported by the finding that each cell in the primary visual cortex responds only to one very precise stimulus, so its response is not at all ambiguous.
    c. is disproved by the observation that visual cortical cells respond only to sine-wave gratings, and not at all to bars and edges.
    d. is now known to be true for cells in area V1, but not for any other visual processing area.

20. The inferior temporal cortex
    a. has receptive fields that always include the fovea.
    b. is concerned with advanced pattern analysis and complex shapes.
    c. may provide our sense of shape constancy.
    d. all of the above.

21. A person with visual agnosia
    a. may have lost recognition only for a few kinds of stimuli, such as faces, as in prosopagnosia.
    b. has lost the ability to read.
    c. is blind.
    d. has had damage limited to the primary visual cortex (area V1).

22. Area V4
    a. seems to be especially important for face recognition.
    b. seems to be especially important for color constancy.
    c. seems to be especially important for shape constancy.
    d. receives input only from the magnocellular system.

23. Occipital area V5 (MT, middle-temporal cortex) analyzes
    a. complex shapes.
    b. colors.
    c. speed and direction of movement.
    d. stereoscopic depth cues.

24. Cells in the dorsal part of MST that respond to expansion, contraction, or rotation of a large visual scene
    a. probably help to record the movement of the head with respect to the world.
    b. probably help to keep track of a single object.
    c. are very particular about the specific objects in their receptive field.
    d. receive input primarily from the parvocellular system.

25. Cells in the ventral part of MST
    a. receive input from cells that record movement of single objects.
    b. also receive input from cells that record movement of the entire background.
    c. respond whenever an object moves in a certain direction relative to its background.
    d. all of the above.

26. Which of the following is true?
    a. Shifting visual attention is associated with activity in the frontal and parietal cortex.
    b. Recognition of complex objects, especially faces, is associated with activity in the fusiform gyrus of the inferior temporal cortex.
    c. The dorsal stream, ending in the parietal cortex, helps the motor system find objects, move toward them and grasp them.
    d. all of the above

27. Human infants
    a. are unable to see any patterns for at least several weeks.
    b. spend more time looking at patternless displays than at faces.
    c. have trouble shifting their attention before about 6 months of age.
    d. all of the above.

28. If a kitten's eyelid is sutured shut for the first 6 weeks of life, and the sutures are then removed, the kitten
    a. is totally blind in the inactive eye only if the other eye had normal visual input.
    b. is totally blind in the inactive eye regardless of the other eye's visual experience.
    c. is able to see horizontal and vertical lines, but not diagonal lines or curves.
    d. sees normally out of the eye, since all of its connections were formed before birth.

29. Children with lazy eye (amblyopia)
    a. should have the active eye covered continuously until adulthood.
    b. should have the active eye covered as early as possible, but only until the lazy eye becomes functional.
    c. should have the active eye covered only after they have reached normal adult size, in order to avoid reorganization of connections.
    d. should not be treated at all, since they will eventually outgrow the condition.

30. Retinal disparity
    a. is an abnormal condition that should be treated as early as possible.
    b. is a cue for depth perception only in people with strabismus.
    c. can be used as a cue for depth perception regardless of the organism's early experience.
    d. can normally be used for stereoscopic depth perception because cortical cells respond differentially to the degree of retinal disparity.

31. Experiments on abnormal sensory environments have shown that
    a. if kittens are reared in an environment in which they see only horizontal lines, at maturity all cells are completely normal, because receptive field characteristics are fully determined at birth.
    b. if kittens are reared with only horizontal lines, they will become so habituated to that stimulus that they soon lose their ability to see horizontal lines.
    c. if kittens are reared with only horizontal lines, they will lose the ability to see vertical lines.
    d. if the environment is illuminated only with a strobe light during development, kittens lose their ability to see either horizontal or vertical lines.

32. Astigmatism
    a. is caused by asymmetric curvature of the eyes and results in blurring of vision for lines in one direction.
    b. is caused by strabismus and results in color blindness.
    c. is caused by amblyopia and results in loss of binocular cells in the cortex.
    d. is caused by too much retinal disparity and results in loss of depth perception.

33. A cataract on the left eye that was present for several months during infancy
    a. did not result in any noticeable problem, as long as it was removed by age 9 or 10.
    b. resulted in mild impairments in face recognition, even though it was removed after the first few months of infancy.
    c. caused less impairment than a cataract on the right eye.
    d. resulted in a great facility for skiing.

Helpful Hint

Here is an analogy of the selective absorption of different wavelengths by the three types of cones. Think of three tennis nets with different sized holes. The one with the largest holes will easily "catch" a red foam-rubber ball about the same size as its holes. Larger or smaller balls will tend to either bounce back off the net or to go through it, though if they are hit just right, they may be caught in the net. A net with medium-sized holes will easily catch a yellow tennis ball, and a net with even smaller holes will catch a blue golf ball.

Solutions

True/False Questions

1. F
2. T
3. F
4. F
5. T
6. F
7. T
8. T
9. T
10. F
11. T
12. T
13. F
14. F
15. T
16. F
17. T
18. F
19. F
20. T
21. F
22. T
23. T
24. F
25. T

Fill In The Blanks

1. receptor potential
2. bipolar; ganglion
3. fovea; blood vessels; ganglion cell axons
4. greater; more; larger
5. 11-cis; all-trans
6. trichromatic
7. opponent-process
8. retinex
9. ganglion; blind spot
10. lateral geniculate nucleus
11. horizontal; enhancing
12. Parvocellular
13. Magnocellular
14. shape; movement; action; brightness; color
15. inferior temporal
16. V4
17. middle temporal; MT; or V5
18. medial superior temporal; MST
19. superior colliculus
20. GABA
21. amblyopia
22. stereoscopic depth
23. motion

24. face recognition

Matching Items

1.	I	7.	A	13.	B
2.	G	8.	P	14.	E
3.	M	9.	F	15.	L
4.	O	10.	H	16.	D
5.	K	11.	J		
6.	N	12.	C		

Multiple-Choice Questions

1.	B	12.	B	23.	C
2.	C	13.	C	24.	A
3.	B	14.	D	25.	D
4.	C	15.	B	26.	D
5.	A	16.	D	27.	C
6.	D	17.	B	28.	A
7.	B	18.	C	29.	B
8.	D	19.	A	30.	D
9.	C	20.	D	31.	C
10.	B	21.	A	32.	A
11.	A	22.	B	33.	B

THE OTHER SENSORY SYSTEMS

Introduction

Sensory systems have evolved to provide information most useful for each species. Although humans can perceive a relatively wide range of stimuli, our sensory systems also show certain specializations.

The sense of hearing uses air vibrations to move the tympanic membrane and three middle ear bones (the hammer, anvil, and stirrup), which focus the force of the vibrations so that they can move the heavier fluid inside the cochlea. The basilar membrane forms the floor of a tunnel, the scala media. Receptor cells are embedded in the basilar membrane; hairs in the top of the receptors are in contact with the overlying tectorial membrane. Inward pressure of the stirrup on the oval window increases pressure in scala vestibuli, which presses down on scala media, which in turn bulges downward into scala tympani and pushes the round window outward. The opposite happens when the stirrup moves outward. The movement of the basilar membrane (the floor of scala media) relative to the tectorial membrane produces a shearing action that bends the hair cells, thereby generating a potential.

Pitch perception depends on a combination of three mechanisms. At low frequencies, neurons can fire with each vibration. At medium frequencies, neurons split into volleys, one volley firing with one vibration, another with the next, and so on. At higher frequencies the area of the basilar membrane with greatest displacement is used as a place code. The characteristics of the basilar membrane vary along the length of the cochlea. At the basal end a bony shelf occupies most of the floor of scala media, and the basilar membrane, which attaches to the shelf, is thin and stiff. At the apex, there is almost no bony shelf, and the basilar membrane is larger and floppier, even though the cochlea as a whole is smaller. The size and stiffness of the basilar membrane determine which part of the basilar membrane will respond to various frequencies of sound with the greatest-amplitude traveling wave. High-pitched tones cause maximal displacement near the base, and low-pitched tones cause maximal displacement closer to the apex. There is considerable overlap of pitches coded by frequency of firing and by place.

After passing through several subcortical structures, auditory information reaches the primary auditory cortex in the temporal lobes. Neurons in one area respond selectively to the location of sound, and those in another area respond selectively to tones. Neurons with similar preferred tones cluster together there.

Damage to the primary auditory cortex does not impair responses to simple sounds but does impair responses to combinations or sequences of sounds.

There are two categories of hearing impairment. Conductive, or middle ear, deafness results from failure of the middle ear bones to transmit sound waves to the cochlea. It can be caused by diseases, infections, or tumorous growths in the middle ear. Nerve, or inner ear, deafness is caused by damage to the cochlea, the hair cells, or the auditory nerve. Prenatal infections or toxins, inadequate oxygen during birth, diseases, reactions to drugs, and exposure to loud noises are frequent causes of nerve deafness.

Sound localization is accomplished by three methods. The difference in loudness between the two ears is used for high-frequency sounds, while the phase difference for sound waves arriving at the two ears is used for low-frequency sounds. In addition, time of arrival at the two ears is useful for sounds with a sudden onset. However, for animals with small heads, there is little phase difference in the sound waves reaching the two ears. Therefore, it is difficult for them to localize low-frequency tones. These animals have evolved the ability to perceive sounds that they can localize easily.

Our auditory system may have evolved from the touch receptors of primitive animals. Vestibular sensation, based on the otolith organs and the semicircular canals in the inner ear, contributes to our sense of balance and guidance of our eye movements.

The sense of touch is composed of several modalities, some of which are fairly well correlated with activity in specific receptor types. For example, free nerve endings are involved in sensations of pain, warmth, and cold. Hair-follicle receptors respond to movement of hairs; Meissner's corpuscles and Pacinian corpuscles signal sudden displacement of skin. Merkel's disks produce a prolonged response to steady indentation of the skin, while Ruffini endings respond to skin stretching.

Sensory nerves enter and motor nerves exit the spinal cord through each of 31 openings in the vertebral canal. These nerves innervate overlapping segments of the body (dermatomes). Several well defined pathways ascend from the spinal cord to separate areas of the thalamus, and thence to appropriate areas of somatosensory cortex in the parietal lobe. Thus, the various aspects of somatosensation are at least partially separate, from the receptor level to the cerebral cortex. Bodily sensations are mapped onto four parallel strips, two of which respond mostly to touch and the other two, to deep pressure and movement of joints and muscles. In some patients damage to the somatosensory cortex may result in impairment of body perception.

Pain information is transmitted to the spinal cord by axons that use glutamate and substance P as their transmitters. Mild pain releases only glutamate; stronger pain releases both. Pain sensations can be inhibited by release of the brain's endogenous opiates (endorphins), including leu- and met-enkephalin, and beta-endorphin. According to the gate theory, various kinds of nonpain stimuli can modify pain sensations.

Endorphins released in the periaqueductal gray area of the midbrain result in excitation of neurons that block the release of substance P in the spinal cord and brainstem.

Capsaicin, derived from hot peppers, elicits the release of substance P and thereby produces a sensation of pain or heat. However, following application of capsaicin, there is a prolonged decrease in pain sensations. Placebo procedures may decrease the emotional response to painful stimuli by inhibiting a pathway through the hypothalamus, amygdala, and cingulate cortex. Pain may be increased as a result of sensitization in damaged or inflamed tissue. Histamine, nerve growth factor, and other chemicals that promote healing also increase sodium gates in pain receptors and may thereby enhance pain sensitivity. Anti-inflammatory drugs, such as ibuprofen, and the neurotrophin GDNF decrease pain by reducing the release of chemicals from damaged tissue. Morphine administered for serious pain is almost never addictive. It is more effective at blocking thin axons that carry dull post-surgical pain than the larger axons that carry sharp pain. The sensation of itch is poorly understood. It is generated by the release of histamines in the skin that activate a very slow-conducting path in the spinal cord. It can be relieved by mild pain from scratching.

Taste and olfactory stimuli activate some receptors better than others; however, vertebrate sensory systems do not have any pure "labeled lines." Instead, the brain analyzes patterns of firing across populations of neurons. Studies of cross-adaptation suggest that we have at least four types of taste receptor: sweet, sour, salty, and bitter. There may also be a receptor for glutamate, termed umami by the Japanese, and additional receptors for bitter and sweet. The mechanisms of activation of some taste receptors have been discovered. Sodium ions activate salty receptors; acids close potassium channels in sour receptors; and sweetness, bitterness, and umami receptors respond to molecules that activate G proteins, which then release a second messenger within the cell. The anterior two-thirds of the tongue sends information via the chorda tympani, a branch of the seventh cranial nerve (facial nerve) to the nucleus of the tractus solitarius in the medulla. The posterior third of the tongue and the throat send input via branches of the ninth and tenth cranial nerves to different parts of the nucleus of the tractus solitarius. From there the information is sent to numerous areas, including the pons, lateral hypothalamus, amygdala, ventral-posterior thalamus, and two areas of the cerebral cortex. There are individual differences in sensitivity to tastes. "Supertasters" have more fungiform papillae near the tip of the tongue. Estradiol increases women's taste sensitivity at mid-cycle and during the early stages of pregnancy.

Olfactory cells have cilia that extend into the mucous lining of the nasal passages. Odorant molecules must diffuse through a mucous fluid in order to reach the receptor sites on the cilia. Humans have several hundred types of olfactory receptor proteins, whereas rats and mice have about 1000 olfactory receptor proteins, which operate on the same principles as metabotropic neurotransmitter receptors. When activated by an odorant molecule, the receptor triggers a change in a G protein, which in turn elicits chemical activities within the cell. People with specific anosmias lack one or more of these receptors. Because there are so many types of receptor, olfaction has more of a labeled-line system of coding than does, for example, color vision, which has only three types of cones. However, even in olfaction, each receptor responds to other odorants that are similar to its preferred stimulus. Therefore, a single receptor can provide an approximate classification of an odorant, but related receptors provide more exact information. A population of varied receptors can provide information about complex mixtures of odors. Pheromones are chemicals released by members of a species that affect the behavior of other members of that species. They are detected by the vomeronasal organ (VNO), located near, but separate from the olfactory receptors. Each VNO receptor responds to only one pheromone and is linked to a G-protein. The VNO in humans is vestigial; however, humans do respond to pheromones, perhaps via receptors in the main olfactory mucosa.

Learning Objectives

Module 7.1 Audition

1. Be able to describe the physical structures of the ear and their contributions to hearing.

2. Understand the mechanisms of pitch perception and sound localization.

3. Know the types of hearing loss and the conditions that can cause them.

Module 7.2 The Mechanical Senses

1. Understand the roles of the otolith organs and semicircular canals in vestibular sensation.

2. Be able to describe the somatosensory receptors and the stimuli they respond to.

3. Be able to describe the cortical processing of somatosensory information.

4. Understand the roles of the various neurotransmitters in the production and the alleviation of pain and itch sensations.

Module 7.3 The Chemical Senses

1. Understand the concepts of the labeled-line and across-fiber pattern principles and how they apply to each of the senses.

2. Understand the mechanisms of the taste receptors and be able to describe the pathways of taste coding in the brain.

3. Be able to describe the operation and numbers of olfactory receptors, and the implications of the numbers of receptors for coding olfactory information.

4. Understand the types of stimuli that the vomeronasal organ responds to and differences between the vomeronasal and olfactory systems.

5. Be able to describe synesthesia and its possible anatomical basis.

Key Terms and Concepts

Module 7.1 Audition

1. Sound and the ear

   Physical and psychological dimensions of sound

   Sound waves: Periodic compressions of air, water, or other media
   Amplitude (physical intensity)

   Loudness (perception of intensity)
   Frequency (compressions per second, hertz: HZ)

   Pitch (perception related to frequency)

   Structures of the ear

   Outer ear

   Pinna → help localize source of a sound
   Middle ear

   Tympanic membrane (eardrum)

   Middle ear bones

   Hammer (malleus)

   Anvil (incus)

   Stirrup (stapes)

   Tympanic membrane: 20 X larger than footplate of stirrup → greater pressure on oval window
   Inner ear

   Oval window
   Cochlea

   Scala vestibuli
   Scala tympani
   Scala media

   Basilar membrane

   Hair cells (auditory receptors)

   Tectorial membrane

   Auditory nerve (part of eighth cranial nerve)

2. Pitch perception

   Frequency theory and place theory

   Frequency theory

Action potentials in synchrony with sound
Problem: Neurons cannot fire fast enough
Volley principle: Effective to ~4000 Hz
Place theory

Each frequency activates hair cells at only one place on basilar membrane
Problem: Basilar membrane parts bound too tightly
Base of basilar membrane: Thin, stiff
Apex of basilar membrane: Larger, floppier
Compromise: Frequency theory below 4000 Hz, place theory above that
Amusia: Tone deafness

3. The auditory cortex

Primary auditory cortex (area A1: Superior temporal cortex)

Includes area MT

Important for visual motion

Damage to parts of superior temporal cortex → motion deafness
Auditory imagery: Fills in gaps in familiar songs
Requires experience for development
Damage to A1 → deficits in advanced processing, not total deafness

Unlike damage to V1, which → blindness
Cells → prolonged response to preferred sound

Tonotopic map
Complex sounds better than pure tones for many cells
Other areas that detect motion of sounds

Part of parietal cortex ("where" stream) → location of sounds and visual stimuli
Areas surrounding A1

Respond more to changes in sounds than to single prolonged sound
Animal cries, machinery noises, music

4. Hearing loss

Conductive deafness (middle-ear deafness)

Certain diseases or infections
Tumorous bone growth in middle ear
Can hear sounds that bypass middle ear, including own voice

Nerve deafness (inner-ear deafness)

May be inherited
Prenatal exposure to rubella, syphilis, or other contagious diseases or to toxins

Inadequate oxygen to brain during birth
Inadequate thyroid activity
Diseases, including multiple sclerosis and meningitis
Childhood reactions to drugs, including aspirin
Repeated exposure to loud noises

Tinnitis: Frequent or constant ringing in ears

Similarity to phantom limb

5. Sound localization

Difference in intensity

Sound shadow
High frequencies

Difference in time of arrival

Sudden onset sounds
Useful for any frequency

Phase difference

Low frequencies

Size of head

Small heads—high frequencies
Large heads—low frequencies

6. In closing: Functions of hearing

Module 7.2 The Mechanical Senses

1. Vestibular sensation

Vestibular organ (adjacent to cochlea)

Otolith organs

Saccule
Utricle
Otoliths: calcium carbonate particles next to hair cells
Semicircular canals (three planes): Filled with jellylike substance, lined with hair cells

Eighth cranial nerve, vestibular component

Brain stem and cerebellum

2. Somatosensation

Somatosensory receptors

    Bare (or free) nerve ending

        Pain, warmth, cold

    Hair-follicle receptors

        Movement of hairs

    Meissner's corpuscles

        Sudden displacement of skin, low frequency vibration

    Pacinian corpuscles

        Sudden displacement of skin, high frequency vibration

    Merkel's disks

        Indentation of skin

    Ruffini endings

        Stretch of skin

    Krause end bulbs

        Uncertain function

    Touch receptors (bare nerve endings, Ruffini endings, Meissner's corpuscles, Pacinian corpuscles):

        Opening of sodium channels

    Heat receptors: Also respond to capsaicin

    Cold receptors: Also respond to menthol and mint

    Tickle: Poorly understood

        Can't tickle oneself

        Motor areas signal somatosensory areas

Input to the spinal cord and the brain

    31 sets of spinal nerves

    Dermatome

Somatosensory thalamus

Somatosensory cortex

    Parietal lobe

    Four parallel strips

        Two for touch

        Two for deep pressure and joint and muscle movement

    Most input from contralateral side, but some from opposite hemisphere via corpus callosum

    Damage to somatosensory cortex → impaired perception of body

3. Pain

    The neurotransmitters of pain

        Glutamate (mild pain)

Substance P (strong pain)
Opioid mechanisms: Inhibit pain

Candace Pert and Solomon Snyder
Inhibit effects of substance P
Met-enkephalin and Leu-enkephalin
β-endorphin (endogenous morphine)
Gate theory: Nonpainful stimuli decrease pain
Endorphins in periaqueductal gray area → medulla

Both areas → spinal cord → block release of substance P

Painful heat

Capsaicin (induces release of substance P, stimulates heat receptors)

Depletes substance P → analgesia
High doses → damage to pain receptors

Pain and emotion

Pain → activation of hypothalamus, amygdala, and cingulate cortex, in addition to somatosensory cortex

→ Emotional responses

Placebo → relief of subjective distress of pain

Somatosensory cortex: Response decreases slightly or not at all
Cingulate cortex: Response decreases substantially, only in area where decrease is expected
Block endorphin synapses → placebos ineffective

Sensitization of pain

Damage to tissue → release of histamine, nerve growth factor → repair damage

Also increase sodium gates → magnify pain response
Facilitate activity at capsaicin receptors
Potentiation of receptors after barrage of stimulation
Similar to learning and memory

Pain control

Morphine before surgery

Rarely addicitve

Blocks activity of thin, unmyelinated axons → blocks postsurgical pain
Doesn't block acute pain carried by large-diameter axons
Marijuana → midbrain neurons with receptors for anandamide and 2-AG → pain relief
Nonsteroidal anti-inflammatory drugs → decrease release of these chemicals
Neurotrophin GDNF → blocks pain sensitivity

4. Itch

Histamines in skin → slow-conducting pathway

Mild pain (scratching) → blocks itch

Opiates decrease pain, increase itch

Novocain effects wear off faster for itch than touch and pain

    Therefore, itch not form of pain

5. In closing: The mechanical senses

Module 7.3 The Chemical Senses

1. General issues about chemical coding

    Labeled-line principle

    Across-fiber pattern principle

2. Taste

    Taste receptors (modified skin cells)

        Taste buds (about 50 receptors per taste bud)
        Papillae (0-10 taste buds per papilla)

    How many kinds of taste receptors?

        Four main types: Sweet, sour, salty, bitter
        Miracle berries and modification of taste receptors

            Miraculin: Acids → sweet
            Sodium laurel sulfate: Intensifies bitter, decreases sweet
        Gymnena sylvestre: Blocks sweet

            Aspartame (NutraSweet®): Sweetness only partially blocked

                Therefore, must stimulate additional receptor
        Adaptation within a taste; little cross-adaptation
        Monosodium glutamate

            Umami
        Different rhythms of action potentials

    Mechanisms of taste receptors

        Salty: Sodium influx

            Amiloride: blocks sodium entry → decreases salty taste
        Sour: Acid closes potassium channels → depolarize membrane
        Sweet, bitter, umami: G protein and second messenger

            Multiple bitter receptors

Taste coding in the brain

  Pattern across fibers
  Information from anterior two-thirds of tongue

    Chorda tympani: Branch of seventh cranial nerve (facial nerve)
  Information from posterior third of tongue and throat

    Ninth and tenth cranial nerves
    Anesthetize chorda tympani

      Lose taste in anterior tongue
      Increase bitter and salt sensitivity in posterior tongue
      "Phantoms" due to release from inhibition
  Nucleus of the tractus solitarius (NTS, in medulla)
  Pons
  Lateral hypothalamus
  Amygdala
  Ventral-posterior thalamus
  Two areas of cerebral cortex

    Insula → taste
    Somatosensory → touch
  Mostly ipsilateral input

Individual differences in taste

  Phenylthiocarbamate (PTC)

    Bitter, very bitter, or little taste
    Supertasters: Most fungiform papillae
  Women's taste sensitivity correlated with estrogen

3. Olfaction

  Behavioral methods of identifying olfactory receptors

    Olfactory cells
    Olfactory epithelium
    Cilia: From cell body into mucous surface
    Rapid adaptation
    Anosmia: Lack of olfaction
    Specific anosmia: Insensitivity to a single chemical

      Isobutyric acid (odor in sweat)
      Musky, fishy, urinous, spermous, malty
      Up to 26 others
  Biochemical identification of receptor types

    Similar to metabotropic neurotransmitter receptors

Seven transmembrane sections

G proteins

About 1000 receptor proteins in rodents

Several hundred in humans

One receptor type per cell

Inhibition of less strongly activated receptors

Implications for coding

Each receptor: Identify approximate nature of molecule

Receptor population: More precise; identify complex mixture

Variety of airborne chemicals, not one single dimension

Space for many receptors not a problem

Messages to the brain

Olfactory bulb

Coding by area of olfactory bulb excited

Several parts of cortex

Clusters of neurons responsive to similar smells

Similar across individuals

Olfactory receptors susceptible to damage

Average survival: ~ one month

Stem cell → new neuron in same place

Axon contains receptor protein → find target in olfactory bulb

Damage to entire olfactory surface → incomplete recovery

Individual differences

Women more sensitive and attentive to odors

Young adult women become more sensitive with experience

Effect of hormones

Deletion of gene for potassium channel → increased sensitivity

4. Vomeronasal sensation and pheromones

Vomeronasal organ (VNO): Receptors located near, but separate from, olfactory receptors

Pheromones: Chemicals released by animals, affect conspecifics

Fewer receptor types

Each receptor responds to one pheromone

Nonadapting

Lack of vomeronasal receptors → impaired mating in mice

Vestigial in humans

Pheromone receptors in olfactory mucosa

Human pheromones

Skin secretions → increased activity in hypothalamus → autonomic responses
Unconscious effects
Synchronized menstrual cycles
Man's pheromones → more regular cycles in partner

5. Synesthesia

Experience one sense in response to stimulation of a different sense

fMRI: Speech activated both auditory and visual cortex

6. In closing: Different senses offer different ways of knowing the world

Taste and smell more important than we realize

Short-Answer Questions

Module 7.1 Audition

1. *Sound and the ear*

   a. What is the relationship between amplitude and loudness? Between frequency and pitch?

   b. What is the role of the tympanic membrane and the hammer, anvil, and stirrup?

   c. Where are the auditory receptors located? How are they stimulated?

2. *Pitch perception*

   a. What led to the downfall of the frequency theory of pitch discrimination in its simple form?

   b. What is the volley theory?

   c. What observation led to the downfall of the place theory as originally stated?

   d. What is the current compromise between the place and frequency theories of pitch discrimination?

   e. At which end of the cochlea is the basilar membrane stiffest?

   f. Describe the location of the primary auditory cortex. To what two aspects of auditory stimuli do parts of primary auditory cortex respond?

   g. What are the effects of damage to the primary auditory cortex?

3. *Hearing loss*

   a. For which type of deafness can one hear one's own voice, though external sounds are heard poorly?

   b. For what type of deafness is hearing impaired for a limited range of frequencies?

c. What are some causes of nerve deafness? Of conductive deafness?

4. *Localization of sounds*

    a. For which frequencies is the "sound shadow" method of localization best? Why?

    b. What characteristic of sound is necessary to be able to localize sounds on the basis of difference in time of arrival? Are some frequencies easier to localize on this basis than others?

    c. Describe localization on the basis of phase difference. For which frequencies is it most effective?

    d. Which method of sound localization is best for a species with a small head? Why?

Module 7.2 The Mechanical Senses

1. *Vestibular sensation*

    a. What are the main parts of the vestibular organ? What are otoliths? What is their function?

    b. What are the semicircular canals? How do they differ from the otolith organs?

2. *Somatosensation*

    a. List the somatosensory receptors and their probable functions.

    b. How many sets of spinal nerves do we have?

    c. What is a dermatome?

    d. Describe briefly the cortical projections of the somatosensory system.

    e. Describe the loss of body sense that may accompany Alzheimer's disease.

3. *Pain*

    a. What is the role of glutamate in pain sensation? What is substance P?

    b. What is capsaicin? How does it work? What food contains capsaicin?

    c. What theory did Melzack and Wall propose to account for variations in pain responsiveness? What is its main principle?

    d. What are endorphins? How was the term derived?

    e. Where are endorphin synapses concentrated? What is their function there?

    f. What is a placebo? What aspect of pain does it sometimes relieve? Which areas of the brain are important for this effect?

    g. Describe the process by which tissue damage results in pain sensitization. Which drugs or natural chemicals can decrease pain sensitization?

    h. In which type of axons does morphine decrease activity? How addictive is morphine when used for pain relief in hospital settings?

4. *Itch*

    a. What is the physiological mechanism of itch sensation?

Module 7.3 The Chemical Senses

1. *General issues about chemical coding*

   a. Describe the labeled-line type of coding. Do vertebrate sensory systems have any pure labeled-line systems?

   b. Describe the across-fiber pattern type of coding. Give an example.

2. *Taste*

   a. Where are the taste receptors located? What is the relationship between taste buds and papillae?

   b. How can cross-adaptation be used to help determine the number of taste receptors?

   c. What are the four major kinds of taste receptor? What additional kinds may we have?

   d. What are the mechanisms of activation of salty, sour, sweet, bitter, and umami receptors? How does amiloride affect salty tastes?

   e. Describe the changes in taste sensitivity that occur if the chorda tympani is anesthetized.

   f. Which structures in the brain process taste information? Is taste analysis primarily ipsilateral or contralateral?

   g. Describe the individual differences in taste of phenylthiocarbamate (PTC). What is the physiological basis of increased sensitivity in supertasters?

3. *Olfaction*

   a. Describe the olfactory receptors. Where do their axons project.

   b. What is a specific anosmia? What can we conclude about the number of olfactory receptors, based on information about specific anosmias?

   c. How are olfactory receptors similar to neurotransmitter receptors? How many olfactory receptor proteins are estimated to exist in rodents, based on isolation of these proteins? in humans?

   d. What can we say about the labeled-line theory vs. the across-fiber pattern theory for smell?

   e. What is the vomeronasal organ? What type of molecules does it detect?

   f. What are some functions of pheromones in mice?

   g. What are two functions of pheromones that have been demonstrated in humans?

4. *Synesthesia*

   a. What is synesthesia? What is one possible explanation for it?

True/False Questions

1. The function of the middle ear bones is to focus the force of vibrations of the eardrum onto the smaller oval window, in order to move the viscous fluid behind the oval window.

   TRUE or FALSE

2. The basilar membrane at the base of the cochlea is larger and floppier than at the smaller apex of the cochlea.

   TRUE or FALSE

3. Two areas of the primary auditory cortex are sensitive to location and frequency of sounds.

   TRUE or FALSE

4. Extensive damage to the primary auditory cortex results in profound deafness for all sounds.

   TRUE or FALSE

5. People with inner-ear deafness can hear their own voices.

   TRUE or FALSE

6. Localization of high-frequency sounds depends mainly on a sound shadow created by the head.

   TRUE or FALSE

7. Pacinian corpuscles are the primary receptors for heat and pain.

   TRUE or FALSE

8. A dermatome is an area on the cortex that receives input from a peripheral structure, such as an arm.

   TRUE or FALSE

9. The somatosensory cortex receives input primarily from the contralateral side of the body, although many neurons also receive input via the corpus callosum from the ipsilateral side.

   TRUE or FALSE

10. Mild pain releases only glutamate in the spinal cord; intense pain releases both glutamate and substance P.

    TRUE or FALSE

11. Endorphins in the periaqueductal gray lead to the activation of neurons that decrease the release of substance P in the spinal cord.

    TRUE or FALSE

12. Capsaicin is an endorphin that that is released in the spinal cord and immediately decreases the release of substance P.

    TRUE or FALSE

13. A placebo decreases the emotional response to pain by decreasing activity in a pathway through the hypothalamus, amygdala, and cingulate cortex.

    TRUE or FALSE

14. Histamine, nerve growth factor, and other chemicals released from inflamed tissue inhibit pain in the area.

    TRUE or FALSE

15. Opiates are even more effective at inhibiting itch than at inhibiting pain.

    TRUE or FALSE

16. Saltiness receptors permit sodium ions on the tongue to cross their membrane and depolarize the neuron.

    TRUE or FALSE

17. Sweet, bitter, and umami receptors close potassium channels, keeping more of the positive ions inside the cell and thereby depolarizing it.

    TRUE or FALSE

18. Taste nerves project to the nucleus of the tractus solitarius in the medulla, which in turn projects to the pons, lateral hypothalamus, amygdala, ventral-posterior thalamus, and two areas of cerebral cortex.

    TRUE or FALSE

19. Each olfactory axon branches widely to provide input to a large percentage of the olfactory bulb.

    TRUE or FALSE

20. Vomeronasal receptors respond to species-specific pheromones that regulate sexual interest, and, in humans, timing of the menstrual cycle.

    TRUE or FALSE

Fill In The Blanks

1. The three middle ear bones are the _____ , the _____ , and the _____ .

2. The basilar membrane in located in the scala _____ .

3. Pitch perception depends on aspects of both the _____ theory and the _____ theory.

4. The two kinds of deafness are _____ and _____ deafness.

5. Phase differences are most useful for localizing _____ -frequency sounds.

6. The vestibular organs consist of the _____ , the _____ , and the _____ .

7. Bare (or free) nerve endings convey information about _____ , _____ , and _____ . Stimulation of these neurons opens _____ channels.

8. The transmitters that convey pain information are _____ and _____ .

9. According to the _____ theory, nonpainful stimuli can decrease the intensity of pain by releasing endorphins in the _____ of the midbrain.

10. _____ is a chemical found in red peppers that activates pain and heat receptors.

11. A drug or procedure that has no pharmacological effect, but that can ease the psychological distress of pain is called a _____ .

12. Sensitization of pain occurs when _____ , _____ , and other chemicals that promote healing also increase the number of _____ gates in pain neurons.

13. Itch is occasioned by release of _____ in the skin.

14. Taste buds are located in _____ on the surface of the tongue.

15. _____ receptors are activated by sodium on the tongue; _____ receptors respond by closing potassium gates; _____ , _____ , and _____ receptors activate G-proteins that release second messengers within the cell.

16. Olfactory receptors are located on _____ that extend into the mucous surface of the nasal passage.

17. Olfactory coding relies more on a _____ principle than does taste coding, because there are so many types of receptor proteins, and each receptor projects to a specific area of the olfactory bulb.

18. Receptors sensitive to pheromones are located in the _____ organ.

Matching Items

1. _____ Amplitude
2. _____ Frequency
3. _____ Sound shadow
4. _____ Time of arrival
5. _____ Phase difference
6. _____ Capsaicin
7. _____ Endorphins
8. _____ Histamine
9. _____ Substance P
10. _____ Pheromone
11. _____ Experience of one sense after stimulation of a different sense

a. Localize low-frequency sounds
b. Localize high-frequency sounds
c. Localize sudden onset sounds
d. Stimulates heat and pain receptors
e. Synesthesia
f. Pitch
g. Loudness
h. Decrease pain
i. Major transmitter for intense pain
j. Increases both healing and pain in sensitization
k. Vomeronasal organ

Multiple-Choice Questions

1. Which of the following is true of auditory perception?
    a. Loudness is the same thing as amplitude.
    b. Pitch is the perception of intensity.
    c. Perception of low frequencies decreases with age and exposure to loud noises.
    d. Perception of high frequencies decreases with age and exposure to loud noises.

2. The function of the tympanic membrane and middle-ear bones is to
    a. directly stimulate the auditory receptors.
    b. move the tectorial membrane to which the stirrup is connected.
    c. focus the vibrations on a small area, so that there is sufficient force to produce pressure waves in the fluid-filled cochlea.
    d. none of the above.

3. The auditory receptors
    a. are called hair cells.
    b. are embedded in the basilar membrane below and the tectorial membrane above.
    c. are stimulated when the basilar membrane moves relative to the tectorial membrane; displacement of the hair cells by about the diameter of one atom opens ion channels in the membrane of the neuron.
    d. all of the above.

4. The frequency theory
    a. in its simplest form cannot describe coding of very high-frequency tones because the refractory periods of neurons limit their firing rates.
    b. can be modified by the volley principle to account for pitch discrimination of all frequencies, up to 20,000 Hz.
    c. is now thought to be valid for high-frequency tones, whereas the place theory describes pitch coding of lower tones.
    d. is a form of labeled-line theory.

5. The place theory
    a. received experimental support from demonstrations that the basilar membrane was composed of a series of separate strings.
    b. has been modified so that a given frequency produces a greater displacement at one area of the basilar membrane than at others.
    c. cannot be true at all, because the basilar membrane is the same throughout its length and therefore cannot localize vibrations.
    d. cannot be true at all, because the basilar membrane is too loose and floppy to show any localization.

6. The basilar membrane
    a. is smallest and stiffest at the apex (farthest, small end) of the cochlea.
    b. is smallest and stiffest at the base (large end) of the cochlea.
    c. has the same dimensions and consistency throughout its length.
    d. shows maximum displacement for low tones near its base.

7. Pitch discrimination
    a. depends on a combination of mechanisms: frequency coding for low pitches, place coding for high pitches, and both mechanisms for intermediate pitches.
    b. depends on a combination of mechanisms: frequency coding for high pitches, place coding for low pitches, and both mechanisms for intermediate pitches.
    c. cannot be satisfactorily explained by any theory.
    d. is accomplished only by place coding.

8. Damage to primary auditory cortex results in
    a. inability to hear anything.
    b. inability to hear high tones, but not low tones.
    c. inability to hear low tones, but not high tones.
    d. inability to recognize combinations or sequences of sounds, as in music or speech.

9. Inner-ear deafness
    a. is frequently temporary; if it persists, it can usually be corrected by surgery.
    b. is characterized by total deafness to all sounds.
    c. may result from exposure of one's mother to rubella or other contagious diseases during pregnancy.
    d. is characterized by being able to hear one's own voice but not external sounds.

10. A "sound shadow"
    a. is useful for sound localization only for low-pitched sounds.
    b. is useful for sound localization only for wavelengths shorter than the width of the head (that is, higher pitches).
    c. is a means of sound localization that uses differences in time of arrival between the two ears.
    d. cannot be used at all by small-headed species such as rodents.

11. Vestibular sensation
    a. arises from free nerve endings in the inner ear.
    b. is produced by a pressure wave along a membrane in the otolith organs.
    c. arises from hair cells in the otolith organs and the semicircular canals.
    d. plays only a minor role in balance and coordination.

12. Which of the following pairs of receptors and sensations is most correct?
    a. free nerve endings: pain, warmth, cold
    b. Merkel's disks: sudden movement across skin
    c. Pacinian corpuscles: steady indentation of skin
    d. Ruffini endings: movement of hairs

13. Dermatomes
    a. are sharply defined, nonoverlapping areas innervated by single sensory spinal nerves.
    b. are overlapping areas innervated by single sensory spinal nerves.
    c. are symptoms of a skin disorder, much like acne.
    d. are found only on the trunk of the body, not the arms, legs, or head.

14. Somatosensory information
    a. travels up a single pathway to one thalamic nucleus, which projects to one strip in the parietal lobe.
    b. travels up different pathways to separate thalamic areas, which project to four parallel strips in the parietal lobe.
    c. travels directly from the spinal cord to the parietal lobe, without any synapses on the way.
    d. travels to separate thalamic areas, which project to four parallel strips in the temporal lobe.

15. Substance P
    a. is an endogenous opiate.
    b. activates receptors that are normally blocked by capsaicin.
    c. is a neurotransmitter that signals intense pain.
    d. none of the above.

16. The gate theory of pain
    a. was proposed by Melzack and Wall.
    b. states that nonpain input can close the "gates" for pain messages.
    c. can be demonstrated by gently rubbing the skin around an injury or concentrating on something else.
    d. all of the above.

17. Leu- and met-enkephalin
    a. have chemical structures virtually identical to morphine.
    b. are transmitters that produce a sensation of pain.
    c. are peptide neurotransmitters, consisting of five amino acids each, that have opiate-like effects.
    d. all of the above.

18. Which of the following is true of the periaqueductal gray area?
    a. Stimulation of enkephalin receptors there leads to blockade of substance P release in pain pathways.
    b. It is an area in the spinal cord where substance P is released to cause pain.
    c. Stimulation of it reduces sharp pain, but not slow, dull pain.
    d. It is a major site for the induction of pain sensitization.

19. The labeled-line principle
    a. states that each receptor responds to a wide range of stimuli and contributes to the perception of each of them.
    b. states that each receptor responds to a narrow range of stimuli and sends a direct line to the brain.
    c. describes color coding better than does the across-fiber pattern principle.
    d. describes most sensory systems in vertebrates.

20. Which of the following is true concerning taste receptors?
    a. There are about 50 receptor cells in each taste bud, and 0 to 10 or more taste buds in each papilla.
    b. Each receptor has its own taste bud.
    c. Taste receptor cells are true neurons that send axons directly to the thalamus.
    d. In adult humans taste buds are located mainly in the center of the tongue.

21. Cross-adaptation studies have suggested that
    a. there are at least four kinds of taste receptors.
    b. there may be a separate receptor for monosodium glutamate.
    c. there may be more than one kind of receptor for both bitter and sweet tastes.
    d. all of the above.

22. Which of the following is an appropriate pairing of receptor type with its method of activation?
    a. salty: sodium inflow
    b. sweet: closing potassium channels
    c. sour: activation of G protein
    d. bitter: sodium outflow

23. Amiloride
    a. facilitates sodium flow across the membrane and intensifies salty tastes.
    b. blocks sodium flow across the membrane and intensifies salty tastes.
    c. blocks sodium flow across the membrane and reduces the intensity of salty tastes.
    d. facilitates potassium flow across the membrane and intensifies sweet tastes.

24. The across-fiber pattern principle of taste
    a. assumes that there are seven basic taste qualities.
    b. holds that taste is coded in terms of a pattern of neural activity across many neurons.
    c. has been disproven by the finding that every receptor responds only to one taste.
    d. none of the above.

25. The nucleus of the tractus solitarius (NTS)
    a. is located in the medulla and sends taste information to the pons, lateral hypothalamus, amygdala, thalamus, and cerebral cortex.
    b. is responsible for analyzing pheromones.
    c. is located in the medulla and sends its output primarily to cranial nerves.
    d. is located in the cerebral cortex and projects to the medulla.

26. Olfactory receptors
    a. are not replaceable, once they die.
    b. each responds to only one specific odor.
    c. respond equally well to a great many odors.
    d. are located on cilia that extend into the mucous surface of the nasal passage.

27. Specific anosmias
    a. are usually very debilitating.
    b. have shown that there are only 4 kinds of olfactory receptors.
    c. suggest that there are probably a fairly large number of kinds of olfactory receptors.
    d. suggest that identification of odors depends entirely on an across-fiber pattern code.

28. Which of the following is true of olfactory receptors?
    a. They are similar to metabotropic neurotransmitter receptors in that they have seven transmembrane sections and trigger changes in a G protein, which then provokes chemical activities inside the cell.
    b. There are as many as 1000 olfactory receptor proteins in mice and several hundred in humans.
    c. They send their axons to specific areas of the olfactory bulb.
    d. All of the above are true.

29. Pheromones
    a. are detected by standard olfactory receptors, which have an especially rapid adaptation.
    b. can synchronize or regularize women's menstrual cycles.
    c. are used in lower mammals, but not in humans.
    d. are especially important for locating sources of food.

Crossword Puzzle

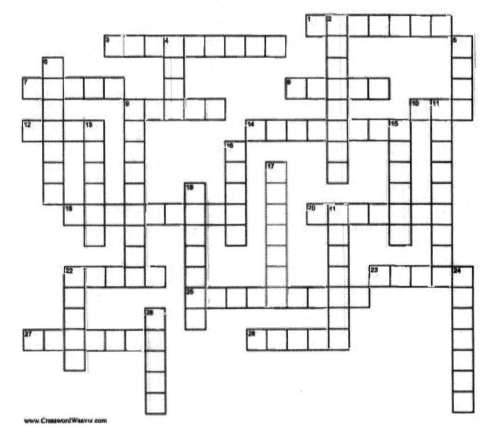

Sensational Senses

www.CrosswordWeaver.com

ACROSS

1 Inability to recognize particular objects
3 Chemical in hot peppers that stimulates pain receptors
7 Scala _____: one of 3 cochlear canals, the floor of which is the basilar membrane
8 _____cellular: large cell in visual system, provides most input to "where" or "how" pathway
9 _____cellular: small cell in visual system, sensitive to color and detail
10 Cortex area responding to expansion, contraction, or rotation of large scene (abbr.)
12 Sensation produced by histamines in the skin, carried by slow-conducting axons
14 Frequent or constant ringing in ears
19 Portion of body innervated by a nerve
20 Organ consisting of 3 canals and containing auditory receptors
22 A taste mediated by G proteins and second messengers
23 Area of retina with no rods and high acuity
25 Endogenous opiate
27 11-cis-_____: part of photopigment in dark-adapted state
28 Quality of tone determined by frequency of vibration of sound waves

DOWN

2 Type of cell whose axons go to lateral geniculate nucleus or tectum
4 Taste mediated by closing of potassium channels
5 Type of visual information processed by ventral stream
6 Neural stream (path) of visual input to inferior temporal lobe
9 A chemical released by animals that affects conspecifics
11 _____ P: Neurotransmitter that signals strong pain
13 Outermost of 3 bones in middle ear
15 Type of visual cortex cell whose receptive field can be mapped with a spot of light
16 Visual receptors mediating color vision
17 Retinal neuron between receptor and ganglion cell
18 Type of visual cortex cell responding to bar of light anywhere in its receptive field
21 Calcium carbonate particle next to hair cell
22 Taste mediated by sodium influx
24 Inability to smell a substance
26 _____ spot: site where ganglion cell axons leave the retina

Crossword Puzzle Solution

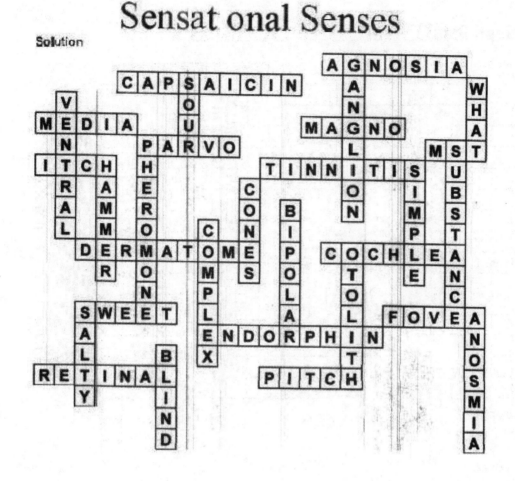

Sensat onal Senses

Solution

Solutions

True/False Questions

1.	T	9.	T	17.	F
2.	F	10.	T	18.	T
3.	T	11.	T	19.	F
4.	F	12.	F	20.	T
5.	F	13.	T		
6.	T	14.	F		
7.	F	15.	F		
8.	F	16.	T		

Fill In The Blanks

1. hammer (malleus); anvil (incus); stirrup (stapes)
2. media
3. frequency; place
4. conductive (middle-ear); nerve (inner-ear)
5. low
6. saccule; utricle; semicircular canals
7. pain; heat; cold; sodium
8. glutamate; substance P
9. gate; periaqueductal gray
10. Capsaicin
11. placebo
12. histamine; nerve growth factor; sodium
13. histamine
14. papillae
15. Saltiness; sourness; sweetness; bitterness; umami
16. cilia
17. labeled-line
18. vomeronasal

Matching Items

1.	G	5.	A	9.	I
2.	F	6.	D	10.	K
3.	B	7.	H	11.	E
4.	C	8.	J		

Multiple-Choice Questions

1.	D	11.	C	21.	D
2.	C	12.	A	22.	A
3.	D	13.	B	23.	C
4.	A	14.	B	24.	B
5.	B	15.	C	25.	A
6.	B	16.	D	26.	D
7.	A	17.	C	27.	C
8.	D	18.	A	28.	D
9.	C	19.	B	29.	B
10.	B	20.	A		

CHAPTER

8

MOVEMENT

Introduction

All movements of the body result from muscle contractions. Acetylcholine is the neurotransmitter released at the neuromuscular junction; it always results in contraction of the recipient muscle. Myasthenia gravis is a disease characterized by weakness and fatigue. It results from autoimmune destruction of acetylcholine receptors on muscle fibers. We manage to move our limbs in two opposite directions by alternately contracting antagonistic muscles, such as flexors and extensors. There are three categories of muscle: smooth, skeletal (or striated), and cardiac. Skeletal muscles may be either fast or slow. Fish have three types of muscle: red, slow, fatigue-resistant; pink, intermediate-speed, moderately fatigue-resistant; and white, fast, easily fatigued. Mammals have muscles composed of mixed fast-twitch and slow-twitch fibers. Muscles consist of many fibers, each of which is innervated by one axon; however, each axon can innervate more than one fiber. Greater precision of movement can be achieved if each axon innervates few muscle fibers.

Two kinds of receptors signal change in the state of muscle contraction. The muscle spindle is a stretch receptor located in fibers parallel to the main muscle. Whenever the main muscle and spindle are stretched, the spindle sends impulses to the spinal cord that excite the motor neurons innervating the main muscle. This results in contraction of the main muscle, opposing the original stretch. The Golgi tendon organ is located at both ends of the main muscle and responds to increased tension in the muscle, as when the muscle is contracting or being actively stretched by an external stimulus. Its impulses to the spinal cord inhibit the motor neuron, leading to relaxation of the muscle. Combinations of activity in these two receptors allow one to maintain steady positions, to resist external forces, and to monitor voluntary movement.

Most behaviors are complex mixtures of voluntary and involuntary, or reflexive, components. Some movements are ballistic, which means that they proceed automatically once triggered. Other movements require constant sensory feedback. Central pattern generators control rhythmic movements, such as wing flapping and scratching. Motor programs are fixed sequences of movements; they may be learned or innate, rhythmic or not.

The cerebral cortex coordinates complex plans of movement. The primary motor cortex sends axons to the brainstem and spinal cord, which in turn innervate the muscles. It has overlapping areas that control

different parts of the body. These areas are activated ev...
in the inferior parietal cortex of monkeys respond durir...
monkey perform the same movement. They enable t...
movements. Neurons in the posterior parietal cortex...
current movements, or to a mixture of sensory inpu...
converting perception into action. The primary so...
with sensory information and also sends axons di...
hand grasps an object, responding to the object's...
areas guide the preparation for movement. Pref...
to movement; it also calculates the likely outc...
movement and, to some extent, during the movem...
a rapid series of movements. There is evidence that the mo...
before we are aware of making a decision to act.

The symptoms of Parkinso...
initiating physical or me...
degeneration of dopam...
nucleus and putame...
ultimately in less...
genes have bee...
more commo...
the form o...
dopamin...
diseas...
dise...

Output from the cortex to the spinal cord can be divided into two tracts. The dorsolateral tract con... movements in the periphery of the opposite side of the body. It includes axons from the primary motor cortex and adjacent areas and from the red nucleus, all of which cross from one side to the other in bulges in the medulla called the pyramids. These axons extend without synapsing to targets in the medulla and spinal cord. The ventromedial tract controls movements near the midline of the body that require bilateral control. It consists of some axons from primary and supplementary motor cortex, others from widespread areas of cortex, and those from the midbrain tectum, reticular formation, and vestibular nucleus. Axons branch to both sides of the cord; they control muscles of the neck, shoulders, and trunk, whose movements are necessarily bilateral.

The cerebellum is important for learning, planning and coordinating complex movements, especially rapid sequences that require accurate timing and aiming. It also contributes to sensory and cognitive processes. Damage to the cerebellum impairs rapid alternating movements, saccades, the ability to touch one's nose with one's finger, and the ability to shift attention. Parallel fibers in the cerebellar cortex activate Purkinje cells, which in turn inhibit the cerebellar and vestibular nuclei. Inhibiting these nuclei for shorter or longer times determines the duration and distance of a movement. Information from these nuclei is then sent to the midbrain and thalamus.

The basal ganglia are a group of subcortical structures that contribute to the selection and organization of movements and to habit learning. The caudate nucleus and putamen receive input from the cerebral cortex and send information to the globus pallidus, which in turn sends output to the thalamus, which finally sends its output to motor and prefrontal cortex. The globus pallidus constantly inhibits the thalamus; the caudate nucleus and putamen select certain movements by telling the globus pallidus to stop inhibiting them. The basal ganglia are especially important for self-initiated movements not controlled by an external stimulus. They are also important for learning motor skills.

's disease include muscle rigidity and tremor, slow movement, difficulty al activity, depression, and cognitive deficits. Parkinson's disease results from ne neurons ascending from the substantia nigra in the midbrain to the caudate , which are part of the basal ganglia. Loss of dopamine in the basal ganglia results xcitation of the cortex. Therefore, the cortex is less able to initiate movements. Several implicated in early-onset Parkinson's disease, but they have little influence on the much late-onset disease. A possible cause of this disease is MPTP in the environment, possibly in herbicides and pesticides. MPTP is converted in the body to MPP+, which accumulates in e neurons and destroys them. On the other hand, nicotine and caffeine may decrease risk of the . Damage to mitochondria, caused by clusters of α-synuclein, is the ultimate cause of Parkinson's ase. The symptoms of Parkinson's disease can be lessened with L-dopa, the precursor of dopamine, hough such treatment frequently results in undesirable side effects. Furthermore, L-dopa does not prevent, and may even hasten, the further loss of neurons. Other possible treatments include antioxidants, drugs that stimulate dopamine receptors, drugs that decrease apoptosis, and high-frequency stimulation of the globus pallidus. Brain grafts of fetal substantia nigra tissue have produced promising results in laboratory animals, but have produced only modest benefits in humans. Research is continuing on the possible use of genetically altered stem cells and neurotrophins.

Whereas Parkinson's disease results from degeneration of the dopaminergic input to the basal ganglia, Huntington's disease results from degeneration of the postsynaptic neurons there and in the cortex. Symptoms begin with a facial twitch and progressively lead to tremors in other parts of the body and to writhing movements and psychological disorders. An autosomal dominant gene on chromosome 4 has been identified as the ultimate cause of the disease. In people with Huntington's disease this gene contains extra repetitions of a sequence of bases (CAG) in the genetic code for a protein called huntingtin. These repetitions lead to production of long chains of glutamine, which aggregate into clusters that impair mitochondria. Cells with abnormal huntingtin also fail to release BDNF, which results in impaired function of other cells. Several drugs for treatment of this disorder show promise in animal models.

Learning Objectives

Module 8.1 The Control of Movement

1. Be able to list the three categories of muscle and understand the need for antagonistic muscles.

2. Understand the difference between fast and slow muscles and conditions under which each is most useful.

3. Be able to name and know the functions of proprioceptors.

Module 8.2 Brain Mechanisms of Movement

1. Understand the roles of the primary motor cortex, inferior parietal cortex, posterior parietal cortex, and the prefrontal, premotor, and supplementary motor cortex in the control of movement.

2. Understand the implications of the timing of the readiness potential before the person is aware of making a decision.

3. Understand the functions and cellular organization of the cerebellum.

4. Be able to list the structures that comprise the basal ganglia and know the function of each and the general contribution of the whole system.

Module 8.3 Disorders of Movement

1. Know the symptoms and immediate physiological cause of Parkinson's disease.

2. Understand the genetic and environmental causes of Parkinson's disease.

3. Know the most common treatment for Parkinson's disease and a problem with that treatment.

4. Be able to describe the symptoms and immediate physiological cause of Huntington's disease.

5. Understand the genetic cause of Huntington's disease.

Key Terms and Concepts

Module 8.1 The Control of Movement

1. Muscles and their movements

   Categories of muscle

      Smooth
      Skeletal or striated
      Cardiac

   Precise movements: Few muscle fibers innervated by each axon

   Neuromuscular junction

      Acetylcholine → excitation and muscle contraction

   Antagonistic muscles

      Flexor
      Extensor

   Myasthenia gravis

      Autoimmune attack on acetylcholine receptors at neuromuscular junctions
      Progressive weakness and rapid fatigue
      Depletion of acetylcholine after several action potentials in rapid succession

   Fast and slow muscles

Fish

Red, slow, resistant to fatigue

Pink, intermediate speed, moderately resistant to fatigue

White, fast, forceful, fatigue quickly

Humans and other mammals: Mixed fibers in each muscle

Fast-twitch fibers

Anaerobic → oxygen debt → muscle fatigue

Use fatty acids

Slow-twitch fibers

Aerobic → slow to fatigue

Use glucose, activate gene to inhibit further glucose use when supplies dwindle

People: Varying percentages of fast- and slow-twitch fibers

Human specializations for locomotion

Shape of toes, leg bones, muscles, and tendons

High percentage of slow-twitch muscles in legs

Extensive sweat glands and reduced body hair → temperature control

Larger buttocks → better balance

Muscle control by proprioceptors

Proprioceptor: Receptor that detects position or movement

Muscle spindle: Stretch receptor parallel to muscle

Stretch reflex

When stretched, causes muscle to contract → decreases stretch

Contributes to walking: Raise upper leg → lower leg moves forward

Golgi tendon organ

In tendons at opposite ends of muscle

Responds to increased muscle tension

Inhibits muscle: Brake against too vigorous contraction

2. Units of movement

Voluntary and involuntary movements

Reflexes: Consistent automatic responses to stimuli

Involuntary

Infant reflexes

Grasp reflex

Babinski reflex

Rooting reflex

Cerebral cortex damage in adults → infant reflexes released from inhibition

Allied reflexes: Several reflexes elicited together
Many behaviors: mixture of voluntary and involuntary influences

Movements with different sensitivity to feedback

Ballistic movement: Executed as a whole; cannot be altered after initiated

Stretch reflex
Contraction of pupil
High sensitivity to feedback

Threading needle
Singing

Delayed auditory feedback

Sequences of behaviors

Central pattern generators

Rhythmic movements
Frequency of repetition governed by spinal cord

Cat scratch: 3 to 4 strokes per second
Motor program: Fixed sequence of movements

Learned or built in
Birds: Wing extension when dropped
Humans: Yawning

3. In closing: Categories of movement

Spinal motor neuron: Final common path

Many brain areas control different patterns

Module 8.2 Brain Mechanisms of Movement

1. The cerebral cortex

Primary motor cortex: Precentral gyrus

No direct connections to muscles

Axons synapse in brainstem and spinal cord
General movement plans

Each movement associated with activity in scattered population of cells
Brief electrical stimulation of cortex → twitches
Longer (.5 sec) stimulation → complex movements
Active when we imagine movements
Inferior parietal cortex

Mirror neurons: Active during movement and while watching another monkey do same movement

Areas near the primary motor cortex

Posterior parietal cortex

Position of body relative to the world
Converting perception into action

Primary somatosensory cortex

Sensory information to motor cortex
Direct output to spinal cord

Prefrontal cortex

Response to sensory signals that lead to a movement
Calculates probable outcome, plans movement
Inactive during dreams

Premotor cortex

Preparation for movement
Gets information about target relative to body
Output to primary motor cortex and spinal cord

Supplementary motor cortex

Preparation for rapid series of movements
Light stimulation → urge to move body part, expectation of movement
Stronger stimulation → movements

Conscious decisions and movements

Decision to move: ~200 ms before actual movement
Readiness potential: ~500 ms before movement

~300 ms before conscious decision

Damage to parietal cortex → intention at same time as movement

Parietal cortex → feeling of intention to move before actual move

Damage to primary motor cortex of right hemisphere → anosognosia

Don't realize that they can't move left arm or leg
Motor cortex normally monitors feedback from muscles

Connections from the brain to the spinal cord

Dorsolateral tract of spinal cord

Axons from primary motor cortex and surrounding areas and from red nucleus of midbrain
Direct connection to spinal cord
Cross in pyramids of medulla
Controls peripheral movements on opposite side of body

Newborn humans: Bilateral control

MOVEMENT

During first year and a half: Contralateral displaces ipsilateral control

Cerebral palsy: Contralateral paths do not mature → competition between the two sides

Ventromedial tract of spinal cord

Axons from primary and supplementary motor cortex, other cortical areas, tectum, reticular formation and vestibular nucleus

Axons branch to both sides of spinal cord

Controls midline movements requiring bilateral influence

Stroke in left primary motor cortex → loss of control of right side of body

Some recovery: A few undamaged neurons in dorsolateral tract, learned use of ventromedial tract and connections between left and right spinal cord

2. The cerebellum ("little brain")

More neurons than rest of brain combined

Rapid movements that require accurate aim and timing

Effects of damage to the cerebellum

Difficulty with aiming and timing
Difficulty imagining sequences of movement
Normal at continuous motor activity

Tests of cerebellar functioning

Saccades
Finger-to-nose test

Move function: Cerebellar cortex
Hold function: Cerebellar nuclei
Slow movement: Not dependent on cerebellum

Damage → effects similar to alcohol intoxication

Evidence of a broad role

Response to sensory stimuli that direct movement
Precise timing of brief intervals
Aspects of attention
Programming sequence of actions as a whole

Cellular organization

Input from spinal cord, sensory cranial nerve nuclei, and cerebral cortex
Cerebellar cortex: Precise geometrical pattern with multiple repetitions of same units

Parallel fibers (axons parallel to each other) activate Purkinje cells one after another
Purkinje cells (flat cells in sequential planes) inhibit cerebellar nuclei and vestibular nuclei of brain stem

These then send information to midbrain and thalamus

Controls duration of response

3. The basal ganglia

Component structures

Caudate nucleus
Putamen
Globus pallidus

Input from cerebral cortex → caudate nucleus and putamen → globus pallidus → thalamus → motor and prefrontal cortex

Transmitter from globus pallidus to thalamus: GABA

Much spontaneous activity → constant inhibition of thalamus
Input from caudate nucleus and putamen → which movements to *stop inhibiting*
Damage to globus pallidus → lack of inhibition → involuntary, jerky movements

Functions

Select correct movement and inhibit other movements
Self-initiated behaviors

Not activated if action is guided by a stimulus

4. Brain areas and motor learning

All motor areas important for learning new skills

Motor cortex

Increased firing rate and consistency
Increased signal-to-noise ratio

Basal ganglia

Organizing sequences of movement into a whole
Alter response patterns as skills become automatic

5. In closing: Movement control and cognition

Behavior: Integrated contributions of numerous areas

Posterior parietal cortex → position of body in visual space → guides movement

Sensory, cognitive, and motor functions
Cerebellum → both motor functions and timing sensory processes
Basal ganglia → select or start movement, enhance cognitive function

Selecting and organizing a movement: Intertwined with sensory and cognitive processes

Module 8.3 Disorders of Movement

1. Parkinson's disease

Symptoms

Rigidity
Muscle tremors
Slow movements
Difficulty initiating physical and mental activity
Depression and cognitive deficits

Less problem if external stimuli guide action

Degeneration of dopamine projections from substantia nigra to caudate nucleus and putamen

Less inhibition of inhibitory neurons → decreased excitation of motor cortex → slow movement onset
Steady loss of substantia nigra neurons after age 45
Less than 20-30% of normal → Parkinson's disease

Possible causes

Early-onset Parkinson's disease: Several genes implicated
Low heritability of late-onset Parkinson's disease
Five genes slightly more common in those with Parkinson's disease
Exposure to toxins

Heroin-like drug: MPTP → MPP+
Postsynaptic neurons increase dopamine receptors

Compensation for loss of dopamine

Result in over-responsiveness

Herbicides, pesticides (including rotenone): One factor
Cigarette smoking, caffeine: Decrease risk
Marijuana: Increases risk
Common factor: α-synuclein → damage to mitochondria

Dopamine neurons more vulnerable

L-dopa treatment

Precursor to dopamine
Effectiveness varies
Does not prevent, and may increase, loss of dopamine neurons
Side effects: Nausea, restlessness, sleep problems, low blood pressure, repetitive movements, hallucinations, delusions

Therapies other than L-dopa

Antioxidant drugs

Drugs that stimulate dopamine receptors

Neurotrophins

Drugs that decrease apoptosis

High-frequency stimulation of globus pallidus or subthalamic nucleus

Brain grafts

Patient's adrenal gland → little benefit

Brain tissue from aborted fetuses

Neurons survive and some make connections

Expensive, requires tissue from 4 to 8 fetuses

No improvement, only lack of further deterioration

Brain tissue together with neurotrophins → greater improvement

Genetically altered fetal cells: Produce much L-dopa

Especially if those cells are stem cells

So far, modest benefits

Transplanted tissue that produces neurotrophins

Effective in rats and monkeys

2. Huntington's disease (Huntington's chorea)

Symptoms

Twitches and tremors

Writhing movements

Impaired ability to learn new movements

Extensive brain damage, especially in caudate nucleus, putamen, globus pallidus, and cortex

Psychological symptoms: Depression, memory impairment, anxiety, hallucinations and delusions, poor judgment, alcoholism, drug abuse, sexual disorders

Stimulating environment may delay onset of symptoms

Heredity and presymptomatic testing

Autosomal dominant gene on chromosome #4

Extra repetitions of sequence of bases (CAG)

The more repetitions, the earlier the onset

Protein encoded: Huntingtin

Mutant form → excess glutamine aggregates into clusters → impairment of mitochondria

Vulnerable to damage from numerous sources

No release of BDNF → impairment of other cells

Promising drugs

Block glutamine chains from clustering

Interfere with expression of huntingtin gene

3. In closing: Heredity and environment in movement disorders

Short-Answer Questions

Module 8.1 The Control of Movement

1. *Muscles and their movements*

    a. List the three categories of muscle.

    b. What is the transmitter at the neuromuscular junction? What is its effect? How do we move our limbs in two opposite directions?

    c. Describe the symptoms and cause of myasthenia gravis.

    d. List the types and functions of skeletal muscle in fish.

    e. How are mammalian muscles different from those of fish? Contrast the muscles of sprinters and marathon runners.

    f. What is a proprioceptor? A stretch reflex?

    g. What is a muscle spindle? What is its effect on the spinal motor neuron that innervates its associated muscle?

    h. Explain the knee-jerk reflex in terms of the above mechanism.

    i. What is a Golgi tendon organ? What is its effect on the spinal motor neuron that innervates its associated muscle? What is its functional role?

2. *Units of movement*

    a. What is a reflex?

    b. Describe some of the involuntary components of "voluntary" behaviors, such as walking or talking.

    c. What is a ballistic movement?

    d. What is the effect of delayed auditory feedback on a singer's ability to hold a single note for a long time?

    e. What is a motor program? Give examples of "built-in" and learned motor programs.

    f. Do humans have any built-in motor patterns?

Module 8.2 Brain Mechanisms of Movement

1. *The cerebral cortex*

a. Describe the role of the primary motor cortex in the control of movement.

b. What did researchers observe when they increased the duration of electrical stimulation of the motor cortex to half a second?

c. What are mirror neurons? Where are they located? What is their apparent function?

d. To what two processes do neurons in the posterior parietal cortex respond? What is the result of damage there?

e. Describe the roles of the prefrontal, premotor, and supplementary motor cortex.

f. Where does the dorsolateral tract begin? Where does it cross from one side to the other?

g. From what structures does the ventromedial tract originate? What is the relationship between this tract and the two sides of the spinal cord?

h. Which movements are controlled by the dorsolateral tract, and which by the ventromedial tract?

i. What happens to the partially bilateral innervation by the primary motor cortex during the first year and a half of life? How may that be affected by cerebral palsy? What is the behavioral result?

2. *The cerebellum*

a. What kinds of movements are especially affected by cerebellar damage?

b. What are saccades? Describe the effect of cerebellar damage on the control of saccades.

c. Describe the motor control required to touch one's finger to one's nose as quickly as possible.

d. Why may a police officer use the finger-to-nose test to check for alcohol intoxication?

e. Describe the evidence for a broad role for the cerebellum, beyond motor performance.

f. From what sources does the cerebellum receive input?

g. Describe the relationship between the Purkinje cells and the parallel fibers. How does this affect movement?

3. *The basal ganglia*

a. What structures comprise the basal ganglia?

b. Which are the main receptive areas? The main output area? Where does the major input come from, and where does the output go?

c. Describe the way in which the basal ganglia select movements. Which transmitter does the globus pallidus release?

d. Are the basal ganglia more important for self-initiated or stimulus guided movements?

e. What is the role of the basal ganglia in the learning of motor patterns?

Module 8.3 Disorders of Movement

1. *Parkinson's disease*

a. Describe the symptoms of Parkinson's disease.

b. What is its immediate cause? How does loss of dopamine in the caudate nucleus and putamen affect activity in the cortex?

c. How strong is the evidence for a genetic predisposition for Parkinson's disease?

d. How did the experience with a heroin substitute lead to suspicion of an environmental toxin as a cause of this disease?

e. How may herbicides and pesticides be implicated?

f. What is a problem with the toxin-exposure hypothesis?

g. What was the unexpected finding concerning cigarette smoking, coffee drinking, and Parkinson's disease?

h. What is the role of α-synuclein in causing damage to dopamine neurons?

i. What is the rationale for treatment of Parkinson's disease with L-dopa? What are the side effects of this treatment?

j. List some other possible treatments for Parkinson's disease.

k. How successful have brain grafts been in treating Parkinson's disease in humans? What are some of the problems with the use of fetal tissue? From where in the brain is fetal tissue taken?

l. What other kinds of tissue have been used for brain grafts to treat Parkinson's disease? What are some potential additional sources for tissue for such grafts?

2. *Huntington's disease*

a. What are the physical and psychological symptoms of Huntington's disease?

b. Which neurons degenerate in Huntington's disease?

c. Discuss the role of genetics in Huntington's disease. On which chromosome is the gene for Huntington's disease located?

d. What is huntingtin? What do we know about the base sequence of the gene that codes for it? What may it do inside the cell?

e. What are two potential treatments for Huntington's disease that have shown promise in animal models?

True/False Questions

1. Acetylcholine is the transmitter at all neuromuscular junctions; however, it has excitatory effects at some muscles, and inhibitory effects at others, depending on the type of receptor on the muscle.

TRUE or FALSE

2. Myasthenia gravis is caused by an autoimmune attack on acetylcholine receptors.

TRUE or FALSE

3. Muscle spindles are receptors at opposite ends of a muscle; activation of them inhibits muscle contraction.

   TRUE or FALSE

4. Ballistic movements are those that have especially high sensitivity to feedback while they are being executed.

   TRUE or FALSE

5. The primary motor cortex is located in the precentral gyrus, at the posterior end of the frontal lobe.

   TRUE or FALSE

6. The posterior parietal cortex is especially important for preparation for a rapid series of movements.

   TRUE or FALSE

7. The prefrontal cortex responds to signals that lead to a movement.

   TRUE or FALSE

8. The dorsolateral tract descends from primary motor cortex and surrounding cortical areas and from the red nucleus; its axons cross in the pyramids of the medulla.

   TRUE or FALSE

9. The ventromedial tract controls peripheral movements on the opposite side of the body.

   TRUE or FALSE

10. The cerebellum is especially important for linking motions rapidly and smoothly, especially those that require accurate aim and timing. However, it is also important for aspects of attention.

    TRUE or FALSE

11. Purkinje cells in the cerebellar cortex inhibit parallel fibers, which are the main output cells of the cerebellum.

    TRUE or FALSE

12. The globus pallidus is the main receiver of input to the basal ganglia; the caudate nucleus and the putamen provide the main output.

    TRUE or FALSE

13. Parkinson's disease results from degeneration of dopamine projections from substantia nigra to the caudate nucleus and putamen.

    TRUE or FALSE

14. L-dopa provides some relief from symptoms of Parkinson's disease, but may also hasten the loss of dopamine neurons.

    TRUE or FALSE

15. Only the earliest-onset form of Huntington's disease shows any heritability.

    TRUE or FALSE

16. Huntington's disease is characterized by excessively long repeats of CAG in the gene that codes for huntingtin.

    TRUE or FALSE

Fill In The Blanks

1. The three categories of muscle are _____ , _____ , and _____ .

2. Antagonistic skeletal muscles are _____ and _____ .

3. Myasthenia gravis results from the loss of _____ receptors, as a result of autoimmune attack.

4. In humans a high ratio of _____ to _____ fibers is more characteristic of sprinters than marathon runners.

5. A stretch receptor located in parallel to a muscle, and that causes the muscle to contract, is called a _____ .

6. A receptor located in tendons at opposite ends of a muscle, and that inhibits muscle contraction, is called a _____ .

7. A movement executed as a whole, without intervening feedback, is a _____ movement.

8. A fixed sequence of movements is called a _____ .

9. The primary motor cortex is located in the _____ gyrus.

10. The brain area that helps to convert perception into action is the _____ cortex.

11. The brain area that responds to sensory signals that lead to a movement and calculates the outcome of that movement is the _____ cortex.

12. Neurons in the inferior parietal cortex that fire when a monkey performs an act, and also when it watches another monkey perform the same act, are called _____ .

13. Neurons in the _____ cortex respond to visual or somatosensory stimuli or to current or future movements and keep track of the body in relation to the world. _____

14. The brain area in front of primary motor cortex that receives information about the position of the target in space as well as the position of the body is the _____ cortex.

15. The supplementary motor cortex is especially important for planning and organizing _____ .

16. The _____ tract controls peripheral movements on the opposite side of the body; the _____ tract controls midline movements that require bilateral influence.

17. The brain area that links movements rapidly and smoothly and contributes to aspects of attention is the _____ .

18. The three structures that comprise the basal ganglia are the _____ , the _____ , and the _____ .

19. Parkinson's disease results from degeneration of the tract from the _____ to the _____ and _____ .

20. The usual treatment for Parkinson's disease is _____ ; however, this may hasten the loss of dopamine neurons.

21. _____ disease is characterized by twitches and tremors, writhing movements, and impaired ability to learn new movements.

22. This disorder results from mutation in the gene on chromosome _____ that codes for the protein called _____ ; as a result a mutant form of the protein is produced, which impairs the neuron's mitochondria and its release of _____ .

Matching Items

1. _____ Long-distance running
2. _____ Golgi tendon organ
3. _____ Muscle spindle
4. _____ Primary motor cortex
5. _____ Posterior parietal cortex
6. _____ Primary somatosensory cortex
7. _____ Dorsolateral tract
8. _____ Ventromedial tract
9. _____ Cerebellum
10. _____ Caudate nucleus, putamen
11. _____ Globus pallidus
12. _____ Parkinson's disease
13. _____ L-dopa
14. _____ Hunington's disease

a. Causes associated muscle to contract
b. Precentral gyrus
c. Receive dopamine from substantia nigra
d. Disease with excessive CAG repeats in a gene
e. Treatment for Parkinson's disease
f. Contains Purkinje cells and parallel fibers
g. Inhibits contraction of associated muscle
h. Keeps track of the body relative to the world
i. Provides sensory information to motor cortex
j. Degeneration of dopamine neurons
k. A human specialization for locomotion
l. Crosses in the pyramids of medulla
m. Main output from basal ganglia
n. Controls midline movements

Multiple-Choice Questions

1. Which of the following is true of nerves and muscles?
   a. There is always a one-to-one relationship between axons and muscle fibers.
   b. Each axon innervates several or many muscle fibers.
   c. Each muscle fiber receives many axons.
   d. Some muscle fibers are not innervated by any axons.

2. Acetylcholine
   a. has only inhibitory effects on skeletal muscles.
   b. has excitatory effects on some skeletal muscles and inhibitory effects on others.
   c. has only excitatory effects on skeletal muscles.
   d. is released only onto smooth muscles, never onto skeletal muscles.

3. Myasthenia gravis
   a. results from destruction of acetylcholine receptors at neuromuscular junctions by an autoimmune process.
   b. is characterized by excessive, jerky movements.
   c. is helped by drugs that greatly increase the production of antibodies to acetylcholine receptors.
   d. all of the above.

4. Which of the following is a typc of skeletal muscle in fish?
   a. slow, white, fatigue-resistant
   b. fast, white, fatigue-resistant
   c. slow, pink, fatigue-prone
   d. slow, red, fatigue-resistant

5. Mammalian muscles
   a. can be classified as red, pink, and white, as in fish.
   b. contain either fast-twitch or slow-twitch fibers, but not both.
   c. contain both fast-twitch and slow-twitch fibers in the same muscles.
   d. show only genetic, and not any environmental, determination of the ratio of fast-twitch to slow-twitch fibers.

6. The muscle spindle
   a. is a stretch receptor located in parallel to the muscle.
   b. inhibits the motor neuron innervating the muscle when it is stretched; this leads to relaxation of the muscle.
   c. responds only when the muscle contracts.
   d. synapses onto the muscle to excite it directly.

7. The Golgi tendon organ
   a. is also located in the muscle spindle.
   b. affects the motor neuron in the same way as the muscle spindle, thereby enhancing its effect.
   c. responds when the muscle contracts.
   d. excites the motor neuron that innervates the muscle.

8. Ballistic movements
   a. are required when a singer holds a note for a long time.
   b. require feedback as they are being executed.
   c. are always highly complex and never simple reflexes.
   d. proceed automatically once triggered.

9. The frequency of repetition of a cat's scratch reflex
   a. varies, and is controlled by pattern generators in the brain.
   b. is constant at three to four scratches per second, and is determined by cells in the lumbar spinal cord.
   c. is constant and is determined by pattern generators in the brain.
   d. is an example of feedback control.

10. Which of the following is true?
    a. Feedback control must be at the root of all movements; otherwise we would be unable to modify our behavior.
    b. Singing a single note does not require feedback, although singing several notes in a sequence does require feedback.
    c. Even ballistic movements are in reality feedback controlled.
    d. There are involuntary components of many voluntary behaviors.

11. Which of the following is true of motor programs?
    a. Grooming behavior of mice is an example of a built-in motor program.
    b. Grooming behavior of mice is an example of a learned motor program.
    c. Species of birds that have not used their wings for flight for millions of years still extend their wings when dropped.
    d. Humans have only learned, and not built-in, motor programs.

12. The primary motor cortex
    a. sends axons to the brainstem and the spinal cord to execute movements.
    b. includes the somatomotor, prefrontal, premotor, and supplementary motor cortex, as well as the basal ganglia.
    c. controls isolated movements of individual muscles.
    d. all of the above.

13. The order of activity in preparing for and executing a movement is
    a. primary motor, premotor, prefrontal cortex.
    b. prefrontal, premotor, primary motor cortex.
    c. premotor, primary motor, prefrontal cortex.
    d. primary motor, prefrontal, premotor cortex.

14. The posterior parietal cortex
    a. is the main receiving area for somatosensory information.
    b. helps us to program a series of rapid movements.
    c. helps us to keep track of the position of the body relative to the world and convert perception into action.
    d. is part of the primary motor cortex.

15. A readiness potential
    a. has been recorded in people's motor cortex several hundred milliseconds before their conscious decision to move.
    b. has been recorded in supplementary motor cortex several hundred milliseconds after the conscious decision to move.
    c. has been recorded in the cerebellum several hundred milliseconds after the movement began.
    d. all of the above.

16. The dorsolateral tract of the spinal cord
    a. originates mostly in the primary motor cortex and adjacent areas and in the red nucleus of the midbrain.
    b. controls movements in the periphery of the body.
    c. controls movements on the side of the body opposite the brain area where the fibers originate.
    d. all of the above.

17. Partial innervation of both sides of the body by the primary motor cortex
    a. occurs in newborn humans.
    b. decreases over the first year and a half, as the contralateral control displaces the ipsilateral control.
    c. remains in cerebral palsy, because the contralateral control does not develop properly; the resulting competition between the contralateral and ipsilateral paths may contribute to clumsiness.
    d. all of the above.

18. The ventromedial tract of the spinal cord
    a. contains crossed fibers from the primary motor cortex and adjacent areas and from the red nucleus of the midbrain.
    b. controls movements near the midline of the body that are necessarily bilateral.
    c. controls movements on the side of the body opposite the brain area where the fibers originate.
    d. works independently from the dorsolateral tract.

19. The pyramids of the medulla
    a. contain the cell bodies of the dorsolateral tract.
    b. contain the cell bodies of the ventromedial tract.
    c. are the site where axons of the dorsolateral tract cross from one side to the other.
    d. are the site where axons of the ventromedial tract cross from one side to the other.

20. The cerebellum
    a. is especially important for performance of movement sequences that require accurate aiming and timing.
    b. is more important for continuous motor activities than for movements that require rhythmically starting and stopping.
    c. is important only for innate, not learned, motor responses.
    d. contains relatively few neurons and synapses, compared to the cerebral hemispheres.

21. Damage to the cerebellum produces
    a. Parkinson's disease.
    b. Huntington's disease.
    c. deficits in saccadic movements of the eyes.
    d. deficits in slow feedback-controlled movements.

22. In executing the "finger-to-nose" movement quickly
    a. the cerebellar cortex is important in the initial rapid movement.
    b. the cerebellar nuclei are important in maintaining the brief hold pattern.
    c. other structures are important in the final slow movement.
    d. all of the above.

23. Purkinje cells in the cerebellum
    a. receive input from parallel fibers.
    b. send output to parallel fibers.
    c. excite cells in the cerebellar nuclei.
    d. send output to the basal ganglia and cerebral cortex.

24. The cerebellum
    a. shows most activity during purely motor tasks.
    b. contributes to any motor, perceptual, or cognitive task that requires careful timing of brief intervals.
    c. is now thought to contribute only to cognitive tasks, and not to motor tasks.
    d. is especially important for controlling muscle force and determining which tone is louder.

25. The basal ganglia consist of
    a. the caudate nucleus, the cerebellum, and the thalamus.
    b. the cerebellum, the putamen, and the thalamus.
    c. the caudate nucleus, the putamen, and the globus pallidus.
    d. the putamen, the globus pallidus, and the pyramids of the medulla.

26. Which of the following is true?
    a. Neurons in the globus pallidus send GABA-containing axons to the thalamus.
    b. Neurons in the globus pallidus show much spontaneous activity.
    c. The caudate nucleus and putamen tell the globus pallidus which movements to stop inhibiting.
    d. All of the above are true.

27. The basal ganglia are important for
    a. actions guided by a stimulus.
    b. learning motor skills, selecting movements, and organizing them into a whole.
    c. wing flapping in birds.
    d. fine control of movement.

28. Parkinson's disease
    a. results from too much dopamine in the basal ganglia.
    b. results from too little acetylcholine at the neuromuscular junction.
    c. results from too little dopamine in the basal ganglia.
    d. is almost completely determined genetically.

29. MPTP
    a. has been used with some success in treating Parkinson's disease.
    b. may be an environmental cause of Parkinson's disease.
    c. may be an environmental cause of myasthenia gravis.
    d. has been used with some success in treating Huntington's disease.

30. α-synuclein
    a. is a promising new treatment for Parkinson's disease.
    b. is a promising new treatment for Huntington's disease.
    c. clots into clusters that damage neurons containing dopamine.
    d. results in destruction of acetylcholine receptors.

31. Which of the following is **not** a current or potential treatment for Parkinson's disease?
    a. dopamine pills.
    b. L-dopa.
    c. neurotrophins.
    d. antioxidants.

32. Brain grafts
    a. are currently the best treatment for Parkinson's disease.
    b. are most effective if they use tissue from the patient's own adrenal gland in order to prevent rejection.
    c. are able to produce beneficial effects only if the implanted tissue survives and makes functional synapses.
    d. currently use fetal substantia nigra tissue, but may someday use stem cells genetically altered to produce large quantities of L-dopa.

33. Huntington's disease
    a. results from destruction of dopaminergic input to the basal ganglia.
    b. is characterized by great weakness.
    c. is caused by a dominant gene on human chromosome number 4.
    d. is caused by a recessive gene on human chromosome number 10.

34. Which of the following are not symptoms of Huntington's disease?
    a. weakness and difficulty initiating movements
    b. depression, anxiety, memory impairment, hallucinations, and delusions
    c. poor judgment, alcoholism, and drug abuse
    d. facial twitch and tremors

35. The gene associated with Huntington's disease
    a. in its normal form, contains a sequence of bases repeated at least 40 times; many of those repeats are lost in patients with Huntington's disease.
    b. in its normal form, does not contain any repeated sequences of bases.
    c. is now known to code for acetylcholine receptors.
    d. is now known to code for huntingtin, a protein, the mutant form of which has long chains of glutamine, which form clusters that impair the neuron's mitochondria.

36. Cells with abnormal huntingtin
    a. release an excessive amount of BDNF, thereby causing uncontrolled growth.
    b. fail to release BDNF along with their neurotransmitter, thereby impairing the function of other cells.
    c. produce as much damage throughout the body as it does in the brain.
    d. produce too little glutamine for normal function.

Solutions

True/False Questions

1.	F	7.	T	13.	T
2.	T	8.	T	14.	T
3.	F	9.	F	15.	F
4.	F	10.	T	16.	T
5.	T	11.	F		
6.	F	12.	F		

Fill In The Blanks

1. smooth; skeletal (striated); cardiac
2. flexors; extensors
3. acetylcholine
4. fast-twitch; slow-twitch
5. muscle spindle
6. Golgi tendon organ
7. ballistic
8. motor pattern
9. precentral
10. posterior parietal
11. prefrontal
12. mirror neurons
13. posterior parietal ;
14. premotor
15. a rapid series of movements
16. dorsolateral; ventromedial
17. cerebellum
18. caudate nucleus; putamen; globus pallidus
19. substantia nigra; caudate nucleus; putamen
20. L-dopa
21. Huntington's
22. 4; huntingtin; BDNF

Matching Items

1.	K	3.	A	5.	H
2.	G	4.	B	6.	I

7. L   10. C   13. E
8. N   11. M   14. D
9. F   12. J

Multiple-Choice Questions

1. B   13. B   25. C
2. C   14. C   26. D
3. A   15. A   27. B
4. D   16. D   28. C
5. C   17. D   29. B
6. A   18. B   30. C
7. C   19. C   31. A
8. D   20. A   32. D
9. B   21. C   33. C
10. D   22. D   34. A
11. A   23. A   35. D
12. A   24. B   36. B

WAKEFULNESS AND SLEEP

Introduction

Animals ranging from insects to humans exhibit endogenous rhythms of behavior. Circannual (approximately year-long) cycles govern hibernation, migration, and seasonal mating in some species. Circadian (approximately 24-hour) cycles regulate activity and sleep as well as other bodily functions. The "clock" governing these cycles generates the rhythm internally, although the external light cycles affect the specific settings. Light influences the suprachiasmatic nucleus (SCN) of the hypothalamus, which provides the main control of rhythms of sleep and temperature. If the SCN is isolated from the rest of the brain, it continues to generate a circadian rhythm of approximately 24 hours. The biochemical mechanism of the clock is based on two genes, initially discovered in fruit flies. These genes, *period* (*per*) and *timeless* (*tim*) produce protein products (Per and Tim) that build up during the day and produce sleepiness. High levels then feed back to decrease production of the proteins. Similar genes have been found in mammals. Melatonin, a hormone produced by the pineal gland, is one means by which the SCN regulates sleeping and waking. Increased melatonin secretion begins 2 to 3 hours before the onset of sleepiness. The SCN can be reset by various stimuli, including light, tides, exercise, noises, meals, etc. Light is the most important stimulus (zeitgeber: time giver) for most mammals. People traveling across several time zones suffer from jet lag, which is worse traveling east than traveling west. People who work night shifts are also stressed and are plagued by more errors and injuries than people who work during their normal waking period. Very bright lights during the new day time and complete darkness during the new night help travelers and shift workers adapt to their schedules. Some axons in the optic nerve form the retinohypothalamic path, which innervates the SCN. Even animals with little or no vision can use retinal ganglion cells that contain their own photopigment (melanopsin) to regulate the biological clock.

The electroencephalogram (EEG) is used to record the average of the electrical potentials of neurons near each electrode on the scalp. Relaxed wakefulness (with the eyes closed) is characterized by alpha waves at a frequency of 8 - 12 per second. Stage 1 of sleep is signaled by irregular, low-voltage waves, after which progression through stages 2, 3, and 4 is correlated with increasingly slow, large-amplitude waves. Throughout the night, there is a cyclic progression back and forth through the four stages approximately every 90 minutes. However, after the first period of stage 1, each return to stage 1 is correlated with rapid eye movements, relaxed muscles, and rapid and variable heart rate and breathing. Rapid eye movement (REM) sleep has also been called paradoxical sleep, because the EEG shows fast, low amplitude waves, as during wakefulness, and heart rate and breathing are variable, but the postural muscles are completely relaxed. Dreams during REM sleep tend to be more intense than those during non-REM (NREM) sleep. Stages 3 and 4 of slow wave sleep predominate early in the night, whereas REM periods are longer and comprise a larger portion of sleep time late in the night.

Wakefulness and behavioral arousal depend, in part, on the reticular formation, a group of large, branching neurons running from the medulla into the forebrain. The pontomesencephalon is the part of the reticular formation that contributes to cortical arousal. It receives input diffusely from many sensory systems and generates spontaneous activity of its own. It sends output to the thalamus and basal forebrain. There are different types of arousal, requiring many brain areas. The locus coeruleus, in the pons, is active in response to meaningful events and may help to form memories. It sends widely branching axons containing norepinephrine to the cortex. The basal forebrain is the site of nuclei that send GABA-containing axons to the thalamus and cortex; GABA inhibits neurons there and promotes sleepiness. The basal forebrain also sends acetylcholine-containing axons to the thalamus and cortex; these neurons promote wakefulness. Separate paths from the hypothalamus increase arousal by releasing the neurotransmitter histamine. Finally, another path from the hypothalamus releases orexin (hypocretin) widely throughout the forebrain and brainstem. Orexin stimulates acetylcholine-containing cells, thereby allowing an individual to remain awake for a longer time, as opposed to alternating between sleep and wakefulness.

Sleep results in part from cooling the brain and core of the body by directing blood to the periphery, where it is cooled by exposure to the environment. In addition, sensory input and activity in arousal systems are reduced. Adenosine accumulates during wakefulness and shuts off the basal forebrain neurons that produce arousal. Caffeine increases arousal by blocking adenosine receptors. Prostaglandins also increase during the day and inhibit hypothalamic cells that increase arousal. Prostaglandins are also produced throughout the body when the immune system fights infection.

During REM sleep, high-amplitude potentials can be recorded in the pons, geniculate, and occipital cortex (PGO waves). Animals maintain nearly constant amounts of PGO waves. If deprived of REM, PGO waves intrude into other sleep stages and even wakefulness. Animals compensate for lost PGO waves when allowed to sleep freely. In addition to initiating REM episodes, cells in the pons inhibit the motor neurons that control postural muscles. Other sites that are active during REM are the limbic system and parts of parietal and temporal cortex. However, the primary visual, motor, and dorsolateral prefrontal cortex, become less active during REM. Acetylcholine induces the onset of REM, as well as of wakefulness, and serotonin and norepinephrine interrupt or shorten it.

Insomnia may be caused by uncomfortable environmental conditions, abnormalities of biological rhythms, and withdrawal from tranquilizers. A phase-delayed temperature rhythm may cause difficulty getting to sleep, whereas a phase-advanced rhythm may cause early awakening. Sleep apnea, the inability to breathe during sleep, may be caused by obesity, genetics, hormones, or impairment of brain mechanisms for respiration. People with sleep apnea often have brain areas that have lost neurons. It is not clear whether the apnea is the cause or the result of the brain damage, but animal studies suggest that apnea causes the damage.

Narcolepsy refers to periods of extreme sleepiness during the day. Additional symptoms of narcolepsy are cataplexy (extreme muscle weakness while awake), sleep paralysis (inability to move during transition into or out of sleep), and hypnagogic hallucinations (dreamlike experiences that are difficult to distinguish from reality). All of these symptoms can be interpreted as intrusions of REM sleep into wakefulness. Narcolepsy results from a deficit in orexin (hypocretin), which maintains wakefulness. Animals lacking orexin spend the same total time in waking and sleeping as normal animals; however, they cannot stay awake for prolonged periods. Periodic limb movement disorder, in which the legs kick every 20 to 30 seconds for minutes or hours, can lead to insomnia. In REM behavior disorder people appear to act out their dreams, possibly as a result of damage to the neurons in the pons that inhibit movement during REM. Nightmares are unpleasant dreams that occur during REM sleep; night terrors are experiences of extreme anxiety, occurring during NREM sleep, from which a person wakens in terror. Sleep talking occurs with similar probability in REM and NREM sleep, whereas sleepwalking occurs mostly during stages 3 and 4 slow-wave sleep.

Sleep serves several functions. The primary function of sleep during early evolution was to conserve energy during times when activity would be either inefficient or dangerous. Both body temperature and energy expenditure are decreased during sleep, and animals that hibernate decrease energy needs even more. Animals that eat nutrition-rich foods and face little threat from attack sleep longer than those that eat plants and must avoid predators. Some species have developed specializations in their sleep, such as decreasing the need for sleep during migration or sleeping with one side of the brain at a time. Another function of sleep is restoration, especially for the brain, such as rebuilding proteins and replenishing energy supplies. People who sleep irregularly or poorly often feel depressed and have decreased alertness and performance. Immune responses may also be altered. A third function of sleep is to promote memory storage. People who slept after learning a task performed better than those who stayed awake. The brain apparently activates the same areas during sleep that were used in the initial learning.

The function of REM sleep is not well understood. In general, the percentage of sleep spent in REM correlates positively with the total amount of sleep. REM deprivation has resulted in increased REM time on subsequent uninterrupted nights. REM may facilitate the consolidation of motor skills; whereas NREM sleep may strengthen verbal memories. The eye movements that characterize REM may also increase oxygen supply to the corneas. Dreams may result from the brain's attempt to make sense of its increased activity during REM episodes (activation-synthesis hypothesis). A clinico-anatomical hypothesis rests in part on the observations that during REM, neural activity in primary visual, motor, and prefrontal cortex is suppressed. Therefore, normal visual input cannot compete with self-generated stimulation, and motor activity is suppressed. Also, working memory and "use of knowledge," functions of prefrontal cortex, are inhibited. On the other hand, increased activity in inferior parietal cortex and higher visual areas may increase spatial perception and visual imagery. Finally, increased activity in the hypothalamus, amygdala, and other areas may increase the emotional intensity of dreams.

Learning Objectives

Module 9.1 Rhythms of Waking and Sleeping

1. Understand the functions of endogenous rhythms and our difficulty with altered rhythms.

2. Be able to describe the anatomical location of the biological clock and its biochemical and hormonal signals.

3. Be able to explain how light can reset the biological clock.

Module 9.2 Stages of Sleep and Brain Mechanisms

1. Know the characteristics of the stages of slow-wave and REM sleep.

2. Know the brain areas and neurotransmitters that promote wakefulness, slow-wave sleep and REM sleep.

3. Know the various sleep disorders, their possible causes, and their treatments.

Module 9.3 Why Sleep, Why REM? Why Dreams?

1. Understand the proposed functions of sleep in general and of REM sleep.

Key Terms and Concepts

Module 9.1 Rhythms of Waking and Sleeping

1. Endogenous cycles

   Endogenous circannual and circadian rhythms

      Bird migration
      Squirrel food storage and fat deposition
      Student sleepiness and wakefulness
      Flying squirrel in total darkness
      Highly constant for given individual in given environment
      Changes with age not due simply to learning

   Duration of the human circadian rhythm

      Difficulties with experiments
      Constant light → rhythms faster than 24 hours
      Constant dark → rhythms slower than 24 hours
      People with choice of light schedule → closer to 25 hours

         Problem: Bright light late in day lengthens cycle
      Ability to adapt to 23- or 25-hour days, but not 22- or 28-hour days
      28-hour light cycle → 24.2 hour wake/sleep cycle
      6-hour wake/12-hour rest cycle → 24.3 – 24.4 hour cycle

2. Mechanisms of the biological clock

    Interfering with the biological clock

        Curt Richter

            Lack of effect of most procedures

    The suprachiasmatic nucleus (SCN)

        Main control of rhythms of sleep and temperature
        Endogenous rhythm

            Disconnected SCN still generates rhythms
            Single SCN cells generate rhythm

                Less steady than group of cells
            Genetic mutation that produces 20-hour rhythm

                Transplantation of mutant or normal SCN: Animals followed rhythm of SCN

    The biochemistry of the circadian rhythm

        Drosophila genes

            Period (per)
            Timeless (tim)
            Proteins Per and Tim build up during day
            Interact with Clock protein → sleepiness
            Light at night → inactivate Tim → decrease sleepiness → reset clock
            Similar genes in mammals (slight differences)

                Per and Tim → increase activity of certain neurons in SCN
                Mutations → altered rhythms

    Melatonin

        Pineal gland
        Peak 2 to 3 hours before sleepiness
        Melatonin pill in afternoon → phase advance
        Repeated melatonin pills in morning → phase delay
        Antioxidant
        Increased movement deficits in Parkinsonian rats
        Impaired reproduction in rats

3. Setting and resetting the biological clock

    Free-running rhythm

    Zeitgeber ("time giver") → resets clock

        Light (most effective for land animals), tides, exercise, noises, meals, temperature

Hamsters in constant light → two hemispheres out of phase

Jet lag

Worse going east
Phase-delay going west
Phase-advance going east
Stress of jet lag → cortisol → degeneration of hippocampus neurons

Shift work

Exposure to bright lights helps

How light resets the SCN

Retinohypothalamic path

Axons from optic nerve
Animals with little or no vision: Light still resets rhythms

Mice with genetic defects
Blind mole rats

Retinal ganglion cells with own photopigment (melanopsin)

Respond slowly to average amount of light

Mice lacking melanopsin gene: Reset clock less effectively

Normal retinal input → partial substitute

4. In closing: Sleep-wake cycles

Sleepiness not voluntary

Work when sleepy → errors and injuries

Module 9.2 Stages of Sleep and Brain Mechanisms

1. The stages of sleep

Electroencephalogram (EEG)

Average of electrical potentials of neurons near scalp electrode
Alpha waves (8 − 12 per second): Relaxed wakefulness

Stage 1 sleep

Irregular, low-voltage EEG waves

Stage 2 sleep

Sleep spindle: 12 − 14-Hz waves in burst of 0.5 second
K-complex: Sharp, high-amplitude negative wave, followed by smaller positive wave

Stages 3 and 4 slow-wave sleep (SWS)

Synchronized EEG: Slow, large amplitude waves

Less input to cortex

2. Paradoxical or REM sleep

   Characteristics

      Paradoxical sleep

         In some ways deepest and in some ways lightest sleep
      Rapid eye movements (REM)
      Irregular, low-voltage fast (desynchronized) EEG
      Postural relaxation
      Variable heart rate, blood pressure, and breathing
      Penile erection or vaginal moistening
      Facial twitches
      Polysomnograph: EEG and eye movement records
      Sleep cycles

         90-minute cycles
         Stages 3 and 4 predominant early in night
         REM predominant late in night

            Governed by time, not length of sleep
            Depressed people: REM soon after going to sleep
         REM sleep and dreaming

            Dement & Kleitman: Dreams reported on 80 - 90% of awakenings from REM
            Some kind of thought process during non-REM sleep (NREM)
            REM: intensifies dreams but not synonymous with dreaming

3. Brain mechanisms of wakefulness and arousal

   Brain structures of arousal and attention

      Cut through midbrain → prolonged sleep

         Not due to loss of sensory input
      Reticular formation: Network from medulla into forebrain
      Pontomesencephalon

         Widespread sensory input
         Spontaneous activity
         Axons to thalamus and basal forebrain

            Acetylcholine and glutamate → excitatory effects
            Arousal then relayed to cortex
      Arousal not a unitary process

         Four kinds of attention

Waking up
Directing attention to a stimulus
Storing a memory
Increasing goal-directed effort
Locus coeruleus ("dark blue place") in pons

Bursts of impulses in response to meaningful events
Norepinephrine
May aid in memory formation, increase wakefulness
Basal forebrain nuclei (anterior and dorsal to hypothalamus)

Provides input to thalamus and cortex
Some neurons: GABA → inhibitory effects → sleep
Input from anterior and preoptic hypothalamus
Temperature regulation
Fever increases output to sleep-related cells
Some neurons: Acetylcholine → mostly excitatory effects → arousal
Damage (including Alzheimer's disease) → impairments of alertness and attention
Paths from hypothalamus

Histamine → arousal
Orexin (hypocretin) → staying awake
Stimulate acetylcholine-containing cells

Getting to sleep

Decrease temperature

Shift blood to periphery
Decrease stimulation

Gentle rocking may help
Inhibit arousal systems

Adenosine inhibits basal forebrain arousal systems

Metabolism: Adenosine monophosphate (AMP) → adenosine → inhibition of arousal neurons in basal forebrain
Caffeine → inhibit adenosine → wakefulness; also → constrict blood vessels in brain
Prostaglandins

Build up during day, decline during sleep
Stimulate neurons that inhibit hypothalamic cells that increase arousal

4. Brain function in REM sleep

Increased activity in pons and limbic system and in parietal and temporal cortex

Pons → onset of REM

Decreased activity in primary visual, motor, and dorsolateral prefrontal cortex

PGO (pons-geniculate-occipital) waves

  Compensation for lost PGO waves

Pons → spinal cord → inhibition of motor neurons

Neurotransmitters

  Acetylcholine → REM onset

    Carbachol
    Important for both waking and REM → activate brain
  Serotonin → interrupts or shortens REM
  Norepinephrine from locus coeruleus → blocks REM

5. Sleep disorders

  Insomnia

    Causes: Noise, uncomfortable temperatures, stress, pain, diet, medications

      Also epilepsy, Parkinson's disease, brain tumors, depression, anxiety
    Trouble falling asleep

      Possible cause: Phase-delayed temperature rhythm
    Awakening too early

      Possible cause: Phase-advanced temperature rhythm
    Withdrawal from tranquilizers

  Sleep apnea (stop breathing for 9 seconds to a minute)

    Low oxygen → loss of neurons in cerebral cortex and hippocampus
    Causes: Obesity, alcohol, tranquilizers

  Narcolepsy

    Attacks of daytime sleepiness
    Cataplexy: Muscle weakness while awake
    Sleep paralysis
    Hypnagogic hallucinations
    May be due to intrusion of REM into wakefulness
    Orexin

      Peptide neurotransmitter → maintain wakefulness
      Cells in lateral hypothalamus
    Treated with stimulants

      Pemoline (Cylert) or methylphenidate (Ritalin)

  Periodic limb movement disorder (mostly during NREM sleep)

  REM behavior disorder

    Acting out dreams

Damage in pons

Motor neurons no longer inhibited

Night terrors, sleep talking, and sleepwalking

Night terrors different from nightmares (bad dreams)

Occur in NREM sleep

Sleep talking

Occurs in REM or NREM sleep

Sleepwalking

Most common in children

Mostly in Stages 3 and 4 (not during REM)

6. In closing: Stages of sleep

Usefulness of EEG recordings in identifying internal experiences

Module 9.3 Why sleep? Why REM? Why dreams?

1. Functions of sleep

Sleep and energy conservation

Decreased temperature and muscle activity → save energy

Similar to hibernation

Hibernation → retard aging

Decrease vulnerability to infection and trauma

Time required for food search

Safety from predators

Migratory birds

Decreased need for sleep during migration

Primates: Stimulation of glutamate receptors → decrease sleep need

Swifts

First flight ~ two years

Both days and nights in the air

Restorative functions of sleep

Effects of sleep deprivation

Human (voluntary) experiments

One night deprivation→ dizziness, impaired concentration, irritability, hand tremors, hallucinations, increased immune function

Winter living in Antarctica (long term) → poor sleep, depression, decreased immune response

Animal (nonvoluntary) experiments

Few days deprivation → increased temperature, metabolism, and appetite

Longer deprivation → decreased immune function, decreased brain activity

Sleep and memory

Sleep → enhanced memory

During sleep: Increased activity in same brain areas activated while learning a skill

Correlation between amount of activity during sleep and amount of improvement

Similar result for birds learning to sing

2. Functions of REM sleep

Individual and species differences

Percent of time in REM correlated with length of sleep

The effects of REM sleep deprivation

Humans

Increased attempts to REM

REM rebound (increased REM in uninterrupted nights)

Hypotheses

Memory storage

Deprivation of sleep early in night (mostly SWS) → impaired verbal learning

Deprivation of sleep late in night (much REM) → impaired consolidation of motor skills

MAO inhibitors (antidepressants) → decrease REM, but don't impair memory

Increase oxygen to eyeballs

3. Biological perspectives on dreaming

The activation-synthesis hypothesis

Cortex synthesizes story from stimuli processed in activated areas of cortex

Primary visual and primary somatosensory cortex inactivated

No sensory input to interfere

Pons → amygdala → emotional content

Prefrontal cortex inactivated → can't remember dreams

Role of the pons

Partial damage to pons: Can still dream, but no REM

Maybe surviving areas → dreams

Extensive damage to pons: Paralyzed, unconscious, or dead

Vague and hard to test

A clinico-anatomical hypothesis

Arousing stimuli processed in unusual ways
Suppression of activity in primary visual, motor, and prefrontal cortex and spinal cord

No normal visual stimuli or motor responses
Inhibited working memory and "use of knowledge"
Increased activity in inferior parietal cortex

Damage there → poor visual-spatial perception and no dreams
Increased activity in "higher" visual areas → visual imagery
Increased activity in hypothalamus, amygdala, and other areas that process emotions
Also vague and hard to test

4. In closing: Our limited self-understanding

No need for conscious understanding of evolutionary reasons for behavior

Short-Answer Questions

Module 9.1 Rhythms of Waking and Sleeping

1. *Endogenous cycles*

a. What do we know about the factors that do, or do not, initiate migration in birds?

b. What are endogenous circannual rhythms? endogenous circadian rhythms? How consistent are circadian rhythms within individuals in a given environment? between individuals?

c. How can circadian rhythms be demonstrated experimentally? What are some bodily and behavioral changes that occur in circadian rhythms?

d. How easily can humans adapt to a new cycle length? What are the limits of adaptation?

2. *Mechanisms of the biological clock*

a. What sorts of attempted interference with the biological clock were not effective?

b. What brain structure is the source of the circadian rhythms? What is its relationship to the visual system?

c. What is the evidence that the suprachiasmatic nucleus (SCN) generates rhythms itself?

d. What happened when SCN tissue from hamsters with a mutant gene for a 20-hour rhythm were transplanted into normal hamsters?

e. What two genes, discovered in Drosophila (fruitflies), govern circadian rhythms? How do they work? How common is this mechanism in other animals?

f. What is melatonin? From which gland is it secreted? When does increased secretion of melatonin occur?

3. *Setting and resetting the biological clock*

a. What is a zeitgeber? What is the most effective zeitgeber for land animals? for many marine animals?

b. Is it easier to cross time zones going east or west? Why?

c. What is the best way to reset the biological clock when working a night shift?

d. By what path does the retina influence the SCN? What is unusual about the ganglion cells whose axons make up this path? How rapidly do they respond to light? How are blind mice and mole rats able to use light to reset their SCN?

Module 9.2 Stages of Sleep and Brain Mechanisms

1. *The stages of sleep*

a. What is an electroencephalogram?

b. What accounts for rapid, low-voltage EEG activity? slow, high-voltage activity?

c. Describe the usual behavioral correlate of alpha waves. What is their frequency?

d. Describe the EEG in stage 1 sleep.

e. What are the EEG characteristics of stage 2 sleep?

f. Which stages of sleep are classed as slow-wave sleep (SWS)?

2. *Paradoxical or REM sleep*

a. Why is REM sleep sometimes called paradoxical sleep? What are its characteristics?

b. What is a polysomnograph?

c. What is the typical duration of the sleep cycle? During which part of the night is REM predominant? During which part are stages 3 and 4 SWS predominant?

d. How good is the correlation between REM and dreaming?

3. *Brain mechanisms of wakefulness and arousal*

a. What is the effect of a cut through the midbrain on sleep and waking cycles? Was this result due simply to loss of sensory input or to damage to a particular brain structure?

b. Describe the input and output of the pontomesencephalon. What is its relation to the reticular formation?

c. Name four kinds of attention.

d. Give the location, neurotransmitter, and a major function of the locus coeruleus.

e. What is the major neurotransmitter released by neurons in the basal forebrain that contributes to sleep? To arousal?

f. What is the neurotransmitter of separate paths from the hypothalamus that stimulate arousal? What is the implication of this for allergy treatments?

g. What is the location of neurons that produce orexin? What is the main function of orexin?

h. What is a good indicator of how fast a person will get to sleep? Explain this finding.

i. How does adenosine contribute to sleepiness? How does caffeine increase arousal?

j. What are prostaglandins? How do they promote sleep?

4. *Brain function in REM sleep*

a. What are PGO waves? Where are they recorded? What happens to PGO waves after a period of REM deprivation?

b. What brain area inhibits motor activity during REM sleep?

c. Which neurotransmitter is important for REM onset? Which two neurotransmitters interrupt or shorten REM? What is one effect of the drug carbachol?

5. *Sleep disorders*

a. How may shifts in circadian rhythm cause insomnia? Describe the different effects of phase advanced vs. phase delayed rhythms.

b. How may sleeping pills contribute to insomnia?

c. Describe the symptoms of sleep apnea. What are three factors that may contribute to sleep apnea?

d. What four symptoms are commonly associated with narcolepsy?

e. Define cataplexy. What tends to trigger it?

f. Define hypnagogic hallucinations.

g. The lack of what transmitter has been associated with narcolepsy?

h. Describe the symptoms of periodic limb movement disorder.

i. What are the symptoms and a possible cause of REM behavior disorder?

j. How do night terrors differ from nightmares? During which type of sleep are night terrors most common?

k. During which stages does sleep talking occur? sleepwalking?

Module 9.3 Why sleep? Why REM? Why Dreams?

1. *Functions of sleep*

a. What was probably the original function of sleep?

b. In what ways does sleep conserve energy?

c. What are some advantages of hibernation?

d. How do dolphins manage their need for sleep and their prolonged time under water?

e. How is the need for sleep altered in migrating birds?

f. How can we study the restorative functions of sleep?

g. What are some effects of sleep deprivation in humans? in rats?

h. What did researchers discover when they recorded brain activity while people learned a motor skill and then again while the people slept?

2. *Functions of REM sleep*

a. What is the relationship between percentage of time in REM and total sleep time?

b. What is one way that people, rats, and cats respond to selective deprivation of REM sleep?

c. To what kind of learning may REM sleep contribute? To what kind of learning may NREM contribute?

d. Do the effects of MAO inhibitors (antidepressant drugs) on REM sleep and memory support or bring into question a role of REM sleep in memory formation?

e. How may REM contribute to oxygen supply for the cornea?

3. *Biological perspectives on dreaming*

a. What is the current view of Freud's assumptions concerning dreaming?

b. State the activation-synthesis hypothesis. What evidence supports this hypothesis?

c. Describe the controversy concerning the role of the pons in dreaming. What is another criticism of the theory?

d. Summarize the basic ideas of the clinico-anatomical hypothesis.

e. What three cortical areas are suppressed during dreams? What would be the effects of these suppressions?

f. What two cortical areas are active during dreams? What would they contribute to dreams?

g. Which subcortical areas are active during dreams? What do these areas contribute?

True/False Questions

1. Day length is the most powerful stimulus for bird migration; if birds are kept in a constant environment, they would eventually migrate, but only after a delay of months.

   TRUE or FALSE

2. Humans can adapt to 23- or 25-hour days, but not to 22- or 28-hour days.

   TRUE or FALSE

3. The suprachiasmatic nucleus can generate circadian rhythms, even if it is disconnected from the rest of the brain.

   TRUE or FALSE

4. The genes *per* and *tim* produce proteins, high levels of which interact with the Clock protein to induce wakefulness.

   TRUE or FALSE

5. Melatonin is a hormone produced by the pituitary gland that induces sleepiness within minutes after being introduced into the body.

   TRUE or FALSE

6. A zeitgeber resets the circadian rhythm, but is not the actual generator of the rhythm.

   TRUE or FALSE

7. Jet lag is worst traveling east.

   TRUE or FALSE

8. The SCN receives branches of the same axons that project to the lateral geniculate nucleus of the thalamus and carry normal visual information.

   TRUE or FALSE

9. Sleep spindles and K-complexes are characteristic of REM sleep.

   TRUE or FALSE

10. Sleep stages 3 and 4 predominate early in the night, and REM periods take up more time late in the night.

    TRUE or FALSE

11. GABA-containing neurons of the basal forebrain produce arousal.

    TRUE or FALSE

12. Acetylcholine triggers the onset of REM sleep, and serotonin and norepinephrine inhibit REM sleep.

    TRUE or FALSE

13. Falling asleep easily but awakening early may be caused by a phase-delayed temperature rhythm.

    TRUE or FALSE

14. Narcolepsy may result from a lack of orexin neurons in the hypothalamus.

    TRUE or FALSE

15. REM deprivation may impair primarily verbal learning.

    TRUE or FALSE

16. Activity in primary visual cortex (V1) is increased in REM sleep, thereby giving rise to the visual content of dreams.

    TRUE or FALSE

Fill In The Blanks

1. The site of the biological clock is the _____ .

2. The drosophila genes _____ _____ and _____ _____ produce proteins that interact with the _____ protein to induce sleepiness.

3. Melatonin is produced by the _____ gland and peaks _____ before the onset of sleepiness.

4. A stimulus that resets the circadian rhythm is called a _____ .

5. The tract that carries input concerning light to the biological clock is the _____ path, which arises from _____ cells with their own photopigment.

6. The EEG waves characteristic of relaxed wakefulness are _____ waves.

7. Sleep cycles last approximately _____ minutes.

8. The _____ is a part of the reticular formation that sends axons to the thalamus and basal forebrain that release _____ and _____ to produce arousal.

9. Two chemicals that build up during waking and induce sleepiness are _____ and _____ .

10. REM sleep is associated with high-amplitude electrical potentials called _____ .

11. The transmitter that stimulates REM onset is _____ ; two that inhibit REM are _____ and _____ .

12. _____ is a peptide neurotransmitter that stimulates acetylcholine neurons that, in turn, produce wakefulness.

13. The theory that dreams are caused by the brain's attempt to make sense out of neural activity is the _____ theory.

14. The clinico-anatomical hypothesis observes that suppressed activity in primary _____ , _____ and _____ cortex leaves the brain without normal sensory input and motor output and without normal working memory and "use of knowledge."

Matching Items

1. _____ Suprachiasmatic nucleus
2. _____ Pineal gland
3. _____ Zeitgeber
4. _____ Retinohypothalamic path source
5. _____ Alpha waves
6. _____ Sleep spindle
7. _____ Pontomesencephalon
8. _____ Locus coeruleus
9. _____ Basal forebrain GABA neurons
10. _____ PGO waves
11. _____ Acetylcholine
12. _____ Serotonin
13. _____ Adenosine
14. _____ Trouble falling asleep
15. _____ Awakening too early
16. _____ Orexin

a. EEG sign of REM sleep
b. A transmitter that inhibits REM
c. EEG sign of stage 2 sleep
d. A transmitter that → waking & REM
e. Site of norepinephrine neurons→memory, wakefulness
f. EEG sign of relaxed wakefulness
g. Ganglion cells with own photopigment
h. Site of biological clock
i. Phase-delayed temperature rhythm
j. Transmitter that maintains wakefulness
k. Phase-advanced temperature rhythm
l. Part of reticular formation that → arousal
m. Structure that releases melatonin
n. Stimulus that resets circadian rhythm
o. Neurons that induce sleep
p. Chemical that builds up to → sleepiness

Multiple-Choice Questions

1. Curt Richter suggested the revolutionary idea that
   a. nearly all behavior is a reaction to a stimulus.
   b. the body generates its own cycles of activity and inactivity.
   c. temperature fluctuations are the best zeitgeber.
   d. animals wait till the first frost before preparing for winter so that they can enjoy summer longer.

2. Migratory birds
   a. respond only to temperature signals to begin migration.
   b. respond only to the ratio of light to dark, especially in spring.
   c. respond only to the availability of food.
   d. become more active in the spring, even in the absence of external cues, and fly north if released from captivity.

3. Circadian rhythms
   a. cannot be demonstrated if lights are always on or always off.
   b. always average within a minute or two of 24 hours in length, regardless of the light cycle.
   c. include cycles of waking and sleeping, eating and drinking, temperature, hormone secretion, and urine production.
   d. are very flexible and can be changed as soon as a different light cycle is established.

4. Which of the following can totally disrupt the biological clock?
    a. food or water deprivation
    b. anesthesia
    c. lack of oxygen
    d. none of the above

5. The suprachiasmatic nucleus (SCN)
    a. is located in the brain stem.
    b. no longer generates a rhythm if it is disconnected from input from the optic nerve.
    c. if transplanted from fetal hamsters that have a mutant gene producing a 20-hour cycle, into normal hamsters, will produce 20-hour cycles in the recipients.
    d. is concerned only with the resetting of the clock, not with generating the rhythm.

6. Two genes in Drosophila known as *period (per)* and *timeless (tim)*
    a. produce proteins that are present in only small amounts early in the day, but increase throughout the day.
    b. produce proteins that make the fly sleepy, when present in high levels.
    c. are similar to genes found in mice.
    d. all of the above.

7. Melatonin
    a. is secreted by the pituitary gland just before awakening.
    b. is secreted by the pituitary gland 2 – 3 hours before the time of sleep onset.
    c. is secreted by the pineal gland 2 - 3 hours before the time of sleep onset.
    d. is secreted by the pineal gland at the time of sleep onset.

8. The human circadian rhythm
    a. can easily adjust to 22- or 28-hour days, but not to 20- or 30-hour days.
    b. has a mean of 24.2 hours, but can adjust to 23- or 25-hour days.
    c. can be most easily reset by using only dim lights in the evening.
    d. cannot be reset at all.

9. Which of the following is true?
    a. It is easier to adjust our biological rhythms to longer cycles and to travel across time zones going west.
    b. It is easier to adjust our biological rhythms to shorter cycles and to travel across time zones going east.
    c. People on irregular shifts tend to sleep the longest when they go to sleep in the morning or early afternoon.
    d. People on night shifts that were exposed to normal levels of room lighting found it easy to adjust their cycles.

10. Alpha waves are characteristic of
    a. REM sleep.
    b. alert mental activity.
    c. relaxed wakefulness.
    d. slow-wave sleep.

11. Stages 3 and 4 sleep
    a. are characterized by sleep spindles and K-complexes.
    b. together are known as slow-wave sleep.
    c. are characterized by irregular, jagged, low-voltage waves.
    d. are the stages during which REM occurs.

12. Which of the following is **not** a sign of REM sleep?
    a. tenseness in postural muscles
    b. extreme relaxation of postural muscles
    c. variable heart and breathing rates
    d. irregular, low-voltage, fast EEG activity

13. Paradoxical sleep is paradoxical because brain waves suggest
    a. slow-wave sleep, when one is really dreaming.
    b. dreaming, when one is really in slow-wave sleep.
    c. sleep, when one is really awake.
    d. activation, when one's postural muscles are most relaxed.

14. REM sleep occurs
    a. only early in a night's sleep.
    b. cyclically, about every 90 minutes.
    c. randomly throughout the night.
    d. only after a period of physical exercise.

15. Dreams
    a. are highly correlated with sleep talking.
    b. are of greater duration and frequency during the early part of the night.
    c. may occur in NREM, but are more likely to include vivid visual imagery during REM.
    d. all of the above.

16. A cut through the midbrain
    a. produced prolonged sleep because an area that promotes wakefulness was cut off from the rest of the brain.
    b. left the animal sleeping constantly because most sensory input was cut off from the brain.
    c. left the animal sleeping and waking normally, since structures that control these functions are anterior to the midbrain.
    d. left the animal more wakeful than usual because much of the reticular formation was still connected to the brain, but a sleep-promoting system had been damaged.

17. The pontomesencephalon, a part of the reticular formation,
    a. is very discretely organized, with few interconnections.
    b. is important in generating slow-wave sleep.
    c. is primarily concerned with sensory analysis.
    d. none of the above.

18. The locus coeruleus
    a. is very active during REM sleep.
    b. is very active during slow wave sleep.
    c. is very active during meaningful events, and may be important for storing information.
    d. got its name from its bright red color.

19. Sleep-inducing nuclei in the basal forebrain
    a. use GABA as their neurotransmitter.
    b. use acetylcholine as their neurotransmitter.
    c. have very restricted projections to specific cortical areas.
    d. are inhibited during a fever, resulting in prolonged wakefulness.

20. Neurons in the basal forebrain that promote arousal
    a. use acetylcholine as their transmitter.
    b. use norepinephrine as their transmitter.
    c. use prostaglandin as their transmitter.
    d. are focused only on waking up and are not related to learning, attention, or any other processes.

21. PGO waves
    a. occur during REM sleep.
    b. are recorded in the pons, lateral geniculate, and occipital cortex.
    c. are compensated, if "lost" due to REM deprivation.
    d. all of the above.

22. Neurons that are more active during REM sleep are located in
    a. primary visual, motor, and dorsolateral prefrontal cortex.
    b. parts of the parietal and temporal cortex.
    c. neurons in the basal forebrain that release GABA as their neurotransmitter.
    d. the locus coeruleus.

23. Which of the following is true?
    a. Histamine increases alertness and is released from neurons in the hypothalamus.
    b. Orexin is also released from neurons in the hypothalamus.
    c. Orexin is necessary, not for waking up, but for staying awake.
    d. all of the above

24. Adenosine
    a. is a major neurotransmitter producing arousal.
    b. builds up during wakefulness until it reaches a sufficient level to shut off arousal neurons in the basal forebrain and thereby produce sleepiness.
    c. is the component of coffee that keeps us awake.
    d. is produced by neurons in the cortex during REM sleep.

25. Prostaglandins
    a. build up during the day and promote sleep.
    b. build up during the night and promote awakening.
    c. are present only in neurons in the lateral hypothalamus.
    d. have effects opposite those of adenosine.

26. Inhibition of motor neurons during REM is induced by neurons in
    a. the dorsolateral prefrontal cortex.
    b. the reticular formation.
    c. the pons.
    d. the amygdala.

27. Which of the following is true?
    a. Acetylcholine promotes the onset of REM sleep.
    b. Acetylcholine promotes slow-wave sleep.
    c. Carbachol inhibits REM sleep.
    d. Serotonin promotes the onset of REM sleep.

28. People with phase-delayed temperature rhythms who try to fall asleep at the normal time may experience
    a. excess sleep.
    b. repeated awakenings throughout the night.
    c. awakening too early.
    d. difficulty falling asleep.

29. Which of the following is a cause of insomnia?
    a. narcolepsy
    b. cataplexy
    c. repeated use of tranquilizers
    d. hypnagogic hallucinations

30. Which of the following is more closely associated with REM sleep than NREM sleep?
    a. nightmares and other dreams
    b. night terrors
    c. sleep walking
    d. all of the above

31. When people are deprived of sleep for a week or more,
    a. they usually suffer severe consequences, including death.
    b. they report dizziness, irritability, and difficulty concentrating, but no drastic consequences.
    c. they actually fall asleep early in the deprivation period and only appear to be awake, because their sleepwalking and sleep talking appear to be very realistic.
    d. they report no symptoms whatever.

32. In our evolutionary history the original need for sleep was probably
    a. promotion of memory storage.
    b. energy conservation at times when animals are relatively inefficient.
    c. rebuilding proteins in the brain.
    d. replenishing energy supplies.

33. Comparisons of sleep patterns across individuals and across species indicate that
    a. percentage of time spent in REM remains the same, no matter how long the individual sleeps.
    b. percentage of time in REM decreases as total amount of sleep increases.
    c. percentage of time in REM increases as total amount of sleep increases.
    d. percentage of time spent in REM is extremely variable, and shows no relationship to the total amount of sleep.

34. After about a week of REM deprivation, subjects
    a. became insane.
    b. showed no effects at all, resuming their typical sleep patterns as soon as they were allowed to sleep freely.
    c. spent less sleep time on subsequent nights in REM sleep.
    d. spent more sleep time on subsequent nights in REM sleep.

35. The activation-synthesis hypothesis proposes that dreams result from
    a. unconscious wishes struggling for expression.
    b. the ego's attempt to gain control of the id.
    c. the brain's attempt to make sense of its activity.
    d. the brain's attempt to wake up.

36. The clinico-anatomical hypothesis is based on observations that during dreaming
    a. there is increased activity in the inferior parietal cortex, which contributes to visuo-spatial perception; in visual cortex outside V1, which provides visual imagery; and in the hypothalamus and amygdala, which contribute to emotional intensity.
    b. there is increased activity in prefrontal cortex, which contributes to the fantasy-like experience of dreams.
    c. there is increased activity in primary visual cortex, which contributes to visual dreams.
    d. there is also increased activity in primary auditory cortex, which provides rich auditory content.

Crossword Puzzle

Doing and Dreaming

www.CrosswordWeaver.com

ACROSS

2 Chemical that builds up during day and inhibits arousal systems; it is inhibited by caffeine

7 A peptide neurotransmitter that helps maintain wakefulness

10 The biological clock (abbr.)

12 _____ gyrus: primary motor cortex

13 Type of brain wave produced during rapid eye movement sleep (abbr.)

16 Transmitter at neuromuscular junction; also used in tracts that arouse brain

18 Precursor of dopamine

19 Fast, easily-fatigued muscle in fish

21 Protein, mutation of which causes Huntington's disease

22 EEG wave with 8-12 cycles per second rhythm

DOWN

1 Tendon organ located at both ends of a muscle, responds to muscle contraction

3 Muscle _____: Stretch receptor parallel to muscle; when stretched, it causes muscle to contract

4 Tract from motor cortex to spinal cord, controls peripheral movements on opposite side of body

5 Disorder in which person falls asleep during emotional excitement

6 Tract from numerous cortical areas to both sides of the spinal cord, controls midline movements

8 Hormone produced by pineal gland, promotes sleep

9 Part of hindbrain important for rapid movements that require accurate aim and timing and for aspects of attention

11 Type of muscle connected to bones

14 Stimulus that can reset the biological clock

15 Slow, fatigue-resistant muscle in fish

17 _____ gravis: disorder caused by autoimmune destruction of acetylcholine receptors

20 A chemical in the environment that may be converted to a toxin that kills dopamine neurons, results in Parkinson's disease

Crossword Puzzle Solution

Doing and Dreaming

Solution:

Solutions

True/False Questions

1.	F	7.	T	13.	F
2.	T	8.	F	14.	T
3.	T	9.	F	15.	F
4.	F	10.	T	16.	F
5.	F	11.	F		
6.	T	12.	T		

Fill In The Blanks

1. suprachiasmatic nucleus
2. period; (per); timeless; (tim); Clock
3. pineal; 2-3 hours
4. zeitgeber
5. retino-hypothalamic; ganglion
6. alpha
7. 90
8. pontomesencephalon; acetylcholine; glutamate
9. adenosine; prostaglandins
10. PGO waves
11. acetylcholine; serotonin; norephinephrine
12. Orexin
13. activation-synthesis
14. visual; motor; prefrontal

Matching Items

1.	H	7.	L	13.	P
2.	M	8.	E	14.	I
3.	N	9.	O	15.	K
4.	G	10.	A	16.	J
5.	F	11.	D		
6.	C	12.	B		

Multiple-Choice Questions

1.	B	4.	D	7.	C
2.	D	5.	C	8.	B
3.	C	6.	D	9.	A

10. C
11. B
12. A
13. D
14. B
15. C
16. A
17. D
18. C

19. A
20. A
21. D
22. B
23. D
24. B
25. A
26. C
27. A

28. D
29. C
30. A
31. B
32. B
33. C
34. D
35. C
36. A

INTERNAL REGULATION

Introduction

Homeostatic drives are drives that tend to maintain certain biological conditions within a fixed range. Temperature regulation in mammals and birds is such a drive. Constant relatively high temperatures provide conditions in which chemical reactions can be regulated precisely and, by increasing the metabolic rate, increase capacity for prolonged activity. Several physiological mechanisms, including shivering, sweating, panting, and redirection of blood flow, raise and lower temperature appropriately. These are coordinated primarily by the preoptic area/anterior hypothalamus (POA/AH), which monitors both its own temperature and that of the skin and spinal cord. Behavioral regulation of temperature is used both by animals that are poikilothermic (body temperature matches that of environment) and by those that are homeothermic (body temperature is regulated within a few degrees of a constant setting). Fever is produced when leukocytes (white blood cells) release cytokines, which activate the vagus nerve, which in turn causes the preoptic area to raise body temperature. Moderate fevers are helpful in combating bacterial infections.

Water balance is critical, both for regulating the concentration of chemicals in our bodily fluids (and therefore the rate of chemical reactions) and for maintaining normal blood pressure. If we have ample supplies of palatable fluids to drink, we may drink a great deal of them and let the kidneys discard the excess. If there is a shortage of fluids to drink, or a large loss of water, the posterior pituitary releases vasopressin (also known as antidiuretic hormone, or ADH), which increases both blood pressure and water retention by the kidneys. There are two major types of stimuli for thirst: decreased water content inside cells and decreased blood volume. When there are increased solutes in the blood, the blood and extracellular fluid become more concentrated. Water tends to flow out of cells into the area of higher osmotic pressure (extracellular fluid). The resulting loss of water from cells surrounding the third ventricle, especially in the organum vasculosum laminae terminalis (OVLT) and subfornical organ (SFO), elicits neural responses that are relayed to several hypothalamic nuclei, including the supraoptic and paraventricular nuclei. Input from the stomach also informs the OVLT and SFO about high levels of sodium. The supraoptic and paraventricular nuclei, in turn, produce vasopressin (antidiuretic hormone, ADH), the hormone that is released from the posterior pituitary and that increases blood pressure and urine concentration. Receptors in the OVLT, SFO, and stomach also relay information to the lateral preoptic area and surrounding areas, which give rise to osmotic thirst. Thus, an increase in osmotic signals results in greater water retention, increased water intake, and higher blood pressure. If large amounts of whole blood are lost, the resulting hypovolemia (low volume of blood) is detected by receptors in the large veins. The kidney also detects the hypovolemia and releases renin, which acts in the blood to produce angiotensin II. This hormone causes constriction of blood vessels to maintain blood pressure. It also stimulates neurons in areas around the third ventricle that use angiotensin II as their transmitter to induce thirst. Thus, the cells around the third ventricle both respond to angiotensin II and release it.

Hypovolemic thirst is satisfied best by salt water. A hunger for sodium depends largely on two hormones, aldosterone and angiotensin II. Aldosterone, secreted by the adrenal glands, causes the kidneys, salivary glands, and sweat glands to conserve sodium; it also stimulates an increase in salt intake. Angiotensin II, as noted above, stimulates sodium hunger. The effects of aldosterone and angiotensin II are mediated by the nucleus of the tractus solitarius, which begins to respond to salt in nearly the same way as to sugar.

The factors regulating hunger, satiety, and the selection of specific foods are very complex. Food selection is influenced by the digestive system (including intestinal enzymes), cultural factors, taste, familiarity, and memories of the consequences of consuming a particular food. Hunger and satiety depend on stimuli from the mouth, stomach, and duodenum. Oral factors, stomach or duodenum distension, and nutrient contents of the stomach contribute to satiety. Cholecystokinin (CCK), released by the duodenum, inhibits stomach emptying. CCK also stimulates the vagus nerve, which activates neurons that release a short version of CCK in the brain. Thus, as with angiotensin II's roles in thirst, the brain and periphery use the same (or similar) chemicals to accomplish related tasks. Blood glucose levels are maintained in a relatively narrow range by varying amounts of insulin, which enables glucose to enter cells, and glucagon, which converts stored glycogen into glucose. Leptin is a peptide that is produced by fat cells; it serves as an indicator of the body's fat stores and is also increased after a meal. Therefore, it provides information about both long-term and short-term nutrient availability. It decreases eating, increases general activity and immune function, and can trigger the onset of puberty. However, leptin is not an effective treatment of obese people; apparently they produce leptin, but are insensitive to its effects.

Brain mechanisms use a complex array of signals to regulate food intake. Hunger-sensitive neurons in the arcuate nucleus of the hypothalamus receive input from the taste system and from axons that release ghrelin, a neurotransmitter that binds to the same receptors as growth-hormone releasing hormone (GHRH, from which it gets its name). Ghrelin is also released in the stomach, where it causes contractions. Again, the same molecule accomplishes related functions in the brain and periphery. The arcuate nucleus also has satiety-sensitive neurons that receive inputs concerning intestine distention (using CCK as transmitter), blood glucose (using an insulin-like transmitter), and body fat (using leptin). Axons from satiety-sensitive neurons in the arcuate nucleus stimulate the paraventricular nucleus of the hypothalamus (PVN), using α-melanocyte stimulating hormone (αMSH). The PVN is important for ending a meal. In contrast, hunger-sensitive neurons in the arcuate nucleus send inhibitory input to the PVN, as well as to satiety-sensitive neurons in the arcuate itself, using GABA, neuropeptide Y (NPY), and agouti-related peptide (AgRP) as transmitters. Therefore, different groups of arcuate neurons can end a meal by stimulating the PVN with αMSH or elicit hunger by inhibiting the PVN with GABA, NPY, and AgRP. An additional pathway from the arcuate nucleus activates orexin-containing cells in the lateral hypothalamus that increase activity and, in some circumstances, eating.

Output from the PVN goes to the lateral hypothalamus, which controls insulin secretion, alters taste responsiveness, and facilitates feeding in other ways. Damage to the lateral hypothalamus results in self-starvation, unless the animal is force-fed, in which case it will partially recover. The effects of lesions on feeding are due to cell bodies in the lateral hypothalamus, rather than to axons passing through, which are themselves important for arousal and activity. The intact lateral hypothalamus contributes to feeding by modifying activity in the nucleus of the tractus solitarius (NTS), which influences taste sensations and salivation, and also by increasing insulin release, facilitating ingestion, and increasing autonomic responses, such as the release of digestive juices. On the other hand, damage to the ventromedial hypothalamus (VMH) and surrounding areas results in obesity. This results from increased stomach motility and secretions, faster emptying of the stomach, and increased release of insulin, which promotes fat storage and inhibits its release for use as fuel. As a result, the animal consumes more frequent normal-sized meals. The problem is not so much that the rat gets fat because it overeats, but that it overeats because it is storing so much fat. The multiple messengers and pathways that control food intake and digestion provide an effective system of checks and balances.

Genes control body weight in many ways, including activity levels. Other genetic influences include the sensitivity to, or production of, peptides, such as melanocortin and ghrelin, that regulate eating. However, social and other environmental influences, as well as exercise and eating habits, are important determinants of body weight. Some appetite-suppressant drugs increase levels of norepinephrine, serotonin, and dopamine or block absorption of fats in the intestines.

Anorexia nervosa is a disorder in which people eat much less than they need, sometimes starving themselves to death. They are usually perfectionistic, most frequently women. They are interested in food, but are afraid of losing control and gaining weight. People with bulimia nervosa alternate between overeating and dieting, frequently eating a huge meal and then purging. People with bulimia have decreased release of CCK, increased release of ghrelin, and other changes in hormones and transmitters that affect eating. However, it is not clear whether transmitter abnormalities precede or result from the bulimia. Bulimia may have some similarities to drug addiction. Rats that consumed excessive glucose after a period of deprivation had increased release of dopamine and opiate-like chemicals and increased the levels of dopamine type 3 receptors in their brain. Furthermore, withdrawal from the glucose resulted in some of the symptoms of drug withdrawal.

Learning Objectives

Module 10.1 Temperature Regulation

1. Understand the advantages of constant high body temperatures and the brain mechanisms that maintain temperatures.

2. Know the advantage of moderate fevers and the physiological mechanisms that produce fever.

Module 10.2 Thirst

1. Understand the concepts of osmotic and hypovolemic thirst and stimuli that give rise to each.

2. Know the brain mechanisms that promote osmotic and hypovolemic thirst and salt appetite.

Module 10.3 Hunger

1. Know the functions of the various components of the digestive system and their roles in hunger and satiety.

2. Understand the functions, neurotransmitters, and outputs of the hunger- and satiety-sensitive neurons in the arcuate nucleus of the hypothalamus.

3. Know the functions of the paraventricular nucleus of the hypothalamus, the lateral hypothalamus, and the ventromedial nucleus of the hypothalamus and their major sources of input.

4. Know the various peripheral and central chemicals that contribute to satiety.

5. Know the evidence for genetic, environmental, and neurochemical contributions to obesity.

6. Be able to describe the characteristics of anorexia nervosa and bulimia nervosa and the physiological correlates of bulimia nervosa.

Key Terms and Concepts

Module 10.1 Temperature Regulation

1. Homeostasis and allostasis

   Walter R. Cannon

   Set range

   Set point

   Negative feedback

   Role of behavior

   Differences from simple homeostasis

   Allostasis: Set points vary with conditions

2. Controlling body temperature

Poikilothermic: Body temperature same as environment

Homeothermic: Body temperature almost constant

Mechanisms for cooling

> Sweating
> Panting
> Licking

Mechanisms for heating

> Shivering
> Increased metabolic rate in brown fat
> Decreased blood flow to skin
> Fluffed out fur

Behavioral mechanisms

Surviving in extreme cold

> Problem: Formation of ice crystals → tear blood vessels and cell membranes
> Some insects and fish: Glycerol and other antifreeze chemicals in blood
> Wood frogs: Do freeze
>
> > Withdraw most fluid from organs and blood vessels, store it in extracellular space
> > Chemicals that regulate ice crystal formation
> > Increased blood-clotting

The advantages of constant high body temperature

> Warmer muscles work better
> Hotter than 37°C→greater energy need
> Hotter than 41°C→protein bonds break
> Reproductive cells: Cooler environment

Brain mechanisms

> Hypothalamus
> Preoptic area/anterior hypothalamus (POA/AH)
>
> > Monitors own temperature
> > Monitors temperature of skin and spinal cord

Fever

> Leukocytes → cytokines → vagus nerve → hypothalamus → fever
>
> > Cytokines also attack intruders, some cross blood-brain barrier
> > Moderate fevers helpful
>
> > Physiological and behavioral means
> > High fevers harmful

3. In closing: Combining physiological and behavioral mechanisms

    Redundancy of mechanisms

Module 10.2 Thirst

1. Mechanisms of water regulation

    Increasing intake

    Decreasing output

    Vasopressin or antidiuretic hormone (ADH)

2. Osmotic thirst

    Osmotic pressure

        Semipermeable membrane

        Increase in solute concentration outside cell

            Water leaves cells → osmotic thirst + more concentrated urine

    Brain areas around third ventricle

        Leaky blood-brain barrier: Detect osmotic pressure

            Organum vasculosum laminae terminalis (OVLT)

            Subfornical organ (SFO)

        Input from stomach: High levels of sodium

        Output → supraoptic and paraventricular nuclei → vasopressin release from posterior pituitary

        Output → lateral preoptic area → drinking

        Input from mouth, stomach, intestines → inhibit thirst temporarily

3. Hypovolemic thirst and sodium-specific hunger

    Loss of blood volume

    Vasopressin → constrict blood vessels

    Hormones from kidneys

        Renin: Angiotensinogen in blood → Angiotensin II → constricts blood vessels

        Angiotensin II → areas around third ventricle → Angiotensin II as their transmitter → thirst

        Angiotensin II also → sodium hunger

            Automatic, unlearned (unlike other specific hungers)

        Adrenal glands → aldosterone → salt retention and sodium hunger

        Angiotensin II + aldosterone → nucleus of the tractus solitarius (taste system) → prefer salt

4. In closing: The psychology and biology of thirst

Both behavioral and autonomic controls

Module 10.3 Hunger

1. How the digestive system influences food selection

   Mouth: Enzymes in saliva → carbohydrate digestion

   Stomach: Hydrochloric acid, enzymes → protein digestion

   Small intestine: Enzymes → protein, fat, and carbohydrate digestion

   Absorption of nutrients

   Large intestine

   Water and mineral absorption
   Lubrication

   Enzymes and consumption of dairy products

   Lactose, milk sugar
   Lactase enzyme

   Lack of lactase → inability to digest milk → stomach cramps, gas

   Other influences on food selection

   Carnivore, herbivore, omnivore
   Culture, taste, familiarity, learning

   Select sweet, avoid bitter, eat salty and sour in moderation
   Familiar = safe
   Conditioned taste aversions

2. Short- and long-term regulation of feeding

   Oral factors

   Desire to taste or chew

   Pump liquid diet into stomach → unsatisfying
   Sham feeding: Eat, swallow, eat more
   Mouth sensations contribute to satiety, but not sufficient

   The stomach and intestines

   Vagus nerve (cranial nerve X)

   Information about stretching of stomach: Sufficient but not necessary for satiety
   Splanchnic nerves

   Information about nutrient contents
   The duodenum

   Also sufficient but not necessary for satiety

The hormone CCK (cholecystokinin)

CCK directly inhibits stomach emptying

CCK also → vagus nerve → short version of CCK released as neurotransmitter in brain

Glucose, insulin, and glucagon

Glucose: Main fuel for brain, one of several for rest of body

Excess glucose

Liver: Glucose → glycogen
Fat cells: Glycogen → fat

Low glucose

Liver: Glycogen → glucose

Insulin: Facilitates glucose entry into cells

Rises when getting ready to eat
Decreases appetite
Hibernating species: High insulin → store fat and glycogen
Diabetes: High blood glucose; little enters cells, most is excreted

Glucagon → liver converts stored glycogen to glucose

Insulin drops → glucose enters cells slowly → hunger increases

Leptin

Produced by fat cells → signal to eat less, be more active, increase immune function
Triggers puberty onset
Obese people: High leptin levels, insensitive to it

3. Brain mechanisms

The arcuate nucleus and paraventricular hypothalamus

Arcuate nucleus

Hunger-sensitive neurons

Input from taste system
Input from axons releasing ghrelin
Stomach releases ghrelin → stomach contractions
Same signal in periphery and brain

Satiety-sensitive neurons

Intestine distention → CCK (short term signal)
Blood glucose (short term signal) → insulin secretion
Neurons release peptide similar to insulin
Body fat (long term signal) → leptin

Output to paraventricular nucleus (PVN) of the hypothalamus

Paraventricular nucleus of the hypothalamus

Inhibits lateral hypothalamus

Damage to PVN → larger meals

Interconnections

Arcuate satiety-sensitive cells excite PVN

α-melanocyte stimulating hormone (αMSH, a melanocortin) → end of meal

Arcuate hunger-sensitive cells inhibit paraventricular hypothalamus

Also inhibit satiety sensitive cells in arcuate itself

Transmitters: GABA, neuropeptide Y (NPY), agouti-related peptide (AgRP)

Additional pathway to cells in lateral hypothalamus that release orexin

The lateral hypothalamus

Controls insulin secretion, alters taste responsiveness, facilitates feeding in other ways

Lesions: Starvation or weight loss

Neurons vs. dopamine axons passing through

Damage to cell bodies or lesions in very young rats → loss of feeding

Mechanisms

Axons to NTS (nucleus of the tractus solitarius in medulla) → taste, salivation

Increase insulin secretion

Axons to cerebral cortex → facilitate ingestion

Increase insulin secretion

Stimulation of autonomic responses, including digestive secretions

Medial areas of the hypothalamus

Ventromedial hypothalamus

Lesions → weight gain to a new high set point

Ventromedial hypothalamic syndrome: Includes damage to nearby cells and axons

Ventral noradrenergic bundle

Increased appetite

Finickiness, after weight gain

More normal-sized meals per day

Increased stomach motility and secretions

Faster stomach emptying

Increased insulin and fat storage

Problem not that rat gets fat from overeating; rat overeats because it's storing so much fat

4. Eating disorders

Social and cultural factors

Genetics and human body weight

High heritability of obesity

Melanocortin receptor

Mutation → obesity
Prader-Willi syndrome

Mental retardation, short stature, obesity
Blood ghrelin levels 4 to 5 times higher than average
Multiple gene influences
Environment

Native American Pimas: Typical American diet → obesity
Inactive life style, fast-food restaurants, large helpings
High-fructose sweeteners

Less insulin or leptin release than with glucose or sucrose → less satiety
Stored as fat, not used for immediate needs

Weight loss techniques

Increase exercise
Restraint of eating

Fat-carbohydrate combinations: High calorie, taste good
Appetite suppressant drugs

"Fen-phen"

Fenfluramine →increase serotonin release and decrease reuptake

Phentermine → block norepinephrine and dopamine reuptake

Medical complications

Sibutramine (Meridia):

Blocks reuptake of serotonin and norepinephrine

Orlistat (Xenical): Blocks fat absorption
Anorexia nervosa

Interested in food, fear becoming fat

Hardworking perfectionists (obsessive-compulsive)
Exercise + dieting → restrained eating

Similar to migrating elk
Bulimia nervosa

Eat enormous meal, then purge
High levels of ghrelin
Low levels of CCK
Similar to drug addiction

> Food-deprive rats for first 4 hours of day, then offer glucose → great increase in eating
> Increased dopamine and opiate-like compounds in brain (similar to abused drugs)
> Increased dopamine type 3 receptors
> Deprived of glucose → withdrawal symptoms

5. In closing: The multiple controls of hunger

   Checks and balances

Short-Answer Questions

Module 10.1 Temperature Regulation

1. *Homeostasis and allostasis*

   a. What is a homeostatic process?

   b. What are some of the physiological processes that are controlled near a set point? What are some homeostatic processes that anticipate future needs or that change under various conditions?

   c. Why does the scrotum of most male mammals hang outside the body? Why should pregnant women avoid hot baths?

2. *Controlling body temperature*

   a. Define the terms poikilothermic and homeothermic.

   b. What prevents the temperature of most fish, amphibians, and reptiles from fluctuating wildly?

   c. How do some frogs, fish, and insects adapt to extreme cold?

   d. What is an advantage of a constant relatively high body temperature? What is the cost to the animal for maintaining homeothermy?

   e. What two kinds of stimuli does the preoptic area monitor for temperature control?

   f. What are leukocytes and cytokines? What are their roles in producing a fever?

   g. Of what benefit is a moderate fever?

Module 10.2 Thirst

1. *Mechanisms of water regulation*

   a. Describe the different mechanisms of maintaining water balance that have been developed by desert animals and by animals with an abundant water supply.

   b. What are the two functions of vasopressin when body fluids are low? What is its other name?

INTERNAL REGULATION

2. *Osmotic thirst*

   a. What is osmotic pressure?

   b. How does the body "know" when its osmotic pressure is low?

   c. What are the roles of the OVLT, the subfornical organ (SFO), the supraoptic and paraventricular nuclei, and the lateral preoptic area in osmotic thirst?

3. *Hypovolemic thirst*

   a. Why is hypovolemia dangerous?

   b. Under what circumstances does hypovolemic thirst occur?

   c. Describe the steps leading to the production of antiotensin II. What are its two main effects?

   d. Will an animal with hypovolemic thirst drink more pure water or more salt water with the same concentration as blood? Why?

   e. What two effects of aldosterone are beneficial in cases of sodium deficiency? What other hormone contributes to salt hunger? On what brain area do these two hormones act to increase salt hunger?

Module 10.3 Hunger

1. *How the digestive system influences food selection*

   a. Enzymes for the digestion of what type of nutrient(s) are present in saliva? In the stomach? In the small intestine?

   b. From which structure is digested food absorbed?

   c. Why do newborn mammals stop nursing as they grow older?

   d. Discuss the evidence that humans are a partial exception to the principle of lactose intolerance in adults.

   e. List the factors that may influence food selection.

2. *Short- and long-term regulation of feeding*

   a. Summarize the evidence for the importance of oral factors in hunger and satiety. What is the evidence that these factors are not sufficient to end a meal normally?

   b. How did Deutsch et al. demonstrate the importance of stomach distension in regulating meal size?

   c. Which two nerves convey the stomach's satiety signals?

   d. What is CCK? In what two places is it produced? What are two mechanisms by which it induces satiety?

   e. What is the effect of insulin on blood glucose? In what ways does insulin affect hunger? Compare the effects of glucagon with those of insulin.

   f. Why do people with untreated diabetes eat a lot but gain little weight? How is this similar to, and how is it different from, the effects of high levels of insulin?

g. Where is leptin produced? What are three effects of leptin? Why may it be important for puberty onset? Why can't we treat most obese people with leptin?

3. *Brain mechanisms*

   a. What are the effects on hunger of two kinds of neurons in the arcuate nucleus? What kinds of input does each type receive?

   b. Which neurotransmitters relay the output of the two kinds of arcuate neurons to the paraventricular nucleus (PVN)?

   c. What is the main role of the PVN in the control of feeding? What is the effect of damage to the PVN?

   d. Describe the evidence that the lateral hypothalamus is important for hunger.

   e. What are four mechanisms by which the lateral hypothalamus contributes to feeding?

   f. What is the result of damage to lateral hypothalamic cell bodies? How did researchers separate the roles of cell bodies from those of dopamine-containing axons passing through.

   g. Describe the various behavioral changes produced by lesions of the ventromedial nucleus of the hypothalamus (VMH), ventral noradrenergic bundle, and surrounding areas.

   h. To what factors can we attribute the obesity induced by VMH lesions?

   i. How are the effects of damage to the paraventricular nucleus (PVN) different from those of VMH damage?

4. *Eating disorders*

   a. Give one example of a group of people who demonstrate the relationship of genetic and environmental factors in the control of weight. How important are exercise and restraint of eating?

   b. Compare the symptoms of anorexia nervosa with those of bulimia nervosa.

   c. Describe the personality characteristics of many people with anorexia.

   d. What chemical differences are seen in bulimics, compared to other people? Can we determine whether these differences imply cause and effect relationships between the chemical and the disorder?

   e. What evidence suggests that excessive eating in bulimia has some parallels with drug addiction?

True/False Questions

1. Behavior can act as a negative feedback mechanism to correct homeostatic imbalances.

   TRUE or FALSE

2. Poikilothermic animals are those that maintain almost constant temperature.

   TRUE or FALSE

3. The POA/AH monitors its own temperature and that of the skin and spinal cord.

   TRUE or FALSE

4. During illness, leukocytes produce cytokines, which in turn stimulate the preoptic area to induce a fever.

   TRUE or FALSE

5. Cells in the supraoptic and paraventricular nuclei send input to the OVLT and subfornical organ concerning hypovolemic signals; the OVLT then releases vasopressin from the anterior pituitary.

   TRUE or FALSE

6. Hypovolemic thirst and osmotic thirst are both relieved best by drinking pure water.

   TRUE or FALSE

7. Aldosterone from the adrenal glands increases salt retention and salt hunger.

   TRUE or FALSE

8. Renin from the kidneys splits off a portion of angiotensinogen, forming angiotensin I, which enzymes then convert to angiotensin II, which in turn constricts blood vessels and stimulates drinking.

   TRUE or FALSE

9. Oral factors are sufficient to induce satiety.

   TRUE or FALSE

10. The splanchnic nerve carries information about the nutrient content of the stomach.

    TRUE or FALSE

11. CCK is a powerful stimulus to initiate eating.

    TRUE or FALSE

12. Diabetics have high levels of glucose, but little is able to enter cells.

    TRUE or FALSE

13. Leptin is produced by fat cells; it is a signal to decrease eating, become more active, and increase immune function.

    TRUE or FALSE

14. Ghrelin is a satiety signal in the stomach and the brain.

    TRUE or FALSE

15. Hunger-sensitive cells in the arcuate nucleus send axons containing GABA, neuropeptide Y (NPY), and agouti-related peptide (AgRP) to stimulate the paraventricular nucleus (PVN) in order to begin a meal.

    TRUE or FALSE

16. Satiety-sensitive cells in the arcuate nucleus send axons containing α-melanocyte stimulating hormone (αMSH, a melanocortin) to stimulate the paraventricular nucleus (PVN) in order to end a meal.

    TRUE or FALSE

17. Orexin induces both satiety and sleepiness.

    TRUE or FALSE

18. Lesions of cell bodies in the lateral hypothalamus result in a specific loss of feeding.

    TRUE or FALSE

19. Lesions of the ventromedial hypothalamus result in a voracious appetite that included even foods that were bitter or untasty and produce continued weight gain until the animals died.

    TRUE or FALSE

20. Lesions of the ventromedial nucleus result in more, normal-sized meals; lesions of the paraventricular nucleus result in an unchanged number of larger meals.

    TRUE or FALSE

21. Some cases of obesity may be linked to a mutation in the melanocortin receptor.

    TRUE or FALSE

22. People with Prader-Willi syndrome are severely underweight because they have insufficient ghrelin release.

    TRUE or FALSE

23. People with anorexia nervosa have no interest in food, as a result of a single-gene defect.

    TRUE or FALSE

24. Bulimia nervosa is in some ways like drug addiction.

    TRUE or FALSE

Fill In The Blanks

1. Walter R. Cannon introduced the term _____ to refer to the biological processes that keep certain body variables within a certain range.

2. Animals whose body temperature matches that of the environment are referred to as _____ .

3. The _____ / _____ is the primary brain area that controls body temperature.

4. During illness leukocytes produce _____ , which in turn result in an increase in body temperature.

5. The two kinds of thirst are _____ and _____ .

6. The _____ and _____ _____ are the main brain areas that detect osmotic pressure.

7. Activity in the _____ and _____ nuclei result in the release of vasopressin from the _____ pituitary.

8. Salt hunger is stimulated by _____ from the adrenal glands and by _____ .

9. Low blood pressure stimulates the kidneys to release _____ , which results in the production of _____ from angiotensinogen in the blood.

10. The _____ nerve carries information about stomach distension; the _____ nerve carries information about the stomach's nutrient content.

11. The duodenum releases _____ (_____), which inhibits stomach emptying and also acts via the vagus nerve to promote satiety.

12. _____ facilitates glucose entry into cells; _____ promotes the release of glucose from the liver.

13. Hunger-sensitive neurons in the _____ receive input from _____ −containing axons and inhibit the paraventricular nucleus via axons containing _____ , _____ , and _____ .

14. Satiety-sensitive neurons in the arcuate nucleus stimulate the _____ by releasing _____ , a _____ , thereby ending a meal.

15. Neurons in the _____ promote feeding by increasing insulin secretion, altering taste responsiveness, promoting ingestion, and increasing autonomic responses, such as secretion of digestive juices.

16. Lesions of the _____ hypothalamus increase stomach motility and secretions, increase insulin and fat storage, and speed stomach emptying.

17. _____ is a satiety signal produced by fat cells; it inhibits _____ , increases _____ , and increases _____ system activity. It can also trigger the onset of _____ .

18. A mutation in the _____ receptor gene may underlie some cases of obesity.

19. The _____ syndrome is characterized by mental retardation, short stature, and obesity that is caused at least in part by high levels of ghrelin.

20. _____ has some characteristics similar to drug addiction.

Matching Items

1. _____ Poikilothermic
2. _____ Homeothermic
3. _____ POA/AH
4. _____ Vasopressin
5. _____ OVLT
6. _____ Osmotic thirst
7. _____ Hypovolemic thirst
8. _____ Renin
9. _____ Vagus nerve
10. _____ Splanchnic nerve
11. _____ Duodenum
12. _____ Lateral hypothalamus
13. _____ Ventromedial hypothalamus
14. _____ Paraventricular nucleus
15. _____ Leptin
16. _____ Bulimia nervosa

a. Brain area that controls temperature
b. Brain area that normally promotes eating
c. Brain area that detects osmotic pressure
d. Lesions → larger meals
e. Lesions → more normal-sized meals per day
f. Carries information about stomach distention
g. Hormone from kidney → angiotensin II
h. Releases CCK to inhibit stomach emptying
i. Peptide hormone produced by fat cells
j. Body temperature relatively constant
k. Result of increased extracellular solutes
l. Hormone → increases blood pressure, thirst
m. Result of loss of blood, vomiting, heavy sweating
n. Characterized by binge eating followed by purging
o. Body temperature similar to environment
p. Carries information about nutrient content

Multiple-Choice Questions

1. Temperature regulation
   a. is an example of a homeostatic mechanism.
   b. is important in mammals and birds for increasing capacity for muscle activity.
   c. maintains body temperature at levels that maximize the enzymatic properties of proteins.
   d. all of the above.

2. The preoptic area monitors
   a. only its own temperature.
   b. only skin and spinal cord temperature.
   c. both its own and skin and spinal cord temperature.
   d. the temperature of internal organs via nerve input from those organs.

3. Behavioral means of temperature regulation
   a. are the only means of temperature regulation in poikilotherms.
   b. are the only means of temperature regulation in homeotherms.
   c. do not become functional until adulthood.
   d. are effective only for controlling temperature within the normal range, not to induce a fever.

4. Fever
   a. is harmful and should always be reduced with aspirin.
   b. is produced primarily by prostaglandins E1 and E2 acting on cells in the preoptic area.
   c. is produced directly by bacteria acting on the preoptic area.
   d. is especially high in baby rabbits, in response to infections.

5. Vasopressin
   a. raises blood pressure by constricting blood vessels.
   b. is also known as antidiuretic hormone, because it promotes water retention by the kidney.
   c. is secreted from the posterior pituitary, as a result of control by the supraoptic and paraventricular nuclei of the hypothalamus.
   d. all of the above.

6. The main reason that a salty meal makes us thirsty is that
   a. excess salt in extracellular fluid produces cellular dehydration; such dehydration of cells in the OVLT results in osmotic thirst.
   b. increased salt in extracellular fluid causes the fluid to enter OVLT cells, thus distending them and producing osmotic thirst.
   c. increased salt in the blood causes the liquid portion of the blood to enter cells throughout the body, thus producing hypovolemia.
   d. the salt enters cells in the OVLT and stimulates them directly.

7. The lateral preoptic area
   a. controls hypovolemic, but not osmotic, thirst.
   b. is the site of receptors for osmotic thirst.
   c. receives input from the OVLT and controls drinking.
   d. primarily responds to signals concerning dryness of the throat.

8. After its blood volume has been reduced, an animal
   a. will drink more pure water than salt water of the same concentration as blood.
   b. will drink more slightly salty water than pure water.
   c. will not drink any more than usual, since both liquid and solute have been removed.
   d. will drink only highly concentrated salt water.

9. Salt hunger
   a. depends in part on aldosterone secreted by the adrenal glands.
   b. is enhanced by angiotensin II.
   c. is mediated by neurons in the nucleus of the tractus solitarius that are activated by aldosterone and angiotensin II.
   d. all of the above.

10. Angiotensin II
    a. is secreted by the kidney.
    b. causes water to leave cells in the preoptic area and thereby stimulates osmotic thirst.
    c. stimulates the subfornical organ, which relays the information to the preoptic area, which in turn induces drinking.
    d. all of the above.

11. Which of the following is **not** likely to induce drinking?
    a. application of aldosterone to the lateral preoptic area
    b. application of angiotensin II to the subfornical organ
    c. low blood pressure signals from baroreceptors in the large veins
    d. a salty meal

12. In the stomach
    a. food is mixed with hydrochloric acid and enzymes for the digestion of protein.
    b. food is mixed with hydrochloric acid and enzymes for the digestion of carbohydrates.
    c. food is mixed with enzymes that aid the digestion of fats.
    d. absorption of food through the walls of the stomach occurs.

13. Lactase
    a. is the sugar in milk.
    b. is an intestinal enzyme for the digestion of milk.
    c. is abundant in almost all adult humans, but is lacking in adults of other mammalian species.
    d. is abundant in birds and reptiles, but is lacking in mammals.

14. Oral factors
    a. contribute to satiety but are not sufficient to determine the amount of food consumed.
    b. are irrelevant to satiety.
    c. are the single most important factor in inducing satiety.
    d. include only the taste of food.

15. If a cuff closes the outlet from the stomach to the small intestine
    a. the animal will not eat because of the trauma of the cuff.
    b. the animal will continue eating, since food must pass beyond the stomach to trigger satiety.
    c. the animal will eat a normal-sized meal and stop.
    d. the animal will eat a normal meal, wait for it to be absorbed through the walls of the stomach, and then eat again.

16. Splanchnic nerves
    a. carry information about the nutrient contents of the stomach.
    b. carry information about the stretching of the stomach walls.
    c. are stimulated directly by cholecystokinin (CCK).
    d. secrete CCK into the circulatory system.

17. CCK
    a. is produced by the duodenum in response to the presence of food there.
    b. works, in part, by closing the sphincter muscle between the stomach and duodenum, thus allowing the stomach to fill faster.
    c. is also produced in the brain, where it tends to decrease eating.
    d. all of the above.

18. Which of the following is true?
    a. Diabetes results from a deficit in glucagon.
    b. Obese people produce more insulin than do people of normal weight.
    c. Diabetic people produce more insulin than do non-diabetics.
    d. Glucose levels in the blood are elevated by insulin.

19. Insulin
    a. is secreted in response to low blood sugar.
    b. is released by the liver.
    c. is no longer secreted after VMH lesions.
    d. promotes entry of glucose into cells.

20. People with untreated diabetes eat more food because
    a. the vagus and splanchnic nerves are damaged.
    b. they store too much of their glucose, so it is unavailable for use.
    c. they excrete most of their glucose unused.
    d. their basal metabolic rate is too high.

21. Glucagon
    a. is high in the late autumn in migratory and hibernating species.
    b. is produced by the small intestine.
    c. stimulates the liver to convert stored glycogen to glucose for release into the blood.
    d. stimulates the liver to convert glucose to glycogen for storage.

22. Which of the following is true of lateral hypothalamic damage?
    a. It results in inactivity and decreased responsiveness to stimuli.
    b. At least some of the results are due to damage to axons passing through the area, rather than to cell bodies located there.
    c. At least some of the effects on eating are due to low levels of insulin and digestive juices.
    d. All of the above are true.

23. Obesity resulting from damage to the ventromedial hypothalamus and ventral noradrenergic bundle
    a. can be prevented by letting the animals eat only as much as they ate before the lesion.
    b. occurs because the stomach empties faster than usual and insulin secretion is increased.
    c. results from a dramatic increase in the palatability of all foods, resulting in overeating even of bitter or untasty food.
    d. results from eating much larger meals than usual, because of lack of satiety.

24. Which of the following is true of the paraventricular nucleus (PVN)?
    a. It is important for ending a meal.
    b. It is important for beginning a meal.
    c. NPY excites neurons in the PVN.
    d. Leptin increases eating by increasing NPY release in the PVN.

25. Leptin
    a. increases eating.
    b. is a neurotransmitter produced by the brain.
    c. is produced by fat cells.
    d. is reduced in quantity in overweight people.

26. Neuropeptide Y (NPY)
    a. is produced by fat cells and decreases feeding.
    b. directly increases metabolic rate.
    c. decreases fat storage by decreasing the production of leptin.
    d. inhibits activity in the PVN, thereby increasing meal size.

27. Microdialysis
    a. is a means of detecting the release of neurotransmitters.
    b. is a technique used primarily for damaging cell bodies while leaving axons intact.
    c. is a technique used primarily for damaging axons while leaving cell bodies intact.
    d. has been used to demonstrate that CCK is an important hunger signal.

28. Which of the following is true?
    a. Anorexics are frequently hardworking perfectionists.
    b. Bulimics have higher than normal levels of peptide YY (PYY).
    c. Bulimics have lower than normal levels of CCK and altered serotonin receptors.
    d. All of the above are true.

Solutions

True/False Questions

1. T
2. F
3. T
4. T
5. F
6. F
7. T
8. T
9. F

10. T
11. F
12. T
13. T
14. F
15. F
16. T
17. F
18. T

19. F
20. T
21. T
22. F
23. F
24. T

Fill In The Blanks

1. homeostasis
2. poikilothermic
3. preoptic area; anterior hypothalamus
4. cytokines
5. osmotic; hypovolemic
6. OVLT; subfornical organ; (SFO)
7. supraoptic; paraventricular; posterior
8. aldosterone; angiotensin II
9. renin; angiotensin II
10. vagus; splanchnic
11. cholecystokinin; CCK
12. Insulin; glucagon
13. arcuate nucleus ; ghrelin; GABA; neuropeptide Y; agouti-related peptide
14. paraventricular nucleus ; α-MSH; melanocortin
15. lateral hypothalamus
16. ventromedial
17. Leptin; eating; activity; immune; puberty
18. melanocortin
19. Prader-Willi
20. Bulimia nervosa

Matching Items

1. O

2. A

3. J

4. L	9. F	14. D
5. C	10. P	15. I
6. K	11. H	16. N
7. M	12. B	
8. G	13. E	

Multiple-Choice Questions

1. D	11. A	21. C
2. C	12. A	22. D
3. A	13. B	23. B
4. B	14. A	24. A
5. D	15. C	25. C
6. A	16. A	26. D
7. C	17. D	27. A
8. B	18. B	28. D
9. D	19. D	
10. C	20. C	

REPRODUCTIVE BEHAVIORS

Introduction

Although sexual reproduction is less efficient than nonsexual reproduction, its major advantage may be shuffling genes to adapt to a changing environment. Sexual reproduction and sex differences are regulated largely by steroid hormones, which are derived from cholesterol. Three types of sex steroid hormones are androgens, which are found in higher concentrations in males; estrogens, which are found in higher concentrations in females; and progesterone, which is found mostly in females and is critical for preparing for and maintaining pregnancy. A number of sex differences are produced by sex-limited genes, which are activated by estrogen or androgen. Hormones, released from endocrine glands, travel in the blood throughout the body. Because of their widespread effects they are useful for coordinating long-lasting effects.

Sex hormones have two distinct kinds of effects, depending on the stage of development at which they are present. Organizing effects are produced during a sensitive period early in development and are permanent, whereas activating effects can be produced at any time and are temporary. Androgens administered to a genetic female during an early sensitive period masculinize her genitals and behavior, and the absence of androgens results in female-typical appearance and behavior. Numerous drugs, including alcohol, marijuana, an antipsychotic drug, cocaine, and even aspirin, can interfere with behavioral masculinization. The SRY (sex-determining region on the Y chromosome) gene causes the primitive gonads to develop as testes and to secrete testosterone, which increases growth of the testes and Wolffian ducts (seminal vesicles and vas deferens). The testes also secrete Müllerian inhibiting hormone (MIH), which causes the female reproductive tract to regress. In the absence of the SRY gene, mammals develop as females. Their gonads differentiate into ovaries, their Müllerian ducts differentiate into oviducts, uterus, and upper vagina, and their Wolffian ducts regress. Hormones also have organizing effects on the hypothalamus. A sexually dimorphic nucleus in the hypothalamus is larger in males, and a cyclic pattern of hormone release in females is also organized in the hypothalamus. In rodents androgen exerts its masculinizing effects on behavior mostly by being converted intracellularly to estrogen. A female is not masculinized by her own and her mother's estrogen because it is bound to alpha-fetoprotein, which prevents it from entering cells. However, small amounts of estrogen are necessary for development of female brains. Organizational effects are also found in the cerebral cortex and certain cognitive functions. Women have increased density of neurons in a language area of the temporal lobe, whereas men have more white matter. Girls are, on average, better at reading, while boys excel at spatial tasks.

When sex hormones are administered during adulthood, they tend to activate whatever behavior patterns were organized during development. Estrogens enhance sensory responsiveness of the pubic area of female rats. The ventromedial nucleus and the medial preoptic area (MPOA) of the hypothalamus are important brain areas for the activational effects of hormones. Under the influence of sex hormones, neurons in the MPOA release dopamine, which enhances female-typical behavior in female rats and male-typical behavior in males. Castrated males produce dopamine in the MPOA but fail to release it in response to a female. Moderate levels of dopamine stimulate D_1 or D_5 receptors, which promote erection in males and receptivity in females; higher levels stimulate D_2 receptors and promote orgasm and ejaculation. A sudden increase in dopamine release in several brain areas at the time of orgasm in humans resembles the "rush" produced by addictive drugs. The impairment of sexual arousal and orgasm by some antidepressant drugs results at least in part from their inhibition of dopamine release. Testosterone increases men's sexual interest, and oxytocin may enhance sexual pleasure, especially at orgasm. Although decreases in testosterone generally decrease sexual activity, low testosterone is not usually the source of impotence. Testosterone increases the production of the gaseous molecule nitric oxide, which increases blood flow to the penis and also increases activity in the hypothalamus. The drug sildenafil (Viagra) prolongs the effects of nitric oxide. Treatments that reduce testosterone production or block its receptors have been used to treat sex offenders.

In women and certain other female primates, menstrual cycles result from interaction between the hypothalamus, pituitary, and ovaries. Follicle-stimulating hormone (FSH) from the anterior pituitary stimulates the growth of ovarian follicles and the secretion of estrogen from the follicles. Increasing estrogen at first decreases the release of FSH, but near the middle of the cycle, it somehow causes a sudden surge of luteinizing hormone (LH) and FSH. These hormones cause an ovum to be released. They also cause the remnant of the follicle (the corpus luteum) to release progesterone, which causes the uterine lining to proliferate in preparation for implantation of a fertilized ovum. Progesterone inhibits release of LH; therefore, near the end of the cycle, all hormones are low, resulting in menstruation if fertilization does not occur. If the ovum is fertilized, estradiol and progesterone increase throughout the pregnancy. Combination birth-control pills contain estrogen and progesterone, which prevent the surge of FSH and LH necessary for the release of an ovum. They also thicken the cervical mucus and prevent implantation of an ovum in the uterus. Women's sexual interest is higher during the periovulatory period. Sex hormones also affect women's preference for somewhat masculinized, as opposed to feminized, men's faces, with a peak of preference for masculinized faces in the periovulatory period. Premenstrual syndrome is characterized by anxiety, irritability, and depression in the days preceding menstruation. It may result from low levels of allopregnanolone, a metabolite of progesterone that alters GABA receptors and thereby decreases anxiety.

Parental behavior in rodents can be rapidly induced by hormonal patterns characteristic of the time of delivery, including increased levels of estradiol, prolactin, and oxytocin. This suggests that the immediate maternal behavior that occurs with delivery may be under hormonal control. Hormones increase activity in the medial preoptic area and anterior hypothalamus, which are important for parental behavior, as well as for temperature regulation, thirst, and sexual behavior. Vasopressin can induce male prairie voles to form long-term bonds with females and help rear their young. Repeated exposure to pups can induce parental behavior after about six days, even in females without ovaries. However, pheromones from the young animals initially suppress parental behavior; it is only after the adoptive mother becomes accustomed to their odors that parental behavior occurs. Thus, there are two phases of maternal behavior, an early phase that is elicited by hormones and a later phase that depends on familiarity with the young. However, hormonal changes are not necessary for parental behavior in humans, except to permit a woman to nurse a baby.

There are a number of differences between men and women in some aspects of their sexual activities and in the qualities that they prefer in their mates. An evolutionary explanation for men's greater interest in short-term sexual relationships with many partners suggests that males typically seek to spread their genes, whereas females have a greater investment in a small number of offspring. However, females may also benefit from having multiple sexual partners, including greater fertility and a chance for a better mate. Both men and women prefer a healthy, intelligent, honest, physically attractive mate. In addition, women seek good providers, especially in societies where women have little economic power. On the other hand men tend to seek younger partners, because they are more likely to be fertile. Studies of responses in hypothetical situations have suggested that men are more likely to be upset by sexual infidelity, whereas women are more upset by emotional infidelity. However, a study of people's responses to actual situations found that both men and women were more upset by emotional infidelity. The fact that similar sex differences are found in many cultures does not necessarily imply that there are genetic bases for them.

Humans are variable in their sexual development and gender identity. Early fetal gonadal structures differentiate in either a male or a female direction, depending on the presence or absence of the SRY gene. Some XY males have a mutation of the SRY gene, resulting in poorly developed genitals. Some XX females have an SRY gene translocated from their father's Y chromosome to another chromosome, which may result in some ovary and some testis tissue. If a female is exposed to excess androgen during the critical period for sex differentiation, due to congenital adrenal hyperplasia (CAH), she may develop structures intermediate between those of a normal female and a normal male. A similar condition may occur if a genetic male has low levels of testosterone or is unresponsive to it. Such individuals are called intersexes or pseudohermaphrodites. Most intersexes have been reared as females, since it is easier to feminize the genitals surgically than to masculinize them. However, the surgery often impairs genital sensation. A genetic male may develop a relatively normal female appearance and gender identity because of testicular feminization (androgen insensitivity), due to a lack of androgen receptors. In the Dominican Republic some genetic males lack an enzyme that converts testosterone to dihydrotestosterone. Because dihydrotestosterone is more effective than testosterone for masculinizing the genitals, these boys appeared to be girls early in life; however, they became masculinized by high levels of testosterone at puberty. They then developed male gender identity, which was consistent with their prenatal testosterone. It was not possible for a genetic male, whose penis was accidentally removed at birth, to develop a female identity, despite attempts by his parents to raise him as a girl. These cases suggest that prenatal hormones play an important role in determining gender identity, although environmental factors may have some influence.

Genetic factors may promote homosexual orientation in both men and women. Monozygotic (identical) twins of homosexuals are more likely to be homosexual than are dizygotic (fraternal) twins or other biological or adopted siblings. One study suggested that a gene that contributes to male homosexuality is on the X chromosome, and therefore is inherited from the mother; however, later studies did not replicate these results. A gene that increases homosexuality, and therefore decreases reproductive success, would be expected to be selected against in the course of evolution. However, it may be perpetuated through kin selection, by increasing the tendency of some men to form friendships and alliances, or by increasing the reproductive ability of the women who carry the gene. There is support for the suggestion that women who carry the gene are more fertile. However, survey data cast doubt on the kin selection hypothesis, and the increased friendship hypothesis has not been tested.

Homosexuality is not well correlated with hormone levels in adulthood. However, there is some evidence from animal studies that low levels of prenatal testosterone may predispose males to respond sexually to other males and for excess testosterone in females to increase their mounting of other females. There are studies in humans that show sex differences in the length of bones, finger-length ratios, size of brain structures, and the ability of a weak noise to suppress a startle response to a loud noise. In some of these comparisons homosexual men or women have measurements that fall between those of heterosexual men and women. However, in finger length ratios homosexual men show hypermasculinized measurements. Perhaps the critical factor promoting homosexuality is not an overall increase or decrease in prenatal testosterone, but altered amounts at specific times or different sensitivities of certain brain areas to testosterone.

Men who have older brothers are more likely to be homosexual than are oldest sons. Perhaps the mother's immune system reacts to a protein in a son and then attacks that protein in later sons. In rats, prenatal stress or alcohol feminized the adult behavior of the male offspring; the combination of stress and alcohol demasculinized, as well as feminized, the offspring. These effects appeared to be mediated by endorphins, which antagonize the effects of testosterone, and by corticosterone, which decreases testosterone levels. Some brain structures show sex differences in size. For some of these structures, including the anterior commissure, the suprachiasmatic nucleus, and the interstitial nucleus 3 of the hypothalamus, homosexual men have structures more similar in size to those of women than to those of heterosexual men. We do not know whether these differences are a cause or an effect of homosexuality, or indeed, if they are relevant at all.

Learning Objectives

Module 11.1 Sex and Hormones

1. Know the three types of sex hormones and the three ways they can exert their effects.

2. Understand the roles of genes and hormones in the organization of physical and behavioral sex differences in mammals.

3. Understand the activating roles of hormones on reproductive behaviors and neurotransmitters in certain brain areas.

4. Understand the hormonal processes that control women's menstrual cycles and pregnancy, including the effects of birth-control pills.

5. Know the endocrine influences on parental behaviors.

Module 11.1 Variations in Sexual Behavior

1. Be familiar with evolutionary interpretations of mate choice and jealousy.

2. Know the genetic and hormonal factors that can produce intersexes and other discrepancies in sexual appearance.

3. Understand the genetic and hormonal influences on gender identity and sexual orientation.

Key Terms and Concepts

Module 11.1 Sex and Hormones

1. Organizing effects of sex hormones

   What good is sex?

      Reshuffles genes to adapt to changing environment

   Steroid hormones

      Four carbon rings
      Derived from cholesterol
      Three ways to exert effects

         Bind to membrane receptors
         Enter cell, activate proteins in cytoplasm
         Activate or inactivate specific genes

      Types of sex hormones

         Androgens
         Estrogens
         Progesterone

   Sex differences

      Sex-limited genes: Activated by estrogen or androgen

         Estrogen → breast development
         Androgen → beard growth
         Hormones → different rates of apoptosis (cell death)
      Three genes on Y chromosome: Active in specific brain areas
      One gene on X chromosome: Active only in female brains

   Organizing effects of hormones

Permanent change
Sensitive stage of development

Activating effects

Temporary activation of a response
May last longer than hormone remains in organ, but not indefinitely

Sex differences in the gonads

Chromosomes

Female: XX
Male: XY

Gonads: identical in very early stage

Male (XY)

SRY gene (sex-determining region on the Y) → testes → testosterone →
Wolffian ducts → seminal vesicles and vas deferens
MIH (Müllerian inhibiting hormone) → degeneration of Müllerian ducts
Penis, scrotum

Female (XX)

Ovaries (egg-producing organs)
Müllerian ducts mature → oviducts, uterus, upper vagina
Wolffian ducts degenerate

Sensitive period for testosterone's effects

Humans: Third and fourth months of pregnancy
Rats: Last few days of pregnancy and first few postnatal days
Masculinization of female rats by testosterone injections
Low levels of sex hormones → female development
Block androgen effects or remove hormones → demasculinization

Alcohol, marijuana, haloperidol (antipsychotic drug), cocaine, aspirin
Small amounts of estradiol necessary for female brain development
Estradiol or estradiol-like compounds → malformation of prostate in males

Sex differences in the hypothalamus

Anterior hypothalamus

Sexually dimorphic nucleus: Larger in males

Cyclic pattern of hormone release in females
Aromatization of testosterone to estradiol

Alpha-fetoprotein: Protects some female mammals from prenatal estradiol
Primates: Protected by metabolism of estradiol
Estradiol injection → masculinizes female rodents

Exceeds normal binding by alpha-fetoprotein or metabolism

Sex differences in the cerebral cortex and cognition

Women > men

  Increased density of neurons in language area of temporal lobe
Men > women

  White matter
Girls > boys

  School grades, especially in reading
Boys > girls

  Mental rotation tasks, line orientation tasks
Organizational, not activational effects
Males > females at maze tests in numerous species

  Women use landmarks; men use compass directions

2. Activating effects of sex hormones

  Relationship to behavior

    Doves: Behavior → hormone change → behavior → hormone change, etc.
    Hormones → alter responsiveness of brain, peripheral structures to certain stimuli

  Rodents

    Dependent on hormones
    Testosterone and its metabolites, dihydrotestosterone and estradiol → masculine behavior
    Estrogen followed by progesterone → feminine behavior
    Pudendal nerve: Tactile stimulation from pubic area to brain

      Estradiol increases its sensitivity
    Ventromedial nucleus
    Medial preoptic area

      Sexually dimorphic nucleus: Exact importance unclear

        Stimulation → sexual behavior in rats
        Lesions → only mild deficits
      Dopamine

        Released in male MPOA in presence of female
        Facilitates copulation
        Males: Testosterone → release of dopamine in MPOA
        Castration → normal production of dopamine, but no release with female
        Moderate dopamine levels → D_1 and D_5 receptors → erection in male and receptivity in
          female
        Higher dopamine levels → D_2 receptors → ejaculation and orgasm
    Orgasm → dopamine in several brain areas similar to "rush" of addictive drugs
    Female rats: Sex is reinforcing only if she controls the pace

Humans

  Effects of hormones on brain

    Testosterone (and maybe estrogen) decreases pain and anxiety
    Estrogen → increased dendritic spines in hippocampus
    Estrogen → increased certain dopamine and serotonin receptors in several brain areas
  Men

    Correlation of testosterone levels and sexual excitement
    Oxytocin release during orgasm → sexual pleasure
    Impotence

      Not usually due to low testosterone
      Impaired blood circulation, neurological problems, reactions to drugs, psychological tension
    Mechanism of erection

      Testosterone → nitric oxide in hypothalamus and penis → blood flow to penis

        Sildenafil (Viagra) → prolonged effect of nitric oxide

      Melanocortin receptors → sexual arousal in males and females
    Sex offenders: Reduce testosterone → reduced sexual activities

      High testosterone levels don't explain offenders' behavior
      Cyproterone: Blocks testosterone receptors
      Medroxyprogesterone: Inhibits gonadotropin and testosterone
      Triptorelin: Blocks gonadotropin and decreases testosterone and deviant behaviors more
        effectively than cyproterone or medroxyprogesterone
  Women

    Menstrual cycle
    FSH (follicle stimulating hormone)

      Promotes growth of follicle, which nurtures ovum
      Increases secretion of estradiol by follicle
    Estradiol

      Decreases FSH, then causes surge of LH (luteinizing hormone) and FSH
    LH and FSH

      Release ovum
      Increase secretion of progesterone by corpus luteum (remnant of follicle)
    Progesterone

      Prepares lining of uterus
      Inhibits LH release
    Menstruation: Due to decreased hormone levels
    If pregnancy: Estrogen and progesterone increase

Fluctuating activity at serotonin 5-HT$_3$ receptors → nausea

Birth-control pills

Combination pill: Both estrogen and progesterone

Prevents FSH and LH surge

Thickens cervical mucus → sperm can't reach egg

Prevents ovum from implanting

Periovulatory period

Increased estrogen levels

Maximum fertility and sexual interest

Preferred more masculine-looking faces during periovulatory period

Premenstrual syndrome (premenstrual dysphoric disorder)

Anxiety, irritability, depression in days before menstruation

Estrogen and progesterone decrease, cortisol increases before menstruation

Women with PMS: Less hormonal fluctuation

Allopregnanolone (metabolite of progesterone)
Modifies GABA synapses → decrease anxiety
Low in women with PMS

3. Parental behavior

Species differences

Monkeys: Increased interest in babies as pregnancy progresses

Rats: Less responsive late in pregnancy; after birth → very responsive

Hormone-dependent early phase

Estradiol

Prolactin → milk production, maternal and paternal behavior

Oxytocin → maternal behavior, sexual arousal, social attachment, enhancement of learning

Increased estrogen receptors in medial preoptic area, anterior hypothalamus → maternal behavior

Vasopressin: Synthesized in hypothalamus, secreted by posterior pituitary

Male prairie voles: Vasopressin → pair bonding, paternal behavior

Male meadow voles with increased activity of gene for vasopressin → preference for mate, paternal behavior

Experience-dependent later phase

Not hormone-dependent

Decreased response to aversive pheromones from pups

Vomeronasal organ

Hormones not necessary in humans

4. In closing: Reproductive behaviors and motivations

    No need to understand purpose of behavior

        Sexual activity feels good
        Mother rat licks pups to get salt

Module 11.2 Variations in Sexual Behavior

1. Evolutionary interpretations of mating behavior

    Interest in multiple mates

        Men: More interest in short-term sexual relations with multiple partners → spread genes
        Women: May sometimes gain from multiple partners

            Infertile mate; gifts; "trade up"

    What men and women seek in a mate

        Both prefer healthy, intelligent, honest, attractive mate
        Women

            Prefer good provider
        Men

            Prefer younger partner: Greater fertility

    Differences in jealousy

        Men: Hypothetically more upset by sexual infidelity
        Women: Hypothetically more upset by emotional infidelity
        Actual infidelity: Both men and women more upset at emotional infidelity

    Evolved or learned?

        Difficult to separate genetic influences from learned tendencies

    Conclusions

        Morality different from scientific questions

2. Gender identity and gender-differentiated behaviors

    Coral goby: Changes sex if partner dies and no new partner of opposite sex appears

    Sex differences: Biological

    Gender identity: Sexual identification

        Human characteristic

    Intersexes

Atypical chromosomes

    XY, with mutation of SRY

    XX, with translocated SRY from father's Y onto another chromosome

Atypical hormone pattern

    Males: Low testosterone, mutation of androgen receptors

    Excess androgens in females: Congenital adrenal hyperplasia (CAH)

        Adrenal glands: Insufficient cortisol → lack of feedback → excess ACTH → testosterone and other androgens from adrenal gland

True hermaphrodites: Some testicular and some ovarian tissue

Intersexes or pseudohermaphrodites: Intermediate appearance

Their interests

    Genetic females with CAH: Usually reared as girls

        Intermediate preferences for girl-typical and boy-typical toys

        Slight increase in boy-typical toys even in normal girls whose mothers had high normal testosterone during pregnancy

        Fewer sexual experiences with men or sexual fantasies

Testicular feminization or androgen insensitivity

    XY genotype

    Lack of androgen receptors

    Varying degrees of feminization

    Some appear to be normal females

        Puberty: Breast development, broadening hips, but no menstruation

        Internal testes

Issues of gender assignment and rearing

    1950s: All intersexes reared as girls

    Surgery → genitals look normal, but no sensation

    Many resent deception

Discrepancies of sexual appearance

    Penis development delayed until puberty

        Decreased 5α-reductase 2 (enzyme that converts testosterone to dihydrotestosterone)

        Dihydrotestosterone more effective in masculinizing genitals

        Puberty → different enzyme to convert testosterone to dihydrotestosterone → masculinize genitals

        Male gender identity after puberty, perhaps due to testosterone effects on brain

Accidental removal of the penis, reared as a girl

    Later: Male gender identity

3. Possible biological bases of sexual orientation

Genetics

    Drosophila (fruit flies) with *fruitless* gene → males court only males

    Greater similarity of orientation in monozygotic (identical) twins

    Gene on X chromosome → increased male homosexuality

        Not replicated in later studies

    Evolutionary selection

        May be perpetuated by kin selection: Not supported by one study

        "Homosexual" gene may → tendency in some men to form friendships and alliances: Untested

        May increase reproductive success of women relatives: Supported by one study

Hormones

    No consistent differences in adult hormone levels

    Animal models

        Decreased testosterone during early development of males → sexual interest in males

        Excess testosterone in females → mounting other females

    Length of bones: Homosexual men partly "feminized," homosexual women partly "masculinized"

        Finger length

            Sex difference in ratio of index finger to ring finger

            Homosexual men: Ratio hypermasculinized

    Size of brain structures: Sometimes shifted toward size of opposite sex, sometimes not

    Prepulse inhibition: Weak noise decreases startle response to louder noise

        Stronger in men than women

        Homosexual men ~ heterosexual men

        Homosexual women → male direction

    Not an overall increase or decrease in prenatal testosterone

        Altered amounts of testosterone at specific times?

        Different sensitivities of certain brain areas to testosterone?

Prenatal events

    Increased probability of homosexuality in men with older brothers

        Mother's immune system attacks a certain protein in later sons?

    Prenatal stress or alcohol in rats → males' sexual behavior feminized

        Both stress and alcohol › sexual behavior also demasculinized

        Endorphins → antitestosterone effects

        Stress → corticosterone → decrease testosterone release

    Uncertain relationship in humans between stress and homosexual sons

Brain anatomy

    Anterior commissure

        Larger in women and homosexual men

Suprachiasmatic nucleus (SCN)

Larger in homosexual than heterosexual men
Deprivation of testosterone during development

Male rats: Abnormailties in SCN
Sexual advances to both males and females early in day, mostly to females later
Interstitial nucleus 3 of anterior hypothalamus

Larger in heterosexual men than in women and homosexual men
Differences not due to AIDS
Cause vs. effect?
Functions unclear

4. In closing: We are not all the same

Biological understanding may increase acceptance of diversity

Short-Answer Questions

Module 11.1 Sex and Hormones

1. *Organizing effects of sex hormones*

   a. What is an advantage of sexual, as opposed to asexual, reproduction?

   b. What is an advantage of hormonal communication, compared to communication by neurotransmitters?

   c. Name the three types of sex hormones. What are three ways in which they exert their effects?

   d. What is a sex-limited gene? How do sex-limited genes produce sex differences in physical characteristics and behavior?

   e. Distinguish between organizing effects and activating effects of hormones.

   f. What is the SRY gene? Describe the chain of events that result from its presence during development.

   g. What are Müllerian ducts? What are Wolffian ducts? What directs the survival or regression of these ducts in males and females?

   h. When is the sensitive period for testosterone's effects on rats? On humans?

   i. Describe the effects of testosterone injections on female rats during the last few days before birth and the first few days after birth.

   j. What happens if a developing mammal is exposed to neither androgens nor estrogens during early development? Which hormone is required in low amounts for brain differentiation in females?

k. By what mechanism does testosterone exert its effects on the hypothalamus in rodents?

l. What are two sex differences in the structure or function of the hypothalamus?

m. What is the role of alpha-fetoprotein?

n. What are some nonreproductive characteristics that may be influenced by prenatal hormones?

2. *Activating effects of sex hormones*

a. Which hormones can restore male-typical sexual behavior in rodents following castration? What is the most effective hormone treatment for restoring female-typical behavior?

b. What is the pudendal nerve? What are estrogen's effects on its function?

c. What brain area may facilitate male-typical behavior in males?

d. What neurotransmitter in the MPOA stimulates male sexual activity? How does castration affect the release of that neurotransmitter in the MPOA?

e. What may be its role in the progression from the early stages of copulation, which require erection in males and the receptive posture in females, to the stage of orgasm?

f. What factor is important in determining whether sexual activity is reinforcing in female rats?

g. What are some nonsexual effects of hormones on the brain?

h. Describe the relationship between testosterone levels and sexual activity in men. Which other hormone contributes to sexual pleasure?

i. How does nitric oxide contribute to erection? What is the role of sildenafil (Viagra)? What type of receptor is stimulated by an experimental drug that increases sexual arousal in both males and females?

j. Which two drugs have been used to treat sex offenders? What promising drug has more recently been used? What are the effects of these drugs?

k. List the chain of hormonal processes in the menstrual cycle.

l. What are the two effects of follicle-stimulating hormone (FSH)?

m. Rising levels of which hormone cause a sudden surge of LH and FSH near the middle of the cycle? What is the effect of the surge of LH and FSH on the ovum?

n. What is the corpus luteum, and what hormone does it release?

o. What are the effects of progesterone? Describe the levels of the major hormones shortly before menstruation.

p. How do combination birth-control pills work?

q. Describe the effect of women's menstrual cycle on their sexual interest and their preference for masculinized vs. feminized faces.

r. Low levels of which metabolite of progesterone may be associated with premenstrual syndrome? Which neurotransmitter does this metabolite affect?

3. *Parental behavior*

a. Which three hormones have been shown to promote maternal behavior in birds and mammals? Which of these hormones also promotes paternal behavior in some species? Which other behaviors are increased by oxytocin?

b. What brain area is important for these hormonal effects?

c. Describe the differences between male prairie voles and male meadow voles in their relationships to females with which they have mated and to their offspring. What hormone is responsible for this difference?

d. Compare the roles of hormones and experience in parental behavior of rodents. Are the effects of experience mediated by hormonal changes?

e. What are the effects of pheromones released by infant rats on females that have not had hormonal priming?

Module 11.2 Variations in Sexual Behavior

1. *Evolutionary interpretations of mating behavior*

    a. What are some differences between men and women in mate preference?

    b. Give an evolutionary explanation for each of these.

    c. How did the results of studies of sex differences in jealousy differ when hypothetical vs. actual cases of infidelity were examined?

    d. How certain can we be that sex differences that are fairly consistent across cultures have a genetic basis?

2. *Gender identity and gender-differentiated behaviors*

    a. What is an intersex?

    b. What are some developmental influences that may produce an intersex individual?

    c. What is the most common cause of the intersex condition? Describe the normal relationship between the adrenal gland and the anterior pituitary. How is this relationship altered in congenital adrenal hyperplasia (CAH)?

    d. What is the difference between a true hermaphrodite and an intersex?

    e. Describe the choice of toys by girls with CAH.

    f. Describe the chromosomal pattern and the genital appearance of individuals with androgen insensitivity, or testicular feminization. What causes the unresponsiveness to androgen? What two abnormalities appear at puberty?

    g. Why have most intersexes been reared as females?

    h. How successful is the surgical treatment of intersexes?

i.   Describe two situations in which children were exposed to the prenatal hormonal pattern of one sex and then reared as the opposite sex. What can we infer from these situations about the relative importance of early rearing experiences and hormones as determinants of gender identity?

3.   *Possible biological bases of sexual orientation*

a.   Describe the evidence for a genetic predisposition towards homosexuality.

b.   Describe the evidence for increased incidence of homosexuality among maternal relatives of homosexual men. How would this implicate a gene on the X chromosome? Has the early finding been replicated?

c.   Discuss the problems concerning evolutionary selection of any genes predisposing toward homosexuality.

d.   What are three possible explanations for the continued existence of genes that predispose toward homosexuality? Which of these has received support from survey data?

e.   Can hormone levels in adulthood account for sexual orientation? What is a more plausible hypothesis concerning hormonal influence on sexual orientation?

f.   Describe the findings regarding the length of arm, leg, and hand bones in heterosexual and homosexual men and women. Were these differences likely due to prenatal or pubertal hormonal differences?

g.   Describe one study suggesting that some homosexual men had unusually high testosterone levels during development.

h.   What is prepulse inhibition? Is it usually stronger in men or women? Are such measures in homosexual men or women shifted from those of heterosexual men or women?

i.   What do these observations suggest about the effects of prenatal exposure to testosterone in humans?

j.   What explanation may account for the greater probability of homosexuality in men with older brothers than in men who were the oldest son?

k.   Describe the experiments on the effects of stress and alcohol on sex differentiation of rats. What were their results?

l.   How may endorphins be implicated in the effects of stress? How may corticosterone mediate the effects of stress?

m.   How good is the evidence regarding possible prenatal stress effects on homosexual men?

n.   What are three brain structures that show a sex difference in size? In which direction is the size difference for each? How do homosexual men compare with heterosexual men and with women regarding the size of these structures?

o.   Describe LeVay's evidence implicating the interstitial nucleus 3 of the hypothalamus in homosexuality.

p.   If there is a consistent difference between homosexual and heterosexual men in the size of various brain nuclei, what can we conclude about the role of these nuclei in determining sexual orientation?

True/False Questions

1. Some receptors for steroid hormones are in the cell membrane and activate second messenger systems similar to those of metabotropic neurotransmitters; others activate proteins in the cytoplasm; and still others move to the nucleus when bound to hormone and alter gene expression.

   TRUE or FALSE

2. The Wolffian ducts are precursors to the internal female reproductive structures.

   TRUE or FALSE

3. The SRY gene on the Y chromosome causes the primitive gonads to differentiate into testes, which secrete testosterone, which in turn leads to masculine development of the genitals and, either directly or through its metabolites, the brain.

   TRUE or FALSE

4. The sexually dimorphic nucleus (SDN) of the hypothalamus is larger in females, because it generates a cyclic pattern of hormone release.

   TRUE or FALSE

5. Female rodents are not masculinized by their own and their mother's estrogen because the aromatase enzyme rapidly converts it to progesterone.

   TRUE or FALSE

6. Hormones activate behavior, in part, by altering the responsiveness of certain brain areas and of the genitals to sexually relevant stimuli.

   TRUE or FALSE

7. Moderate concentrations of dopamine in the MPOA of rats stimulate D_1 and D_5 receptors, which facilitate erections in males and sexually receptive postures in females.

   TRUE or FALSE

8. Sildenafil (Viagra) promotes erections by increasing testosterone release.

   TRUE or FALSE

9. Birth-control pills containing estrogen and progesterone prevent the mid-cycle surge of LH and FSH and also thicken the mucus of the cervix and prevent implantation of an ovum.

   TRUE or FALSE

10. Premenstrual syndrome is caused by stronger fluctuations of hormones across the menstrual cycle and by excess allopregnanolone.

    TRUE or FALSE

11. Hormones promote maternal behavior by increasing activity in the MPOA and anterior hypothalamus.

    TRUE or FALSE

12. Hormones that promote parental behavior in some species include estrogen, prolactin, oxytocin, and vasopressin.

    TRUE or FALSE

13. A major stimulus for maternal behavior is the detection of attractant pheromones produced by the infant rat.

    TRUE or FALSE

14. Although both men and women seek mates that are healthy, intelligent, honest, and physically attractive, women also seek mates that will be good providers, and men seek mates that are young.

    TRUE or FALSE

15. Although men say that they would be more upset by sexual infidelity than emotional infidelity, a recent study found that both men and women are more upset by emotional infidelity.

    TRUE or FALSE

16. Intersexes have been usually reared as boys, because it has long been known that even moderate amounts of prenatal testosterone will lead to a male gender identity.

    TRUE or FALSE

17. Congenital adrenal hyperplasia (CAH) is the most common cause of the intersex condition.

    TRUE or FALSE

18. Testicular feminization occurs when the testes secrete large amounts of estrogen, rather than testosterone.

    TRUE or FALSE

19. The lack of the enzyme that converts testosterone to dihydrotestosterone results in children that appear to be boys at birth, but who start secreting estrogen at puberty, causing them to switch to a female identity.

    TRUE or FALSE

20. There is some evidence that female relatives of gay men have more offspring than do other women, providing a possible explanation for why a gene that seems to be disadvantageous for reproduction might have survived.

    TRUE or FALSE

21. It is now generally accepted that some gay men have inherited a gene on the Y chromosome, passed on to them from their father, which predisposed them to homosexuality.

    TRUE or FALSE

22. A major factor in predisposing men to homosexuality is that they have low levels of testosterone in adulthood.

    TRUE or FALSE

23. Prenatal stress may alter brain development, in part, by increasing the release of endorphins, which can affect the fetus's hypothalamus, and in part by increasing release of corticosterone, which decreases the release of testosterone.

TRUE or FALSE

24. The INAH-3 nucleus is larger in heterosexual men than in women and homosexual men.

TRUE or FALSE

Fill In The Blanks

1. Three types of sex hormones are _____ , _____ , and _____ .

2. The gene that directs the primitive gonad to become a testis is the _____ gene.

3. The _____ ducts develop into the oviducts, uterus, and upper vagina.

4. The _____ ducts develop into the seminal vesicles and vas deferens.

5. The protein that binds estradiol in the blood of some immature animals, thereby protecting females from their own and their mother's estradiol, is _____ .

6. The enzyme that converts testosterone to estradiol is _____ .

7. The neurotransmitter _____ is released in the _____ of male rats and promotes sexual behavior.

8. Sildenafil (Viagra) prolongs the effects of _____ and thereby increases blood engorgement of the penis.

9. _____ , a drug that blocks gonadotropin release, has been used to treat sex offenders.

10. Combination birth control pills work by preventing the surge of _____ and _____ that would normally release an ovum, by _____ the _____ of the cervix, and by preventing implantation of the ovum in the uterus.

11. Increased levels of _____ , _____ , and _____ around the time of birth increases maternal behavior by activating neurons in the _____ and _____ .

12. _____ promotes pair bonding and paternal behavior in male prairie voles.

13. Men tend to prefer a _____ partner; women tend to prefer a mate who is a good _____ .

14. A person who develops genitals intermediate between those of typical males and females is known as a(n) _____ .

15. The condition in which insufficient cortisol production in female fetuses results in excessive production of androgens by the adrenal gland is _____ .

16. People with an XY chromosome pattern but who lack androgen receptors and appear to be female have a condition known as _____ .

17. Delay of development of a penis until puberty can result from a genetic defect in the enzyme _____ , which converts testosterone into _____ .

18. Evidence favoring a genetic predisposition to homosexuality includes the observation that the concordance rate for homosexuality among _____ (or _____) twins is higher than that for _____ (or _____) twins; however, these data also show environmental factors to be important, because the concordance rate is less than 100%.

19. Prenatal stress increases the release of _____ and of _____ , which can impair masculine development of the brain.

20. The _____ is a brain nucleus that is larger in heterosexual men than in women and homosexual men. However, the interpretation of this finding is not clear.

Matching Items

1. _____ Allopregnanolone
2. _____ Estrogen, prolactin, oxytocin
3. _____ Pudendal nerve
4. _____ Müllerian ducts
5. _____ Wolffian ducts
6. _____ Alpha-fetoprotein
7. _____ Aromatase
8. _____ Dopamine in MPOA
9. _____ LH and FSH surge
10. _____ Progesterone
11. _____ 5α-reductase
12. _____ INAH-3

a. Binds estradiol in blood during development
b. Seminal vesicles, vas deferens
c. Testosterone → estradiol
d. Hormones that promote maternal behavior
e. Carries tactile stimulation from pubic area to brain
f. Metabolite of progesterone that is low in women with PMS
g. Oviducts, uterus, upper vagina
h. Testosterone → dihydrotestosterone
i. Releases ovum
j. Facilitates male and female sex behavior
k. Larger in men than in women and gay men
l. Prepares uterus for embryo, inhibits LH

Multiple-Choice Questions

1. Which of the following is <u>not</u> true of sex hormones?
   a. They are peptide hormones.
   b. They are derived from cholesterol.
   c. They consist of androgens, estrogens and progesterone.
   d. They mediate the effects of sex-limited genes.

2. The SRY gene
   a. is present on the X chromosome and is responsible for the tendency of mammals to become female, unless the gene's effects are overridden by high levels of testosterone.
   b. is present on the Y chromosome and causes the gonads to differentiate into testes, which then secrete testosterone, which in turn masculinizes the organism.
   c. has been linked to homosexuality.
   d. is the major gene that directly specifies the size of sexually dimorphic brain structures.

3. Wolffian ducts
   a. are the precursors of the oviducts, uterus, and upper vagina.
   b. are the precursors of the seminal vesicles and vas deferens.
   c. are the precursors of the external genitals.
   d. none of the above.

4. Sex differences in the hypothalamus include
   a. the sexually dimorphic nucleus of the medial preoptic area, which is larger in males.
   b. parts of the hypothalamus that generate a cyclic pattern of hormone release in females.
   c. both a and b.
   d. none of the above.

5. If a female rat receives testosterone injections during the last few days before birth or the first few postnatal days, then in adulthood
   a. she will exhibit neither masculine nor feminine sexual behavior.
   b. she will exhibit normal feminine sexual behavior in spite of the full masculinization of her genitals.
   c. she will exhibit normal feminine sexual behavior, and her genitals will appear fully feminine.
   d. her pituitary and ovary will produce steady levels of hormones rather than cycling in the normal manner, and she will exhibit masculinized sexual behavior.

6. A female pattern of development can be produced
   a. by giving a female mammal large amounts of estrogen during the sensitive period.
   b. in normal males by giving them estrogen in adolescence.
   c. in mammals of either sex by depriving the animal of testosterone during the sensitive period, although some estrogen is necessary for feminine differentiation of the brain.
   d. all of the above.

7. Which of the following is true?
   a. Testosterone's organizing effects occur throughout the entire period of gestation.
   b. Alpha-fetoprotein is the enzyme that converts testosterone to estradiol.
   c. Estradiol masculinizes the hypothalamus largely by being aromatized to testosterone.
   d. Testosterone masculinizes the hypothalamus of rodents largely by being aromatized to estradiol.

8. High levels of androgens during prenatal development of females
   a. result in steady levels of sex hormones in adulthood, instead of the typical female cycles.
   b. will cause female rats to mount other females in adulthood.
   c. may contribute to choice of male-typical toys by girls.
   d. all of the above.

9. The sexually dimorphic nucleus (SDN) of the MPOA
   a. is larger in males than in females.
   b. is necessary for males to be able to perform any male-typical behavior.
   c. is the area that controls the production of testosterone.
   d. all of the above.

10. Activation of female sex behavior by hormones
    a. is most easily elicited by injections first of progesterone and then dihydrotestosterone in females whose ovaries were removed.
    b. may be mediated in part by increasing the sensitivity of the pudendal nerve, which transmits tactile stimulation from the pubic area to the brain.
    c. is mediated by a decrease in stimulation of D_1 and D_5 dopamine receptors in the MPOA.
    d. is mediated by an increase in serotonin activity.

11. Dopamine in the MPOA of male rats
    a. is released when a gonadally intact male is exposed to a receptive female.
    b. is not released in normal amounts by castrated males.
    c. may act through different receptors to promote erection first and then ejaculation.
    d. all of the above.

12. Cyproterone, medroxyprogesterone, and a newer drug, triptorelin
    a. are common treatments for impotence.
    b. are common treatments for premenstrual syndrome.
    c. can be used to decrease sexual fantasies and offensive sexual behaviors of sex offenders.
    d. can be used to increase sexual interest in women.

13. The corpus luteum
    a. is the remnant of the ovarian follicle, which releases progesterone.
    b. releases estrogen during the early part of the cycle, which causes the pituitary to release a surge of progesterone at midcycle.
    c. is the primary source of FSH.
    d. is the primary source of LH.

14. FSH
   a. is secreted from the uterus.
   b. is secreted from the follicle.
   c. stimulates the follicle to grow, nurture the ovum, and produce estrogen.
   d. stimulates the follicle to grow and produce LH.

15. Combination birth control pills
   a. contain both estrogen and progesterone.
   b. suppress the release of FSH and LH.
   c. thicken cervical mucus.
   d. all of the above.

16. Which of the following is true?
   a. The effects of sex hormones are limited to the control of reproductive behavior and the endocrine system.
   b. Early hormones control the relative rates of apoptosis in different brain areas, leading to sex differences in size of those areas; some are larger in males and others, in females.
   c. Estrogen in adulthood produces major enhancements in spatial performance, so that females outperform males on maze tasks.
   d. Estrogen inhibits the growth of dendritic spines on neurons in the hippocampus, thereby preventing distracting stimuli from bothering a woman.

17. Premenstrual syndrome may be related to
   a. low levels of allopregnanolone, a metabolite of progesterone that decreases anxiety by altering GABA receptors.
   b. low levels of estrogen, coupled with high levels of progesterone.
   c. low levels of progesterone, coupled with high levels of estrogen.
   d. excessive testosterone.

18. Which is true concerning rodent parental behavior?
   a. Maternal behavior depends on hormones for the first few days after giving birth.
   b. Hormones continue to be the most important factor in eliciting parental behavior throughout the entire period of care of the young.
   c. The odor of newborn rat pups is naturally very attractive to female rats.
   d. Parental behavior is enhanced by lesions of the MPOA, since that area is concerned only with male sexual behavior, which would interfere with parental behavior.

19. Which of the following is true of prairie voles and meadow voles?
   a. Male prairie voles form long-term pair bonds and help take care of their young.
   b. Male meadow voles tend to be loners and do not care for their young.
   c. Male meadow voles that have experimentally increased gene activity for vasopressin in one part of their brain form pair-bonds and help care for their young.
   d. all of the above.

20. Which of the following is true of mate selection?
    a. It is now clear that women are more jealous about their husbands' sexual infidelity, whereas men are more jealous of their wives' emotional infidelity.
    b. Men tend to have a stronger preference for a young partner, whereas women prefer a mate who can be a good provider.
    c. Women never have anything to gain from having more than one sex partner, since they can have only a limited number of pregnancies.
    d. Women tend to prefer more feminized faces during their periovulatory period than at other times.

21. Intersexes
    a. are extremely rare, no more than one in several million.
    b. usually have complete sets of both male and female structures.
    c. include genetic females who were exposed to elevated levels of androgens during fetal development, due to congenital adrenal hyperplasia (CAH).
    d. are usually genetic males who have been exposed to estrogens during fetal development.

22. Intersexes
    a. should always have surgical "correction" of their genitals immediately after birth.
    b. are sometimes resentful that surgical "correction" of their genitals destroyed sexual sensation and makes them feel violated.
    c. should be reared as males if they have an XY chromosome configuration, and as females if they have an XX configuration, regardless of the appearance of their external genitals.
    d. provide clear evidence that prenatal hormones are unimportant in gender identity.

23. Androgen insensitivity (testicular feminization)
    a. is characterized by normal testosterone levels, but a lack of androgen receptors.
    b. results in an individual who appears to be completely female but fails to menstruate at puberty and has no pubic hair.
    c. cannot be alleviated by giving injections of testosterone.
    d. all of the above.

24. Certain genetic males in the Dominican Republic
    a. lack the enzyme that converts testosterone to dihydrotestosterone.
    b. lack the enzyme that converts testosterone to estradiol.
    c. are usually reared as boys, but adapt easily to a feminine sexual identity when they begin to produce high levels of estrogen at puberty.
    d. are usually reared as girls, but are completely unable to adapt to their new male gender identity when high levels of testosterone at puberty cause growth of a penis.

25. A genetic predisposition to homosexuality
    a. may be carried by a gene on the X chromosome that promotes homosexuality in males, although the evidence is not consistent.
    b. may be carried by a gene on the Y chromosome that promotes homosexuality in males, although the evidence is not consistent.
    c. is now known to be controlled by the same gene in male and female homosexuals.
    d. has been disproven, since evolution strongly selects against any genes that would interfere with reproduction.

26. Male homosexuality
    a. is highly correlated with low levels of testosterone in adulthood.
    b. is highly correlated with high levels of estrogen in adulthood.
    c. may be associated with increased stress during prenatal development.
    d. may be redirected to heterosexuality by injections of testosterone in adulthood.

27. Which of the following is true?
    a. It is now clear that low levels of testosterone during gestation are the major cause of homosexuality in males.
    b. There is considerable support for the hypothesis that kin selection has ensured the survival of genes for homosexuality, despite their apparent decrease in reproductive ability.
    c. Alcohol, administered prenatally during the same time as a stressor, may overcome the effects of stress, because it helps to calm the mother.
    d. The probability of a homosexual orientation is higher among men with older brothers, perhaps because the mother's immune system attacks a protein in the later sons.

28. The interstitial nucleus 3 (INAH-3) of the anterior hypothalamus
    a. is larger in women and homosexual men than in heterosexual men.
    b. is smaller in women and homosexual men than in heterosexual men.
    c. is smaller in homosexual men than in either women or heterosexual men, primarily because the AIDS virus is known to kill neurons in that site more than in the rest of the brain.
    d. is now known to be the primary brain center that determines sexual orientation.

Crossword Puzzle

Heat, Sex, and Gluttony

www.CrosswordWeaver.com

ACROSS

4 Type of thirst caused by loss of body fluids

8 Hormone from anterior pituitary that stimulates ovum to mature and causes the follicle to secrete estrogen (abbr.)

10 Tendency to maintain a variable within a set range

12 Brain area that inhibits lateral hypothalamus and controls meal size (abbr.)

14 Brain area sensitive to osmotic stimuli (abbr.)

16 Hormone from kidney that produces angiotensin in response to hypovolemia

18 Hormone that facilitates glucose entry into cells

20 Chromosomal male

21 Syndrome characterized by irritability before menstruation (abbr.)

24 Hypothalamic area that contains both satiety- and hunger-sensitive cells

25 Transmitter in MPOA that facilitates copulation

26 Hormone that inhibits stomach emptying and stimulates vagus nerve to induce satiety (abbr.)

27 Tract that differentiates into female internal genitals

28 _____ nervosa: eating disorder characterized by restrained eating, perfectionism

30 Nerve sensitive to nutritive content of stomach

and leads to release of the ovum

2 Tract that differentiates into male internal genitals

3 Enzyme necessary to digest milk

5 Nerve that provides information about stretching of stomach

6 Brain area important for temperature regulation, sexual behavior, and parental behavior (abbr.)

7 Another name for vasopressin (abbr.)

9 Hormone produced by fat cells that decreases hunger

11 Gene on Y chromosome that initiates formation of testes (abbr.)

13 Area of hypothalamus, lesion of which leads to obesity; it also contributes to female sexual behavior

15 _____ nervosa: Eating disorder characterized by eating huge meals, followed by purging

17 Hormone released with orgasm, promotes sexual pleasure; also promotes sexual arousal, maternal behavior, and social attachment

18 Individual with appearance between that of male and female

19 Initial segment of small intestine

22 Chemical produced by a leukocyte that activates the vagus nerve and causes the POA/AH to produce a fever

23 Hypothalamic area that facilitates eating in several ways, also contains dopamine neurons passing through

29 Chromosomal female

DOWN

1 Hormone from anterior pituitary that surges just before ovulation

Crossword Puzzle Solution

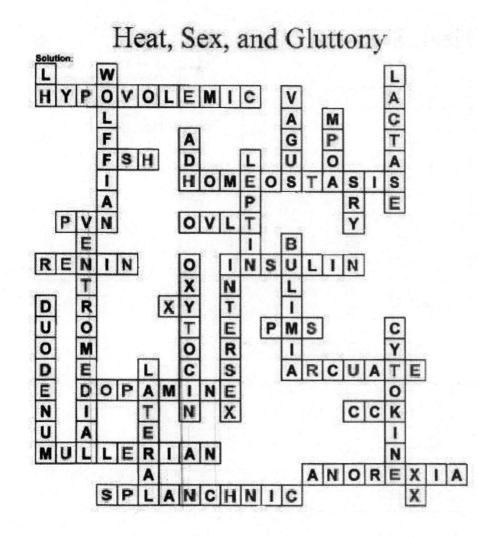

Heat, Sex, and Gluttony

Solutions

True/False Questions

1. T
2. F
3. T
4. F
5. F
6. T
7. T
8. F
9. T
10. F
11. T
12. T
13. F
14. T
15. T
16. F
17. T
18. F
19. F
20. T
21. F
22. F
23. T
24. T

Fill In The Blanks

1. estrogens; androgens; progesterone
2. SRY
3. Müllerian
4. Wolffian
5. alpha-fetoprotein
6. aromatase
7. dopamine; medial preoptic area
8. nitric oxide
9. Triptorelin
10. LH; FSH; thickening; mucus
11. estrogen; oxytocin; prolactin; medial preoptic area; anterior hypothalamus
12. Vasopressin
13. younger; provider
14. intersex
15. congenital adrenal hyperplasia
16. testicular feminization
17. 5α-reductase; dihydrotestosterone
18. monozygotic ; identical; dizygotic ; fraternal
19. endorphins; corticosterone
20. INAH-3

Matching Items

1. F
2. D
3. E

4.	G	7.	C	10.	L
5.	B	8.	J	11.	H
6.	A	9.	I	12.	K

Multiple-Choice Questions

1.	A	11.	D	21.	C
2.	B	12.	C	22.	B
3.	B	13.	A	23.	D
4.	C	14.	C	24.	A
5.	D	15.	D	25.	A
6.	C	16.	B	26.	C
7.	D	17.	A	27.	D
8.	D	18.	A	28.	B
9.	A	19.	D		
10.	B	20.	B		

12

EMOTIONAL BEHAVIORS

Introduction

Emotional states include three aspects: cognition, readiness for action, and feeling. Readiness for action depends on the autonomic nervous system, composed of the sympathetic and parasympathetic divisions. Sympathetic activity prepares for vigorous or emergency activity, whereas the parasympathetic system promotes digestion and conserves energy. Each situation requires a different combination of sympathetic and parasympathetic activity. There has been debate about the role of autonomic arousal in emotions. The James-Lange theory proposes that autonomic and skeletal activity occurs first, and emotions result from our perception of those responses. There is evidence for the importance of physiological responses in determining the intensity of emotions, and extreme sympathetic nervous system arousal during panic attacks is interpreted as fear. However, it is possible to feel some blunted emotions, even after injuries that prevent autonomic responses. Also, there are not clear distinctions among autonomic responses that would allow us to identify specific emotions, based only on the autonomic responses.

The frontal and temporal lobes of the cerebral cortex are strongly activated during various emotions, and the insular cortex is activated during feelings of disgust and fear. The frontal and temporal lobes of the left hemisphere mediate what Jeffrey Gray termed the Behavioral Activation System. It includes low to moderate autonomic arousal, a tendency to approach new objects, and a pleasant mood. In contrast, the frontal and temporal lobes of the right hemisphere are associated with the Behavioral Inhibition System, which increases attention and arousal, decreases action, and elicits disgust and fear. People with greater activity in the left hemisphere tend to be happy and out-going, while those with greater right hemisphere activity are more withdrawn and have more unpleasant emotions. The right hemisphere also helps to recognize emotions in others. Emotions provide a useful guide for quick decisions. Damage to the prefrontal cortex results in a lack of emotions. People with such damage make stupid decisions, despite being able to predict the outcomes; they are also impulsive and fail to behave morally. However, emotions can also prompt unwise decisions.

Many kinds of situations can trigger aggressive attacks, including pains, threats, and even dispassionate attacks for financial or other gains. Increased aggressiveness is influenced by heredity and by prenatal influences, including maternal smoking during pregnancy. Postnatal environment and body size at age three are also factors that influence aggressiveness. Testosterone level is correlated with aggressiveness, although its effect is relatively weak. It may affect the way people react to various stimuli. Stimulation of some brain areas can promote aggressive responses. Some people with temporal-lobe epilepsy have violent outbursts as a result of seizures that involve the amygdala. This tendency is referred to as intermittent explosive disorder. Antiepileptic drugs and tranquilizers frequently control the epilepsy and the violence; however, for extremely violent individuals who were not helped by drugs, lesions of the amygdala have sometimes reduced the violence and/or the epilepsy. Low serotonin turnover may also be associated with aggressiveness in both animals and people. Turnover is inferred from levels of 5-HIAA, a serotonin metabolite. Low serotonin turnover was observed in mice that showed isolation-induced aggression and in monkeys that were naturally aggressive. Low serotonin turnover in humans may be associated with violent crimes and suicide. However, low serotonin turnover is also associated with impulsiveness and depression. Serotonin synthesis can be affected by diet. Tryptophan, the precursor of serotonin, competes with other amino acids for transport into the brain. Therefore, foods like maize (American corn) and aspartame (NutraSweet), which are high in the amino acid phenylalanine and low in tryptophan, can increase aggressive or suicidal tendencies. Similarly, several genes that control serotonin synthesis, its transport back into cells, or its breakdown can affect the amount of serotonin in synapses. Increases of serotonin typically decrease depression, aggressiveness, impulsiveness, and even drug cravings. Strangely, serotonin is also released during aggression, although it is also released during all social encounters in rats.

Fear is a temporary tendency to escape from an immediate threat, whereas anxiety is generalized and longer lasting. The basolateral and central nuclei of the amygdala are important for learned fear responses, including enhancement of the startle reflex. The amygdala receives input concerning pain, vision, and hearing. Its output to the hypothalamus controls autonomic responses; its output to prefrontal cortex influences approach and avoidance responses; and its connections to the central gray in the midbrain elicit the startle response. Damage to the amygdala reduces or eliminates fears and also impairs the interpretation of social signals. The amygdala is activated by emotional expressions and scenes, even if the person does not consciously recognize the picture. People with Urbach-Wiethe disease suffer atrophy of the amygdala and have a resultant loss of the experience or perception of fear. One reason that people with damage to the amygdala fail to recognize fearful expressions may be that they focus on the nose and mouth, rather than the eyes. On the other hand, genes that enhance amygdala responsiveness are associated with fearful and anxious personalities.

Drugs that are used to control anxiety affect synapses in the amygdala. CCK (cholecystokinin) excites the amygdala and is also released in the prefrontal cortex in stressful situations. Injections of drugs that stimulate CCK receptors into the amygdala enhance the startle reflex, and drugs that block CCK type B receptors block anxiety. The main inhibitory transmitter in the amygdala is GABA; drugs that block GABA type B receptors produce panic. Anxiety is commonly treated with benzodiazepine tranquilizers. These drugs exert their effect at benzodiazepine binding sites on the $GABA_A$ receptor complex, thereby facilitating the binding of GABA to its own sites at the complex. The binding of GABA increases the flow of chloride ions across the membrane and thereby inhibits neural activity. Alcohol also binds to the $GABA_A$ complex and facilitates GABA binding. An experimental drug can block the effects of alcohol on the $GABA_A$ complex and on behavior. However, this drug is not marketed because of its potential for misuse.

Diazepam-binding inhibitor (DBI) is an endozepine (endogenous antibenzodiazepine). It is released by glia cells and blocks the effects of diazepam and other benzodiazepines, thereby increasing anxiety.

Stress was defined by Hans Selye as the nonspecific response of the body to any demand made upon it. In addition to specific responses to stressors, the body mounts a general adaptation syndrome, characterized by three stages: alarm, resistance and exhaustion. Stress activates the autonomic nervous system, especially the sympathetic "fight or flight" response, and also the HPA axis (the hypothalamus, pituitary gland, and adrenal cortex). During stress, the hypothalamus directs the anterior pituitary to secrete ACTH (adrenocorticotropic hormone), which in turn stimulates the adrenal gland to secrete cortisol. Cortisol shifts energy metabolism to increase blood sugar and metabolic activity. Moderate levels of cortisol improve attention and memory, but very high or low levels of cortisol impair these functions.

Three important elements of the immune system are B cells, which produce antibodies that attach to and inactivate specific antigens; T cells, which attack specific "foreign" cells or stimulate proliferation of other immune cells; and natural killer cells, which kill tumor cells and cells infected with viruses in a nonspecific way. These immune cells are leukocytes (white blood cells); they produce cytokines, which fight infections and communicate with the brain by stimulating receptors on the vagus nerve, which conveys a message to the hypothalamus and hippocampus, which in turn release cytokines in the brain. Cytokines induce fever, which helps fight infections, and promote fatigue, which leads to conservation of energy. Although brief stressors activate the immune system, chronic stressors may depress its functioning and leave an individual more vulnerable to disease. Prolonged stress, with its high cortisol levels, can also increase the vulnerability of hippocampal neurons, with resultant impairment of memory. Post-traumatic stress disorder (PTSD) occurs in some people who have had traumatic experiences. They have flashbacks, nightmares, and exaggerated arousal to noises and other stimuli. We do not know why some people do, and others do not, succumb to PTSD. Those who do have been found to have a smaller than usual hippocampus and low cortisol levels. Although cause and effect have not been clearly established, there is evidence that in some cases the small hippocampus preceded, and may have increased vulnerability to, the PTSD.

Learning Objectives

Module 12.1 What Is Emotion?

1. Be able to describe the influences of the autonomic nervous system on emotions.

2. Know the effects of damage or inactivation of cortical structures and of the right vs. left hemisphere on emotional responsiveness.

3. Understand the role of emotions in decision making and the brain areas that promote wise decision making.

Module 12.2 Attack and Escape Behaviors

1. Know the genetic, environmental, and hormonal contributions to aggressiveness.

2. Understand the roles of brain abnormalities and serotonin turnover in aggressive behavior.

3. Understand the ways in which the amygdala promotes fear and anxiety.

4. Be able to explain the effects of anxiety-reducing drugs.

Module 12.3 Stress and Health

1. Understand the concept of the General Adaptation Syndrome, including its three stages and its implications for today's crises.

2. Understand the components and functions of the hypothalamus-pituitary-adrenal (HPA) axis.

3. Know the components and functions of the immune system and the effects of brief or prolonged stressors on immune function.

4. Be able to list the symptoms of post-traumatic stress disorder (PTSD) and describe the relation between size of hippocampus, cortisol levels, and vulnerability to PTSD.

Key Terms and Concepts

Module 12.1 What Is Emotion?

1. Emotions, autonomic arousal, and the James-Lange Theory

   Emotional state: Three aspects

      Cognition
      Readiness for action
      Feeling

   Autonomic nervous system arousal

      Sympathetic nervous system→ vigorous, emergency activity
      Parasympathetic nervous system → digestion, conservation of energy
      Each situation → mixture of sympathetic and parasympathetic activity

   James-Lange theory: Appraisal → action → emotional feeling

      Prefrontal cortex: Responds differently to "pleasant" or "unpleasant" photos within 1/8th second

   Is physiological arousal necessary for emotions?

      Feedback from muscle movements unnecessary for emotion
      Autonomic response not affected by paralysis
      Pure autonomic failure

         Report cognitive aspects of emotions; decreased emotional intensity

   Is physiological arousal sufficient for emotions?

Panic attack

Extreme sympathetic nervous system arousal → interpreted as fear

Smiling → increases happiness

Brain stimulation during surgery → laughter interpreted as emotion

Supplementary motor cortex of frontal lobe

Frowning → photographs rated more unpleasant

Certain breathing patterns or postures → mild emotional feelings

James-Lange correct: Perception of bodily reactions increases emotional intensity

Small physiological differences among mild emotions: Hard to differentiate

Feedback from body not sufficient to identify emotions

2. Brain areas associated with emotion

Attempts to localize specific emotions

PET or fMRI: Frontal or temporal cortex activated during varied emotions

Variability

EEG: Different emotions → different brain areas in first half-second

Transcranial magnetic stimulation to inactivate an area

Inactivation of medial frontal cortex → impaired recognition of angry faces

Insular cortex (insula): Disgust

Dis-gust = bad taste

Also responds to frightening pictures

Contributions of the left and right hemispheres

Left hemisphere (especially frontal and temporal lobes)

Behavioral Activation System (BAS)

Low to moderate autonomic arousal

Tendency to approach new objects

Pleasant mood

Right hemisphere

Behavioral Inhibition System (BIS)

Increased attention and arousal

Decreased action

Increased fear and disgust

More responsive to emotional stimuli than left

Both detecting and expressing emotion

Personality differences

Greater activity in left frontal cortex → outgoing, fun-loving

Greater activity in right → shy, less satisfied, more unpleasant emotions

Left hemisphere damage → improved detection of others' emotions

Inactivating right hemisphere (Wada procedure) → recall facts, not emotions

3. The functions of emotions

"Gut feelings" based on autonomic responses: Useful guide for quick decision

Prefrontal cortex damage → lack of emotions

Stupid decisions, despite predicting outcomes

No moral behavior

Gambling task

Damage to prefrontal cortex or amygdala → little or no emotion; choose riskier decks of cards

Emotions can also interfere with good decisions

4. In closing: Emotions and the nervous system

A few basic emotions vs. continuous dimensions

If there are separate brain locations → suggest a few basic emotions

If emotion areas overlap → continuous dimensions

Module 12.2 Attack and Escape Behaviors

1. Attack behaviors

"Play" behavior: Compromise between attack and escape

Corticomedial amygdala

Priming for further attacks

Heredity and environment in violence

Heritability

Monozygotic = dizygotic in juvenile crimes

Family, neighborhood more important than genes

Monozygotic > dizygotic in adult crimes

More control over environment: Choice of friends, environment → violence

Maternal smoking during pregnancy

Effect compounded with complications during pregnancy

Correlational, not causational effect

Body size: Tall at age 3 → fearless, aggressive at age 11

Even if not tall at age 11

Combination: Biological parents with criminal record + adoptive parents with discord, depression, substance abuse, legal problems

Hormones

    Male-female differences

        More crime in men 15-25 years of age: Highest testosterone levels
        Higher testosterone correlated with more violent acts

            Interpretation difficult
        Testosterone may $\rightarrow$ attend longer, respond more vigorously to conflict

Brain abnormalities and violence

    Intermittent explosive disorder

        Outbursts of violent behavior with little provocation
        Temporal lobe epilepsy

            Hallucinations, lip smacking, repetitive acts, emotional behaviors
            Most people with temporal lobe epilepsy not violent

Serotonin synapses and aggressive behavior

    Nonhuman animals

        Social isolation of male mice $\rightarrow$ lower serotonin turnover, correlated with aggression
        5-HIAA (5-hydroxyindoleacetic acid): Measure of serotonin turnover
        Social isolation of female mice $\rightarrow$ no change in serotonin turnover or aggression
        Male monkeys: Low serotonin turnover correlated with high aggression, short lives
        Possible evolutionary explanations

            Evolution $\rightarrow$ intermediate aggressiveness: Both fearless and highly fearful die young
            Rats: Greatest fear $\rightarrow$ early death from natural causes
            Overreact to stressful events
            High-risk, high-payoff $\rightarrow$ a few sire many young

    Humans

        Low serotonin turnover: Correlation with violent crimes or suicide
        Higher suicide rates in spring: Serotonin turnover lowest
        Low tryptophan diet $\rightarrow$ increase in aggressiveness

            Other amino acids compete with tryptophan for transport channel
            Aspartame, maize (corn): High in phenylalanine $\rightarrow$ competes with tryptophan
        Relevant genes

            Gene for tryptophan hydroxylase: Tryptophan $\rightarrow$ serotonin
            Gene for serotonin transporter

                "Short" form $\rightarrow$ decreased activity of transporter $\rightarrow$ prolong serotonin in synapse $\rightarrow$ anxiety + decreased aggression
            Gene for monoamine oxidase (MAO): Enzyme breaks down serotonin

                Less MAO + mistreatment as children $\rightarrow$ violence
                Puzzle: Less MAO should $\rightarrow$ more serotonin, which should $\rightarrow$ less aggression

Low serotonin → depression, aggression, impulsivity

    Addicts → drug craving
    Effects are complicated
Another complication

    Serotonin release during aggression

        Possible explanation: Low basal levels → receptor supersensitivity
        Possible explanation: Serotonin released during all social encounters

2. Escape, fear, and anxiety

  Fear, anxiety, and the amygdala

    Fear: Tendency to escape from immediate threat
    Anxiety: General sense of possible danger
    Startle reflex

        Auditory input → cochlear nucleus of medulla → pons → tense muscles
        Stronger if already tense
    Studies in rodents

        Pain, vision, hearing → basolateral, central amygdala
        Output to hypothalamus → autonomic responses
        Output to prefrontal cortex → approach and avoidance responses
        Output to midbrain → pons → skeletal responses
        Damage to amygdala → no enhancement of startle reflex by conditioned fear signal
        Two possible explanations:

            Amygdala damage destroys fear
            Amygdala damage → difficulty understanding emotional consequences
        Protozoan parasite → reproduce in cat → excrete eggs in feces → rat picks up eggs from ground
          → new parasites → damage rat's amygdala → lose fear → eaten by cat → reproduce in cat
    Studies in monkeys

        Amygdala damage

            Klüver-Bucy syndrome: Little fear or avoidance
            Fall to bottom of social hierarchy
            Increased friendliness
            Similar to people taking tranquilizers
  Activaton of the human amygdala

    Expressions that require emotional processing → amygdala response
    Emotions elicited by angry or fearful faces: Depend on gaze direction
    Amygdala response: Also depends on gaze direction

        Complex: Depends on need for emotional interpretation, subject's mood
        Responds even if stimulus not identified consciously

Cortical blindness: Better-than-chance identification of emotion in pictures, via right amygdala, even though no cortical response

Damage to the human amygdala

Urbach-Wiethe disease (genetic disease → calcium accumulation in amygdala)

Strokes or brain surgery

Report normal emotions, but are impaired at processing emotions when signals are subtle

Inability to judge trustworthiness

Inability to focus attention on emotional stimuli

Difficulty recognizing fear and disgust in photos

Some difficulty with anger, surprise, arrogance, guilt, admiration and flirtation

Can recognize emotions in movies and everyday life

Focus mostly on nose and mouth—not eyes

Personality differences

Gene interferes with serotonin uptake in amygdala → strong negative emotions

Anxiety-reducing drugs

Hyperactive amygdala → exaggerated fears

Transmitters in amygdala: CCK, excitatory; GABA, inhibitory

"Intruder" rats

CCK in prefrontal cortex → anxiety

CCK type B antagonist → no anxiety

CCK type A receptors → opposite effects (maybe), less abundant

CCK-stimulating drugs in amygdala → enhance startle reflex

GABA type B antagonist → panic

Benzodiazepines

Barbiturates: Habit forming, easy to take fatal overdose

Common benzodiazepine tranquilizers

Diazepam (Valium)

Chlordiazepoxide (Librium)

Alprazolam (Xanax)

$GABA_A$ receptor complex

Chloride channel → hyperpolarization

Benzodiazepines and alcohol → enhance GABA binding

Benzodiazepine effects

Amygdala, hypothalamus, midbrain → decrease learned shock avoidance

Cerebral cortex, thalamus → sleepiness, decrease epilepsy, impair memory

Diazepam-binding inhibitor (DBI), an endozepine: Endogenous antibenzodiazepine

Isolation → increase in endozepines in several brain areas → fearfulness, aggression

Released mainly by glia cells

Alcohol as a tranquilizer

Cross-tolerance: Alcohol, benzodiazepines, barbiturates
Alcohol $\rightarrow$ increased flow of chloride ions through $GABA_A$ receptor complex
Antianxiety effects: Similar to benzodiazepines
Ro15-4313: Blocks effects of moderate amounts of alcohol on $GABA_A$ receptors and behavior

Not marketed because of potential for misuse

3. In closing: Doing something about emotions

Problem: How to use new understanding

Module 12.3 Stress and Health

1. Concepts of stress

Behavioral medicine: Effects on health of diet, smoking, exercise, stressful experiences

Hans Selye: Stress is nonspecific response of body to any demand made upon it

Any threat $\rightarrow$ specific effects + generalized response to stress
General adaptation syndrome

Three stages

Alarm: Increased sympathetic nervous system activity
Resistance: Adrenal cortex secretes cortisol $\rightarrow$ prolonged alertness, fight infections, heal wounds
Exhaustion: Tired, inactive, vulnerable

Robert Sapolsky: Today's crises more prolonged $\rightarrow$ harmful

Bruce McEwen: Stress = threatening events that elicit behavioral and physiological responses

2. Stress and the hypothalamus-pituitary-adrenal cortex axis

Slower than autonomic nervous system

Hypothalamus $\rightarrow$ anterior pituitary $\rightarrow$ adrenocorticotropic hormone (ACTH) $\rightarrow$

human adrenal cortex $\rightarrow$ cortisol (rat adrenal cortex $\rightarrow$ corticosterone) $\rightarrow$
increased blood sugar and metabolism
Useful in short term, harmful if prolonged

The immune system

Autoimmune disease: Immune system attacks "self"
Leukocytes (white blood cells)

B cells

Mature in bone marrow

Plasma cells → antibodies
B memory cells
T cells

Mature in thymus
Some directly attack intruder
Others stimulate other T or B cells to multiply
Natural killer cells: Relatively nonspecific in their targets
Cytokines

Example: Interleukin-1 (IL-1)
Attack infections
Peripheral cytokines → vagus nerve → hypothalamus and hippocampus →

Release cytokines in brain → anti-illness behaviors
Fever → fight infections
Sleepiness → conserve energy

Effects of stress on the immune system

Psychoneuroimmunology
Inescapable, temporary stressors → response similar to illness
Brief stressors → brief activation of immune system

Also symptoms resembling illness
Long-term stressors → decreased protein synthesis, including immune system proteins

High cortisol → hippocampal damage

Decreased learning and memory
Early stress in rats → fewer hippocampal neurons in adulthood

3. Post-traumatic stress disorder (PTSD)

Symptoms

Flashbacks and nightmares
Avoidance of reminders
Exaggerated arousal in response to noises and other stimuli

Vulnerability

Small hippocampus (cause or effect?)
Low cortisol levels → ill-equipped to combat stress?
Small hippocampus in both twins

Only one was in war and had PTSD
Therefore, small hippocampus predisposed to PTSD

4. In closing: Emotions and body reactions

Stress → adrenal cortex and immune system → reactions similar to illness

Short-Answer Questions

Module 12.1 What Is Emotion?

1. *Emotions, autonomic arousal, and the James-Lange theory*

    a. What are the roles of the sympathetic and parasympathetic nervous systems?

    b. Describe the James-Lange theory of emotions.

    c. Is physiological arousal necessary for emotions? What is the implication of the very rapid response of the prefrontal cortex to emotional stimuli?

    d. Describe the condition of pure autonomic failure.

    e. Describe the experience of panic attack.

    f. Describe the findings of the experiment in which subjects held a pencil between their teeth or with their lips.

    g. Summarize the current understanding of the importance of physiological arousal for emotions.

2. *Brain areas associated with emotion*

    a. Describe the responses of the frontal and temporal lobes to photographs, stories, or recalled personal experiences associated with particular emotions. On the basis of these data, can we localize specific emotions to particular brain areas?

    b. Describe the effects of damage to or inactivation of the frontal cortex, the temporal cortex, and the insular cortex.

    c. What are the roles of the right and left hemispheres in the detection and expression of emotion?

3. *The functions of emotions*

    a. Describe the findings of the experiment in which people were shocked after either snake or spider pictures that were presented too fast for conscious identification. What can we conclude about the value of "gut feelings"?

    b. Describe the behavior of people with damage to the prefrontal cortex.

Module 12.2 Attack and Escape Behaviors

1. *Attack behaviors*

    a. What is one explanation of a cat's "play" behavior with its prey?

b. What are the effects of stimulation of the amygdala on aggressive behavior? Which area of the amygdala is especially important for this effect?

c. Describe the evidence for heritability of violence in adulthood, but not in childhood.

d. What environmental risk factor is compounded with complications during pregnancy in determining predisposition toward violence?

e. How strong is the correlation between testosterone levels and aggressive behavior? By what psychological effect may testosterone promote aggression?

f. Describe intermittent explosive disorder. What physiological disorder may be linked to intermittent explosive disorder?

g. What are the symptoms of temporal lobe epilepsy? Are most people with temporal lobe epilepsy violent?

h. What transmitter abnormality appears to be associated with aggressive behavior? How can it be measured?

i. Describe the experimental evidence in mice for the relationship between a transmitter abnormality and aggressive behavior.

j. How was serotonin turnover related to behavior in male monkeys in a natural-environment study?

k. What evidence implicates low serotonin turnover in humans as a factor in aggressive behavior?

l. What dietary factors influence serotonin synthesis?

m. Which three genes have been implicated in a tendency toward aggressiveness?

n. What other mood or behavior disorders are associated with low serotonin turnover?

o. Describe the complication concerning the timing of serotonin release relative to aggression. What are two possible explanations for this complication?

2. *Escape, fear, and anxiety*

a. Why should researchers be interested in the startle response?

b. What is a key brain area for learned fears? What kinds of sensory input does it receive? Which two nuclei appear to be most important for conditioned fear responses?

c. What are the main output connections of the amygdala? What does each control?

d. Describe the effects of a protozoan parasite on rats. How may the behavioral change lead to the reproduction of the parasite?

e. What are the usual effects of amygdala damage? Describe the Klüver-Bucy syndrome.

f. Describe the responses of the human amygdala to photographs depicting various emotions. Does the amygdala respond even if the stimulus is not identified consciously?

g. What causes Urbach-Wiethe disease? Under what conditions do people with amygdala damage have trouble processing emotional information? How do their social judgments of other people differ from those of normal people?

h. Why may people with amygdala damage fail to identify fearful expressions in photographs?

i.   What genetic abnormality is implicated in anxiety disorders?

j.   Name one excitatory and one inhibitory transmitter in the amygdala that have been implicated in the control of anxiety.

k.   What type of drug blocked anxiety in male mice placed into a resident male's cage? What type of drug enhanced the startle reflex when injected into the amygdala?

l.   What is the most common type of drug used to reduce anxiety? What was a major problem with the use of barbiturates for anxiety?

m.   When a benzodiazepine molecule attaches to its binding site on the GABAA receptor, how is the binding of GABA affected? What effect does this have on the flow of chloride ions across the cell membrane?

n.   What are the behavioral effects of benzodiazepines on the amygdala? On the cerebral cortex and thalamus?

o.   What is one endogenous chemical that affects the benzodiazepine receptors? Why is the term endozepine confusing? Which type of cell releases it?

p.   What is the effect of alcohol on the GABAA receptor? What are the advantages and disadvantages of a drug that blocks alcohol's effects on the GABAA receptor? What is your opinion of the decision not to market the drug?

Module 12.3 Stress and Health

1.   *Concepts of stress*

a.   What is the main emphasis of behavioral medicine?

b.   What was Hans Selye's definition of stress? What symptoms did Selye notice in patients with a wide variety of illnesses?

c.   What are the three stages of the General Adaptation Syndrome, and what occurs in each?

2.   *Stress and the hypothalamus-pituitary-adrenal cortex axis*

a.   Describe the steps in the control of cortisol secretion from the adrenal cortex.

b.   What is the role of cortisol in the body's response to stress?

c.   What are three of the most important cells of the immune system?

d.   What are antigens? How was the name "antigen" derived?

e.   What are the roles of B cells and of T cells?

f.   What is the role of natural killer cells?

g.   What are cytokines? How do cytokines produced in the periphery communicate with the brain?

h.   What are the roles of fever and fatigue in fighting illness?

i.   What is the effect of short-term stress on the immune system?

j. Describe the evidence suggesting that long-term stress impairs the function of the immune system.

k. What are cortisol's major effects on blood sugar and metabolism? How does this affect the immune system?

l. How do high cortisol levels affect the hippocampus? How does this affect memory?

3. *Post-traumatic stress disorder (PTSD)*

a. What are the symptoms of posttraumatic stress disorder (PTSD)?

b. Is the hippocampus of people who suffer from PTSD likely to be larger or smaller than average? What can be inferred about cause and effect in this relationship? What may we infer about the relationship of low cortisol levels and vulnerability to PTSD?

True/False Questions

1. Students who very briefly viewed pictures of snakes or spiders showed a physiological reaction only if they could identify the object.

    TRUE or FALSE

2. Various situations call for different amounts and combinations of sympathetic and parasympathetic nervous system activity.

    TRUE or FALSE

3. According to the James-Lange theory, our conscious identification of an emotion occurs first and instructs the autonomic nervous system to respond appropriately.

    TRUE or FALSE

4. Three cortical areas that are very responsive in emotional situations are the frontal lobe, the temporal lobe, and the insular cortex.

    TRUE or FALSE

5. The right hemisphere is more responsive to emotions, especially unpleasant emotions, than is the left.

    TRUE or FALSE

6. People with damage to their prefrontal cortex showed a lack of emotions and made stupid decisions, in spite of being able to predict the outcome of their actions.

    TRUE or FALSE

7. Monozygotic twins show a greater concordance than dizygotic twins for juvenile crimes, but not for adult crimes.

    TRUE or FALSE

8. Testosterone may increase aggressiveness by causing the individual to attend longer and respond more vigorously to conflict.

    TRUE or FALSE

9. People with damage to the prefrontal cortex may be more aggressive because they have a general loss of inhibitions.

   TRUE or FALSE

10. Low serotonin turnover in people is correlated with violent crimes and suicides.

    TRUE or FALSE

11. Output from the amygdala to the hypothalamus controls skeletal responses.

    TRUE or FALSE

12. People with Urbach-Wiethe disease show an increased tendency for panic disorder.

    TRUE or FALSE

13. CCK is a major excitatory transmitter in the amygdala and tends to promote anxiety; GABA is the main inhibitory transmitter and tends to decrease anxiety.

    TRUE or FALSE

14. Benzodiazepines directly open the chloride channel in the $GABA_A$ receptor, so that GABA is no longer needed. Therefore, it is easy to take a fatal overdose.

    TRUE or FALSE

15. Alcohol, benzodiazepines, and barbiturates exhibit cross-tolerance; an individual that develops tolerance to one will show partial tolerance to the others.

    TRUE or FALSE

16. Endozepines are powerful natural benzodiazepines and therefore inhibit fear and anxiety.

    TRUE or FALSE

17. The three stages of Selye's General Adaptation Syndrome are alarm, resistance, and exhaustion.

    TRUE or FALSE

18. B cells of the immune system release cytokines that directly kill invading bacteria.

    TRUE or FALSE

19. T cells mature in the thymus; some directly attack intruders and others stimulate other B or T cells to multiply.

    TRUE or FALSE

20. Natural killer cells release antibodies that are tailored to attack specific invaders.

    TRUE or FALSE

21. Peripheral cytokines stimulate the vagus nerve, which relays input to the hypothalamus and hippocampus; cytokines are then released in the brain to produce anti-illness behaviors.

    TRUE or FALSE

22. Brief stressors inhibit the immune system, and prolonged, intense stressors inhibit it even more.
    TRUE or FALSE

23. High cortisol concentrations damage the hippocampus, resulting in memory problems.
    TRUE or FALSE

24. People with PTSD have very high cortisol levels, because they are so frequently under a lot of stress.
    TRUE or FALSE

Fill In The Blanks

1. According to the _____ theory, autonomic arousal and skeletal actions come first; our experience of emotion is the label we give to our responses.

2. Evidence for the James-Lange theory is that people with _____ failure can report the cognitive aspects of emotions, but they do not feel emotions intensely.

3. The _____ and _____ lobes of the cortex are activated during varied emotions; the _____ cortex responds during feelings of disgust and fear.

4. The _____ hemisphere is associated with the Behavioral Activation System, which is characterized by low to moderate autonomic arousal, a tendency to approach new objects and _____ mood.

5. The _____ hemisphere is more responsive to emotional stimuli, both in detecting and expressing emotion.

6. People with damage to the _____ cortex or _____ showed little or no emotion and made riskier choices.

7. Stimulation of the _____ amygdala primes an animal for attack.

8. _____ twins were more similar in their commission of adult crimes than were _____ twins, but the two groups of twins were similar in commission of juvenile crimes.

9. _____ disorder is sometimes associated with temporal lobe epilepsy, although most people with temporal lobe epilepsy are not violent.

10. Levels of _____ are a measure of serotonin turnover. Low serotonin turnover is associated with _____ .

11. Three genes that have been associated with aggressiveness in humans are those that direct production of _____ , the _____ , and _____ .

12. Damage to the _____ resulted in a lack of enhancement of the startle reflex by conditioned fear signals.

13. Monkeys with the _____ syndrome, as a result of damage to the amygdala, show little fear or avoidance.

14. In humans, the _____ disease results in degeneration of the _____ and a resultant difficulty in expressing or recognizing _____ .

15. A major excitatory neurotransmitter in the amygdala is _____ ; the main inhibitory neurotransmitter is _____ .

16. _____ bind to their own site on the $GABA_A$ receptor and enhance the binding of GABA; this tends to increase the flow of _____ ions.

17. Diazepam-binding inhibitor (DBI) is a(n) _____ ; it increases _____ and _____ .

18. _____ defined stress as a nonspecific response of the body to any demand made upon it.

19. The _____ consists of three stages: alarm, resistance, and exhaustion.

20. Activation of the hypothalamus stimulates the anterior pituitary to produce _____ , which in turn stimulates the adrenal cortex to secrete _____ .

21. Leukocytes that attack tumor cells and cells infected with viruses are called _____ .

22. _____ , including interleukin-1, are released by leukocytes to combat infection; they also stimulate the _____ nerve, which leads to cytokine release in the brain, which in turn produces a _____ and _____ .

23. PTSD victims tend to have a smaller _____ and, surprisingly, also have low levels of _____ .

Matching Items

1. _____ Prefrontal cortex damage		a.	Alarm, resistance, exhaustion
2. _____ Panic disorder		b.	Leukocytes that mature in the thymus, attack intruders, help B or T cells multiply
3. _____ General adaptation disorder		c.	Extreme sympathetic activity interpreted as fear
4. _____ B cells		d.	Make stupid decisions, no moral behavior
5. _____ T cells		e.	Damages hippocampus
6. _____ Cytokine		f.	Leukocytes that secrete antibodies
7. _____ Brief stressor		g.	Behavioral Inhibition System
8. _____ High cortisol		h.	Main inhibitory transmitter in amygdala
9. _____ Small hippocampus		i.	Brief activation of immune system
10. _____ 5-HIAA		j.	Endogenous antibenzodiazepine
11. _____ Right hemisphere		k.	Released by lympocytes, fight infection, inform brain
12. _____ CCK		l.	Metabolite of serotonin
13. _____ GABA		m.	A major excitatory transmitter in amygdala
14. _____ DBI		n.	Possible predisposition to post-traumatic stress disorder (PTSD)

Multiple-Choice Questions

1. Which of the following is true?
   a. A lack of emotions, as in people with prefrontal cortex damage, promotes rational decision making.
   b. The James-Lange theory proposed that autonomic arousal and skeletal actions precede emotions.
   c. Responses based on "gut feelings" are almost always wrong.
   d. Sympathetic nervous system activity prepares the body for digestion and relaxation.

2. Which of the following cortical areas is **not** highly activated during emotional perceptions?
   a. frontal cortex
   b. temporal cortex
   c. insular cortex
   d. occipital cortex

3. People with pure autonomic failure
   a. report the cognitive aspects of emotions, but feel emotions much less intensely.
   b. have little or no cognitive ability.
   c. express extreme panic at being unable to move.
   d. All of the above are true.

4. What is the current state of acceptance of the James-Lange theory?
   a. It is no longer thought to have any validity.
   b. It is correct in that physiological arousal is sufficient to distinguish between emotions, such as fear and anger.
   c. It is incorrect in that decreasing autonomic responses actually increases intensity of emotions.
   d. It is largely correct in that physiological arousal is both necessary and sufficient to influence the intensity of our emotions.

5. Which of the following is true?
   a. Damage to or inactivation of frontal cortex increases the perception of anger.
   b. Inactivation of the right hemisphere interferes greatly with the recall of facts but has little effect on the recall of emotion.
   c. The insular cortex is important for feelings of disgust.
   d. People with greater activity in their right hemisphere tend to be more outgoing and loving.

6. Which of the following is true?
   a. Cats that "play" with their prey are really sadistically torturing the smaller animal.
   b. Increased aggressiveness can be elicited by stimulation of the corticomedial amygdala.
   c. There is greater evidence for heritability in juvenile crimes than in adult crimes.
   d. Smoking during pregnancy primarily increases the likelihood that the offspring will be arrested for nonviolent crimes, rather than violent crimes.

7. Which of the following is true?
   a. The correlation between testosterone and aggression in humans is real, but of modest size.
   b. Both genetics and environmental factors contribute to the predisposition to commit crimes and aggressive behaviors.
   c. Many people with damage to the prefrontal cortex have a tendency toward many socially inappropriate behaviors.
   d. All of the above are true.

8. Lesions of the amygdala
   a. usually produce difficulty in interpreting social stimuli as well as decreased fear.
   b. usually cause temporal lobe epilepsy.
   c. lead to a state that resembles panic disorder.
   d. usually result in decreased serotonin turnover.

9. Which of the following has **not** been implicated in aggressiveness?
   a. the corticomedial nucleus of the amygdala
   b. the entire hippocampus
   c. being a boy who was taller than usual at age 3
   d. maternal smoking during pregnancy

10. Temporal-lobe epilepsy
    a. is invariably associated with violence.
    b. is generally untreatable except by surgery.
    c. symptoms include hallucinations, lip smacking or other repetitive acts, and, in some cases, violence.
    d. can frequently be improved with antipsychotic drugs.

11. Which of the following is true?
    a. Mice with low levels of serotonin turnover are abnormally placid.
    b. Serotonin turnover has been found to be lower than normal in impulsive, aggressive humans.
    c. 5-HIAA is a drug that has been used successfully to treat uncontrollable violence.
    d. All of the above are true.

12. Which of the following is true?
    a. Social isolation increased aggressiveness in female mice as much as in males.
    b. Almost all monkeys with low serotonin turnover had longer lifespans, because they killed off their competitors.
    c. Low serotonin turnover in humans has been associated with depression, impulsivity, and drug craving, as well as with aggression.
    d. People who have a tendency toward aggressiveness should consume a lot of aspartame and maize (corn), in order to increase their serotonin synthesis.

13. Output from the amygdala to the hypothalamus controls
    a. the intensity of sensory input to the organism.
    b. the interpretation of potentially frightening stimuli.
    c. skeletal movements of the startle response.
    d. autonomic fear responses, such as increased blood pressure.

14. After damage, inactivation, or atrophy of the amygdala
    a. a person has difficulty recognizing or portraying fearful expressions.
    b. a rat no longer shows any startle reflex.
    c. people with Urbach-Wiethe disease are unusually aggressive and fearful.
    d. monkeys rise to the top of the social hierarchy, because they successfully threaten others.

15. Librium, Valium, and Xanax
    a. are more habit-forming than barbiturates and more likely to lead to a fatal overdose.
    b. are benzodiazepines.
    c. act exclusively on CCK synapses.
    d. All of the above are true.

16. The benzodiazepines
    a. block $GABA_A$ synapses.
    b. decrease the membrane's permeability to chloride ions.
    c. attach to binding sites on the $GABA_A$ receptor complex, thereby facilitating GABA binding.
    d. directly open chloride channels.

17. Which of the following is true?
    a. Alcohol displaces benzodiazepines from their binding sites, thereby disrupting GABA transmission.
    b. Endozepines, including diazepam-binding inhibitor (DBI), are actually endogenous antibenzodiazepines, which inhibit GABA transmission.
    c. The most effective anti-anxiety drugs stimulate CCK receptors.
    d. Alcohol produces its antianxiety effects by blocking chloride channels.

18. Cortisol
    a. is secreted by the anterior pituitary gland.
    b. serves primarily to activate a sudden burst of "fight or flight" activity.
    c. serves primarily to decrease metabolic activity in order to save energy for later stresses.
    d. shifts energy away from synthesis of proteins, including those necessary for the immune system, and towards increasing blood sugar.

19. T cells
    a. are specialized to produce antibodies.
    b. mature in the thymus and either attack intruder cells or stimulate other B or T cells to multiply.
    c. are cells in the hypothalamus that produce cytokines.
    d. are useless until they are activated by B cells.

20. Cytokines
    a. in the periphery activate receptors on the vagus nerve, which relays input to the hypothalamus and hippocampus, which then release cytokines themselves in the brain.
    b. help overcome typical illness symptoms, such as fever and sleepiness, after illness is over.
    c. increase appetite and energy expenditure to better fight the illness.
    d. easily cross the blood-brain barrier, in order to coordinate peripheral and central effects.

21. Stress
    a. is by far the major factor in the activity of nonhuman animals' immune response; however, humans are not susceptible to stress effects.
    b. impairs the immune system from the first moments of the stressor's presence.
    c. produces a brief activation of the immune system, followed by inhibition of immune response if the stressor continues for a long time and is sufficiently intense.
    d. All of the above are true.

22. Prolonged high levels of cortisol
    a. make hippocampal neurons vulnerable to damage, which results in decreased learning and memory.
    b. lead to an increase in protein synthesis, which helps the immune system during long-term stressors.
    c. are found in almost all people with PTSD.
    d. All of the above are true.

23. PTSD
    a. occurs in almost all people who are subjected to traumatic experiences.
    b. includes symptoms of flashbacks, nightmares, avoidance of reminders, and exaggerated response to noises or other stimuli.
    c. is usually accompanied by a larger than usual hippocampus, because the memory of the trauma is so firmly established.
    d. All of the above are true.

Solutions

True/False Questions

1. F	10. T	19. T
2. T	11. F	20. F
3. F	12. F	21. T
4. T	13. T	22. F
5. T	14. F	23. T
6. T	15. T	24. F
7. F	16. F	
8. T	17. T	
9. T	18. F	

Fill In The Blanks

1. James-Lange

2. pure autonomic

3. frontal ; temporal ; insular

4. left; pleasant

5. right

6. prefrontal; amygdala

7. corticomedial

8. Monozygotic; dizygotic

9. Intermittent explosive

10. 5-HIAA; aggressiveness

11. tryptophan hydroxylase; serotonin transporter; monoamine oxidase

12. amygdala

13. Klüver-Bucy

14. Urbach-Wiethe; amygdala; fear

15. CCK; GABA

16. Benzodiazepines; chloride

17. endozepine; fearfulness; aggression

18. Hans Selye

19. general adaption syndrome

20. ACTH; cortisol

21. natural killer cells

22. Cytokines; vagus; fever; fatigue

23. hippocampus; cortisol

Matching Items

1.	D	7.	I	13.	H
2.	C	8.	E	14.	J
3.	A	9.	N		
4.	F	10.	L		
5.	B	11.	G		
6.	K	12.	M		

Multiple-Choice Questions

1.	B	10.	C	19.	B
2.	D	11.	B	20.	A
3.	A	12.	C	21.	C
4.	D	13.	D	22.	A
5.	C	14.	A	23.	B
6.	B	15.	B		
7.	D	16.	C		
8.	A	17.	B		
9.	B	18.	D		

THE BIOLOGY OF LEARNING AND MEMORY

Introduction

Learning depends upon changes within single cells, which then work together as a system to produce adaptive behavior. Different kinds of learning and memory may rely on different neural mechanisms. Classical conditioning establishes a learned association between a neutral (conditioned) stimulus (CS) and an unconditioned stimulus (UCS) that evokes a reflexive response (UCR). As a result, the previously neutral stimulus comes to evoke a conditioned response (CR), which is often, but not always, similar to the reflexive response. Operant conditioning is the increase or decrease in a behavior as a result of reinforcement or punishment. Other forms of learning, such as bird song learning, may fall outside the categories of classical or operant conditioning.

Ivan Pavlov hypothesized that all learning is based on simple neural connections formed between two brain areas active at the same time. Karl Lashley tested this hypothesis by making various cuts that disconnected brain areas from each other and by removing varying amounts of cerebral cortex after rats had learned mazes or discrimination tasks. To his surprise, he found that no particular connection or part of the cortex was critical for any task. Lashley assumed that all learning occurred in the cortex and that all types of learning relied on the same physiological mechanism. Recent evidence suggests that certain subcortical nuclei may be important for specific types of learning and that several different neural mechanisms underlie different types of learning. For example, one simple type of conditioning, the eye-blink response, relies on the lateral interpositus nucleus of the cerebellum. The red nucleus, a midbrain motor center, is necessary for the motor expression of the eye-blink response, but not formation of the memory. Similar mechanisms appear to underlie eye-blink conditioning in rats and in humans.

Memory can be divided into several types: short-term vs. long-term, explicit vs. implicit, and declarative vs. procedural. Short-term memories have relatively low capacity and fade rapidly, unless they are rehearsed. When an item in short-term memory is forgotten, it cannot be reconstructed. Long-term memory has a vast capacity, can be recalled even years later, and can often be reconstructed if an item is forgotten. Working memory is the temporary storage of information while we are using it. Working memory has three components: a "phonological loop" for storing auditory information, a "visuospatial sketchpad" for storing visual information, and a "central executive" that directs attention and determines which items will be stored. The prefrontal cortex seems to be especially important for working memory. A common test of working memory is the delayed response task, in which one must respond to a stimulus presented a short time earlier. Neurons in the prefrontal cortex are active during the delay. Aged monkeys have fewer neurons in the prefrontal cortex. Aging humans with declining memory have declining prefrontal activity, while aging humans with intact memory show greater activity than in young adults.

Information about memory has been obtained from studies of three major syndromes involving amnesia in humans. A main cognitive deficit in all three syndromes is the inability to form new long-term declarative or explicit memories. Declarative memory is memory that people can state in words, whereas procedural memory consists of motor skills. Explicit memory is deliberate recall of information that one recognizes as a memory; implicit memories can be detected as indirect influences on behavior, and do not require recollection of specific information. One syndrome results from hippocampal damage and is exemplified by the patient H. M., who had bilateral removal of the hippocampus to relieve incapacitating epilepsy. Following surgery, H. M. has suffered extensive anterograde amnesia and moderate retrograde amnesia; however, his working memory remains intact. The cases of H. M. and other patients with hippocampal damage suggest that the primary function of the hippocampus is to promote storage of declarative, explicit memory, especially episodic memory—memory for single events or episodes. Nonhuman animals with hippocampal damage show memory impairments on delayed matching tasks, which are somewhat similar to human declarative memory. In addition, they are impaired on tasks that measure spatial memory, suggesting a second hypothesis, that a major function of the hippocampus is spatial memory. Rats with hippocampal damage forget which arms of a radial arm maze they have already entered in search of food; they also forget the location of a platform submerged in murky water. Among related species of birds that live in different habitats, those that are most dependent on finding previously hidden food have the largest hippocampus. Humans also use their hippocampus to solve spatial problems. Apparently, some portions of the hippocampus code spatial information and others code nonspatial aspects. A third hypothesis is that the hippocampus is important for configural learning, in which the meaning of a stimulus depends upon other stimuli that are paired with it. Thus, the hippocampus may bind together the pieces of an experience or lay out a map of where the pieces are stored, so that they can later be remembered together. However, hippocampal damage may also impair nonconfigural learning if it is complicated and difficult.

Another function of the hippocampus is to consolidate short-term memories into long-term memories. Donald Hebb proposed that reverberating circuits of neuronal activity allow the brain enough time to synthesize proteins, grow new connections, or otherwise make long-lasting changes. Electroconvulsive shock was used to disrupt any reverberating circuits, and many memories were, indeed, impaired. However sometimes the procedure impaired memories that were already well established, and other memories that were initially disrupted could be retrieved after a reminder. Highly emotional events are easily remembered because of the effects of epinephrine and cortisol. Small to moderate amounts of cortisol stimulate the amygdala, which in turn activates the hippocampus and cerebral cortex. However, prolonged or excessive stress, and its accompanying high cortisol level, impairs memory.

Another human disorder, Korsakoff's syndrome, occurs almost exclusively in severe alcoholics and is characterized by apathy, confusion, confabulation (accepting guesses as if they were memories), and both retrograde and anterograde amnesia. It is caused by prolonged thiamine deficiency, which results in loss of neurons throughout the brain, especially in the mamillary bodies of the hypothalamus and the dorsomedial thalamus, which projects to prefrontal cortex. In addition to their deficit in explicit memory, Korsakoff's patients have difficulty recalling the temporal order of events. They also confabulate, or make a guess to fill in the memory gaps.

A third human memory disorder is Alzheimer's disease, which is characterized by memory loss, confusion, depression, restlessness, hallucinations, delusions, and loss of sleep and appetite. People with Down syndrome, who have three copies of chromosome 21, almost always get Alzheimer's disease if they survive into middle age. Mutations of other genes account for a small percentage of late-onset Alzheimer's disease. However, half of all patients have no relatives with the disease. Alzheimer's disease is associated with the accumulation of amyloid deposits in the brain. Amyloid precursor protein is normally cleaved to form a smaller protein of 40 amino acids, amyloid-β 40 ($A\beta_{40}$), which probably has a useful function. In people with Alzheimer's disease, the precursor is cleaved to form a slightly larger protein consisting of 42 amino acids ($A\beta_{42}$), which accumulates and damages the membranes of axons and dendrites. Amyloid plaques, formed in the extracellular space from degenerating axons and dendrites, lead to atrophy of the cerebral cortex, hippocampus, and other areas. An abnormal form of tau protein, which forms part of the intracellular support structure of neurons, also accumulates in Alzheimer's patients, forming tangles within cell bodies. The brains of Alzheimer's victims reveal widespread neural degeneration, including loss of acetylcholine neurons in the basal forebrain, which leads to impaired attention and arousal. Drugs that stimulate acetylcholine receptors or prolong acetylcholine release may help to relieve symptoms. Stimulation of cannabinoid receptors can limit overstimulation of glutamate receptors, thereby protecting neurons. Antioxidants and curcumin (a component of Indian curry) may block amyloid-β formation and guard against brain degeneration. Vaccination against $A\beta_{42}$ may someday be used to avoid Alzheimer's disease. One lesson from amnesic patients is that there are somewhat independent kinds of memory that depend on different brain areas.

Many researchers have studied the cellular mechanisms of learning in invertebrates, which have simple, well-defined nervous systems. Studies using Aplysia have demonstrated changes in identified synapses during habituation and sensitization. Long-term potentiation (LTP) is increased synaptic responsiveness in cells of the mammalian hippocampus. LTP shows specificity, in that only the active synapses become strengthened. It also shows cooperativity, in which near simultaneous stimulation by two or more axons increases responsiveness. A third characteristic is associativity, which refers to the increased responsiveness to a weak stimulus as a result of its being paired with a strong stimulus. The opposite change, long term depression (LTD), occurs in both the hippocampus and cerebellum. It is a decrease in responsiveness to a synaptic input that has been repeatedly paired with another input at low frequency. LTP depends on stimulation of two types of glutamate receptors. Stimulation of AMPA receptors depolarizes the neuron, thereby displacing the magnesium ions that normally block the ion channels of nearby NMDA receptors. As a result, the NMDA receptors are able to respond to glutamate, allowing both sodium and calcium ions to enter the cell. The calcium, in turn, activates certain chemicals and genes inside the postsynaptic neuron. These changes result in either increased numbers or responsiveness of AMPA or NMDA receptors and increased dendritic branches. Finally, a retrograde neurotransmitter may increase the responsiveness and size of presynaptic terminals and increase the number of transmitter release sites. Genetic alterations producing abnormal NMDA receptors result in impaired learning in mice, whereas alterations producing excess NMDA receptors result in better than normal memory. Other mice that overproduce the protein GAP-43 in the presynaptic neuron also show enhanced ability to learn and solve problems. Drugs that enhance LTP also enhance memory. For example, caffeine increases arousal and enhances memory, and drugs that facilitate acetylcholine in people with Alzheimer's disease also result in increased memory. Finally, ginko biloba and other "natural" drugs touted to enhance memory do increase blood flow and produce small benefits, but only in those with circulatory problems.

Learning Objectives

Module 13.1 Learning, Memory, Amnesia, and Brain Functioning

1. Know the differences between classical and operant conditioning and the terms used in each.

2. Be able to describe Lashley's search for the engram and his conclusions and why Richard Thompson's search arrived at a different conclusion.

3. Know the characteristics of short-term and long-term memory and a current theory of working memory.

4. Be able to describe the theories of the function of the hippocampus in declarative memory, spatial memory, configural learning, and consolidation.

5. Know the symptoms and causes of Korsakoff's syndrome and Alzheimer's disease.

Module 13.2 Storing Information in the Nervous System

1. Understand the mechanisms of habituation and sensitization in Aplysia.

2. Be able to describe the characteristics of long-term potentiation (LTP) and long-term depression (LTD).

3. Understand the roles of AMPA and NMDA receptors in LTP.

Key Terms and Concepts

Module 13.1 Learning, Memory, Amnesia, and Brain Functioning

1. Localized representations of memory

   Classical conditioning

   Ivan Pavlov
   Conditioned stimulus (CS)

Unconditioned stimulus (UCS)
Unconditioned response (UCR)
Conditioned response (CR)

Operant conditioning

Reinforcer
Punishment

Bird-song learning: Neither classical nor operant

Lashley's search for the engram

Engram: Physical representation of what has been learned
Amount of damage, not location

Equipotentiality: All parts of cortex contribute equally to complex behaviors
Mass action: Cortex works as a whole
Unnecessary assumptions:

Cerebral cortex is the only site of the engram
All kinds of memory are the same

The modern search for the engram

Richard F. Thompson

Rabbit eye-blink response
Lateral interpositus (LIP) nucleus of cerebellum: Site of conditioning

Last structure in the circuit that had to be awake during conditioning
Red nucleus: Motor expression
Classical conditioning of eye-blink in humans

PET scans: increased activity in cerebellum, red nucleus, and other areas
Damage to cerebellum → impaired eye-blink conditioning

2. Types of memory

Short-term and long-term memory

Donald Hebb

Short-term memory

Seven unrelated items
Fades quickly without rehearsal or meaningful context
Once forgotten, it is lost
Long-term memory

Vast capacity
Hints → reconstruction of memory

Working memory

Weakened distinction between short-term and long-term memory

Phonological loop: Stores auditory information

Visuospatial sketchpad: Stores visual information

Central executive: Directs attention and picks items for storage

Delayed response task

Dorsolateral prefrontal cortex → high activity during delay → working memory

Older people

Declining activity in prefrontal cortex → impaired working memory

Those with intact memory: Greater activity than young adults

Stimulant drugs → enhanced activity in prefrontal cortex of aging monkeys → improved memory

3. The hippocampus and amnesia

Amnesia: Memory loss

Amnesia after hippocampal damage

H. M.: Surgery for severe epilepsy

Severe anterograde amnesia (loss of memory for events after surgery)

Moderate retrograde amnesia (loss of memory for events shortly before surgery)

Normal short-term or working memory

No episodic memories (memories of single events)

A few weak semantic (factual) memories

Improvement with repeated practice if linked to something he already knew

Severe anterograde declarative memory (ability to state memory in words)

Intact procedural memory (development of motor skills)

Improvement on Gollins picture test

Distinction between declarative and procedural memory not firm

Better implicit than explicit memory

Explicit memory: Deliberate recall of information one recognizes as a memory

Implicit memory: Influence of recent experience on behavior, even without realizing one is using memory

Individual differences in hippocampus and memory

Children, adolescents, and young adults: Smaller hippocampus → better memory

Hypothesis: Apoptosis weeds out ineffective neurons

Older adults: Inconsistent results regarding size of hippocampus

Hippocampal activity

Gene that controls BDNF (a neurotrophin)

Performance better with valine at one location, rather than methionine

Theories of the function of the hippocampus

    The hippocampus and declarative memory

        Damage to the hippocampus in rats

            Impairs memory of when they smelled an odor

        Damage to the hippocampus in monkeys

            Delayed matching-to-sample test: Impaired

            Delayed nonmatching-to-sample test: Impaired

            Minor procedural changes: Variable results

                Varied objects in test: Hippocampal damage impairs

                Same two objects: Little effect of lesions

                Interpretation: Hippocampus and entorhinal cortex (input) more important for processing novel stimuli

    The hippocampus and spatial memory

        Rats: Hippocampal neurons tuned to spatial locations

            "Remap" environment after a change

        London taxi drivers

            Hippocampus activated by answering spatial questions

            Posterior hippocampus larger than in other people

        Damage to the hippocampus in humans → impairments on spatial tasks

        Damage to the hippocampus in rats

            Radial maze: Forget which arms they already tried

            Morris search task: Forget location of platform

        Closely related species that differ in spatial memory

            Clark's nutcracker: Most dependent on buried food

                Largest hippocampus

                Best performance on spatial tasks

            Pinyon jays: Moderately dependent on buried food

                Second largest hippocampus

                Second best performance on spatial tasks

            Scrub jay and Mexican jay: Least dependent on buried food

                Smallest hippocampus

                Worst performance on spatial tasks

        Some parts of hippocampus: Nonspatial aspects of task

    The hippocampus, configural learning, and binding

Configural learning: Meaning of a stimulus depends on other stimuli
Hippocampal damage → impaired performance

> Complicated nonconfigural learning: Also impaired
> Hippocampus not necessary for configural learning, but assists

Theory: Hippocampus → quickly record single combination of stimuli

> Cortex → detect repeated combinations
> Hippocampus → Bind pieces of memory together; → map separate pieces

The hippocampus and consolidation

Consolidation of long-term memories
Donald Hebb: Reverberating circuit

> Theory: Electroconvulsive shock → disrupt reverberations that → long term memory
> Problem: Electroconvulsive shock sometimes wiped out much older memories
> Problem: Some "lost" memories later restored by reminders

Emotional events easy to remember

> Epinephrine (adrenalin)
> Cortisol
>
> > Moderate amounts: Amygdala → hippocampus → memory storage
> > Excessive or prolonged → memory impairment
>
> Damage amygdala: Emotional arousal does not enhance storage

Brain works harder to remember more recent events

4. Other types of brain damage and amnesia

Korsakoff's syndrome and other prefrontal damage

Wernicke-Korsakoff syndrome
Prolonged thiamine (vitamin B_1) deficiency

> Chronic alcoholics

Widespread loss of neurons, especially in:

> Mamillary bodies of hypothalamus and
> Dorsomedial thalamus (projects to prefrontal cortex)

Both anterograde and retrograde amnesia, apathy, confusion
Better implicit than explicit memory

> Priming

Poor recall of temporal order of events
Confabulation: Guess to fill in gaps in memory

Alzheimer's disease

Memory loss, confusion, depression, restlessness, hallucinations, delusions, sleeplessness, loss of
appetite

Better procedural than declarative memory

Better implicit than explicit memory

Genetic and nongenetic causes

    Relationship to Down syndrome (3 copies of chromosome 21)

        Genes on chromosome 21 and others linked to early-onset Alzheimer's

        Several genes linked to late-onset Alzheimer's: Account for small percentage of cases

        Half of patients: No known relatives with Alzheimer's

    Cross-cultural differences

        Yoruba people of Nigeria: Low-calorie, low-fat, low-sodium diet → low risk

    Amyloid precursor protein → amyloid beta protein 40 (amyloid-β, or $A\beta_{40}$)

        Alzheimer's disease: Amyloid beta protein 42 ($A\beta_{42}$, longer form, impairs function)

        Amyloid plaques (degenerating axons and dendrites in space between neurons) → atrophy of cerebral cortex, hippocampus, other areas

    Tau protein: Part of intracellular support

        Abnormal tau → tangles (degeneration within cell bodies)

    Main problem: Probably amyloid-β, though tau contributes

Widespread atrophy

    Loss of acetylcholine neurons in basal forebrain → impaired attention, arousal

Prevention or alleviation

    Stimulate acetylcholine receptors or prolong acetylcholine release

    Stimulate cannabinoid receptors → limits overstimulation of glutamate receptors

    Block formation of amyloid-β

    Antioxidants: Dark fruits and vegetables

    Curcumin (component of turmeric, in Indian curry)

    "Vaccinate" with amyloid-β

        Inject young mice with a little $A\beta_{42}$ → immune attack → no Alzheimer's

        Similar effect in some people

        Life-threatening side effects in a few people → research stopped

What amnesic patients teach us

    Somewhat independent kinds of memory: Dependent on different brain areas

5. In closing: Different types of memory

    "Overall intelligence" as measured by IQ tests: Convenient fiction

    Different abilities: Different brain processes

Module 13.2 Storing Information in the Nervous System

1. Blind alleys and abandoned mines

    Wilder Penfield: Each neuron stores particular memory

    "Memories" vague, not accurate

    G. A. Horridge: "Learning" in decapitated cockroaches

    Process slow, variable

    James McConnell and others: Transfer of memories by feeding or injecting "trained" RNA

    Variable results

2. Learning and the Hebbian synapse

    Simultaneous pre- and postsynaptic activity → increased synaptic efficiency

3. Single-cell mechanisms of invertebrate behavior change

    Aplysia as an experimental animal

    Plasticity
    Touch siphon, mantle, or gill → withdrawal response

    Habituation in Aplysia

    Decreased ability of sensory neuron to activate motor neuron

    Sensitization in Aplysia

    Increase in response to mild stimuli after more intense stimuli
    Facilitating interneuron: Serotonin (5-HT) → presynaptic terminals of many sensory neurons
    Presynaptic receptors → closing of potassium channels → prolonged action potential → more
        transmitter release
    Protein synthesis → long-term sensitization

4. Long-term potentiation in mammals (LTP)

    Brief but rapid series of stimuli → increased responsiveness for minutes, days, or weeks

    Characteristics

    Specificity: Only active synapses strengthened
    Cooperativity: Nearly simultaneous stimuli more effective than single stimuli
    Associativity: Pairing weak and strong inputs → enhanced later response to weaker one

    Long term depression (LTD) in hippocampus and cerebellum

    LTD: Prolonged decrease in response to inputs presented at low frequencies

    LTP in one synapse → decreased responsiveness in neighbors

    Biochemical mechanisms

Actions at AMPA and NMDA synapses

AMPA glutamate receptors

Open sodium channels

NMDA glutamate receptors: Depends on degree of polarization across membrane

Magnesium blockade of ion channel

Removal of magnesium by depolarization

Sodium and calcium influx into postsynaptic neuron

Calcium → activation of genes and many chemicals →

Increase in later responsiveness to glutamate

CaMKII (α-calcium-calmodulin-dependent protein kinase II) activation →

New AMPA receptors or old ones moved to better location

New NMDA receptors

Dendrite: New branches

Some AMPA receptors: More responsive

LTD: Opposite of LTP

NMDA receptors: Establish, not maintain, LTP

Presynaptic changes

Retrograde neurotransmitter → presynaptic neuron →

Decrease threshold for action potentials

Increase neurotransmitter release

Expand its axon

Release transmitter from additional sites on axon

LTP and behavior

Genes causing abnormal NMDA receptors → slow learning in mice

Genes causing extra NMDA receptors → better learning in mice

LTP → GAP-43 in presynaptic neuron → better learning

Similar effects of drugs on LTP and on memory

Caffeine → arousal → memory

Alzheimer's disease: Drugs that facilitate acetylcholine → memory

Increase in dopamine or glutamate may → memory

Ginko biloba and other chemicals → increase blood flow → small benefits in those with circulatory problems

5. In closing: The physiology of memory

Requirement of memory: Record what we need to remember, not everything

Short-Answer Questions

Module 13.1 Learning, Memory, Amnesia, and Brain Functioning

1. *Localized representations of memory*

   a. Describe the relationships among the conditioned and unconditioned stimuli and the unconditioned and conditioned responses in classical conditioning.

   b. Who discovered classical conditioning? What were the conditioned and unconditioned stimuli in his experiments? What was the unconditioned, and eventually the conditioned, response?

   c. What is the fundamental difference between classical and operant conditioning? Define reinforcement and punishment in terms of operant conditioning.

   d. Why is bird-song learning difficult to classify?

   e. What is an engram? What two principles did Lashley propose based on his search for the engram?

   f. What two assumptions did Lashley make, which later investigators rejected?

   g. What brain area was found by Richard F. Thompson to be important for classical conditioning of the eye-blink response in rabbits?

   h. What area was important for the expression of the motor response, but not for the initial conditioning?

   i. Which areas showed increased activity on PET scans during eye-blink conditioning in humans?

2. *Types of memory*

   a. Define short-term memory and long-term memory.

   b. What is working memory? What are its three hypothesized components?

   c. What is the delayed response task? Which brain area is especially important for performance on this task?

   d. Compare activity in the prefrontal cortex in older people who have declining memory with that of young adults. Describe prefrontal activity in older people who have intact memory.

3. *The hippocampus and amnesia*

   a. Why was H. M.'s hippocampus removed bilaterally? How successful was this treatment at relieving epilepsy? What were the other effects of the surgery?

   b. What is the difference between retrograde and anterograde amnesia? Which is more evident in H. M.?

   c. What is episodic memory? How was that affected by HM's surgery?

   d. Distinguish between declarative and procedural memory. Which is impaired in H. M.? What is a test for procedural memory?

e. Distinguish between explicit memory and implicit memory. What is one test of implicit memory?

f. What can we say about the relationship of memory to hippocampal size? Hippocampal activity?

g. For what three types of memory is the hippocampus hypothesized to be important?

h. Describe the delayed matching-to-sample and delayed nonmatching-to-sample tasks.

i. Under what conditions does hippocampal damage impair performance on matching- or nonmatching-to-sample tasks?

j. What type of memory is tested by the radial maze and the Morris search task? What two kinds of errors can rats make in the radial maze? Which type of error do rats make after damage to the hippocampus?

k. Describe the Morris search task. What deficits on this task are seen in hippocampally damaged rats?

l. Describe the relationship between birds' dependence on finding previously hidden food and the size of their hippocampus.

m. What is configural learning? Describe the likely role of the hippocampus in configural learning.

n. How did Donald Hebb explain consolidation?

o. What problems were encountered with the interpretation of experiments using electroconvulsive shock?

p. How do exciting experiences enhance memory consolidation?

q. What brain areas are stimulated by the amygdala after an emotional experience? What is the effect of long term or excessive stress?

r. Which ages are considered the "autobiographical memory bump?" Are events remembered better or worse during these ages?

4. *Other types of brain damage and amnesia*

a. What is the immediate cause of Korsakoff's syndrome? What are its symptoms? In what group of people does it usually occur?

b. Which brain areas show neuronal loss in Korsakoff's syndrome?

c. Describe the symptoms of Korsakoff's syndrome in terms of anterograde vs. retrograde amnesia and explicit vs. implicit memory. What is priming, and what type of memory can show priming effects?

d. What symptoms do Korsakoff's patients have in common with patients with frontal-lobe damage?

e. What is confabulation? On what kind of questions do people with Korsakoff's syndrome confabulate?

f. Describe the symptoms of Alzheimer's disease.

g. Why are some cases of early-onset Alzheimer's disease thought to be related to a gene on chromosome 21?

h. How important are genetic factors in late-onset Alzheimer's disease?

i.   What is amyloid precursor protein? What are the two forms of amyloid beta protein? Which form is implicated in the formation of amyloid deposits?

j.   What other protein is implicated in Alzheimer's disease? What is its normal function? What is the relative importance of these two proteins in causing the disease?

k.   Which brain area is a prominent site of atrophy in Alzheimer's disease? What physical signs are present in areas of atrophy?

l.   What are two temporary means of alleviating Alzheimer's disease? What dietary factors may guard against Alzheimer's disease?

m.   What have we learned about memory from amnesic patients?

Module 13.2 Storing Information in the Nervous System

1.   *Blind alleys and abandoned mines*

a.   What did Wilder Penfield conclude from his brain stimulation experiments? What are some problems with his conclusion?

b.   Describe G. A. Horridge's experiments with headless cockroaches. Why was this experimental approach abandoned?

c.   Describe the experiments in planaria and rats that seemed to show transfer of training from one individual to another via RNA or protein. Why were these experiments abandoned?

2.   *Learning and the Hebbian synapse*

a.   How did Donald Hebb explain consolidation?

b.   What is a Hebbian synapse? How is it related to classical conditioning?

c.   What problems were encountered with the interpretation of experiments using electroconvulsive shock?

d.   How do exciting experiences enhance memory consolidation?

e.   What brain areas are stimulated by the amygdala after an emotional experience? What is the effect of long term or excessive stress?

f.   Single-cell mechanisms of invertebrate behavior change

g.   Why should anyone be interested in the cellular mechanisms of habituation or sensitization in the lowly Aplysia?

h.   What possible mechanisms of habituation were ruled out? What mechanism does seem to account for habituation in Aplysia?

i.   How is sensitization produced experimentally in Aplysia?

j.   Describe the cellular events that explain sensitization in Aplysia. How does a decrease in potassium outflow increase transmitter release?

k.   How does long-term sensitization differ from the short-term variety?

3. *Long-term potentiation in mammals*

   a. How is long-term potentiation (LTP) produced? How long does it last? In what brain area was it first discovered?

   b. What is meant by specificity? Cooperativity? Associativity?

   c. What is long term depression (LTD)? Where has it been observed? How does it differ from LTP?

   d. Which transmitter stimulates both NMDA and AMPA receptors? Why must AMPA receptors be stimulated, in addition to NMDA receptors, in order to produce LTP?

   e. Describe the sequence of events that follows the successful activation of NMDA receptors.

   f. What is CaMKII?

   g. List four changes in the postsynaptic neuron that contribute to LTP.

   h. Are NMDA receptors important for the establishment or maintenance of LTP?

   i. What is a retrograde neurotransmitter? What changes in the presynaptic terminal may contribute to LTP?

   j. What kinds of experiments have shown the relevance of NMDA receptors for establishing memories in intact organisms?

   k. What is GAP-43? What is the effect of a genetic mutation that results in overproduction of this protein?

   l. What kinds of drugs can enhance memory?

   m. How beneficial is ginko biloba to memory? What is its mechanism of action? In what group of people is it beneficial?

True/False Questions

1. In some classical conditioning experiments the UR resembles the UCR, and in other cases it does not.

   TRUE or FALSE

2. Lashley proposed the principles of Equipotentiality and Mass Action.

   TRUE or FALSE

3. Richard F. Thompson presented data showing that Lashley's principles were indeed true.

   TRUE or FALSE

4. Donald Hebb successfully showed that electroconvulsive shock completely prevented consolidation of new memories into long-term storage, but never affected older memories; furthermore, the "lost" memories could never be restored.

   TRUE or FALSE

5. Working memory is thought to have three components: a phonological loop, a visuospatial sketchpad, and the central executive.

   TRUE or FALSE

6. During the delayed response task in monkeys, activity in the amygdala is especially high, because the amygdala is the main site for working memory.

   TRUE or FALSE

7. H. M.'s major problems are severe retrograde amnesia and deficits in implicit memory.

   TRUE or FALSE

8. A *smaller* hippocampus was correlated with better memory in children, adolescents, and young adults, but the relationship was less clear in older adults.

   TRUE or FALSE

9. The hippocampus may quickly record single combinations of stimuli and bind the pieces of memory together, whereas the cortex requires repeated presentation of those combinations in order to form long-term memories of them.

   TRUE or FALSE

10. London taxi drivers have especially large amygdalas, which help them find their way around the city.

    TRUE or FALSE

11. Korsakoff's syndrome is characterized by widespread loss of neurons, especially in the mamillary bodies of the hypothalamus and the dorsomedial thalamus.

    TRUE or FALSE

12. Early-onset Alzheimer's disease is primarily caused by thiamine deficiency, as a result of prolonged heavy drinking.

    TRUE or FALSE

13. Decapitated cockroaches show very impressive "learning" when injected with "trained" RNA from intact cockroaches.

    TRUE or FALSE

14. Aplysia show sensitization when serotonin from a facilitating interneuron closes potassium channels on presynaptic terminals of sensory neurons, thereby prolonging the action potential and releasing more neurotransmitter.

    TRUE or FALSE

15. The influx of magnesium through NMDA receptors triggers many intracellular changes that result in LTP.

    TRUE or FALSE

16. Activation of CaMKII sets in motion many processes, including increasing AMPA and/or NMDA receptors, growing more dendritic branches, and increasing responsiveness of some AMPA receptors.
    TRUE or FALSE

17. Activation of NMDA receptors is necessary for both establishing and maintaining LTP.
    TRUE or FALSE

18. In some cases LTP depends on changes in the presynaptic neuron, produced by a retrograde transmitter.
    TRUE or FALSE

Fill In The Blanks

1. In _____ conditioning the individual's response determines the outcome; in _____ conditioning the CS and UCS are presented independently of the individual's behavior.

2. An _____ is the physical representation of what has been learned.

3. The _____ of the cerebellum is the site of conditioning of the eye-blink response. The _____ is required for motor expression of this response.

4. The _____ stores auditory information; the _____ stores visual information; and the _____ directs attention and picks items for storage.

5. The deliberate recall of information one recognizes as a memory is _____ memory.

6. HM shows severe _____ amnesia and moderate _____ amnesia.

7. Damage to the hippocampus impairs _____ memory, _____ memory, and _____ learning.

8. During emotional situations moderate increases in the hormone _____ activate the _____ , which relays the information to the _____ and _____ .

9. _____ syndrome results from thiamine deficiency, which causes widespread loss of neurons, especially in the _____ of the hypothalamus and the _____ thalamus, which projects to the prefrontal cortex.

10. Alzheimer's disease is characterized by _____ , formed from degenerating axons and dendrites, and _____ , resulting from abnormal _____ protein, which normally forms part of the intracellular support network.

11. Some possible means of preventing or alleviating Alzheimer's disease are stimulating _____ or _____ receptors, blocking the formation of amyloid-β, and including _____ or _____ in the diet.

12. The main difference between LTP and LTD is the _____ of stimulation of the two inputs.

13. Stimulation of AMPA receptors is needed to remove the _____ ions that normally block the ion channels of NMDA receptors.

14. LTP may increase the number of _____ and/or _____ receptors, increase _____ , and increase sensitivity of some _____ receptors.

15. A _____ neurotransmitter from the postsynaptic neuron to the presynaptic neuron may decrease the threshold for _____ , increase _____ release, expand the size of the _____ , and increase the number of sites of transmitter release.

16. Genes that result in extra _____ receptors or overproduction of _____ result in better than normal learning and memory.

17. _____ increases blood flow in people with circulatory problems and may thereby produce small increases in memory.

Matching Items

1.	_____ Bird song learning	a.	Hebb: basis of consolidation
2.	_____ Mass action	b.	Site of eye-blink conditioning
3.	_____ Lateral interpositus nucleus	c.	Lashley: Cortex works as a whole
4.	_____ Reverberating circuits	d.	Moderate amounts facilitate memory
5.	_____ Cortisol	e.	Severe anterograde amnesia
6.	_____ Phonological loop	f.	Neither classical nor operant conditioning
7.	_____ Dorsolateral prefrontal cortex	g.	Responses tuned to spatial locations
8.	_____ H. M.	h.	$A\beta_{42}$, abnormal Tau, plaques, and tangles
9.	_____ Rat hippocampal neurons	i.	Stores auditory information
10.	_____ Korsakoff syndrome	j.	Severe thiamine deficiency
11.	_____ Alzheimer's disease	k.	Site of working memory
12.	_____ Aplysia sensitization	l.	Protein in the presynaptic neuron that enhances learning
13.	_____ NMDA receptors	m.	Serotonin from facilitating interneurons
14.	_____ GAP-43	n.	Establish, not maintain, LTP

Multiple-Choice Questions

1. In classical conditioning
   a. the meat used by Pavlov was the conditioned stimulus.
   b. the learner's behavior controls the presentation of reinforcements and punishments.
   c. a stimulus comes to elicit a response that may be similar to a response elicited by another stimulus.
   d. bird-song learning can be fully explained in terms of CS and UCS.

2. Ivan Pavlov showed that
   a. after some pairings of the CS and the UCS, the individual begins to make a new, learned response to the CS.
   b. all parts of the cortex contribute equally to complex learning.
   c. the cortex works as a whole—the more cortex, the better.
   d. learning occurs when cells in the UCS center degenerate and cells in the CS center branch diffusely.

3. Lashley successfully demonstrated that
   a. the lateral interpositus nucleus is the site of all engrams.
   b. all learning takes place in the cerebral cortex.
   c. the same neural mechanisms underlie all types of learning.
   d. none of the above.

4. The lateral interpositus nucleus of the cerebellum
   a. is important for the motor expression of eye-blink conditioning in rabbits, but not the actual conditioning.
   b. is important for the actual conditioning of the eyelid response.
   c. is more important for explicit than implicit memory formation.
   d. is an area that shows a great deal of damage in Korsakoff's syndrome.

5. Hebb's distinction between short-term and long-term memory
   a. was initially supported by data showing that electroconvulsive shock disrupted the reverberating circuits that stored short-term memories during the process of consolidation into long-term memories; however, problems later arose with those experiments.
   b. is supported by data showing that short-term memories are stored in the amygdala and long-term memories are stored in the lateral interpositus nucleus of the cerebellum.
   c. has been rejected by researchers because short-term and long-term memory merge so gradually that they are considered to be a single type of memory.
   d. has recently been attributed to Pavlov, instead of Hebb.

6. Working memory consists of
   a. a phonological loop.
   b. a visuospatial sketchpad.
   c. a central executive.
   d. all of the above.

7. The delayed response task for monkeys
   a. showed that visual memories are stored in primary visual cortex.
   b. showed that high activity in prefrontal cortex during the delay was correlated with successful performance on the task, suggesting that this area does store working memory.
   c. showed that cells in the prefrontal cortex are more important for initiating movement than for storing information about the stimulus.
   d. is no longer used as a test for working memory.

8. H. M.
   a. had his hippocampus removed because of his uncontrollable violence.
   b. acquired severe epilepsy as a result of the surgery.
   c. has a terrific memory for numbers but can learn no new skills.
   d. has more severe problems with declarative than with procedural memory.

9. Which of the following statements applies to H. M.?
   a. He has more severe anterograde than retrograde amnesia.
   b. He has more trouble with implicit than with explicit memory.
   c. His deficits show that the hippocampus is the storage site for all factual memories.
   d. All of the above are true.

10. Your memory of what you had for dinner last night is an example of
    a. explicit memory.
    b. implicit memory.
    c. procedural memory.
    d. short-term memory.

11. Priming is useful for
    a. producing memory consolidation.
    b. testing short-term memory.
    c. testing implicit memory.
    d. testing explicit memory.

12. Damage to the hippocampus produces impairment on tasks requiring
    a. declarative, explicit memory.
    b. configural learning and complicated nonconfigural learning.
    c. spatial memory.
    d. all of the above.

13. Damage to the hippocampus results in
    a. rats going down a never-correct arm of the radial maze.
    b. rats forgetting which arms they have already explored.
    c. inability to climb onto a platform in the Morris search task because of motor impairment.
    d. monkeys that cannot choose a nonmatching stimulus under any conditions.

14. Which of the following is true?
    a. Clark's nutcracker birds are very dependent on previously hidden food and have a large hippocampus.
    b. Mexican jays are also dependent on previously hidden food, but have a small hippocampus.
    c. The use of color memory in solving problems is a better predictor of hippocampal size than is dependence on previously hidden food.
    d. Hippocampal damage impairs performance on all tasks that use spatial memory, but does not impair any other tasks.

15. Experiments on consolidation have shown that
    a. after electroconvulsive shock, all memories from the previous several days are totally lost and cannot be retrieved.
    b. more brain activity may be required to remember recent events than those that were consolidated years ago.
    c. prolonged high elevations of cortisol levels are even more effective than brief moderate elevations for promoting memory storage.
    d. all of the above are true.

16. Which of the following is true?
    a. Electroconvulsive shock increases memory formation by causing circuits to reverberate.
    b. Testing rats in the Morris water maze is difficult, because rats enjoy swimming so much that they don't try to find the hidden platform.
    c. The role of the hippocampus in configural learning may be to bind the various pieces of the experience or lay out a map of where the pieces are stored.
    d. Recent experiments show that the hippocampus is important only for spatial memories.

17. Korsakoff's syndrome
    a. occurs because alcohol dissolves proteins in the brain, thereby shrinking presynaptic endings.
    b. is caused by prolonged thiamine deficiency.
    c. results from damage primarily to the hippocampus.
    d. all of the above.

18. Patients with Korsakoff's syndrome
    a. have damage in the mamillary bodies of the hypothalamus and the dorsomedial nucleus of the thalamus, which projects to prefrontal cortex.
    b. have symptoms somewhat similar to those of patients with damage to the prefrontal cortex.
    c. have better implicit memory than explicit memory.
    d. all of the above.

19. Alzheimer's disease
    a. results from three copies of chromosome 21.
    b. results from a long history of excessive alcohol consumption.
    c. occurs much less frequently in the Yoruba people of Nigeria than in Americans, probably because of their low-fat, low-calorie, low-sodium diet.
    d. have too much GAP-43, which is a particularly destructive chemical.

20. Patients with Alzheimer's disease
    a. have plaques and tangles in damaged areas of their brains.
    b. unlike H. M. and Korsakoff's patients, have more problems with implicit than explicit memory.
    c. have a nearly 100% probability of passing the disease on to their offspring.
    d. all of the above.

21. Which of the following is true concerning Alzheimer's disease?
    a. Amyloid precursor protein can be cleaved to produce amyloid beta protein 42 ($A\beta_{42}$), which accumulates in the brain and impairs the function of neurons.
    b. An abnormal form of the tau protein, which forms part of the intracellular support structure in neurons, also accumulates in Alzheimer's patients.
    c. Certain genes have been implicated in either early- or late-onset Alzheimer's disease.
    d. All of the above are true.

22. Techniques for alleviating or preventing Alzheimer's disease include
    a. totally avoiding curcumin, an ingredient in Indian curry.
    b. eating a diet rich in antioxidants.
    c. giving drugs that block acetylcholine receptors or decrease acetylcholine release.
    d. injecting large amounts of $A\beta_{42}$ into the brains of aging people.

23. Donald Hebb proposed that
    a. a cellular basis of memory is the strengthening of synapses by simultaneous activity in the pre- and postsynaptic neurons.
    b. having two different axons stimulating a given dendrite at the same time is confusing to the dendrite and leads to long-term depression.
    c. short-term and long-term memory are the same thing.
    d. Hebbian synapses can explain operant, but not classical, conditioning.

24. Aplysia are studied because
    a. they are the intellectual giants of the ocean.
    b. they have simple nervous systems with large neurons that are virtually identical among individuals.
    c. they have the most complex brains of all invertebrates.
    d. we can automatically infer the principles of learning in complex vertebrates.

25. Habituation in Aplysia is the result of
    a. a decrease in the firing rate of a facilitating interneuron.
    b. a decrease in the firing rate of the sensory neuron.
    c. decreased ability of the sensory neuron to activate the motor neuron.
    d. muscle fatigue.

26. The mechanism mediating sensitization in Aplysia includes
    a. the release of dopamine from the sensory neuron onto the facilitating interneuron.
    b. the release of serotonin by the sensory neuron onto the motor neuron.
    c. release of serotonin by the facilitating interneuron onto the presynaptic terminals of sensory neurons → decreased potassium outflow in the sensory neurons → prolongation of transmitter release.
    d. synthesis of new proteins in short-term, but not long-term sensitization.

27. Long-term potentiation (LTP)
    a. was first discovered in Aplysia.
    b. results from increased inflow of magnesium through AMPA receptors.
    c. requires depolarization via NMDA receptors in order to allow calcium outflow through AMPA receptors.
    d. requires depolarization via AMPA receptors in order to dislodge magnesium ions from NMDA receptors.

28. LTP
    a. is very powerful but lasts only a few seconds.
    b. may result from increased responsiveness of AMPA receptors, increased numbers of AMPA or NMDA receptors, and/or increased dendritic branching.
    c. depends on NMDA receptors for its maintenance, but not for its establishment.
    d. may result from decreased sensitivity of the postsynaptic cell to the inhibitory transmitter glutamate.

29. Presynaptic changes in LTP
    a. are mediated by a retrograde neurotransmitter.
    b. may include a decreased threshold for action potentials and increased transmitter release.
    c. may include expansion of axons and release of transmitter from new sites on the axon.
    d. all of the above.

30. Which of the following is evidence for the relevance of LTP to behavior?
    a. Abnormalities in the gene for NMDA receptors impaired memory.
    b. Genes that resulted in excess NMDA receptors also impaired memory.
    c. Overproduction of GAP-43 impaired memory.
    d. Ginko biloba is one of the best facilitators yet discovered for memory.

Crossword Puzzle

Emotions and Memories

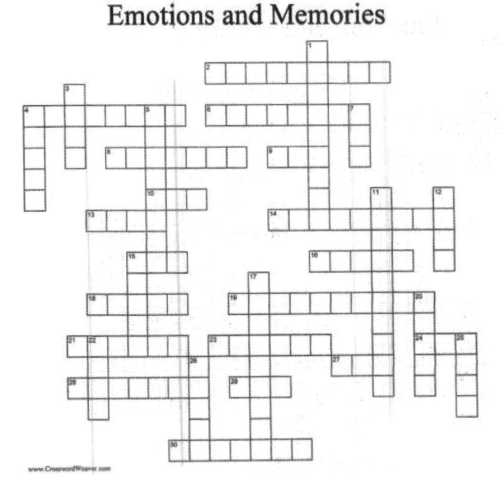

www.CrosswordWeaver.com

ACROSS

2 Transmitter that may inhibit aggressiveness
4 Lobe in which epilepsy leads to hallucinations, lip smacking, repetitive acts, and, in a few people, intermittent explosive disorder
6 Hormone released during stress; can damage the hippocampus and inhibit immune system if present in high levels for a prolonged time
8 A protein, one form of which forms plaques, which lead to atrophy of the cerebral cortex, hippocampus and other brain areas
9 Excitatory transmitter in the amygdala (abbr.)
10 An endozepine; may increase fearfulness and aggression (abbr.)
13 5-____: metabolite of serotonin, used as measure of serotonin turnover (abbr.)
14 Type of memory that does not change from time to time
15 Behavior system mostly in left hemisphere, characterized by low to moderate arousal, pleasant mood, and tendency to approach new objects (abbr.)
16 _____-Lange: theory that appraisal leads to action, followed by emotional feeling
18 Immune system cell that produces antibodies
19 Disease with symptoms of impaired memory formation, plaques and tangles, and general neural degeneration
21 Researcher who studied classical conditioning in dogs
23 Area of cortex that mediates disgust
24 Prolonged increase in responsiveness following brief but rapid series of electrical stimuli (abbr.)
27 A protein that is part of intracellular support; an abnormal form leads to tangles within cells and contributes to Alzheimer's disease
28 Small marine invertebrate studied for single cell mechanisms of learning

29 Behavior system mostly in right hemisphere, characterized by increased attention and arousal, decreased action, and increased fear and disgust (abbr.)
30 Researcher who searched for the engram

DOWN

1 Syndrome in alcoholics in which memory consolidation is impaired
3 Glutamate receptor normally blocked by magnesium; if activated it allows calcium influx, which leads to long term potentiation (abbr.)
4 Immune system cell that matures in the thymus; may attack intruder or stimulate other immune system cells to multiply
5 Brain area, damage to which decreases fear and the ability to interpret emotional stimuli
7 Prolonged decrease in response to input presented at low frequencies (abbr.)
11 Site of neurons in interpositus nucleus that mediate eyeblink conditioning
12 Researcher who proposed that reverberating circuits mediate consolidation of memories
15 Type of leukocyte that produces antibodies
17 Type of conditioning based on stimulus-stimulus associations
20 Pioneer of stress research; proposed general adaptation syndrome
22 Glutamate receptor that opens a sodium channel; may become more responsive or move to better location as part of long term potentiation (abbr.)
25 Disorder characterized by flashbacks and nightmares, avoidance of reminders, exaggerated arousal responses to noises (abbr.)
26 Receptor complex associated with a chloride channel; activated by benzodiazepines (abbr.)

Crossword Puzzle Solution

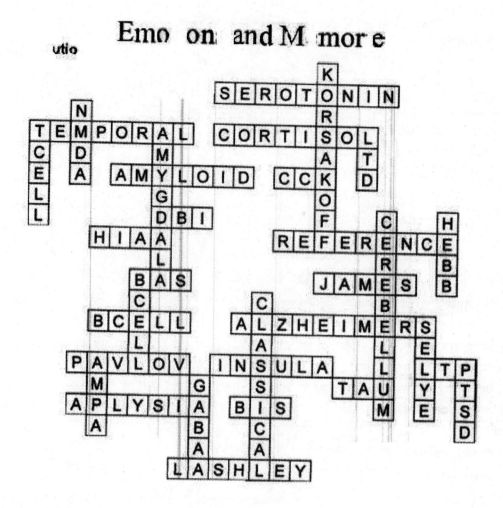

Emotion and Memory

Solutions

True/False Questions

1. T
2. T
3. F
4. F
5. T
6. F

7. F
8. T
9. T
10. F
11. T
12. F

13. F
14. T
15. F
16. T
17. F
18. T

Fill In The Blanks

1. operant; classical
2. engram
3. lateral interpositus nucleus; red nucleus
4. phonological loop; visuospatial sketchpad; central executive
5. explicit
6. anterograde; retrograde
7. declarative; spatial; configural
8. cortisol; amygdala; hippocampus; cerebral cortex
9. Korsakoff's; mamillary bodies; dorsomedial
10. plaques; tangles; tau
11. acetylcholine; cannabinoid; antioxidants; curcumin
12. frequency
13. magnesium
14. AMPA ; NMDA; dendrite branching; AMPA
15. retrograde; action potentials; neurotransmitter; axon
16. NMDA; GAP-43
17. Ginko biloba

Matching Items

1. F
2. C
3. B
4. A
5. D
6. I

7. K
8. E
9. G
10. J
11. H
12. M

13. N
14. L

Multiple-Choice Questions

1.	C	11.	C	21.	D
2.	A	12.	D	22.	B
3.	D	13.	B	23.	A
4.	B	14.	A	24.	B
5.	A	15.	B	25.	C
6.	D	16.	C	26.	C
7.	B	17.	B	27.	D
8.	D	18.	D	28.	B
9.	A	19.	C	29.	D
10.	A	20.	A	30.	A

COGNITIVE FUNCTIONS

Introduction

Approximately 90% of people are strongly right-handed. Of the remaining 9 − 10%, most are somewhat ambidextrous, and a few are strongly left-handed. Chimpanzees are also mostly right-handed, especially for communicative gestures. Early damage to the left hemisphere can result in non-right-handedness. A dominant gene predisposes to right-handedness and a clockwise hair whorl; a recessive gene produces random handedness and random hair whorls. Therefore, handedness has a strong genetic component, but environmental factors can modify the genetic predisposition.

Each hemisphere of the brain receives sensory input primarily from the opposite side of the body and controls motor output to that side as well. The hemispheres are connected by a large bundle of fibers, the corpus callosum, as well as several smaller bundles. In humans, the eyes are connected with the brain in such a way that the left half of each retina supplies input to the left hemisphere, and vice versa. Furthermore, the left half of each retina receives input from the right half of the visual field. Therefore, the right half of the visual field projects to the left hemisphere, and vice versa. The auditory system projects bilaterally, although the projection to the opposite side is stronger. This relationship has allowed researchers to test the roles of the two hemispheres in people whose corpus callosum had been severed in order to relieve epilepsy. Such studies have shown that the left hemisphere is specialized for language and details, whereas the right hemisphere is particularly adept at emotional expression and perception, complex spatial problems, and overall patterns. Split-brain people sometimes seem to have two "selves" occupying the same body. In these people each half of the brain processes information and solves problems more or less independently of the other, although cooperation can be learned, thanks to enhanced function of subcortical connections. Even in intact people, evidence for hemispheric specialization can be seen. One possible basis for the lateralization of language functions in the left hemisphere is that in 65 percent of people a portion of the left temporal lobe, the planum temporale, is larger on the left side than on the right. The size difference is apparent even shortly after birth, and is correlated with performance on language tests.

The corpus callosum matures gradually, and experience determines the survival of the axons that make the best functional connections through the corpus callosum. People born without a corpus callosum are different from those who had split-brain surgery in adulthood. They can verbally describe sensory input from either hand and from either visual field. They may rely on greater development of the anterior, hippocampal, and posterior commissures to convey information from one hemisphere to the other. In addition, each hemisphere develops connections to both sides of the body. About 10% of people are either left-handed or ambidextrous; most of them have mixed hemispheric control of speech, though the left is usually dominant. Although there may be hemisphere specialization, almost all tasks require cooperation by both hemispheres. Recovery of language ability after damage to the left hemisphere is variable and depends in part on age at the time of damage and also on the cause and suddenness of the damage. Early damage tends to result in greater reorganization of the right hemisphere for language, whereas any recovery in adulthood tends to be accomplished by reorganization of surviving parts of the left hemisphere. Rasmussen's encephalography progresses slowly and allows the opposite hemisphere to reorganize gradually.

Because new features evolve from older ones that may have served similar functions, researchers have studied the language abilities of our nearest relatives, the chimpanzees. A number of chimpanzees have been taught to communicate with their trainers, a computer, or each other using various nonspoken language systems. However, even after years of training, their linguistic abilities fall far short of those of young children. Bonobos (Pan paniscus, or pygmy chimpanzees) have shown the most impressive linguistic abilities among our primate relatives. They have learned by imitation, have used words to describe objects (as opposed to making a request) or to refer to a past event, and have created original sentences. In addition, some have learned to understand spoken English sentences. Elephants, dolphins, and parrots also show some language-like abilities. Studies of nonhuman language abilities may provide insights about how best to teach language to brain-damaged or autistic people; they may also stimulate consideration of the unique versus shared abilities of humans and of the nature of language. Language may have evolved as a by-product of larger brains and increasing intelligence. However, some people with normal brains and intelligence have severely impaired language. Conversely, people with Williams syndrome have severe mental retardation and abnormally developed brains, but nearly normal language, social, and musical abilities. On some tests they even have better than average abilities. An alternative view is that language arose as an extra brain module. This view is supported by the ease with which children develop language. Indeed, if children do not learn some language when they are young, they will always be disadvantaged. However, much of the brain is involved in language processing, and parts of the brain important for language are also important for memory, music perception and other abilities. Therefore, increasing intelligence may have occurred because of the growing importance of language for social interaction. In general, children learn new languages more easily than do adults, especially pronunciation and unfamiliar grammar. On the other hand, adults are better at memorizing vocabulary.

Paul Broca discovered that damage to an area of the left frontal lobe results in difficulties with language production and with the use of grammatical connectives and other closed-class grammatical forms. People with such damage can usually understand both written and spoken language better than they can produce it, although they do have difficulty understanding the closed class words that they have most trouble producing. Carl Wernicke, on the other hand, described a pattern of deficits almost the opposite of Broca's aphasia: poor language comprehension, anomia (difficulty finding the right word), but articulate (though frequently meaningless) speech. This syndrome results from destruction of an area in the left temporal lobe near the primary auditory cortex. Although Wernicke's area and surrounding areas are specialized for language comprehension, connections to other areas, including the motor cortex, are also important.

Dyslexia, a reading disorder in otherwise normal people, may result from having a bilaterally symmetrical cortex, microscopic abnormalities, weak connections among areas of the left hemisphere, subtle hearing deficits, or differences in attention. There are many kinds of dyslexia, which have different underlying causes. Dysphonetic dyslexics have difficulty sounding out words, whereas dyseidetic dyslexics have trouble recognizing words as a whole. Some dyslexics' reading ability may be improved by focusing on one word at a time.

Within the first 200 to 250 milliseconds (ms), stimuli that will become conscious are processed similarly to those that will remain unconscious. However, during the next several hundred ms, stimuli that will become conscious receive enhanced processing. Factors that determine which stimuli will become conscious include stimulus intensity, similarity to previous stimuli, and deliberate focusing of attention. Certain brain areas respond more strongly to their preferred stimuli when those stimuli are presented with an incongruent distracting stimulus. This suggests that the major function of attention is to enhance the processing of relevant stimuli rather than to inhibit processing of irrelevant stimuli. Damage to parts of the right hemisphere may result in spatial neglect, a tendency to ignore the left side of the body and its surroundings or the left side of objects. The deficit is in attention, not sensation. There are several ways to increase attention to the neglected stimuli. Many patients with neglect also have problems with spatial working memory and with shifting attention in non-spatial contexts.

Attention-deficit hyperactivity disorder (ADHD) is characterized by attention deficits, hyperactivity, impulsivity, mood swings and other psychological problems. Several tasks can differentiate people with ADHD from other people. ADHD probably depends on multiple genes as well as environmental influences, including maternal smoking during pregnancy. There are small differences in the brains of ADHD people; however, these differences are not consistent. The stimulant drugs methylphenidate (Ritalin) and amphetamine are able to increase attentiveness and improve school performance. They act by increasing the amount of dopamine available to receptors. Some behavioral treatments also improve the ability to attend to and perform tasks. However, neither ADHD nor attention in general is well understood.

Learning Objectives

Module 14.1 Lateralization of Function

1. Know the evidence for genetic influences on handedness.

2. Be able to describe the visual and auditory connections to the hemispheres.

3. Know why some people have had their corpus callosum cut and how that operation affected their everyday lives and their ability to do conflicting tasks with their two hands.

4. Be able to describe the methods of testing hemispheric dominance for speech.

5. Be able to describe the functions of the right and left hemispheres.

6. Understand the relationship of handedness and language dominance to the anatomical differences between the hemispheres.

7. Know the factors that affect recovery of speech after brain damage.

Module 14.2 Evolution and Physiology of Language

1. Be able to describe the language abilities of common chimpanzees, bonobos, elephants, dolphins, and parrots.

2. Understand the problems with the hypothesis that language is a product of overall intelligence.

3. Understand the evidence for and against the development of language as a special module.

4. Know the symptoms and causes of Broca's aphasia and Wernicke's aphasia.

5. Be able to describe the symptoms of dyslexia and some contributing anatomical, physiological, and functional factors.

Module 14.3 Attention

1. Know the similarities and differences in the early processing of conscious vs. unconscious stimuli and some factors that can select certain stimuli for consciousness.

2. Be able to describe examples of brain processing of attended vs. ignored stimuli and the implications for the role of attention in this processing.

3. Be able to describe the symptoms and physical causes of sensory neglect.

4. Know the symptoms, possible brain correlates, and treatments of attention-deficit hyperactivity disorder (ADHD).

Key Terms and Concepts

Module 14.1 Lateralization of Function

1. Handedness and its genetics

   ~90% of people strongly right-handed

   > Remaining ~10% somewhat ambidextrous
   > A few strongly left-handed

   Chimpanzees mostly right-handed, especially for communicative gestures

   Early left hemisphere damage can → non-right-handed

   Dominant gene → right-handedness and clockwise hair whorl

Recessive gene → random handedness and random hair whorl

2. The left and right hemispheres

Primarily contralateral control of the body

Exceptions: Taste and smell
Evolutionary hypothesis: Torso "flipped" relative to legs and brain

Hemispheric connections

Corpus callosum
Anterior commissure
Hippocampal commisure
Posterior commisure

Lateralization

Left hemisphere specialized for language
Right hemisphere: Functions difficult to summarize

3. Visual and auditory connections to the hemispheres

Right visual field → left half of both retinas → left hemisphere (and vice versa)

Small vertical strip in center of retina → both hemispheres
Optic chiasm

Both ears → both hemispheres

Opposite side stronger

4. Cutting the corpus callosum

Decreases frequency of epileptic seizures

Epilepsy: Repeated episodes of excessive synchronized neural activity

Causes

Decreased release of GABA
Mutation of gene for GABA receptor
Trauma, infection, tumor, toxic substance

Antiepileptic drugs

Block sodium flow across membrane
Enhance effects of GABA

Surgical removal of focus (origin)
Cut corpus callosum if more than one focus

Restricts seizures to one side
Decreases number of seizures

Split-brain people

    Independent control of two sides of body
    Abnormal behavior only if input is restricted to one side
    No problem with familiar tasks, new tasks difficult
    Can use two hands independently

        Conflicting tasks: Cognitive, not motor problem for intact-brain people

            Easier if clear targets direct movement

Left hemisphere: Speech comprehension and production

    95% of right-handers
    80% of left-handers
    Some speech understanding in both hemispheres
    Canary Island shepherds: Whistle communication → mostly left hemisphere

        People who don't understand the language → react as if music
    Bilateral control of speech → stuttering in some people

Split hemispheres: Competition and cooperation

    Hands do conflicting tasks
    Learning to cooperate

        Use of subcortical connections
        Guess with left hemisphere → if wrong, right hemisphere → frown on both sides of face → left
            hemisphere detects frown → changes answer
        Verbal task: One word to each hemisphere

            Right hand drew input to left hemisphere
            Left hand drew two pictures, but not combined concept

The right hemisphere

    Understands simple speech
    Emotional content of speech and facial expression, humor, and sarcasm

        Left hemisphere damage → better detection of lying

            Left hemisphere interferes with right hemisphere emotional perception
        Right hemisphere damage → monotone; can't understand emotional expression, humor, or
            sarcasm
        Right hemisphere: Recognizes both pleasant and unpleasant emotions in others
    Spatial relationships

        Right hemisphere: Overall patterns
        Left hemisphere: Details

Hemispheric specializations in intact brains

    Small differences
    Difficulty doing two things at once when both depend on same hemisphere

5. Methods 14.1: Testing hemispheric dominance for speech

    Wada test: Sodium amytal injected into carotid artery on one side of head

    Dichotic listening task: Earphones → different words to the two ears at same time

    Object naming latency test

        Left hemisphere dominance → faster response to stimulus in right visual field and vice versa

    Record brain activity during speech or listening to speech

        PET, fMRI, electrical or magnetic evoked response
        Some activity in non-dominant hemisphere

6. Development of lateralization and handedness

    Anatomical differences between the hemispheres

        Innate tendency to attend to language sounds
        Planum temporale: Larger in left hemisphere

            Left to right ratio

                Greater in those who are strongly right-handed
                Correlated with language skills
                Left/right difference even in infants
                Smaller, but significant, left/right differences in gorillas and chimpanzees
        Less ability to acquire language after early damage to left than to right

    Maturation of the corpus callosum

        Maturation over first 5 to 10 years
        Survival of functional connections
        Matures enough between ages 3 and 5 to compare stimuli between two hands

    Development without a corpus callosum

        Verbally describe stimuli in either hand
        Speech still in left hemisphere
        Each hemisphere: Increased connections to both sides of body

            Anterior commissure
            Hippocampal commissure
            Posterior commissure

    Hemispheres, handedness, and language dominance

        More than 95% of right-handed: Left hemisphere for speech
        Most left-handers: Left hemisphere for speech, though some mixed control
        Choice of path: Turn away from hemisphere with more dopamine

            Right-handers turn left, and vice versa

Recovery of speech after brain damage

Age at time of left hemisphere damage

Young brain usually more plastic than older brain

Exception: Early amygdala damage → impairment of irony and metaphor, as well as emotion

Left hemisphere damage → less language impairment in children than adults

Adult: Remaining parts of left hemisphere reorganize

Young child: Right hemisphere gains language capacity

Variability in both young and old

Type of medical problem that produced the damage

Rasmussen's encephalopathy

Gradual degeneration of glia, neurons of one hemisphere

Epileptic seizures, deterioration of speech and memory

Remove damaged hemisphere → language recovers slowly

Gradual degeneration of left hemisphere → right hemisphere reorganizes slowly

How speech was lateralized

Speech in both hemispheres → better recovery from left-hemisphere damage

Transcranial magnetic stimulation → inactivation of one hemisphere

Strong lateralization: Inactivation of dominant hemisphere → loss of speech

Bilateral control of speech: Inactivation → no loss of speech

7. Avoiding overstatements

Complicated tasks: Both hemispheres

8. In closing: One brain, two hemispheres

Module 14.2 Evolution and Physiology of Language

1. Nonhuman precursors of language

Productivity: Ability to produce new signals to represent new ideas

Common chimpanzees

Inability to speak

Ability to use visual symbols

Few original combinations: Little productivity

Symbols used to request, not describe

Limited comprehension of others' communications

Bonobos

Pan paniscus (pygmy chimpanzees)
Social order similar to humans'
Language ability of 2- to 2½-year-old child
Understand more than they produce
Name and describe without request
Request what they do not see
Refer to past
Creative requests
Early training by observation and imitation

Nonprimates

Elephants

Imitate sounds they hear → social bonds

Dolphins

Respond to gestures and words, cannot produce language

Parrots

Speak, name, count, form concepts

Implications

How to teach brain-damaged or autistic people
Difficulty of defining language

2. How did humans evolve language?

Language as a product of overall intelligence

First problem: People with normal intelligence and impaired language

Genetic condition → use of posterior areas, rather than frontal cortex
Second problem: Williams syndrome

Mental retardation, skillful use of language
Genes deleted from chromosome 7
Abnormal development of brain areas for visual processing
Severe impairment in numerical and visual-spatial skills
Normal abilities:

Music
Friendliness
Interpretation of facial expressions
Large amygdala, other areas for emotional processing → low social anxiety, more anxiety about inanimate objects
Language: Variable, from near normal to spectacular

Slow development
Sometimes odd grammar

Language not product of overall intelligence

Language as a special module

Language acquisition device
Ease of language development in most children
Poverty of the stimulus argument:

Children hear few examples of some grammatical structures they acquire

Therefore, rules inborn
But: Thousands of languages; can't be born knowing all
Intelligence as a byproduct of language

Does language learning have a critical period?

Adults: Better at memorizing vocabulary
Children: Better at pronunciation and unfamiliar grammar
No age cutoff, but earlier is better

3. Brain damage and language

Broca's aphasia (nonfluent aphasia)

Broca's area: Small part of left frontal cortex, near motor cortex

Serious deficits only with more extensive damage
Deficits in comprehension if meaning is difficult
Difficulty in language production

Articulation, writing, and gestures

Affects production of sign language
Omission of closed-class grammatical forms (prepositions, conjunctions, etc.)
Ability to speak open-class forms (nouns and verbs)
Problem with meanings, not just pronunciation
May leave out weakest elements
Problems comprehending grammatical words and devices

Problems understanding prepositions and conjunctions
Still use normal word order for their language
Comprehension resembles normal people who are distracted
Rely on inferences

Wernicke's aphasia (fluent aphasia)

Wernicke's area: Near auditory cortex
Articulate speech
Anomia: Difficulty finding the right word
Poor language comprehension, especially nouns and verbs
Connections to other brain areas

Reading a verb → activation of motor cortex that would produce the movement

4. Dyslexia

Specific impairment of reading

Adequate vision and other academic skills

More common in boys than girls

More common in English readers than in more phonetic language readers

No single abnormality

Mild microscopic abnormalities

Bilaterally symmetrical cortex, especially planum temporale

In some dyslexics, right larger than left

Weak connections among areas in left hemisphere

Dysphonetic vs. dyseidetic dyslexics

Dysphonetic → difficulty sounding out words
Dyseidetic → difficulty recognizing words as wholes

Little or no visual impairment

Subtle hearing impairment

Difficulty distinguishing temporal order

Spoonerisms
Tapping rhythms

Converting vision to sound, vice versa

Differences in attention

Shifting attention from one word to another
Attentional focus to right of word in visual focus
Treatment: Read one word at a time
Attend to several tasks at once

5. In closing: Language and the brain

Language neither a simple by-product of intelligence nor independent of other functions

Module 14.3 Attention

1. Alterations in brain responses

Conscious and unconscious stimuli → similar brain responses in first 200-250 milliseconds (ms)

Next few hundred ms: Brain enhances response to those stimuli that become conscious

Select on basis of intensity, similarity to previous stimuli, deliberate shift in attention
Binocular rivalry
Change blindness
Increased response to a sound in presence of a distraction
fMRI: Fusiform gyrus response to face increased by distracting name
Attention → enhancing relevant activity more than inhibiting irrelevant activity

2. Neglect

    Spatial neglect: Damage to right hemisphere

        Ignore left side of body and its surroundings
        Damage to inferior right parietal cortex → neglect of everything to left of body
        Damage to superior right parietal cortex → neglect left side of objects, regardless of location
        Problem with attention, not sensation
        Problems with spatial working memory and shifting attention

3. Attention-deficit hyperactivity disorder (ADHD)

    Distractibility, impulsivity, hyperactivity, sensitivity to stress, mood swings, short temper, deficit in planning

    3-10% of children, especially males

    Difficult diagnosis

    Measurements of ADHD behavior

        Choice-delay task: Smaller reward now vs. larger later
        Stop signal task: Disregard previous signal
        Attentional blink task: Miss probe letter after green letter

    Possible causes and brain differences

        Fairly high heritability

            Multiple genes, prenatal environment, especially smoking
        95% of normal brain volume

            Smaller right prefrontal cortex and cerebellum
        Treatments

            Methylphenidate (Ritalin) or amphetamine

                Increase attentiveness, decrease impulsiveness, in children and adults
                Increase dopamine availability to postsynaptic receptors

                    Max effect in 1 hour, when dopamine levels highest

            Stimulants enhance attention, learning, even in normal children and adults
            Behavioral treatments

Reduce distraction

Use lists, schedules

Pace oneself

Learn to relax

4. In closing: Attending to attention

Attention → enhancement of one stimulus after another

Theoretical implications about the nature of consciousness

Short-Answer Questions

Module 14.1 Lateralization of Function

1. *Handedness and its genetics*

   a. Describe the percentages of people who are right-handed, left-handed, and ambidextrous.

   b. Describe the effects of the dominant and recessive genes for handedness and hair whorls.

2. *The left and right hemispheres*

   a. What is an evolutionary explanation for why the brain'→s control of the body is primarily contralateral?

   b. What are the main connections between the hemispheres?

   c. Visual and auditory connections to the hemispheres

   d. To which hemisphere(s) does the right visual field project? To which hemisphere(s) does the right half of both retinas project? To which hemisphere(s) does the right eye project?

   e. To which hemisphere(s) does the right ear project? What ability requires this distribution of input? When the two hemispheres receive different information, which ear does each hemisphere pay more attention to?

3. *Cutting the corpus callosum*

   a. What are the causes of epilepsy? What are several ways in which it can be treated?

   b. What is the corpus callosum? Why is it sometimes severed in cases of severe epilepsy? What are the effects of such an operation on overall intelligence, motivation, and gross motor coordination?

   c. What have we learned from split-brain humans concerning specialization of the two hemispheres? Which tasks are best accomplished by the left hemisphere?

   d. What percentage of right-handed people have left-hemisphere dominance for language? Describe the control of language in left-handed people.

e. What is a cause of stuttering in some people?

f. What is the basis for learned cooperation between the hemispheres in split-brain people?

g. What did the split-brain person draw with his right hand, when two different words were flashed to his right and left visual fields? What did he sometimes draw with his left hand? Could he combine information from his right and left visual fields to form a new concept?

h. Which functions are best performed by the right hemisphere?

i. What is one simple task that can show hemispheric specialization in intact people? How large are the hemispheric differences in intact people?

4. *Methods 14.1: Testing hemispheric dominance for speech*

a. Name four ways of testing hemispheric dominance for speech.

b. Development of lateralization and handedness

c. What is the planum temporale and what is its significance for language?

d. How early is the size difference in the left vs. right planum temporale apparent?

e. Compare the ability of 3-year-olds and of 5-year-olds to discriminate fabrics with either one hand or different hands. What can we infer from this about the development of the corpus callosum?

f. In what ways are people who never had a corpus callosum different from split-brain people?

g. Which other commisures between the two hemispheres may compensate for the lack of a corpus callosum in people born without one?

h. What happens to the language ability of children who suffer damage to their left hemisphere in infancy?

i. How does recovery from left-hemisphere damage differ in adults, compared to children?

j. Describe Rasmussen's encephalopathy. Why does removal of the damaged hemisphere often result in slow, but surprisingly full recovery of language?

k. How valid is the assumption that a given individual relies consistently on one hemisphere or the other?

Module 14.2 Evolution and Physiology of Language

1. *Nonhuman precursors of language*

a. What are some differences between the abilities of common chimpanzees and of humans to use symbols?

b. What was unusual about the ability of some bonobos to learn language?

c. In what ways do bonobos resemble humans more than common chimpanzees in language abilities?

d. What evidence is there that nonprimate species can learn language?

e. How did humans evolve language?

f.   Briefly discuss the proposal that our language may have developed as a by-product of overall intelligence.

g.   How well do the correlations between general intelligence and language hold up? How is this a problem for the view that language evolved as a product of large brains and intelligence?

h.   Describe the pattern of abilities and disabilities in the family with a genetic mutation that produces language deficits. How is this a problem for the view that language evolved as a product of large brains and intelligence?

i.   Describe Williams syndrome. How does this relate to the evolution of language as a product of general intelligence?

j.   What is the main argument for the hypothesis that language evolved as an extra brain module? What is a problem with that hypothesis?

k.   What is an alternative hypothesis regarding the evolution of language and intelligence?

l.   Is there a critical period for language learning? What are some ways of testing this idea?

2.   *Brain damage and language*

a.   Where is Broca's area located?

b.   Describe the effects of damage to Broca's area. What are closed-class words?

c.   Locate Wernicke's area.

d.   Contrast the effects of damage to Wernicke's area with those of damage to Broca's area.

e.   What other brain areas contribute to language comprehension?

3.   *Dyslexia*

a.   What is dyslexia? How consistent are its symptoms?

b.   What are some possible biological causes of dyslexia?

c.   Describe dysphonetic and dyseidetic types of dyslexia.

d.   What other difficulties do people with dyslexia often have?

e.   What is one method of improving the ability of dyslexics to read?

Module 14.3 Attention

1.   *Alterations in brain responses*

a.   In what time frame does the processing of conscious stimuli begin to differ from that of unconscious stimuli?

b.   What factors may lead to the selection of certain stimuli to be processed consciously?

c.   What is binocular rivalry? Change blindness?

d.   What evidence suggests that attention enhances processing of relevant information, rather than inhibiting processing of irrelevant information?

2. *Neglect*

    a. Describe spatial neglect.

    b. Damage to what part of the brain gives rise to spatial neglect?

    c. How may the attention of a person with spatial neglect be directed to objects on his or her left side?

    d. What other deficits do many patients with spatial neglect have?

3. *Attention-deficit hyperactivity disorder*

    a. List the symptoms of attention-deficit hyperactivity disorder (ADHD).

    b. Briefly describe three tests that may be used to diagnose ADHD.

    c. How heritable is ADHD? What are some other factors that can predispose children to ADHD?

    d. What are some differences in the brains of people with ADHD?

    e. Which drugs have been used to treat ADHD? What is their mechanism of action?

    f. What behavioral techniques have been used to treat ADHD?

True/False Questions

1. About 10% of people are strongly left-handed.

    TRUE or FALSE

2. A dominant gene results in right-handedness and a clockwise hair whorl; a recessive gene results in random handedness and a random hair whorl.

    TRUE or FALSE

3. It is impossible to be left-handed and have a clockwise hair whorl.

    TRUE or FALSE

4. The right visual field projects to the left half of both retinas, and from there to the left hemisphere.

    TRUE or FALSE

5. As with the visual system, the right auditory field projects only to the left hemisphere, in order to be able to coordinate auditory and visual input.

    TRUE or FALSE

6. The primary causes of epilepsy are decreased release of the excitatory transmitter glutamate and mutation of a gene for a glutamate receptor.

    TRUE or FALSE

7. Split-brain people can perform familiar tasks with no problem and can use their hands independently to perform competing tasks, which is difficult for intact-brain people.

    TRUE or FALSE

8. Speech is localized in the left hemisphere of 95% of right-handers and in the right hemisphere in 95% of left-handers.

   TRUE or FALSE

9. Specialties of the right hemisphere include emotional expression and interpretation, spatial abilities, humor, and sarcasm.

   TRUE or FALSE

10. The right hemisphere is unable to understand even simple speech.

    TRUE or FALSE

11. The left-to-right ratio of the size of the planum temporale is positively correlated with language ability.

    TRUE or FALSE

12. Some aspects of the behavior of young children are similar to those of split-brain people.

    TRUE or FALSE

13. Rasmussen's encephalopathy results in total inability to understand or produce language.

    TRUE or FALSE

14. Bonobo chimpanzees develop the language ability characteristic of human teenagers.

    TRUE or FALSE

15. People with Williams syndrome are mentally retarded except in language, social, and musical abilities and ability to interpret facial expressions.

    TRUE or FALSE

16. Broca's aphasia results from fairly extensive damage to Broca's area in the frontal lobe and cortical areas surrounding it.

    TRUE or FALSE

17. Wernicke's aphasia results in difficulty speaking and omission of closed-class words.

    TRUE or FALSE

18. Dyslexia may have a variety of types and causes, including mild microscopic abnormalities, bilaterally symmetrical cortex, weak connections among areas in the left hemisphere, and subtle hearing impairment.

    TRUE or FALSE

19. Dyslexics can sometimes be helped by trying to view a whole sentence at a time, rather than focusing on one word at a time.

    TRUE or FALSE

20. Brain responses to conscious and unconscious stimuli are processed differently from the very first few milliseconds.

    TRUE or FALSE

21. Spatial neglect results from extensive damage to the right hemisphere, especially the right parietal cortex.

    TRUE or FALSE

22. The problem in spatial neglect is due to inadequate sensory processing, rather than a deficit in attention.

    TRUE or FALSE

23. Drugs such as Ritalin and amphetamine rarely help children with attention-deficit hyperactivity disorder (ADHD) and should no longer be used.

    TRUE or FALSE

Fill In The Blanks

1. A _____ gene results in right handedness and clockwise hair whorls; a _____ gene results in random handedness and random hair whorls.

2. The major connections between the hemispheres are the _____ , the _____ , and the _____ .

3. The left visual field projects to the _____ half of both retinas, which then project to the _____ hemisphere.

4. Cutting the corpus callosum is an effective treatment for _____ when drugs and simpler surgery are ineffective.

5. The _____ test is used to test hemispheric dominance for speech; sodium amytal is injected into the carotid artery on one side of the head.

6. The _____ hemisphere is more important for expressing and understanding emotional content of speech and facial expression, humor, and sarcasm.

7. The _____ is an area in the temporal lobe that is larger on the left than the right side in most people.

8. _____ produces gradual degeneration of glia and neurons in one hemisphere; as a result of increasing seizures the damaged hemisphere may be removed. If it is the left hemisphere that is removed in childhood, a surprising amount of language may be regained, because the gradual degeneration allowed the _____ hemisphere to be partially reorganized for language.

9. _____ chimpanzees can acquire the ability to use visual symbols to name and describe (even when not requesting something), to refer to the past, to request things they do not see, and to make creative requests.

10. Deletion of genes from chromosome _____ results in abnormal development of brain areas for _____ processing in people with Williams syndrome; as a result they have severe impairment in _____ and _____ skills but near normal to spectacular _____ abilities.

11. _____ aphasia, also known as nonfluent aphasia, is characterized by difficulty in language _____ and in omission of _____ grammatical forms.

12. _____ aphasia, also known as fluent aphasia, is characterized by articulate speech, combined with _____ (difficulty finding the right word) and poor comprehension of nouns and verbs.

13. _____ is a specific impairment of reading, together with adequate vision and other academic skills.

14. Spatial neglect is often the result of extensive damage to the right hemisphere, especially the _____ .

15. Some children with ADHD have somewhat smaller than average brain volumes, especially in the right _____ cortex and the _____ .

Matching Items

1. _____ Split-brain people or animals
2. _____ Left hemisphere
3. _____ Right hemisphere
4. _____ Dichotic listening task
5. _____ Corpus callosum
6. _____ Anterior commissure
7. _____ Planum temporale
8. _____ Productivity
9. _____ Bonobos
10. _____ Williams syndrome
11. _____ Broca's aphasia
12. _____ Wernicke's aphasia
13. _____ Wada test
14. _____ Dyslexia

a. One word to left ear, another to right ear
b. Area larger in left than right temporal lobe
c. Major connection between hemispheres
d. Specialized for spatial, emotional abilities
e. Independent control of two sides of body
f. Specialized for language, details
g. Chimpanzees with good language skills
h. Nonfluent aphasia, difficult closed-class words
i. Minor connection between hemispheres
j. Fluent aphasia, anomia
k. Reading impairment, other skills OK
l. Produce new signals for new ideas
m. Normal language, retarded in other skills
n. Test for hemispheric specialization

Multiple-Choice Questions

1. A strong tendency to left-handedness
   a. is characteristic of chimpanzees, unlike humans.
   b. is found in a minority of people who are not right-handed; most non-right-handers are more ambidextrous.
   c. is promoted by a dominant gene that also confers counterclockwise hair whorls.
   d. all of the above.

2. Severing the corpus callosum
   a. usually destroys language abilities.
   b. usually relieves the symptoms of epilepsy.
   c. has provided evidence that linguistic abilities reside largely in the right hemisphere.
   d. none of the above.

3. People with bisected brains
   a. can use their two hands independently in a way that other people cannot.
   b. develop cooperation between the hemispheres because the corpus callosum grows back.
   c. perform very poorly on intelligence tests.
   d. all of the above.

4. The only way to restrict visual input to only the right hemisphere of a split-brain person is to
   a. flash it briefly to the left eye while the right eye is closed.
   b. flash it briefly to the right eye while the left eye is closed.
   c. flash it briefly in the left visual field while the person is looking straight ahead.
   d. flash it briefly in the right visual field while the person is looking straight ahead.

5. A split-brain person who sees a picture of an object in his left visual field usually
   a. will be able both to point to the correct object with his left hand and to name it.
   b. will not be able to pick out the object or to name it.
   c. will be able to pick it out with his left hand, but will not be able to name it.
   d. will be able to name it but not pick it out.

6. People with right-hemisphere damage
   a. have trouble producing and understanding emotional facial expressions.
   b. have trouble speaking with emotional expression and understanding others' vocal emotional expression.
   c. have trouble with some complex visual and spatial tasks.
   d. all of the above.

7. People with left-hemisphere damage
   a. have great difficulties with spatial relationships.
   b. perform better than chance in detecting lying.
   c. easily begin to use the right hemisphere for language function.
   d. all of the above.

8. Hemispheric specialization in intact people
   a. has not been demonstrated.
   b. can be shown but is small and inconsistent.
   c. is consistent with that observed in split-brain people but is even more dramatic.
   d. is the reverse of specialization in split-brain people.

9. Which of the following is true of the planum temporale?
   a. Children with the biggest ratio of left to right planum temporale performed best on language tests.
   b. It is larger in the right than in the left hemisphere for almost everyone.
   c. It is equal in size in the two hemispheres at birth, indicating that maturation of language causes the size difference in adults.
   d. All of the above are true.

10. What did Galin et al. discover when they asked 3-year-old and 5-year-old children to discriminate two fabrics?
    a. The 3-year-olds were better than the 5-year-olds.
    b. All children made fewer errors with their right hands than with their left.
    c. All children made 90 percent more errors using different hands than when using the same hand.
    d. Three-year-olds made 90 percent more errors using different hands than using the same hand, but 5-year-olds did equally well with one hand or two.

11. People who never had a corpus callosum
    a. are just like split-brain patients.
    b. can verbally describe objects in either visual field and name objects that they touch with either hand.
    c. are especially fast at tasks requiring coordination of both hands.
    d. all of the above.

12. Which of the following is true of handedness and language dominance?
    a. Humans are the only species that show a hand preference.
    b. While hiking in the woods, both right- and left-handers tend to turn to the right when they reach a fork in the path.
    c. Most left-handed people have language dominance in the right hemisphere.
    d. Most left-handed people have language dominance in the left hemisphere, but are more variable than right-handers.

13. Children with Rasmussen's encephalopathy in the left hemisphere
    a. can never learn to speak again, if the left hemisphere is removed.
    b. often can eventually regain speech, because the degeneration was slow enough that the right hemisphere could be reprogrammed for language.
    c. have shown that there is a clear critical period for learning language; no language learning can occur after the age of three or four.
    d. none of the above.

14. Productivity
    a. refers to the ability to produce new language signals to represent new ideas.
    b. is a characteristic of communication systems of most mammals.
    c. refers to the ability to translate one signal into another.
    d. is only a means of increasing ones income, and has nothing to do with language.

15. Ordinary chimpanzees
    a. frequently use symbols in new, original combinations.
    b. frequently use symbols to describe scenes and events.
    c. have a social order much like that of humans.
    d. use symbols almost always to request, only rarely to describe.

16. Bonobos
    a. are unable to put symbols together in new ways to express new meanings.
    b. use symbols only to request objects.
    c. can understand some spoken English sentences.
    d. have learned to speak English fluently.

17. Which of the following is a problem with the theory that human language evolved as a product of overall intelligence and larger brains?
    a. Some people have normal overall intelligence, but have impaired language.
    b. Some people are severely retarded and have abnormal brain development, but have near normal, and sometimes spectacular, language ability.
    c. Selective pressure for social interactions may have favored the evolution of language, and overall intelligence may have developed as a by-product of language.
    d. All of the above are true.

18. People with Williams syndrome
    a. have severe difficulties with even simple grammatical rules.
    b. have good language abilities, but are retarded in nonlinguistic function.
    c. can draw beautifully, but cannot write.
    d. have almost total loss of Wernicke's area.

19. A patient has great difficulty in articulating words and a tendency to omit endings and abstract words, but less difficulty comprehending spoken and written words. The patient probably has damage in
    a. Broca's area.
    b. Wernicke's area.
    c. the corpus callosum.
    d. primary motor cortex controlling muscles of articulation.

20. A second patient has difficulty naming objects and understanding both spoken and written language; speech is fluent but not very meaningful. You suspect that the patient has damage in
    a. Broca's area.
    b. Wernicke's area.
    c. the anterior commissure and hippocampal commisure.
    d. left visual cortex and posterior corpus callosum.

21. Dyslexic people
    a. all have very similar symptoms, and all of the symptoms are limited to difficulties in visual perception.
    b. are sometimes helped by focusing on whole paragraphs at a time, rather than reading one word at a time.
    c. are more likely than normal readers to have a bilaterally symmetrical cerebral cortex or larger language-related areas in the right hemisphere than in the left.
    d. all of the above.

22. Stimuli that are destined to become conscious
    a. are processed similarly to those that remain unconscious for the first $200 - 250$ ms.
    b. then lead to increased neural activity in the next few hundred ms.
    c. are selected for consciousness by having greater intensity, similarity to previous stimuli, or as a result of deliberate focus of attention.
    d. all of the above.

23. Spatial neglect
    a. results from ineffective sensory input, rather than a problem with attention.
    b. results from damage to the right parietal cortex.
    c. results from damage to the left parietal cortex.
    d. is a symptom of ADHD.

24. ADHD
    a. has been associated with a slightly smaller brain volume, especially in the right prefrontal cortex and cerebellum, although these differences are inconsistent.
    b. shows little or no heritability.
    c. is best treated with sedative drugs.
    d. can be treated only with drugs; behavioral treatments are ineffective.

Crossword Puzzle

Words, Brains, and Attention

www.CrosswordWeaver.com

ACROSS

1 _____ encephalopathy, disorder in which one hemisphere degenerates slowly; if it is the left hemisphere, the right hemisphere may have time to reorganize for language.

5 Transmitter whose effects are enhanced by antiepileptic drugs

8 Drug that increases attentiveness and decreases impulsiveness in children and adults

11 _____ class words, those that include prepositions and connectives

12 Hemisphere that specializes in emotional expression and interpretation, spatial ability, humor, and musical ability

13 Chimpanzee with surprisingly good language ability

14 _____ temporale, area in the temporal lobe, usually larger on the left side

16 Man who discovered brain area that supports fluent speech and use of connectives

17 _____ aphasia, characterized by articulate speech, but difficulty finding the right word

18 Reading disorder in otherwise normal people

DOWN

2 Disorder characterized by distractibility, impulsivity, and hyperactivity, more prevalent in boys than girls (abbr.)

3 Spatial _____, disorder characterized by ignoring the left side of the body and its surroundings; caused by damage to the right parietal cortex

4 Test for hemispheric dominance for speech, involves injecting sodium amytal into the carotid artery on one side of the head

6 _____ commissure, a minor bundle of axons connecting the two hemispheres

7 Syndrome characterized by mental retardation but skillful use of language

9 Man who discovered brain area that supports naming and understanding

10 Corpus _____, major bundle of fibers connecting the two hemispheres, occasionally cut to relieve epilepsy

15 Hemisphere specialized for speech

341

Crossword Puzzle Solution

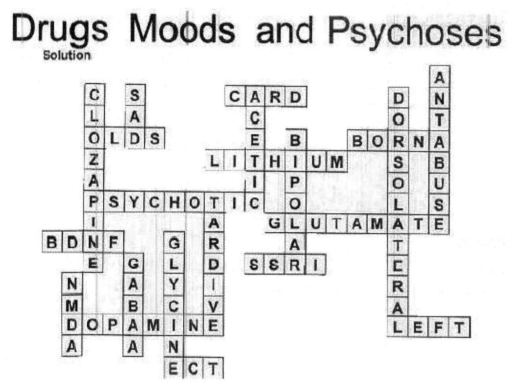

Drugs Moods and Psychoses

Solutions

True/False Questions

1. F
2. T
3. F
4. T
5. F
6. F
7. T
8. F
9. T
10. F
11. T
12. T
13. F
14. F
15. T
16. T
17. F
18. T
19. F
20. F
21. T
22. F
23. F

Fill In The Blanks

1. dominant ; recessive
2. corpus callosum; anterior; commissure; hippocampal commissure
3. right; right
4. epilepsy
5. Wada
6. right
7. planum temporale
8. Rasmussen's encephalopathy; right
9. Bonobo
10. 7; visual; numerical; spatial; language
11. Broca's; production; closed-class
12. Wernicke's; anomia
13. Dyslexia
14. right parietal cortex
15. prefrontal ; cerebellum

Matching Items

1. E
2. F
3. D
4. A
5. C
6. I
7. B
8. L
9. G
10. M
11. H
12. J
13. N
14. K

Multiple-Choice Questions

1. B	10. D	19. A
2. B	11. B	20. B
3. A	12. D	21. C
4. C	13. B	22. D
5. C	14. A	23. B
6. D	15. D	24. A
7. B	16. C	
8. B	17. D	
9. A	18. B	

PSYCHOLOGICAL DISORDERS

Introduction

Substance abuse is a maladaptive pattern of substance use leading to clinically significant impairment or distress. Most abused drugs and most reinforcing activities, including electrical self-stimulation of the brain, are linked to dopamine release in the nucleus accumbens. However, dopamine in the nucleus accumbens may be more related to "wanting" aspects of an event, rather than its pleasurable, or "liking," effects. Repeated use of cocaine increases the ability of cocaine to release dopamine in nucleus accumbens and to increase activity in prefrontal cortex. However, it also decreases the responsiveness to other more natural incentives. One hypothesis suggests that the prefrontal cortex stimulates the nucleus accumbens to support the specific reinforcing activity. Repeated drug use increases background inhibition of the prefrontal cortex, so that only the strongest stimuli get through. In addition, administration of an addictive drug during withdrawal leads to sensitization, so that either stress or the reminder of that drug can elicit craving.

Alcohol is the most commonly abused drug. Alcohol inhibits brain activity through general effects, such as decreasing sodium influx and expanding neuronal membranes, and also by decreasing serotonin activity, facilitating responses at GABAA receptors, blocking glutamate receptors, and increasing dopamine activity. There are two major types of alcoholism. Type I alcoholism is less dependent on genetics, develops gradually, and is equally common in women and men. Type II alcoholism has a stronger genetic basis, a rapid, early onset, a great preponderance of men, and an association with criminality. There is a genetic contribution to alcoholism. Monozygotic twins have a higher concordance rate than do dizygotic twins. Biological children of alcoholics have a higher risk of alcoholism, especially the sons of alcoholic fathers. However, maternal drinking during pregnancy is also a factor. Several genes are weakly correlated with alcoholism. They may increase impulsiveness, which can lead to trying alcohol at an early age, or increase stress responsiveness, which can lead to relapse after attempting to quit. Some factors that may mediate the genetic predisposition to alcoholism include less intoxication from small to moderate amounts of alcohol and greater than average relief from stress after drinking alcohol. In addition, alcoholics tend to have a smaller than normal amygdala in the right hemisphere. Antabuse (disulfiram) is used to treat alcoholism; it inactivates acetaldehyde dehydrogenase, the enzyme that converts acetaldehyde (the toxic metabolic product of alcohol) to acetic acid (a source of energy). A person who drinks after taking Antabuse will become sick. However, many persons who use Antabuse never drink, and therefore never become ill; they use Antabuse as a daily reminder not to drink alcohol. Methadone is used to treat addiction to heroin and morphine. It has effects similar to those of heroin and morphine, but, because it is taken as a pill, its effects rise and fall slowly and do not produce a "rush." Addiction represents a loss of control over one's behavior, blurring the distinction between voluntary and involuntary.

Depression is typified by episodic sadness and helplessness, lack of energy, feelings of worthlessness, suicidal ideas, sleep disorders, and lack of pleasure. While the cause of depression is not fully understood, a number of possible factors have been identified. There may be a genetic component to depression; the risk is highest in relatives of women with early-onset depression. Several genes have been found to have a link to depression, including one linked to an 80% decrease in the ability to produce serotonin and another that controls the serotonin transporter. Women are at greater risk for depression than are men. Although hormone levels are not strongly correlated with depression, decreases in estrogen and progesterone can lead to depression in vulnerable women. Stress may trigger depression in some people; it releases cortisol, which is helpful in the short term, but exhausts energy stores and impairs sleep and the immune system during prolonged stress. Abnormal hemispheric dominance is sometimes associated with mood disorders. Happiness in normal people is associated with activation of the left prefrontal cortex, whereas depressed people have lower metabolic activity in the left, and increased activity in the right prefrontal cortex. Depression may occasionally be caused by exposure to a virus at some point in life. The Borna virus predisposes people to various psychiatric difficulties, including depression.

Most drugs that improve affective disorders act in one of three ways: blocking reuptake of monoamines (tricyclics), blocking reuptake of only serotonin (selective serotonin reuptake inhibitors, or SSRIs) or inhibiting monoamine oxidase (monoamine oxidase inhibitors, or MAOIs). Fluoxetine and other SSRIs have fewer side effects than do the tricyclics. Several atypical antidepressants have other mechanisms of action. Bupropion inhibits reuptake of dopamine and, to some extent, norepinephrine. Venlafaxine inhibits reuptake of serotonin and, to a lesser extent, norepinephrine and dopamine. Nefazodone blocks serotonin type 2A receptors and weakly inhibits serotonin and norepinephrine reuptake. St. John's wort is an herb and is not regulated by the Food and Drug Administration. Its effects are variable but similar to those of SSRIs; however, it may also contribute to more rapid breakdown of beneficial drugs. A major problem with the transmitter hypothesis of depression is that drugs affect transmitter levels almost immediately but exert noticeable effects on mood only after two or three weeks. A possible explanation is that brain-derived neurotrophic factor (BDNF) is released with neurotransmitters and would take a few weeks to increase neurogenesis and incorporation of the new neurons into the hippocampus. To the extent that antidepressants increase neurotransmitter release, they would also increase release of this peptide. There is evidence that the effectiveness of antidepressants is mediated by BDNF, which increases the size of parts of the hippocampus and cerebral cortex that shrink during depression. Blocking BDNF in animals blocks the behavioral effects of antidepressant drugs. In addition to treatment by drug therapy, mood disorders are sometimes treated with electroconvulsive therapy (ECT), sleep alterations, or bright lights. ECT is particularly useful for patients who are unresponsive to antidepressants or who are suicidal and need rapid relief. Memory loss that is sometimes associated with ECT is minimized by administering the ECT only to the right hemisphere. ECT alters the expression of numerous genes, including those that produce neurotrophins, arachidonic acid, generation of new neurons, and responsiveness to exercise. Sleep-deprivation therapy is based on observations that depressed persons enter REM sleep much sooner than normal persons. A regimen of earlier bedtimes following one sleepless night usually offers relief from depression for at least a week, and a combination of sleep alteration and antidepressant drugs produces long-term benefits.

Depression can occur as either a unipolar or a bipolar disorder. A unipolar disorder is one in which an individual varies between normal mood and depression. Bipolar disorder, or manic-depressive disorder, is characterized by cycles of depression and mania. During their manic phase, people are restless, uninhibited, excitable, impulsive, self-confident, and apparently happy. In bipolar I disorder there is a full-blown manic phase; in bipolar II disorder the manic phase is milder and is referred to as hypomania. Bipolar disorder has been linked to genes on several chromosomes; however, the linkage is weak. Lithium is effective in treating bipolar I disorder, and if taken regularly, prevents relapse into either mania or depression. Valproate and carbamazepine are effective treatments for bipolar II disorder; they increase activity at GABA synapses, whereas lithium does not. All three drugs block synthesis of arachidonic acid, which is produced during brain inflammation. An experimental treatment uses echo-planar magnetic resonance spectroscopic imaging to produce weak electromagnetic fields throughout the head; this treatment produces temporary mood benefits. One additional treatment for bipolar disorder is to keep a consistent sleep schedule in a darkened, quiet room.

Seasonal affective disorder (SAD) occurs mostly in areas where nights are long in the winter. SAD patients may have phase-delayed sleep and temperature cycles, unlike other depressed people, who are phase-advanced. Exposure to bright lights for an hour or more per day is usually an effective treatment for SAD. This treatment may affect serotonin synapses and circadian rhythms.

Schizophrenia is an illness in which emotions are "split off" from the intellect. Its positive symptoms (behaviors that are present but should be absent) include a psychotic cluster (hallucinations and delusions) and a disorganized cluster (inappropriate emotions, bizarre behaviors, and thought disorder). Negative symptoms (behaviors that are absent but should be present) include deficits in social interaction, emotional expression, speech, and working memory. The main problem may be disordered thoughts, which result from abnormal connections between the cortex and the thalamus and cerebellum. Approximately 1 percent of people suffer schizophrenia at any given time. There has been a gradual decline in both the prevalence and severity of schizophrenia worldwide, for unknown reasons. Schizophrenia is much less common in the Third World than in the United States and Europe. It is more prevalent and more severe in men than in women. Much evidence favors a genetic predisposition to schizophrenia. There is a higher concordance rate for schizophrenia in monozygotic than in dizygotic twins and in biological than in adoptive relatives. Genetics cannot completely explain the occurrence of schizophrenia, however, since the concordance rate for monozygotic twins is not 100 percent. One confounding factor in genetics studies is that biological parents of schizophrenics are more likely to engage in unhealthy habits, including smoking and drinking, that could impair prenatal development. Some studies have found genes with possible links to schizophrenia. Indeed disrupted forms of two genes have been found to interact, altering the structure of the hippocampus, decreasing its gray matter, and predisposing a person to schizophrenia. Another gene was linked to negative symptoms of schizophrenia. Perhaps several genes contribute to different symptoms and may interact with environmental factors.

The neurodevelopmental hypothesis suggests that schizophrenia results from abnormal early development of the brain. Difficulties surrounding birth or during pregnancy have been linked to increased incidence of schizophrenia. These include poor nutrition during pregnancy, Rh incompatibility, complications during delivery, low birth weight, and fevers due to infections during middle pregnancy. A number of minor brain abnormalities have been found in the brains of schizophrenics. Prefrontal and temporal cortex are smaller than usual; the ventricles are larger; cell bodies in the hippocampus and prefrontal cortex are smaller; and the left hemisphere is smaller and less active. The area of most consistent abnormalities is the dorsolateral prefrontal cortex, one of the latest brain areas to mature. Because there is no evidence of neuronal loss in adulthood, it is thought that the brain abnormalities result from early developmental factors. Since the most affected brain areas are those that mature slowly, the behavioral problems may not emerge until long after the damage occurred. However, neurons may continue to shrink, rather than die, in adulthood.

Antipsychotic drugs, including phenothiazines (chlorpromazine: Thorazine) and butyrophenones (haloperidol: Haldol), block dopamine receptors. Furthermore, some symptoms of schizophrenia can be temporarily experienced by people who take large doses of drugs that stimulate dopamine synapses. On the basis of such observations it has been hypothesized that schizophrenia occurs because of excess activity at dopamine synapses. There is evidence for greater occupation of dopamine D2 receptors in schizophrenic patients in one study, and another study found that the greater the D2 receptor occupation in the prefrontal cortex of schizophrenic patients, the greater the cognitive impairment. There are a number of problems with this hypothesis, however. First, neuroleptic drugs block dopamine receptors almost immediately, but take two or three weeks to produce therapeutic benefits. In addition, there is no consistent evidence of abnormally high levels of dopamine or its metabolites in schizophrenics. A second hypothesis is that there may be a deficit in glutamate activity, especially in the prefrontal cortex. Schizophrenics release less glutamate in prefrontal cortex and hippocampus than do other people, and glutamate has effects that are frequently opposite to those of dopamine. Therefore, any problem observed could be due either to insufficient glutamate or excess dopamine. Phencyclidine (PCP) inhibits NMDA glutamate receptors and produces both positive and negative symptoms similar to schizophrenia. It also produces little psychotic response in preadolescents but produces a long-lasting relapse in recovered schizophrenics. Although there is evidence of glutamate deficiency in schizophrenia, glutamate itself cannot be administered, because too much glutamate can kill neurons. However, the amino acid glycine is a co-transmitter at NMDA glutamate receptors and increases the effectiveness of glutamate. It is not an effective antipsychotic by itself, but it increases the effectiveness of antipsychotic drugs, especially for negative symptoms.

The decision to administer neuroleptic drugs has been complicated by their potentially severe side effects. The most troublesome effect is tardive dyskinesia, which consists of tremors and other involuntary movements. This condition develops gradually and may last long after the drug is discontinued. Recent advances in research have led to the use of new atypical antipsychotic drugs (such as clozapine, amisulpride, risperidone, and olanzapine), which appear to control the negative symptoms of schizophrenia better than the older drugs and do so without causing tardive dyskinesia. These drugs block D4 dopamine receptors more strongly than D2 receptors. They also block serotonin 5-HT2 receptors and increase the release of glutamate. Their major side effects are weight gain, increased risk of diabetes, and an impaired immune system. Schizophrenia does not result from disruption of only one gene or abnormality of a single transmitter. Several genes, several transmitters, and several brain areas have been implicated, as well as environmental factors.

Learning Objectives

Module 15.1 Substance Abuse

1. Understand the relation of dopamine in the nucleus accumbens to motivation ("wanting") and why dopamine does not seem to be related directly to pleasure ("liking").

2. Understand the relationship of the prefrontal cortex to the nucleus accumbens in the development of sensitization to drugs.

3. Know the physiological effects of alcohol and the effects of Antabuse on alcohol metabolism.

4. Be able to describe the evidence for a genetic contribution to alcoholism.

5. Know why methadone can be used to treat addiction to heroin or morphine and why it does not end the addiction.

Module 15.2 Mood Disorders

1. Know the symptoms of depression and the evidence for a genetic contribution to depression.

2. Understand the possible roles of hormones, abnormalities of hemispheric dominance, and viruses in the onset or worsening of depression.

3. Be able to describe the short-term and long-term mechanisms of action of antidepressant drugs.

4. Understand the possible mechanisms of action and the advantages and disadvantages of psychotherapy, electroconvulsive therapy, and altered sleep patterns.

5. Know the symptoms of bipolar disorder and the possible contributions of genetics.

6. Know the mechanisms of action of drugs used to treat bipolar disorder.

7. Be able to describe seasonal affective disorder and a treatment for it.

Module 15.3 Schizophrenia

1. Be able to describe the negative and positive symptoms of schizophrenia.

2. Know the conditions resembling schizophrenia, with which it may be confused, and the demographic factors related to schizophrenia.

3. Be able to describe the evidence for a genetic contribution to schizophrenia.

4. Understand the evidence for the neurodevelopmental hypothesis.

5. Understand the evidence for and against the dopamine hypothesis of schizophrenia.

6. Be able to describe the evidence for the glutamate hypothesis of schizophrenia and the potential role for glycine in treating schizophrenia.

7. Know the undesired effects of antipsychotic drugs and the mechanisms of action of the newer drugs that minimize these effects.

Key Terms and Concepts

Module 15.1 Substance Abuse and Addictions

1. Synapses, reinforcement and addiction

    Substance abuse: Maladaptive pattern of substance use leading to clinically significant impairment or distress

    Reinforcement and the nucleus accumbens

        Electrical self-stimulation of the brain

            James Olds and Peter Milner
        Self-stimulation in several brain areas → dopamine release in nucleus accumbens
        Other reinforcing experiences also → dopamine release in nucleus accumbens

            Sexual excitement, gambling, videogames, men looking at attractive female faces → increased activity in nucleus accumbens
            Men looking at attractive male faces → *decreased* nucleus accumbens activity

    Addiction as increased "wanting"

        Is nucleus accumbens a "pleasure area" and dopamine a "pleasure chemical?"
        Paychecks, videogames, gambling don't → happiness
        Drug addicts: Work hard for drug, even if drug does not → pleasure
        Berridge and Robinson: "Liking" vs. "wanting"

            Mice with increased dopamine: Same "liking," but more work for sweet liquid
            Mice with deficient dopamine: "Liked" food, didn't "want" it enough to move

    Sensitization of the nucleus accumbens

        Repeated cocaine → increased ability of cocaine to release dopamine in nucleus accumbens and increase activity in prefrontal cortex
        Less response to other incentives
        Hypothesis

            Prefrontal cortex stimulates nucleus accumbens → support reinforcing activity
            Repeated drug use → background inhibition of prefrontal cortex → only strongest stimuli get through

Addictive drug during withdrawal → sensitization

Stress or reminder of drug → craving

2. Alcohol and alcoholism

Alcoholism (alcohol dependence): Alcohol interferes with the person's life

Physiological effects

Inhibits flow of sodium and expands membrane surface

Decreases serotonin activity

Facilitates $GABA_A$ receptor

Blocks glutamate receptors

Increases dopamine activity

Genetics

Strong genetic basis for early-onset alcoholism, especially in men

Type I (or Type A) alcoholism

Later onset

Develops gradually

Less dependence on genetics

Fewer genetic relatives are alcoholic

Men and women about equally affected

Generally less severe

Type II (or Type B) alcoholism

Rapid, early onset

Stronger genetic basis

Overwhelmingly men

More severe

More associated with criminality

Evidence for genetic basis

Monozygotic concordance > dizygotic concordance

Biological children of alcoholics: Greater risk than adoptive children

But maternal drinking during pregnancy also a factor

Gene effects →

Impulsive, risk-taking behavior → try alcohol at earlier age

Increase stress response → relapse after attempt to quit

Increase adenosine production → calming → decrease alcohol intake

Risk factors

Impulsive, risk-taking, easily bored, sensation-seeking, outgoing

Son of alcoholic father

Less than average intoxication after moderate amount of alcohol

Greater decrease in stress by alcohol
Smaller amygdala in right hemisphere

3. Medications to combat substance abuse

Antabuse

Ethyl alcohol → acetaldehyde (poisonous) → acetic acid (source of energy)

Acetaldehyde dehydrogenase
Weak gene for acetaldehyde dehydrogenase → metabolize acetaldehyde more slowly → illness
after alcohol
Antabuse (disulfiram): Antagonizes acetaldehyde dehydrogenase → illness after alcohol

Moderately effective
Supplement to alcoholic's commitment to quit

Methadone

Similar to heroin and morphine, but taken as a pill
Gradually enters blood and brain → effects rise and fall slowly → no "rush"
Similar drugs: buprenorphine and levomethadyl acetate (LAAM)
Not an end to addiction: Quit methadone → craving
Pill also has small amount of naloxone (blocks opiate effects)

If dissolved in stomach: Acid breaks down most of the naloxone
If dissolved in water and injected: Naloxone cancels out methadone

4. In closing: Addictions

Blurring of distinction between voluntary and involuntary

Module 15.2 Mood Disorders

1. Major depressive disorder

May be caused by hormonal problems, head injuries, brain tumors, other illnesses

Co-morbid with substance abuse, anxiety, schizophrenia, Parkinson's disease

Symptoms

Sad and helpless for weeks
Little energy, feel worthless, contemplate suicide
Trouble sleeping, concentrating
Little pleasure from sex or food
Cannot imagine being happy again
Absence of happiness more reliable than increased sadness

Incidence

Twice as common in women as men
Any time after adolescence
5% of adults in United States each year: "Clinically significant" depression

Genetics and life events

Moderate heritability
Relatives more likely to suffer from other psychological disorders, as well as depression
Risk highest in relatives of women with early-onset depression
One gene → 80% decrease in ability to produce serotonin
Another gene → controls serotonin transporter

Two copies of "short" type: Increasing stress → increased depression
Two copies of "long" type: Little effect of stress
One copy of each: Intermediate effect of stress

Hormones

Depression episodic, not constant
Stress → cortisol release

Helpful in short term, harmful if prolonged
Sex hormones: Role less certain

Postpartum depression

More common in women depressed at other times or with premenstrual discomfort
Decrease estradiol and progesterone → depression in vulnerable women
Increase estradiol → relieve depression in menopausal women
Increased incidence in women not just due to increased reporting

Abnormalities of hemispheric dominance

Happy mood: Increased activity in left prefrontal cortex
Depression: Decreased activity in left and increased in right prefrontal cortex
Right-hemisphere damage may → manic

Viruses

Borna disease: Frantic activity alternating with inactivity
Virus found in 2% of normal people, 30% of severely depressed
May predispose to psychiatric difficulties in general

Antidepressant drugs

Accidental discoveries of psychiatric drugs

Disulfiram (Antabuse): Helps people avoid alcohol

Originally used in manufacture of rubber
Bromides: Treatment for epilepsy

Originally thought to reduce sexual drive, masturbation
Iproniazid: First antidepressant

Originally used to treat tuberculosis

Chlorpromazine: First antipsychotic

Originally used as tranquilizer

Today: Evaluate new drugs in test tubes or tissue samples

Types of antidepressants

Tricyclics

Decrease reuptake of catecholamines or serotonin → longer in synapse

Imipramine (Tofranil)

Also block histamine and acetylcholine receptors and some sodium channels → side effects

Selective serotonin reuptake inhibitors (SSRIs)

Similar to tricyclics, but selective for serotonin

Fluoxetine (Prozac), sertraline (Zoloft), fluvoxamine (Luvox), citalopram (Celexa) and paroxetine (Paxil or Seroxat)

Fewer side effects

MAOIs

Block monoamine oxidase → monoamines broken down more slowly

Phenelzine (Nardil)

Avoid foods containing tyramine: Tyramine + MAOI → high blood pressure

Atypical antidepressants

Bupropion (Wellbutrin)

Inhibits reuptake of dopamine and, to some extent, norepinephrine, but not serotonin

Venlafaxine

Inhibits reuptake mostly of serotonin, slightly of norepinephrine and dopamine

Nefazodone

Blocks serotonin type 2A receptors

Weakly blocks reuptake of serotonin and norepinephrine

St. John's wort

Herb, not regulated by FDA

Effects similar to SSRIs, but variable

Increases effect of enzyme that breaks down toxins and beneficial drugs

Exactly how do antidepressants work?

Normal serotonin turnover in depressed patients

Dietary decrease in serotonin levels→ temporary depression in patients with history of depression, no effect in normal people

Problem of time course

    Effect on synapses within hours, effect on behavior two to three weeks

    Brain-derived neurotrophic factor (BDNF)

        Released with neurotransmitters
        Promotes survival and growth of hippocampal neurons
        Parts of hippocampus and cerebral cortex shrink during depression
        Animal studies: Block BDNF → block behavioral effects

    Desensitized autoreceptors → increased release of serotonin and other transmitters

Other therapies

    Effectiveness of antidepressants

        Antidepressants → improvement of 50–60% of patients in a few months

        Placebo → improvement of 30% of patients in a few months

    Psychotherapy/cognitive therapy

        Increases metabolism in brain areas similarly to antidepressants

        Effects last longer, but require more time to be effective

        Regular exercise also effective

    Electroconvulsive therapy (ECT)

        Initially used to treat schizophrenia

        Now used for patients who do not respond to drug therapy or who are suicidal

        Works faster than drugs

        Administered every other day for two weeks

        Used with muscle relaxants or anesthetics

        Side effect: memory loss; minimized with shock to right hemisphere only

            Right-hemisphere activity associated with unpleasant mood

        High rate of relapse within a few months

        Alters expression of ~120 genes in hippocampus and frontal cortex

            Neurotrophins

            Arachidonic acid

            Generation of new neurons

            Responsiveness to exercise

    Repetitive transcranial magnetic stimulation

        Temporarily disables all neurons just below magnet

        Similar to ECT in effectiveness

        Not clear how it works

  Altered sleep patterns

    Correlation between sleep problems and depression

    Depressed: REM within 45 minutes

        Increased eye movements per minute during REM

Therapy

Stay awake all night → fastest improvement
Often effective only until next night's sleep
Combine with earlier bedtime → effective for at least a week
Sleep alteration + drug therapy → long-lasting benefits

2. Bipolar disorder

Definitions

Unipolar disorder: One extreme − vary between normal and depression
Bipolar disorder: Manic-depressive disorder

Mania: Restlessness, excitement, laughter, self-confidence, rambling speech, loss of inhibitions
Full-blown mania: Bipolar I disorder
Hypomania: Bipolar II disorder

Also have attention deficits, poor impulse control, verbal memory problems

Glucose metabolism: Higher than normal in mania, lower than normal in depression

Genetics

Greater similarity in monozygotic > dizygotic twins and in biological > adoptive relatives
Apparent linkage to genes on several chromosomes, none strongly linked

Treatments

Lithium salts

Stabilize mood, prevent relapse
May have toxic side effects
Effective for bipolar I disorder

Other drugs

Valproate (Depakene, Depakote), carbamazepine

Effective for bipolar II disorder

How do drugs relieve bipolar disorder?

Increase activity at GABA synapses

Valproate, carbamazepine do
Lithium does not

Valproate → growth of axons and dendrites

Other drugs not tested for this

Block synthesis of arachidonic acid

Produced during brain inflammation
Blocked by lithium, valproate, and carbamazepine
Polyunsaturated fatty acids (abundant in seafood) also block effects of arachidonic acid

Echo-planar magnetic resonance spectroscopic imaging

Weak electromagnetic fields throughout head → temporary mood benefits
Consistent sleep schedule in dark, quiet room

3. Seasonal affective disorder (SAD)

    Common where nights are long in winter

    SAD: Phase-delayed sleep and temperature rhythms, unlike other depressed people, who are
    phase-advanced

    Bright lights for an hour or more per day

        Affects serotonin synapses
        Affects circadian rhythms
        Also helps nonseasonal depression
        As effective as drugs or psychotherapy, less expensive, faster

4. In closing: The biology of mood swings

    Brain structure and chemistry alter reactions to events

    Experience alters brain

Module 15.3 Schizophrenia

1. Characteristics

    Deteriorating function in everyday life; some combination of hallucinations, delusions, thought
    disorder, movement disorder, and inappropriate emotional expressions

        Acute condition: Sudden onset and good prospects for recovery
        Chronic condition: Gradual onset and a long-term course
        Dementia praecox: Premature mental deterioration
        Not dissociative identity disorder (multiple personality)
        Split between emotional and intellectual aspects

    Behavioral symptoms

        Negative symptoms: Behaviors that are absent, but should be present

            Weak social interactions, emotional expression, speech, and working memory
            More stable, less responsive to treatment
        Positive symptoms: Behaviors that are present, but should be absent

            Psychotic cluster: Delusions and hallucinations

                Increased activity in thalamus, hippocampus, and parts of cortex, including auditory areas
            Disorganized cluster: Inappropriate emotion displays, bizarre behaviors and thought disorder

                Difficulty with abstract concepts, attention, working memory
        Main problem: Disordered thinking

Abnormal connections between cortex and thalamus and cerebellum

Differential diagnosis of schizophrenia

Conditions resembling schizophrenia

Mood disorder with psychotic features
Substance abuse

May → visual hallucinations
Brain damage

Temporal or prefrontal cortex
Undetected hearing deficits
Huntington's disease

Catatonic schizophrenia → motor and psychological abnormalities similar to Huntington's disease
Nutritional abnormalities

Deficiency of niacin, vitamin C
Allergy to milk proteins, wheat gluten, other proteins

Demographic data

Approximately 1% of people: Schizophrenia at any given time

Gradual decline in prevalence and severity
10-100 times more common in United States and Europe than in Third World

More common and more severe in men than women
Older father → increased risk of schizophrenia

2. Genetics

Twin studies

Greater concordance for monozygotic (50%) than dizygotic (15-20%) twins

Heredity not the only factor

Monozygotic twins: Gene can be expressed in one twin, suppressed in other
Dizygotic twins: Same genetic resemblance as siblings, but higher concordance

Adopted children who develop schizophrenia

Greater concordance with biological than adoptive parents
Biological mother → genes + prenatal environment

Poor nutrition; smoke, drink; poor medical care

Efforts to locate a gene: No strong links

Natural selection should decrease responsible gene

Schizophrenics: Fewer children

Relatives: Average number
Gene for childhood-onset schizophrenia

But childhood-onset schizophrenia different from other forms, uncommon
One gene → small increase in risk
Different genes in different families?
Complex combinations of genes?

One form of *DISC1* ("disrupted in schizophrenia 1") → alters structure, decreases gray matter in hippocampus
One form of *PDE4B* interacts with *DISC1* → schizophrenia
One gene linked to negative symptoms
Some cases: Environmental influence?

3. The neurodevelopmental hypothesis

Argument for:

Several kinds of pre- or neonatal difficulties linked to later schizophrenia
People with schizophrenia: numerous small brain abnormalities originating early in life
Plausible that early brain abnormalities → adult behavioral abnormalities

Prenatal and neonatal environment

Poor nutrition, premature birth, low birth weight, delivery complications
Head injuries in childhood
Rh-positive child of Rh-negative mother→ immunological rejection

Later-born boys with Rh incompatibility → schizophrenia, hearing & mental problems
Season of birth effect

Winter births → higher risk
Mostly in non-tropical climates
Viral epidemics

Influenza in fall → later schizophrenia in babies born in winter
Fever in mother slows cell division, damages brain
Increased schizophrenia after influenza epidemic in 1967
Blood samples from pregnant women: Increased virus and immune system proteins → later risk of schizophrenic children
Rubella ("German measles"): Increased risk of schizophrenic children
Cat parasite in childhood → impaired brain development and increased risk of schizophrenia

Mild brain abnormalities

Smaller left temporal and prefrontal cortex

Most cortical areas smaller in at least one study
Especially in those with complications during pregnancy or birth
Areas that mature slowly most affected: Dorsolateral prefrontal cortex

Memory and attention deficits similar to those with temporal or prefrontal cortex damage

Enlarged ventricles: Less space taken by brain cells

Microscopic level

Smaller cell bodies, especially in hippocampus and prefrontal cortex

Lateralization

Right planum temporale equal to or larger than left

Lower activity in left hemisphere

More likely left-handed

Brain abnormalities not due to antipsychotic drugs

Alcohol abuse by schizophrenics may contribute to volume deficits

Brain damage may not be progressive

Brain abnormalities similar in older and younger patients

No glial cell proliferation or activation of genes for repair

Cells may shrink but not die

Early development and later psychopathology

Why is it diagnosed after age 20, if early brain development is the cause?

Earlier problems: Deficits in attention, memory, impulse control

Prefrontal cortex: Slow maturing

Neurodevelopmental hypothesis: Plausible, not firmly established

4. Methods 15.1 The Wisconsin card-sorting task

Measures functioning of prefrontal cortex

Deck of cards sorted first by one rule, then by a different (conflicting) rule

Schizophrenia or damage to prefrontal cortex → difficulty shifting to the new rule

5. Neurotransmitters and drugs

Antipsychotic drugs and dopamine

The dopamine hypothesis: Excess activity at certain dopamine synapses

Antispychotic (neuroleptic) drugs: Block dopamine receptors

Phenothiazines

Chlorpromazine (Thorazine)

Butyrophenones

Haloperidol (Haldol)

Correlation between clinically effective dose and dose needed to block dopamine receptors

Drugs that can provoke schizophrenic symptoms

Substance-induced psychotic disorder

Hallucinations and delusions: Positive symptoms

Amphetamine, methamphetamine, cocaine → increase activity at dopamine synapses

LSD → effects at serotonin synapses; increases activity at dopamine synapses

Schizophrenia: Twice as many dopamine D_2 receptors occupied as normal

IBZM: Binds to D_2 receptors

Compare IBZM binding before and after blocking synthesis of dopamine

Difference = number of D_2 receptors occupied by dopamine

Greater D_2 activation in prefrontal cortex → greater cognitive impairment

Problems with the dopamine hypothesis

Approximately normal levels of dopamine and its metabolites

Time course of drugs

Affect synapses quickly

Effects on behavior build up over 2 to 3 weeks

Role of glutamate

The glutamate hypothesis

Deficient activity at glutamate synapses, especially in prefrontal cortex

Relationships between dopamine and glutamate: Opposing effects

Dopamine inhibits glutamate release

Glutamate excites neurons that inhibit dopamine release

Mice with few glutamate NMDA receptors: D_2 antagonist normalized behavior

Measurements of glutamate

Schizophrenia → less glutamate release in prefrontal cortex and hippocampus

Also fewer glutamate receptors

The effects of phencyclidine (PCP, "angel dust")

Inhibits NMDA glutamate receptors

Positive and negative symptoms similar to schizophrenia

PCP and ketamine → little psychotic effect in preadolescents

PCP → long-lasting relapse in people recovered from schizophrenia

LSD, amphetamine, and cocaine → only temporary symptoms

Enhancing glutamate activity

Too much glutamate → toxic effects

Glycine: Co-transmitter at NMDA glutamate receptors

Increases effectiveness of glutamate

Not effective antipsychotic by itself

Increases effectiveness of antipsychotic drugs, especially for negative symptoms

New drugs

Antipsychotic drugs → decrease mesolimbocortical activity → beneficial effects

Decrease activity of dopamine neurons in basal ganglia → undesired effects

Tardive dyskinesia: Tremors and other involuntary movements

May last for years after quitting drug

Second generation (or atypical) antipsychotics

Clozapine, amisulpride, resperidone, olanzapine

Block D_4 receptors

Briefer or less intense blockade of D_2 receptors

Also blocks serotonin 5-HT_2 receptors

Increases glutamate release

Effective on negative, as well as positive, symptoms

Side effects: Weight gain, increased risk of diabetes; impaired immune system

Schizophrenia not a one-gene or a one-transmitter disorder

Also deficits in GABA activity

6. In closing: The fascination of schizophrenia

Search for pattern among many clues and false leads

Short-Answer Questions

Module 15.1 Substance Abuse and Addictions

1. *Synapses, reinforcement and addiction*

   a. How were the brain mechanisms of pleasure and reinforcement discovered?

   b. Which brain area is especially important for reinforcement and addiction? What is the relationship of motivated behaviors, electrical self-stimulation, and drugs of abuse on dopamine release there?

   c. Is dopamine release always associated with pleasure? Describe Berridge and Robinson's distinction between "wanting" and "liking." To which of these is nucleus accumbens dopamine more closely linked?

   d. Describe sensitization of the nucleus accumbens. What is the relation between the prefrontal cortex and nucleus accumbens in this process?

2. *Alcohol and alcoholism*

   a. What are two effects of alcohol on membranes? What type of receptor is facilitated by alcohol? Which other three neurotransmitters are affected?

   b. List the differences between Type I and Type II alcoholism.

   c. Describe the evidence for a genetic risk factor for alcoholism. How strong is that evidence?

3. *Medications to combat substance abuse*

   a. Describe the metabolism of alcohol.

   b. What is the biochemical effect of Antabuse? What is its physiological effect when combined with alcohol use?

   c. How may Antabuse work, in addition to its physiological effect?

   d. What are two characteristics of sons of alcoholics that may predispose them to alcoholism?

   e. What is methadone and how is it used? What prevents addicts from dissolving the pills and injecting themselves with the solution? Does methadone provide an end to addiction?

Module 15.2 Mood Disorders

1. *Major depressive disorder*

   a. List the symptoms of major depression.

   b. What is the evidence for a genetic predisposition for depression?

   c. Are men or women more vulnerable to depression? What may be the role of hormones in depression?

   d. What seems to be the role of stress in the onset of episodes of depression?

   e. What patterns of hemispheric dominance have been associated with happy moods in normal people? What is the pattern in depressed people?

   f. What is Borna disease? What evidence links it to depression?

   g. Name three groups of antidepressant drugs and explain how each exerts its effects.

   h. Why are selective serotonin reuptake inhibitors (SSRIs) preferred over tricyclics and monoamine oxidase inhibitors?

   i. What are three atypical antidepressants?

   j. How effective is St. John's wort in relieving depression? Which class of antidepressants produces effects similar to those of St. John's wort? What is one potential problem with the use of St. John's wort?

   k. Explain the problem of the time course of drugs' effects on neurotransmitters and their effects on depressive symptoms.

   l. What neurotrophin is produced as a result of repeated use of antidepressants? In which brain area is it produced?

   m. What is the effect of repeated use of antidepressants on autoreceptors? How does that affect neurotransmitter release?

   n. How is electroconvulsive therapy (ECT) applied today? How is this an improvement over practices in the 1950s?

   o. For which two groups of patients is ECT most often used?

p. What are the advantages and disadvantages of ECT?

q. What are the effects of ECT on the expression of some genes? What newer treatment is similar to ECT?

r. How does the onset of REM sleep differ in depressed people, compared to nondepressed individuals?

s. What change in sleeping schedules has been found to alleviate depression? How long do the benefits last?

2. *Bipolar disorder*

a. What is the difference between unipolar and bipolar disorder? What is another term for bipolar disorder?

b. Describe the symptoms of mania. What is hypomania? What is the difference between bipolar I and bipolar II disorder?

c. Describe the pattern of glucose metabolism in the two extreme conditions of bipolar I disorder.

d. What can we say about genetic factors in bipolar disorder?

e. What drug is effective for bipolar I disorder? Which two drugs are used to treat bipolar II disorder?

f. What are three possible mechanisms by which one or more of these drugs achieve their effects?

g. What are two possible non-drug treatments for bipolar disorder?

3. *Seasonal affective disorder (SAD)*

a. What is seasonal affective disorder? How is it treated?

b. What is a possible mechanism for improvement as a result of this treatment? How effective is it?

c. How are the sleep and temperature rhythms of SAD patients different from those of other depressed patients?

Module 15.3 Schizophrenia

1. *Characteristics*

a. What is the origin of the term schizophrenia?

b. What are the negative symptoms of schizophrenia? How stable are they?

c. What are the two clusters of positive symptoms of schizophrenia?

d. What is the main cognitive problem in schizophrenia? What is the physiological problem that may underlie this problem?

e. What are some conditions resembling schizophrenia that may be confused with it?

f. What is the overall incidence of schizophrenia? Does this incidence vary among ethnic groups or sexes?

2. *Genetics*

a. What evidence from twin studies suggests a genetic basis for schizophrenia? What are concordance rates?

b. What other factor may explain the greater concordance with biological than adoptive parents?

c. How may one form of the DISC1 and of the PDE4B gene interact to increase the incidence of schizophrenia?

d. What can we conclude about the role of genetics in schizophrenia?

3. *The neurodevelopmental hypothesis*

a. What evidence suggests that schizophrenia may result from abnormalities in the early development of the brain?

b. What specific prenatal and neonatal conditions have been associated with increased risk for schizophrenia?

c. In which season of birth is there a slightly greater likelihood of developing schizophrenia? What factor may account for this effect?

d. What brain abnormalities have been linked with schizophrenia?

e. Which brain areas have been most strongly implicated? What are some psychological functions of those areas? Do schizophrenics show impairment of those functions?

f. Why do researchers believe that these abnormalities resulted from early developmental effects, rather than from gradual brain damage in adulthood?

g. How might one explain the late onset of schizophrenic symptoms, if the brain damage occurred during early development?

4. *Neurotransmitters and drugs*

a. What is the dopamine hypothesis of schizophrenia? What are the main lines of evidence favoring it?

b. What are two chemical families of antipsychotic (neuroleptic) drugs that have been in wide use for many years? What is their major effect on receptors?

c. Which drugs can induce a state similar to schizophrenia? What is their major mechanism of action?

d. What are two problems with the dopamine hypothesis?

e. What other neurotransmitter has been hypothesized to be abnormal in schizophrenia? What is the relationship between these two neurotransmitters?

f. Why may blockade of dopamine receptors have beneficial effects, if the original problem is deficient glutamate?

g. What is phencyclidine (PCP)? What are its effects on receptors? What are its psychological effects?

h. What kinds of evidence suggest an abnormality in glutamate release or receptors?

i. Why would it be unwise to administer glutamate to schizophrenic people?

j. What is glycine? How does it affect NMDA receptors? What are the clinical findings concerning glycine?

k. What is tardive dyskinesia? How rapid is its onset?

l. What are four atypical antipsychotic drugs? What are their effects on receptors and neurotransmitter release?

m. What is a major advantage of atypical antipsychotic drugs? What are their negative side effects?

True/False Questions

1. Electrical stimulation of the brain is usually reinforcing only if it activates dopamine release, especially in the nucleus accumbens.

    TRUE or FALSE

2. Dopamine release in the nucleus accumbens is now thought to be synonymous with pleasure: It always occurs with pleasant stimuli and never with unpleasant stimuli.

    TRUE or FALSE

3. Alcohol inhibits the flow of sodium across membranes, decreases serotonin activity, facilitates the $GABA_A$ receptor, and increases dopamine activity.

    TRUE or FALSE

4. Type II alcoholism is more severe, is associated with criminality, is more prevalent in men than in women, and has a relatively strong genetic basis.

    TRUE or FALSE

5. Antabuse (disulfiram) stimulates acetaldehyde dehydrogenase, thereby decreasing the effects of alcohol.

    TRUE or FALSE

6. During depression there is decreased activity in the left hemisphere and increased activity in the right prefrontal cortex.

    TRUE or FALSE

7. Depression is more common in women than in men; decreases in estrogen and progesterone in vulnerable women may lead to depression.

    TRUE or FALSE

8. Tricyclic antidepressants work by inhibiting monoamine oxidase, which would otherwise metabolize the monoamine neurotransmitters.

    TRUE or FALSE

9. St. John's wort is an especially effective antidepressant that has no bad side effects.

    TRUE or FALSE

10. Brain-derived neurotrophic factor (BDNF) is released with neurotransmitters and may mediate the effects of antidepressant drugs.

TRUE or FALSE

11. ECT increases the expression of at least 120 genes, including those regulating neurotrophins, arachidonic acid, generation of new neurons, and responsiveness to exercise.

TRUE or FALSE

12. Bipolar disorder is usually treated with the same drugs as are used for unipolar depression.

TRUE or FALSE

13. Arachidonic acid is a neurotransmitter that increases dopamine release.

TRUE or FALSE

14. Negative symptoms of schizophrenia include deficits in social interaction, emotional expression, speech, and working memory.

TRUE or FALSE

15. The neurodevelopmental hypothesis of schizophrenia is supported by evidence that the prefrontal and temporal cortex and the hippocampus are smaller in schizophrenics, but there are no signs of damage in adulthood, such as increased glia cells and expression of genes that promote repair.

TRUE or FALSE

16. Support for the dopamine hypothesis includes the observations that schizophrenics have much higher levels of dopamine and its metabolites and that the time courses of neuroleptic drugs on dopamine synapses and on clinical symptoms are similar.

TRUE or FALSE

17. Glycine is a co-transmitter at glutamate synapses and increases the effectiveness of glutamate.

TRUE or FALSE

Fill In The Blanks

1. Almost all addictive drugs and motivated behaviors increase the release of _____ in the _____ .

2. Alcohol decreases _____ activity, facilitates _____ receptors, blocks _____ receptors, and increases _____ activity.

3. The enzyme that metabolizes acetaldehyde to _____ is _____ .

4. Happy moods are associated with _____ activity in the _____ hemisphere.

5. Atypical antidepressants include _____ , _____ , and _____ .

6. _____ is released with neurotransmitters and is increased with repeated administration of antidepressants.

7. ECT and _____ stimulation work faster than drugs but may cause memory loss, which can be lessened by administration only to the _____ hemisphere.

8. Three drugs used to treat bipolar disorder are _____ , _____ , and _____ .

9. _____ is produced during brain inflammation and is blocked by _____ , _____ , and _____ .

10. Seasonal affective disorder is often associated with phase- _____ sleep and temperature rhythms, unlike rhythms in other depressed people.

11. Positive symptoms of schizophrenia are grouped into a _____ cluster and a _____ cluster; the main problem is _____ .

12. Brain abnormalities in schizophrenia include smaller _____ and _____ cortex, especially in the _____ hemisphere, and smaller cells in the _____ and _____ cortex.

13. Atypical antipsychotic drugs block _____ receptors more than _____ receptors, block serotonin _____ receptors, and increase _____ release.

14. Tremors and other involuntary movements that result from prolonged use of neuroleptic drugs are referred to as _____ .

Matching Items

1. _____ "Wanting"
2. _____ Promotes survival of hippocampal neurons
3. _____ Methadone
4. _____ Psychotic cluster of positive symptoms
5. _____ Disulfiram (Antabuse)
6. _____ Rapid, early onset; more men than women
7. _____ Fluoxetine (Prozac)
8. _____ Bupropion (Wellbutrin)
9. _____ Increased activity in right prefrontal cortex, decrease in left
10. _____ Bright lights for at least 1 hour per day
11. _____ Lithium salts
12. _____ Haloperidol (Haldol)
13. _____ Phencyclidine (PCP)
14. _____ Tardive dyskinesia
15. _____ Glycine
16. _____ Clozapine

a. Delusions, hallucinations
b. Inhibits acetaldehyde dehydrogenase
c. Atypical antidepressant
d. Atypical antipsychotic
e. Used to treat heroin addiction
f. Tremors, involuntary movements
g. Associated with depression
h. Treatment for SAD
i. Type II alcoholism
j. Typical antipsychotic
k. Enhances effect of glutamate
l. An SSRI antidepressant
m. Dopamine release in nucleus accumbens
n. Treatment for bipolar I disorder
o. Brain-derived neurotrophic factor (BDNF)
p. Blocks NMDA receptors → psychotic symptoms

Multiple-Choice Questions

1. Addictive drugs
   a. release dopamine in the nucleus accumbens.
   b. have neural effects similar to those of naturally reinforcing behaviors.
   c. lead to sensitization of nucleus accumbens to the drugs after repeated use.
   d. all of the above.

2. Alcohol
   a. inhibits the flow of sodium across the membrane.
   b. expands the surface of membranes.
   c. makes $GABA_A$ receptors more responsive.
   d. all of the above.

3. Type II alcoholism
   a. has a stronger genetic basis than does Type I.
   b. develops gradually over the years.
   c. affects men and women about equally.
   d. all of the above.

4. Acetaldehyde dehydrogenase
   a. is the generic name for Antabuse.
   b. controls the rate of conversion of acetic acid, a toxic product of alcohol metabolism, into acetaldehyde, a source of energy.
   c. controls the rate of conversion of acetaldehyde, a toxic product of alcohol metabolism, into acetic acid, a source of energy.
   d. if present in high levels, would make us feel very ill after drinking alcohol.

5. Which of the following is true?
   a. Sons of alcoholics experience less than average relief from stress after drinking alcohol.
   b. Antabuse acts as a supplement to the alcoholic's commitment to stop drinking.
   c. Sons of alcoholics show greater than average intoxication after drinking a small to moderate amount of alcohol.
   d. Sons of alcoholics tend to have an unusually large amygdala in the right hemisphere.

6. Methadone
   a. is frequently abused because it acts rapidly when taken in pill form, producing a sudden rush of excitement.
   b. is a tricyclic antidepressant.
   c. has effects similar to heroin, but when given in pill form its effects occur gradually, without a "rush."
   d. cures addiction after the first few doses, with no need for further treatment.

7. Which of the following is **not** a common symptom of major depression?
   a. sleeping soundly for at least 10 - 12 hours per night
   b. sadness and helplessness
   c. lack of energy
   d. little pleasure from sex or food

8. Which of the following is true of depression?
   a. A gene on chromosome 11 is now known to be the cause of most cases of depression.
   b. Hormonal changes before menstruation or after childbirth often cause major depression, even in women without a biological predisposition to, or history of, that disorder.
   c. Since no specific genetic abnormality has been linked to depression, it is now commonly agreed that depression does not have any genetic basis.
   d. Genes that control the brain's ability to produce serotonin or the serotonin transporter have been linked to depression in some people.

9. Depression is frequently associated with
   a. increased activity in the left, and decreased activity in the right prefrontal cortex
   b. decreased activity in the left, and increased activity in the right prefrontal cortex.
   c. increased activity in the right, and decreased activity in the left temporal cortex
   d. decreased activity in the right, and increased activity in the left temporal cortex.

10. Research on Borna disease suggests that
    a. a virus causes an autoimmune attack on the brain.
    b. any illness that causes a fever also causes major depression.
    c. a virus may be one cause of depression or bipolar disorder.
    d. the viruses that infect animals cannot infect humans.

11. Which of the following is **not** a type of antidepressant drug?
    a. monoamine oxidase inhibitors
    b. tricyclics
    c. selective serotonin reuptake inhibitors (SSRIs)
    d. dopamine receptor blockers

12. Which of the following is true?
    a. The effects of drugs on transmitter systems occur almost immediately, but their effects on depression are delayed for two to three weeks.
    b. The effects of drugs on transmitter systems are delayed for two to three weeks, but their effects on depression are immediate.
    c. Depression results from having excessive activity of all the monoamine transmitters.
    d. The major effect of fluoxetine (Prozac) is to block serotonin receptors.

13. Repeated use of antidepressant drugs
    a. results in transmitters activating other types of receptors.
    b. sensitizes autoreceptors and thereby *decreases* release of serotonin.
    c. increases production and release of brain-derived neurotrophic factor (BDNF) in the hippocampus.
    d. all of the above.

14. Electroconvulsive therapy (ECT)
    a. is effective because it confuses patients, and they forget their depressing thoughts.
    b. is rarely used anymore because of its bad reputation.
    c. increases the expression of at least 120 genes in the hippocampus and frontal cortex, including those for neurotrophins, arachidonic acid, generation of new neurons, and responsiveness to exercise.
    d. must be administered to the left hemisphere, which produces loss of language ability.

15. Depressed people
    a. enter REM sleep more slowly than do normal people.
    b. are sometimes helped by skipping one night's sleep and then adopting an earlier bedtime.
    c. have their symptoms worsened by exposure to transcranial magnetic stimulation.
    d. all of the above.

16. Bipolar disorder is characterized by
    a. cycles between depression and normal moods.
    b. cycles between depression and mania or hypomania.
    c. higher glucose metabolism in the brain during depression, and lower activity during mania.
    d. Unusually regular sleep habits.

17. Lithium
    a. is more effective than valproate and carbamazepine for bipolar I disorder.
    b. is extremely safe because it is so simple.
    c. is helpful for depression but not for mania.
    d. all of the above.

18. People with seasonal affective disorder (SAD)
    a. become more depressed during winter because of the cold.
    b. are frequently helped by sitting in hot sauna baths for an hour or more each day.
    c. show phase-advanced sleep and temperature rhythms, similar to those of other depressed people.
    d. are frequently helped by exposure to bright lights for an hour or more each day.

19. Schizophrenia
    a. is characterized by multiple personalities.
    b. refers to a split between the emotions and the intellect.
    c. is rarely misdiagnosed because its symptoms are so clearly distinctive.
    d. is typically first diagnosed in the elderly.

20. Which of the following is true of the positive symptoms of schizophrenia?
    a. They are usually associated with increased neural activity in the visual cortex, because almost all hallucinations are visual, and an especially large dorsolateral prefrontal cortex.
    b. They include deficits in social interactions, emotional expression, and speech.
    c. They consist of a disorganized cluster, including inappropriate emotions, bizarre behaviors, and thought disorder, and a psychotic cluster, including delusions and hallucinations.
    d. They are more stable over time and more difficult to treat than are negative symptoms.

21. The prevalence of schizophrenia
    a. is declining, for unknown reasons.
    b. is higher in Third World countries than in the United States and Europe.
    c. is higher in women than in men.
    d. is fairly easy to study, since schizophrenia is one of the easiest disorders to diagnose.

22. Which of the following provides some support for a genetic basis for schizophrenia?
    a. Adopted children have a higher concordance rate with their adoptive than biological kin.
    b. The concordance rate for schizophrenia is greater for dizygotic than monozygotic twins.
    c. The concordance rate for schizophrenia is greater for monozygotic than dizygotic twins.
    d. Mutation of a gene on chromosome 7 has been shown to cause schizophrenia.

23. A problem with estimating the possibility of a genetic basis for schizophrenia is that
    a. monozygotic twins may both have the same gene, but it may be expressed in one twin, but suppressed in the other.
    b. common prenatal factors, such as smoking, drinking, and other poor health habits, may at least partially explain the increased concordance rate with biological parents, compared to adoptive parents, of schizophrenics.
    c. both A and B are true.
    d. none of the above is true.

24. Research on possible causes of schizophrenia has demonstrated that
    a. a prenatal viral infection may cause fever, which results in impaired brain development.
    b. several studies have converged on a single gene as the primary cause of schizophrenia.
    c. conflicting messages from parents are a major cause of schizophrenia.
    d. the season-of-birth effect occurs more often in the tropics, where diseases are harder to control.

25. Studies of the brains of schizophrenics have revealed that
    a. they have shrunken ventricles.
    b. their prefrontal and temporal cortical areas are smaller, especially in the left hemisphere.
    c. they have more abnormalities in rapidly maturing areas, such as the brain stem, than in slowly maturing areas, such as dorsolateral prefrontal cortex.
    d. they have a large proliferation of glia cells and expression of genes activated during repair, indicating that much of the damage is caused during adulthood.

26. Drug-induced psychosis
    a. causes a full-blown state of schizophrenia, with mostly negative, rather than positive, symptoms.
    b. is caused by drugs that block dopamine receptors.
    c. is caused by drugs that increase the stimulation of dopamine receptors.
    d. is caused by drugs that stimulate glutamate receptors.

27. Which of the following is not an effective neuroleptic drug?
    a. haloperidol
    b. chlorpromazine
    c. amphetamine
    d. clozapine

28. According to the dopamine hypothesis of schizophrenia, people with schizophrenia have
    a. excessive activity at dopamine synapses.
    b. deficient activity at dopamine synapses.
    c. glutamate in neurons that should release dopamine.
    d. dopamine in neurons that should release glutamate.

29. A problem with the dopamine hypothesis is that
    a. neuroleptic drugs improve schizophrenic symptoms before they have a significant effect on dopamine synapses.
    b. people with schizophrenia have nearly normal levels of dopamine and its metabolites.
    c. there was actually less occupation of dopamine D_2 receptors in schizophrenics, whereas there should have been more, if excess dopamine was the problem.
    d. amphetamine, cocaine, methamphetamine, and LSD increase activity at dopamine receptors, but are among the best treatments for schizophrenia, suggesting that excess dopamine activity cannot be a cause of that disorder.

30. Which of the following is true?
    a. Phencyclidine (PCP) is an atypical neuroleptic drug that treats schizophrenia by stimulating glutamate receptors.
    b. Since there is too much glutamate in the brains of schizophrenic people, a good way to improve their symptoms is to block glutamate receptors.
    c. Glycine interferes with the binding of glutamate to NMDA receptors, thereby worsening schizophrenic symptoms.
    d. In many brain areas, dopamine inhibits glutamate release, or glutamate stimulates neurons that inhibit dopamine release; therefore, increased dopamine would produce the same effects as decreased glutamate.

31. Tardive dyskinesia
    a. recedes completely once all traces of antipsychotic drugs have left the body.
    b. usually occurs soon after beginning antipsychotic drug treatment.
    c. is characterized by tremors or involuntary movements and may result from blocking of dopamine receptors in the basal ganglia.
    d. is caused by the newer atypical antipsychotics more than the older drugs.

32. Clozapine and other atypical antipsychotic drugs
    a. block dopamine D_4 receptors more than D_2.
    b. also block serotonin $5\text{-}HT_2$ receptors.
    c. have some undesirable side effects, including weight gain, increased risk of diabetes, and impaired immune system.
    d. all of the above.

Solutions

True/False Questions

1.	T	8.	F	15.	T
2.	F	9.	F	16.	F
3.	T	10.	T	17.	T
4.	T	11.	T		
5.	F	12.	F		
6.	T	13.	F		
7.	T	14.	T		

Fill In The Blanks

1. dopamine; nucleus accumbens
2. serotonin; $GABA_A$; glutamate; dopamine
3. acetic acid; acetaldehyde dehydrogenase
4. increased; left
5. bupropion; venlafaxine; nefazodone
6. Brain-derived neurotrophic factor
7. repetitive transcranial magnetic; right
8. lithium salts; valproate; carbamazepine
9. Arachidonic acid; lithium; valproate; carbamazepine
10. delayed
11. psychotic; disorganized; disorganized thinking
12. prefrontal; temporal; left; hippocampus; prefrontal
13. D_4 dopamine; D_2; $5HT_2$ glutamate
14. tardive dyskinesia

Matching Items

1.	M	7.	L	13.	P
2.	O	8.	C	14.	F
3.	E	9.	G	15.	K
4.	A	10.	H	16.	D
5.	B	11.	N		
6.	I	12.	J		

Multiple-Choice Questions

1.	D	3.	A	5.	B
2.	D	4.	C	6.	C

7. A	16. B	25. B
8. D	17. A	26. C
9. B	18. D	27. C
10. C	19. B	28. A
11. D	20. C	29. B
12. A	21. A	30. D
13. C	22. C	31. C
14. C	23. C	32. D
15. B	24. A	